Oliver Cromwell

For

Andrew, Rachel, Sophie,
Amelia, Tim, Nicky and Eleanor

Oliver Cromwell

'Gentleman, General, Politician and Protector'
(FLECKNO)

'A larger soul, I think, hath seldom dwelt in a house of clay'
(JOHN MAIDSTONE TO JOHN WINTHROP)

Pauline Gregg

J. M. Dent & Sons Ltd
London

First published 1988
© Pauline Gregg 1988

This book is set in Linotron 11/13 Bembo
Printed in Great Britain by The Bath Press, Avon for
J. M. Dent & Sons Ltd,
91 Clapham High Street, London SW4 7TA

British Library Cataloguing in Publication Data

Gregg, Pauline
    Oliver Cromwell.
    1. England. Cromwell, Oliver. Biographies.
    I. Title
    942.06′4′0924

    ISBN 0-460-04709-4

Contents

Contents

Contents

Part IX

'For to be Cromwell was a greater thing than ought below, or yet above a king'   307

Illustrations

Preface

When John Morley published his biography of Oliver Cromwell nearly a century ago he prefixed his work with what was, in effect, a justification and an excuse: '... any such career and character as Cromwell's', he said, 'must still be capable of an almost endless range of presentment and interpretation'.

Since Morley's biography, 'presentment' and 'interpretation' have continued in many forms, as the bibliography at the end of this book – albeit only selective – indicates: the present work is but one of many for whom Morley's words are a spur and a justification. In coming to my task, therefore, I have been immeasurably helped by the research and writing that has already been done. It is no truism to say that without it this book would never have been written.

In a class apart are the two massive collections of Cromwell's Letters and Speeches. That by Abbott, published in four volumes between 1937 and 1947, is indispensable and is linked by narrative which, in itself, is a biography. But for me it is the collection by Thomas Carlyle, published between 1845 and 1904, which brings Oliver Cromwell to life as a man of flesh and blood.

In spite of a vast Cromwell literature – almost, it might be said, because of it – the task of the present-day biographer is heavy. I am deeply grateful to Professor Ivan Roots who read a first draft and has not hesitated to let me draw on his wide and detailed knowledge of Cromwell and his times. Needless to say, the deficiencies that remain are all my own.

My work has been done mainly in the Bodleian Library and the History Faculty Library of the University of Oxford. My thanks again go to the helpful and efficient staff of both libraries as well as to the institutions themselves which make working there such a pleasure. I am also glad to record once more my thanks to the

British Library and its staff.

In an exciting weekend in Huntingdon I received much help as well as great enjoyment from the excellent Cromwell Museum and its Librarian, Mrs Miriam Barraud, and also from the town Information Officer, Mrs Christine Gilby. I appreciate their kindness. The Master of Sidney Sussex College and Mr Christopher Parish were most helpful in showing me round the College, and answering my questions. It was a particular pleasure to take lunch under Samuel Cooper's strange and haunting crayon portrait of Cromwell. I am very grateful.

In bringing Huntingdon, Hinchingbrooke and the whole Cromwell area vividly alive my thanks go to Barry and Sylvia Williamson who guided me along the ways Cromwell trod. In Ireland Cromwell's campaigns were made real to me by Alan Barwise, who escorted me round Drogheda, and by Rosalind Barwise who enabled me to understand Wexford and the South. I thank them both.

Too many friends have been kind and helpful in too many ways for me to record them all. I hope they will, nevertheless, be aware of my gratitude.

It is finally my pleasure to thank my publisher and editor, Peter Shellard, for his patience and understanding. It is his expertise, on many levels, that brings this book to life.

As always, I thank my family, and particularly my husband, for their forbearance and help.

May all concerned enjoy Cromwell as much as I have done!

Garsington,
1988

England and Wales

NORTH SEA

Newcastle ●

● Carlisle

● Penrith

Marston Moor ✗ ● York

Preston ✗

Pontefract ● Hull ●

IRISH SEA

Gainsborough ✗

Lincoln ● ✗ *Winceby*

Shrewsbury ●

Ely ●

Huntingdon ●

Naseby ✗ ● St Ives

Worcester ✗ ● Evesham Cambridge ● ● Newmarket

Edgehill ✗

Colchester ●

Milford Haven

Burford ● ● Oxford

Pembroke ► Reading ●

ST GEORGES CHANNEL

● Bristol ✗ LONDON

Newbury

ENGLISH CHANNEL

THE CROMWELL FAMILY TREE

WALTER CROMWELL of Putney = ?
(d.c. 1480)

MORGAN WILLIAMS = KATHERINE CROMWELL
(married 1494)

SIR RICHARD WILLIAMS ALIAS CROMWELL OF HINCHINGBROOKE
(b.c. 1496 d. 1544)

SIR HENRY WILLIAMS ALIAS CROMWELL OF HINCHINGBROOKE
(b. 1537 d. 1603)

who had eleven children, six sons and five daughters.

1 SIR OLIVER CROMWELL OF
  HINCHINGBROOKE (b. 1563.
  d. 1655).
2 †ROBERT, father of Oliver
  Cromwell (b. ? d. 1617).
3 Henry.
4 Richard.
5 Philip, later knighted.
6 Ralph.
7 Joan.
8 Elizabeth.
9 Frances.
10 Mary.
11 Dorothy.

†ROBERT, second son of Sir Henry,
had 10 children:

1 Joan 1592–1598.
2 Elizabeth 1593–1672.
3 Henry, eldest son, died in
  infancy, 1595.
4 Katherine, 1597. Date of death
  unknown.
5 ††OLIVER, 1599–1658. Lord
  Protector of the
  Commonwealth.
6 Margaret, 1601. Date of death
  unknown.
7 Anna, 1603–1646.
8 Jane, 1606–c1656.
9 Robert, 1609. Died in infancy.

10 Robina, date of birth and death
   unknown.

††OLIVER, the only son of Robert
to survive, had nine children:

1 Robert 1621–1639. Died at
  Felsted School, of smallpox.
  Unmarried.
2 Oliver 1623–1644. Unmarried.
3 Bridget 1624–1681. Married.
  (1) Henry Ireton 1646.
  (2) Charles Fleetwood 1652.
4 RICHARD 1626–1712, who
  succeeded his father as
  Protector.
  Married Dorothy Major of
  Hursley 1649.
5 Henry 1628–1674. Married
  Elizabeth, Daughter of Sir
  Francis Russell of
  Chippenham.
6 Elizabeth 1629–1658. Married
  John Claypole of
  Northborough 1645.
7 James 1632. Died in infancy.
8 Mary 1637–1713. Married
  Thomas Belasyse, Viscount
  Fauconberg, 1657.
9 Frances 1638–1721. Married.
  (1) Robert Rich, son of Lord
  Rich, 1657.
  (2) Sir John Russell.

Part I

'But in thine own fields exercisest long . . .'

1

'. . . by birth a gentleman'

At Hinchingbrooke, the imposing mansion just outside the town of Huntingdon belonging to Sir Oliver Cromwell, festivities were in full swing. The ancient stone abbey, restored with red brick by Sir Oliver's father, was warm in the thin April sunshine. As evening fell it was a blaze of light. Notables from town and country were flocking in; Heads of Houses from the University of Cambridge in scarlet robes; courtiers from London, townsfolk, village folk, Sir Oliver's newly married wife, the widow of the wealthy financier Sir Horatio Palavicino, Sir Oliver's younger brother Robert from the town of Huntingdon with his family. The youngest of Robert's five children, barely four years old, was there, a solemn, somewhat aggressive boy who was Sir Oliver's godson and namesake. Food and drink for the guests were unstinted with meat of many kinds and the best wine in great variety. Booths round the house provided unlimited beer with bread and meat for humbler folk.

The occasion of the celebration was the arrival of James VI of Scotland who, after the death of Elizabeth I earlier in 1603, was travelling down the Great North Road to London to assume the crown as James I of England, Scotland and Ireland.

Hinchingbrooke stood near the river Ouse by the old Roman Ermine Street which was the direct route from London to the north and was accustomed to visitors. Queen Elizabeth had many times been a guest. But to honour the new monarch Sir Oliver mustered his considerable wealth to provide hospitality beyond anything King James had yet seen. Opportunely the new bay to the great hall on the first floor, built to celebrate his recent marriage, added just the scale and scope that James and his entourage required. James was impressed: 'Marry, mon, thou hast treated me better than any one syn I left Edinboro!' he exclaimed. What pleased him most were

3

the gifts with which he was showered – 'goodly horses', 'fleet and deep-mouthed hounds', 'hawks of excellent wing', and a standing cup of gold. Not surprisingly he came back many times to enjoy the lavish hospitality of Hinchingbrooke, and its owner was duly knighted in the Coronation honours.

To the little Cromwells of Huntingdon Hinchingbrooke was a second home. There were many parties, much dancing and singing. Uncle Oliver was fond of music and was a friend of John Dowland who had dedicated a book of songs and airs to him. Their own father, Robert, a second son, farmed his land round Huntingdon and was comfortably off; but the difference between him and the eldest son was obvious.

The Cromwells were descended from a wealthy brewer named Morgan Williams who, although his business interests were in Putney, was of Glamorgan stock. Morgan Williams married Katherine, sister to Thomas Cromwell, Earl of Essex, who was engaged in suppressing the English monasteries on behalf of his master, King Henry VIII. The eldest son of Morgan and Katherine took the surname of his illustrious uncle and, as Richard Cromwell, also entered the service of Henry VIII, ably assisting in the work of monastic destruction. Among his rewards were, in 1538, the Benedictine priory of Hinchingbrooke and, two years later, the site of the Benedictine Abbey of Ramsey. The seal was put upon his career in the jousts held before Henry VIII as part of the May Day celebrations of 1540. He appeared in the lists magnificently accoutred, with his horses draped in white velvet, and proceeded to oust all comers. The King was so delighted with his prowess and his appearance that he let drop the diamond ring from his finger exclaiming: 'Formerly thou wast my Dick, but hereafter shalt be my diamond.' The action spoke more clearly than the enigmatic utterance, Richard caught the ring and the Cromwells substituted a diamond for a javelin in the paws of the lion in their family crest. Richard Cromwell was knighted, but the most eloquent sign of royal favour was that he survived the fall and execution of his uncle Thomas Cromwell, the hammer of the monks. He married a daughter of the Lord Mayor of London and when he died in 1546 he was a very rich man.

It was his son, Henry, who built Hinchingbrooke House, partly a conversion from the old priory, partly a new construction of red brick. Here Henry Cromwell with his wife, another Lord Mayor's daughter, entertained Queen Elizabeth and was duly knighted. He was Member of Parliament, marshal, and four times sheriff of his county. He was vigorous in mustering the county against the Spanish Armada, raising twenty-six horsemen at his own cost, besides the four soldiers he was bound by law to furnish. He called upon the trained bands to practise 'the right and perfect use of their weapons' and to fight for 'the sincere religion of Christ' against 'the devilish superstition of the Pope'. His words and his actions would certainly have been recounted to his grandchildren and were to be reflected in the words of at least one of them in a later crisis.

The eldest son of this 'Golden Knight', as he was termed on account of his liberality and the splendour in which he lived, inherited not only Hinchingbrooke and the bulk of his father's wealth but also his liberality in excess as he showed when he entertained King James in 1603. The subsequent frequent visits of the King helped to deplete the fortune of even the wealthy Cromwells of Hinchingbrooke.

The inheritance of Robert, the second son of the Golden Knight, was comparatively small. It consisted mainly of former Abbey estates round Huntingdon and included, with the house in Huntingdon High Street, a dovecote and a brew-house. Robert married a widow, Elizabeth Lynn, who had been born a Steward. On her side, also, the rise of the family had been associated with monastic dissolution and the disintegration of the older Church. Her great-uncle, Robert Steward, was the first Protestant Dean of Ely Cathedral, her father and her uncle worked extensive monastic land round Ely and farmed the Cathedral tythes. The family home, where Elizabeth was born, was a large and attractive half-timbered house in the shadow of Ely Cathedral.

Robert and Elizabeth, though not wealthy, were not badly off and they lived quietly and unostentatiously in a comfortable house in Huntingdon High Street, their farm land stretching round them, their family growing.[1]

The fifth child and second son of Robert and Elizabeth Cromwell was born at Huntingdon on 25 April 1599. Four days later he was christened Oliver, after his uncle, in the church of St John the Baptist, one of four churches which were still standing out of the sixteen which had existed in the Middle Ages. As befitted a member of the upper classes the baptismal entry was in Latin.[2]

It is doubtful whether Robert or Elizabeth Cromwell paid much attention to the birth in Dunfermline, Scotland, one and a half years later, of a second son, christened Charles, to King James VI of Scotland. The death of Queen Elizabeth on 24 March 1603, when the little Oliver was nearly four years old and the baby Charles barely two and a half, was much more emotive, marking the end of an era that had lasted for well on half a century. The plunge from the known to the unknown coloured the general appraisement of James as he came south with his entourage of Scots to take over, as King James I, the government of England, Scotland and Ireland. His entertainment at Hinchingbrooke gave the Cromwells a better opportunity than most to form a judgement of the new King.

The little Prince Charles was not there. It was fifteen months later, on 17 July 1604, that he was borne southwards in a litter, being unable to walk or ride unaided. His parents met him at Easton Neston in Northamptonshire and there is no reason to believe that he touched Hinchingbrooke on his way to London or that he accompanied his father there the following year when James visited Hinchingbrooke from his hunting lodge in Royston. There remains nothing but a nice sense of prophecy-with-hindsight in the story, recounted long after, that about this time there was an encounter between the two little boys in which Oliver gave Charles a bloody nose. But even without a meeting there was enough gossip to enable the Cromwell parents to compare with satisfaction their own hearty second son and the sickly Prince (also a second son) who was afflicted both with rickets and a serious speech defect.

The apocryphal stories told of the childhood of these two children bear some similarity. Charles had had a dark cloak thrown over him by an old man as he lay in his cradle, his father being quick in prophecy: 'Gin he ever be King, there'll be noe gude a' his reign. The deil has cusen his cloak ower him already.' In Oliver's case the devil appeared as a figure in a tapestry that hung in the room where he was born. The cloak motif is taken up in the story told of him when he was a little older, resting on his bed after exercise, when the gigantic figure of a woman drew the curtains back and, after gazing at the boy, told him he would become the greatest man in England.

Oliver had more legendary escapes from death than Charles. During a visit to Hinchingbrooke a tame monkey seized him and carried him over the rooftops without harming him or letting him fall; he was saved from drowning in a local river by a curate, who later regretted his act of succour; he fell into a well at Maldon in Essex while watering his horse but escaped without injury. The story of Oliver playing the part of a monarch in a school play, with the crown upon his head, resembles the story told of Charles that his elder brother crowned him with the Archbishop's mitre: such anecdotes at least indicate boys of entirely different character.

There is little actual information about the childhood of Oliver. It may be assumed that he ran, jumped, wrestled, raided orchards like other country boys, that he rode horses as a matter of course, riding with his father and brother to inspect the family farmland. The absence of recorded illness indicates a robust, sturdy lad.

With Charles it was different: he was a Prince and must needs be recorded, so the picture of his childhood is clearer. It would be strange, indeed, if news from Whitehall concerning the delicate little boy did not come to Huntingdon, and stranger still if Oliver did not compare himself with the unfortunate young Prince – the visits to the bone surgeon, the strong boots that provided support for the weak ankles, the perseverance with riding until the great horse and riding at the ring came naturally to him. The struggle for physical attainment that did so much to mould the character of the Prince was absent in Oliver Cromwell simply because it was not necessary. On the other hand, the mental and spiritual struggle that later showed itself in Oliver had no parallel in Charles, who remained serene and certain.

Oliver had a little pre-school education, first from an old lady, a kind of nurse-governess, who probably did no more than 'mind' him, and then from an elderly clergyman, the Rev Mr Long, who conducted a small kindergarten in Huntingdon. After this he went to the free grammar school of the town where he was under the care of Dr Thomas Beard and his assistant.

Dr Beard was not only the schoolmaster of Huntingdon, he was rector of the church of St John where Oliver was baptised and where he and his family worshipped. He was prominent in local affairs, he was a friend of the family, a witness to Robert Cromwell's will, and a frequent and welcome visitor to the Cromwell home, where his friendliness and charm belied the sternness of the doctrine expressed in his books. For he was learned, a sincere Puritan, and had published in 1597 *The Theatre of God's Judgments, translated from the French and augmented with over 300 examples.* To later editions, published between 1612 and 1631, were added still more examples. All these, and the book itself, witnessed to the glory of the 'elect'. The 'elect', ran the argument, are so ordained by God. Once they realize this they fight on the side of the Lord and, so long as they remain aware of their calling, they will overcome the powers of darkness. Oliver would certainly have known the book which was popular and ran into at least four editions, and he would have imbibed the same teaching at his parish church and at his school. Thus early was Oliver Cromwell shown on which side of the great argument of predestination and free will his path would lie. But having accepted the doctrine of predestination, how would he know whether he was, indeed, one of God's elect? The search to find out, the morbid fear that he was not, perhaps, chosen, conflicted with his naturally boisterous nature to produce a crisis in adolescence which manifested itself in the actions that his detractors later magnified.

For as he grew older Oliver became more exuberant and began to press his physical activity in the dubious directions that fed the pens of later gossip writers and helped to fuel his own spiritual crises with remorse and self-recrimination. He seems to have done nothing particularly endearing during his schooldays: he was of a stubborn disposition that made correction difficult; he played truant, he broke down hedges and stole the birds from the dovecotes. His periods of concentration on his work were few though intense. Dr Beard showed no special favour to the boy. Perhaps he went too far in the other direction, for when Oliver recounted to him the story of the vision by his bed who promised greatness, Dr Beard whipped him soundly. Oliver's father did likewise when the boy repeated the story to him. It is evident that the dream or vision made a strong impression upon Oliver: he never forgot it and recounted it several times in later life. The young Prince Charles was meanwhile proving more tractable and a keen scholar, out to please, and devoted to his tutor, Dr Thomas Murray, with whom he was on the closest terms of affection and respect.

When Oliver was not more than sixteen years old and still at school his elder brother, Henry, died. It is difficult to assess the effect upon the boy. Death was not uncommon among the young in the seventeenth century; and of Oliver's relations with his brother, of the affection or closeness between them, we know nothing. But personal relationships apart, the death of his only brother brought fresh and harsh responsibilities to young Oliver. Still a schoolboy, he was now the only son in a family of six sisters, heir to his father's estate, centre of his father's hopes and ambitions.

Prince Charles, also, had an elder brother named Henry – Prince of Wales and heir to the throne. Henry, Prince of Wales, died in 1612 a few years before young Henry Cromwell, when Charles was only twelve years old. Charles, like Oliver, had to shoulder new and exacting responsibilities, in his case no less than those of heir to the throne; and he had, in addition, to bear the loss of a brother to whom he was devoted and whom he deeply loved.

But death notwithstanding, both boys continued on their way, Charles with ever-increasing duties of state, Oliver to the University of Cambridge. He had evidently imbibed enough Latin under Dr Beard to be admitted to Sidney Sussex College as a Fellow Commoner on 23 April 1616 when he was just seventeen years old. His tutor was Richard Howlett, the Master of the College was Dr Samuel Ward, Lady Margaret Professor of Divinity at the University. Dr Ward had been one of the team who prepared the King James's version of the Bible, he was a strong believer in predestination, and had upheld that view at the Synod of Dort in 1619 against the Arminians who believed in free will. He was a stern disciplinarian requiring his students to memorize the often inordinately long sermons they heard, and was ready to whip them publicly in Hall if they failed to do so. The College under his rule was described as a 'nursery of Puritanism' and some of its spirit must have rubbed off on Oliver Cromwell. Reports, however, indicate much the same interests as in his schooldays, with little time for intellectual pursuits but a great enthusiasm for football, cudgelling, wrestling and an early form of cricket. There is talk of 'a rough and blustering disposition', of 'a dissolute and disorderly course of life'. There is a story, too, that he jumped from the first floor window of his room in College on to a horse standing outside.

But whatever tales accompany his youth Oliver Cromwell did acquire some background of general knowledge and at least a working acquaintance with Latin, for evidence indicates that in later life he both understood and spoke Latin – though 'very viciously and scantily' according to one observer. One early biographer says he was well read in Greek and Latin history; another that he excelled in mathematics. Mathematics then carried something of the prestige of 'technology' in the twentieth century and a certain diligence in studying it would not be surprising or exceptional; while a superficial knowledge of Greek and Roman history is what any normal middle-class Englishman of the seventeenth century would carry with him as part of his stock-in-trade.[3]

With that indefinable attribute we term 'culture' Oliver Cromwell was not endowed; the remark that 'the spirit of the Renaissance was never breathed upon him' may well be apt, emphasizing again the contrast between him and Prince Charles who, after the death of his brother, developed into the Renaissance prince *par excellence*. The 'considerable and well-chosen library' Cromwell was said to have acquired in later life was what might have been expected from any man with money to spend who was not entirely cut off from the intellectual life of his time. It is interesting that when he came to give advice to his son Richard he recommended the study of a little history, mathematics, and cosmography 'with subordination to the things of God'. For reading he recommended Raleigh's *History of the World* which, he said, being 'a body of history' added much more to the understanding than fragments of story.[4] There was no mention of Shakespeare, of Beaumont and Fletcher or Ben Jonson, whose plays and masques gave much pleasure to King Charles; nor of the young Milton who came to Cambridge shortly after Oliver's departure and celebrated the muses within the venerable walls of Christ's College much as Cromwell had memorized sermons within the stern confines of Sidney Sussex, nor of Andrew Marvell, more closely associated with Cromwell through his poems than any other writer but who tutored Fairfax's daughter, not Cromwell's.

Oliver had been at Cambridge for only a year when his father died and family responsibilities compelled him to leave the University. Again, it is difficult to assess the personal loss. Robert Cromwell was of a retiring disposition. Both circumstances and his own character had marked out for him a life very different from that of his father, the 'Golden Knight' of Hinchingbrooke, or of his elder brother, Sir Oliver, who inherited the house and estate. Nevertheless, Robert Cromwell had been educated at Queen's College, Cambridge, and then at Lincoln's Inn. He was said to be 'a man of very good sense and of competent learning', his friendship with Dr Beard indicating, indeed, a man of some intellectual curiosity as well as strong

Puritan beliefs. It is possible that these had been encouraged, if not engendered by Dr Beard, for Queen's College had no particularly strong Puritan tradition. Also like Dr Beard, Robert Cromwell was not averse to meting out the strong punishment which he thought his sons sometimes deserved. He was active in local affairs, being bailiff of the town of Huntingdon, Justice of the Peace for his county, and trustee of the the free school his son attended. He was keenly interested in the drainage of the fenland which was part of his wife's background as well as impinging closely upon his own county, and as Commissioner of Sewers he was signatory to a document which pronounced the drainage of the Great Level to be feasible. He was elected by his fellow-townsmen to Elizabeth's Parliament of 1593, though there is no record of his active participation. Doubtless he was glad to return to the less complicated affairs of Huntingdon and the more private life he enjoyed.[5]

Whatever had been the relationship between this upright and retiring man and his only surviving son, the loss of such a calm and steadying influence was bound to affect young Oliver. He was uncertain of his direction, not fully capable of shouldering the family responsibilities now thrust upon him, disoriented by having to leave Cambridge suddenly, before his time, overwhelmed at finding himself the only male among six women for whose well-being, by the standards of the time, he was now responsible. He appears to have gained little comfort from the acquisition of a brother-in-law, Valentine Walton, the son of a neighbouring squire, who had married his sister Margaret a few days before the death of her father. Ignoring advice from family or friends he took refuge in a life of near debauchery; gambling, drinking, running up debts, demanding drink for himself and his associates without paying for it, accosting women in the town and its neighbourhood, indulging in pranks which were sometimes more than practical jokes if the story of him at a party at Hinchingbrooke can be credited. Here it is said that he daubed himself with excrement, compelled others to dance with him, so fouling their clothes also, and creating such a stench throughout the hall, that his uncle was called and obliged him to be ducked in the pond to cleanse him. This daubing accords so closely with two other later tales – one at his daughter's wedding, one at the signing of the King's death warrant – that one wonders if the later episodes lend authenticity to the the earlier tale or whether the earlier tale is manufactured out of knowledge of the later episodes.[6]

Whether it was out of despair at his conduct, or whether she merely wished her son to acquire the smattering of law which was considered necessary to any family, Elizabeth Cromwell sent Oliver to London, to Lincoln's Inn. There is no record of his enrolment there or at Gray's Inn. His father, grandfather, and two uncles had attended Lincoln's Inn, many of his kinsmen were at Gray's Inn. In either place the company he would keep would not necessarily improve his manners or his way of life, for the Inns of Court were well-known for the type of young blade who attended them. Whether he stayed long enough to acquire a smattering of law is again uncertain. Instead, the stories tell of an early return to Huntingdon and a continuation of a dissolute life, so quarrelsome in his drink that few would bear him company, his chief weapon the quarterstaff at which he was seldom overmatched. It is possible that he went to the Continent, perhaps driven by a lack of friends and his own restless spirit. There is a tradition that he went to Paris and indulged there in the same kind of life he had led at home. Another story, with more justification, says that he was in Amsterdam where he met the Jew, Manessa Ben Israel, whose friendship induced him later to allow the Jews to return to England when he had the power to let them. One would like to think of him enrolling in one of the continental armies and seeing at first hand something of the military strategy that would serve him so well later. There is no evidence of this, though soldiering would have been a likely pursuit for such a physical young man.[7]

Whatever he did could not have lasted long, for within three years of leaving Cambridge Oliver Cromwell was courting in the City of London. The lady in question was Elizabeth Bouchier, the daughter of a wealthy London fur dealer and leather dresser who had been knighted by King James in 1610. Apart from their London house the family possessed lands in Essex and a fine country house, Little Standbridge Hall, near Felsted. Elizabeth's mother was a Suffolk lady named Frances Crane, and these links with the Eastern counties make it likely that Cromwell family connections – the Mashams of Otes or the Barringtons who were relatives and near neighbours of the Bouchiers – had helped to bring the young people together and that they met in Essex as well as London before their betrothal was announced.

The marriage of Oliver Cromwell and Elizabeth Bouchier in the church of St Giles, Cripplegate, on 22 August 1620[8] not only makes it clear that Cromwell's period of debauchery could not have lasted very long, but makes it extremely unlikely that it could have been as vicious as his detractors made out. The husband whom Sir James Bouchier accepted for his daughter would need to reach a certain standard of reputation and conduct. This apart, what Sir James saw was a young man of good country stock and lineage, well connected and with a family tradition of wealth, even if not much wealth was immediately to hand, whose family fortunes, like his own, were founded on the Reformation and the Protestant religion – though without the additional security of trade and industry. That his future son-in-law's education was incomplete would hardly have worried the London tradesman; that the lad had sown some wild oats was only what many young men of good family had done, and was probably a point in his favour. Moreover, Elizabeth was the oldest of six children and, at the age of twenty-three, was ripe for marriage.

These considerations apart, young Cromwell was tall – some 5′ 9″ or 10″ – physically strong, somewhat 'rough hewn' in appearance, blunt in his manner, apt to take offence easily, inclined, indeed, to be quarrelsome. He was not handsome yet the rugged features were attractive, in spite of the heavy nose, the eyes were ardent and expressive and in an age when male dominance was taken for granted he was the kind of man a young woman might well welcome for her husband – the more so in the case of Elizabeth Bouchier who was two years older than Oliver and appears to have been of a gentle, homely disposition.

Oliver for his part saw a well-connected lady of some wealth, prepared to be devoted to him, not beautiful yet plump and pretty enough with eyes that promised a sense of humour – which would be good for him, though he would not have admitted it. He needed to settle down, to achieve some stability, and felt, perhaps, that a wife would be a balancing factor against the other women in his family. Whatever the financial arrangements with his mother and sisters after his father's death, Oliver was able to provide a generous settlement for Elizabeth Bouchier which implies that she, for her part, brought him a considerable dowry.[9]

2

'. . . his native wood-notes wild'

Cromwell's native shire, where he now established himself with a wife and the expectation of a growing family, was a land-locked county some fifty or sixty miles north of the capital. It was enclosed by Bedfordshire to the south and Northamptonshire to the west with Cambridgeshire and the Isle of Ely on its eastern flank. The Great Ouse, on whose northern, gently rising bank stood the county town of Huntingdon, flowed northwards through the county from Bedford in the south to empty itself into the Wash at King's Lynn thirty miles north-east of Huntingdon. The Wash formed a natural basin towards which the land sloped and into which emptied many small streams as well as the Ouse, the Nene and other rivers. The counties of Lincolnshire to the north and Norfolk to the south shared its flat, wide estuary.

The town of Huntingdon owed its importance originally to the Roman Ermine Street which crossed the Ouse at this point on its way from London to Lincoln and York. It consisted mainly of one street, about a mile long, with the houses of poorer people branching off in little lanes to right and left. Sturdier buildings, including the Cromwell house, the grammar school where Cromwell had studied under Dr Beard, and the George, a handsome courtyard inn, owned by his grandfather, stood along its main street. A little behind the George was the town square on which stood the Falcon Inn, another well-known hostelry. A handsome, six-arched bridge of stone, four of the arches of which were large enough for barges to pass through, crossed the Ouse at the southern end of the town; below it, to the East, were the ruins of a small monastery, while on a low nearby hill stood the remains of an ancient castle from the ruined keep of which extensive views opened out over the flat countryside.

The land consisted for the most part of low-lying clay. It was fertile but subject to flooding and was mostly under the plough, though a mixed breed of sheep grazed on a little enclosed pasture; a few cows, used mainly for suckling calves for the London market, provided household milk, and small areas of woodland provided welcome shade in sunny weather and were useful for firing and fencing and small building purposes. The area was sufficiently profitable and near enough to London to have encouraged speculators to move in and buy up acres either to farm themselves or, more likely, to let at a good rent. Despite this there was little enclosure when Oliver Cromwell settled down to the farmer's life in the early years of the seventeenth century.

The pleasant arable that lay near and around the comfortable house in Huntingdon High Street was fertile and yielded good wheat, the cattle in the meadows were fat, their milk flowed freely, there was barley to supply the small breweries on the Cromwell land which were conveniently fed by the small Hitchin Brook that ran behind the house. It was most likely Cromwell's mother who managed these, selling the beer for small profit or merely serving it to refresh the family and their workpeople.

The river Ouse – that 'goodly fair river' – was central to the life of the Cromwell family and, indeed, of the whole region, forming part of an extensive system of inland waterways which had existed for centuries. Apart from stone for building there coursed along these rivers much of the trade of the eastern counties, supplying not only inland towns like St Neots and Huntingdon and St Ives but serving the ports of the eastern seaboard – Boston, King's Lynn, Great Yarmouth – and thus the coastal trade north to Hull and Newcastle, south to London. Corn and other agricultural produce and malt went down the Great Ouse to be shipped coastwise; coal came from Newcastle to be brought upstream to Huntingdon and other towns. Yarmouth, besides its famous herrings, was a great entrepôt for coal from Newcastle. King's Lynn both shipped wool to Hull and received it to pass on to Norfolk clothiers. The prosperous cloth manufacture of Norwich, the light, bright mixtures of wool and silk known as bombazines, and the coarser 'new draperies' were already famous. The Flemings and other Dissenters who had been driven out of the Low Countries a couple of generations earlier, bringing their faith and their skills with them, were a flourishing community both economically and spiritually whose influence spread beyond the looms of Norwich and East Anglia.

Trade, whether inland or to the coast, was fed by the boats that plied the rivers. The horses, led by boys, that towed the boats were a familiar sight up and down the river Ouse. Sometimes, in wet seasons, both boy and beast trudged along up to the knees or even the waist in the swollen river. The hazards created by inadequate care of these water highways were a constant problem to the inhabitants: rivers were foul, overgrown with weeds, full of refuse, impeded by weirs, by mills, by fords, by shallows, by fish nets. A few public-spirited riparian landlords had valiantly tried to maintain their own stretches of river but had been powerless against general neglect and laziness. But these difficulties notwithstanding there was beauty in the river, particularly as it flowed down from Huntingdon to St Ives. Good fish were obtainable in its waters. The wild fowl which nested on its banks provided a good supplement to the family diet. So did the geese, many of which were destined to be taken in droves to the capital, joining the calves on the long, dusty or muddy haul to London in order to titillate the palates of the wealthy.

Wheat was still a profitable crop, though too much dependent on the weather, and its price varied disconcertingly with trade vicissitudes, external wars, outbreaks of plague in the capital and a dozen external factors which had nothing to do with the farmer's skill. Yet, riding round the big, flat, spreading wheat fields, unencumbered by hedge or ditch, with no hill and scarcely any rising ground to impede the vision, the eye travelling to the far horizon in one direction or seeking the distant tower of Ely in another, a man might be content. With hawking and fishing and a little hunting of smaller animals and birds, with his barns full, his orchards and his market gardens yielding well, Oliver Cromwell could lead a simple and uneventful life.

A few miles away stretched the far more dramatic fenland where life was both more difficult and more exciting. Here people lived even closer to a Providence which had cast them for roles in a virtually unique environment. In winter, when the fenlands were flooded, the area was a sea of water farther than the eye could reach, the only means of transport was by boat, diet was confined to fish, the inhabitants lived in huts built precariously on islands of firmer ground, they occupied themselves by making mats and baskets and fish-nets from reeds collected earlier. In the summer, when the waters receded, there could be seen the innumerable ditches, canals, and drains with which the fens were intersected, as well as the alders

16

and willows the fenmen had planted to help contain the floods. Then the rich, fertile earth was not only bright with yellow and purple loosestrife, with rose-purple willow-herb, with ragwort, sow-thistle and an abundance of colourful plants and flowers, but it yielded the luxurious long grass and rank hay called lid with which the fenmen fed the cattle which, with fish and fowl, provided their summer diet. They frequently reaped this harvest upon stilts which carried them high over the rich, sodden earth, they collected the reeds they needed for thatching, the turf and sedge for firing, branches of alder and willow for basket-making. Then, in November, they set fire to what remained in order to make it grow stronger. At this time the blazing marshes were an awesome sight, the fire flaming from horizon to horizon over the flat countryside. A man might see it, wrote a contemporary of Cromwell, 'and wonder thereat'.

The area was famous for its independence, having a long historical record of freedom from at least the time of Hereward the Wake who resisted the Norman invader from within the wild and desolate protection of the fenland. The inhabitants were said to be 'rude' and 'uncouth' (epithets used of Cromwell in his youth) and unprepared for close contact with 'upland-men'. They certainly lived as a race apart, ready to resist any so-called improvements that would reduce their harvest or deprive them of fish or fowl or any of the perquisites of the watery waste they had learned to utilize to their own advantage.[1]

Cromwell and his family, if not actually part of this existence, were close to it geographically and through his mother's connections: she was a fen-woman. His maternal grandfather, and now his uncle, his mother's brother, farmed in the Isle of Ely, a small area of higher ground in the Cambridgeshire fenland, close by the great cathedral of Ely. For the area, though desolate of stone, was notable for its many stone churches and for this splendid cathedral whose building material had been brought along the river highways from Barnock in Northamptonshire. His father, also, had a strong interest in the fenland through his post as Commissioner of Sewers, and it was presumably after some detailed survey of the area that he joined the great controversy over drainage and signed the paper asserting that the drainage of the Great Level of the fens was a feasible project.

Riding, perhaps, to Whitlesmere where kites, buzzards and herons hovered, practising the hawking he loved all his life, watching the annual rise and fall of the waters, gazing over the blazing marshland in November, Oliver Cromwell could feel himself close to elemental forces outside the control of man and look beyond them to the workings of a divine Providence.

It was in Huntingdon, nevertheless, as property-owner and burgess, that his immediate interests lay.

Cromwell fulfilled satisfactorily his role as burgess of Huntingdon and just three months after his marriage was called upon to play his part on a wider stage. His name then headed the list of burgesses, following those of the two bailiffs of Huntingdon, who elected Sir Henry St John and Sir Miles Sandys to the Parliament summoned in November 1620 by King James. The young Cromwell, not yet twenty-one, was beginning to feel his feet not only as a member of the local community but as part of a large and influential family. For St John was related to the Cromwells, Sandys was closely connected to them in many ways, and it required less than Oliver's perspicacity to be aware of the net of other Cromwell kinsmen spreading with interlocking connections round the Eastern and Home counties.[2]

The Parliament which met in 1621 was of more than common interest. The marriage, eight years earlier, of King James's only daughter to the Elector Palatine, the upholder of the Protestant religion in the Holy Roman Empire, had involved the country in a disastrous war in which the forces of Protestantism were suffering humiliating defeat at the hands of a Catholic coalition. James wanted this Parliament to provide more money for the war, and the plight of his daughter and her family, wandering homeless across Europe, offered telling support for his demands. But the Members of Parliament had questions to ask before they granted supply. No longer was it a simple issue of being against the Pope and the Spaniard, fighting the Armada in the name of God and the Queen, bringing back treasure from the Spanish Main. On the contrary, the country was involved in a European land war which was costly in lives, money and honour, in which it found itself on the losing side. Moreover, the heir to the throne, by means of some tortuous reasoning on the part of James which the Members of Parliament failed to understand, was being offered as bridegroom to the King of Spain's daughter. The Commons asked that the Prince of Wales should marry a Protestant Princess, they asserted their right to free speech and declared that affairs concerning the King, the State and the Church of England were proper subjects for debate in Parliament. This 'Protestation' so enraged King James that, having dissolved Parliament, he tore the offending page from the Journal of the House of Commons. News travelled sufficiently widely for Oliver Cromwell to be well aware of the actions of the Parliament he had helped to elect and of the dramatic rebuff it had received at the King's hands. The era of the news-sheet was beginning, and not only English Papers but Dutch *courantos*, translated into English, were finding a ready market among English people anxious to learn of the progress of the war in Europe. So were the pamphlets lampooning the King and deriding him for failing to help his daughter or support the Protestant faith. It would be surprising indeed if none of these reached the household at Huntingdon.

Meanwhile Oliver's personal responsibilities were widening with the birth in October 1621 of his first child, named Robert after his grandfather. A second son, Oliver, after his father, followed in February 1623. But the Cromwells could not quietly enjoy their growing family. The European wars and consequent loss to England of markets in the Low Countries and Germany were affecting trade and in particular the livelihood of the cloth workers of neighbouring East Anglia. At the same time a series of bad winters were straining resources as crops suffered and harvests were poor. It was at this time, in the spring of 1623, that Prince Charles chose to ride across France to Spain to woo the Spanish Infanta in person. The expedition, when the news leaked out, was the subject of horrified speculation round many English hearths. The Cromwell household could hardly avoid the prevailing gloom. Nevertheless, the bonfires in Huntingdon burned as brightly as any others when Prince Charles landed at Portsmouth on October 5 – not so much for his safe return as that he had returned without a Spanish bride.

For Oliver personally, in spite of outward signs of responsibility and maturity, times were difficult. The precarious nature of farming with its fluctuations of yield and profit did not accord with his own instinctive need to control his environment. He may have been worried that his farming did not provide sufficiently for his growing family – Bridget in 1624, Richard in 1626, Henry in 1628: like all the Cromwell women Elizabeth was fecund. It is possible that Oliver found his position in a family of women somewhat daunting. Though his mother might manage the brewhouse and his wife the children there were still his sisters, who perhaps provided too many hands for the rest of the household tasks.

There is no recorded interest by Oliver in wider issues at this time, no indication that he was concerned in the Parliaments which, on the death of James in 1625, Charles I summoned at the beginning of his reign. Instead, whatever the cause, Oliver was being seized by strange fancies, fearing death, seeing visions connected with the cross in Huntingdon High Street, once more encountering, as when a child, an apparition by his bedside which promised him greatness. He summoned help, sometimes in the middle of the night, from the local physician, Dr Simcotts, who noted a rash on his face and pronounced him 'a most splenetic man'.[3] But, more profoundly, a deep religious crisis was shaking him emotionally. Like his parents, and strongly influenced by Dr Beard, he was devoutly Puritan in outlook. In particular Beard's book had made a deep impression on him and he was struggling to discover whether he was, indeed, destined for salvation. Depression settled on him when he thought he was unworthy. Shortly after Richard's birth in 1626 he was cheerful enough to write charmingly to his old Cambridge friend, Henry Downhall, a fellow of St John's, entreating him to stand godfather to the child: 'I am more apt to encroach upon you for new favours than to show my thankfulness for the love I have already found. But I know your patience and your goodness cannot be exhausted by Your friend and servant, Oliver Cromwell.'[4] Richard was duly christened on October 19 with Henry Downhall as one of his distinguished sponsors.

But the following year the sale of Hinchingbrooke House subdued this lightness of touch. As King James returned again and again for renewed hospitality Sir Oliver was paying many times over for his initial entertainment of the King. And even his purse was not bottomless. Oliver was shocked and mortified as he watched the senior side of the family at Hinchingbrooke falling into hard times, particularly when in 1627 the magnificent house, which to him had been a second home, was sold to the Earl of Manchester of the Montagu family, rival landowners in Huntingdonshire. This sale, and his own straitened financial circumstances, could be taken as a sign of God's disapproval. Nevertheless, a second daughter, Elizabeth, was born in 1629.

Cromwell was seeking for Divine guidance at a time when religion was in a state of flux. A century had passed since the English Reforma-

Hinchingbrooke House, Huntingdon – the family mansion (Sylvia Williamson)

Robert Cromwell, Oliver's father
(Cromwell Museum)

Elizabeth Cromwell, Oliver's mother
(Cromwell Museum)

The grammar school, Huntingdon, now the Cromwell Museum (Sylvia Williamson)

Elizabeth Cromwell, Oliver's wife (Cromwell Museum)

Bridget Ireton, Oliver's eldest daughter (Cromwell Museum)

Richard Cromwell, Oliver's elder surviving son (Cromwell Museum)

Henry Cromwell, Oliver's second surviving son (Cromwell Museum)

Elizabeth Claypole, Oliver's second daughter (Cromwell Museum)

Cromwell's 'little wenches' in later life –
Mary Belasyse (above) and Frances Russell
(right) (Cromwell Museum)

The family home at Ely (photo by
C. Nesbitt-Larking)

Portrait of Cromwell
by Sir Peter Lely

tion had removed the English Church from the overlordship of Rome, effecting at the same time those material changes in property and wealth from which Cromwell's forbears had profited. In that time the position of the church, and peoples' relationship to it, had stabilized in some ways but in others was still unresolved.

Henry VIII, while substituting national for Papal supremacy, had made little alteration to dogma or ritual. Elizabeth I had confirmed the position of the English monarch as Head of the Church in the Act of Supremacy of 1559, but basic questions concerning the form and content of worship remained subject to impassioned controversy: the use of English instead of Latin in religious services; the place of 'images', of stained glass, of ornament in churches; the apparel of priests; the acts of bowing, crossing, kneeling; and most importantly the position of the altar and whether it should be called a 'table'. The sacrament itself was at the heart of doctrinal controversy. Many, who could dispense with Papal supremacy, believed fervently in the transubstantiation of the bread and wine into the body and blood of Christ. Others, who also took communion as the central, mystical act of worship, yet believed that Christ was received by them 'in the heart', and entered in 'by faith' and not in any material sense.

Gradually changes were effected. Gospels and Epistles were read, the Litany sung, in English; images and relics were removed from churches, their veneration condemned; bowing and crossing were frowned upon, vestments were simplified, the baptismal ceremony became simpler, general confession took the place of individual auricular confession. A momentous step was taken in the middle of the sixteenth century with the issue of a new Prayer Book in English, the work of Archbishop Cranmer. This made it clear that though the words 'body and blood' as well as 'bread and wine' were retained in the Eucharist the reference was symbolic and the communion service itself was an act of remembrance. As a concession to Protestant extremists the altar was spoken of as the 'table' and it could stand either in the body of the church or in the chancel. But to indicate reverence it should have 'a fair white linen cloth upon it' and the communion should be taken kneeling.

It had been a muddled progression but at least there was some clarity concerning the tenets and position of the Church of England. James I, in whom a rigorous Presbyterian upbringing had ironically engendered a revulsion from that stern church, was disappointed

21

when he found that in England, in spite of the continuing hierarchy of bishops and priests, there existed a very vocal and demanding opposition. Almost on his arrival a petition was presented to him asking for the abolition of ceremonial including the cross in baptism and the ring in marriage. It gave him the opportunity to call a conference at Hampton Court in 1604 to hear both sides and at which he himself could pontificate. He pronounced, with a degree of common sense, that he would have 'one doctrine, and one discipline, one religion in substance and in ceremony' and, with less tact, that those who would not conform would be 'harried out of the land'. The conference confirmed his belief that the power of the monarch, in control of the state, and the bishops, in control of the church, must stand together: 'No bishop, no King,' as he put it.

The Hampton Court conference also resulted in a fresh version of the Bible in English. The translation, at a time when the English language had reached its full flowering, was printed and available to all, taking its place beside, and steadily supplanting, earlier versions. This, with the Prayer Book in English and an increasing number of devotional works and homilies in the native tongue encouraged people to read, to understand, to form their own judgments.

The issue as to how far a man could help himself to salvation was a potent subject of discussion. Had a man 'free will' to believe, to act, to do good works, to achieve his own salvation? Or was he 'predestined' to either salvation or damnation and, if so, how would he know? Such matters were obviously of great significance. Men of learning and stature wrote and talked about them, tempers were raised, they became fundamental to religious thought. At Dort, in Holland, a synod of leading theologians debated the issue in 1618/19. The Dutchman, whose Latinized name was Arminius, was a keen exponent of the doctrine of free will and gave his name to the set of beliefs that embodied both free will and High Church practices. For the two normally went together. Arminianism was the doctrine of High Church English Protestants. The doctrine of predestination was held by the dissenting followers of Calvin who in England came to be known as Puritans.

Charles I firmly endorsed his father's aphorism of 'No bishop no King' while his nature and temperament were receptive to visual beauty and order. None of this could be satisfied by Puritanism. Not for Charles the tortuous seeking after truth that occupied Oliver Cromwell. He was partnered by the man he set on the ladder to preferment and who became his Archbishop of Canterbury in 1636. William Laud believed implicitly, as Charles did, that decency and order were necessary to the House of God. He would not go so far as admitting transubstantiation in the Eucharist but he would have the altar decently and seemly in the chancel in the East end of a church where its very position would call for reverence. Communion would be taken kneeling at it, priests would be robed, stained glass and images would enhance the beauty of the church and of the ceremony, bowing and crossing would express the piety of the individual.

It was against this background of Charles and Laud on the one hand and a burgeoning Puritanism on the other that Oliver Cromwell was working out his personal salvation in the quiet fields of Huntingdonshire and Cambridgeshire. He read the Bible in English; his tutor, Dr Beard, had been a leading proponent of predestination at the Synod of Dort, most of his family and friends were Puritans. The *Mayflower* had sailed in the year he married and he knew personally many who had sought religious freedom in the New World. He could not know, as he sought to still the turmoil within himself, that the turmoil over the four kingdoms was only just beginning, nor that he himself would be instrumental in writing in letters of fire over the whole land the prophetic dictum of King James: No bishop, no King!

3

'Girds yet his sword and ready stands to fight'

While this moody man was increasing his family and riding his acres communing with God and his own spirit in the wide expanse of field and sky, momentous issues continued to shake Europe and his own country. The Prince, so near in age to Oliver, had developed into a personable young man, small and slight yet physically active, with no trace of his infantile infirmities save a slight stammer in his speech. If testimony were needed of his horsemanship and physical endurance his ride across France to Madrid provided it. It would have given Oliver no satisfaction that, although Charles had not taken the Spanish wife of his father's choice, he married, in the year of his succession in 1625, the Roman Catholic Princess, Henrietta-Maria, sister to the King of France. Nor could the continued ascendancy of the favourite, the Duke of Buckingham, with his flamboyance, his personal extravagance and his general ineptitude, have given any comfort to the Huntingdon squire. It was becoming clear that there were issues at stake that went beyond the problems of Huntingdon fields.

Charles I had been King for three years, and foreign policy as devised by him and Buckingham was both foolish and illogical. While words supported the King's sister and the Protestant forces in Europe, Charles and Buckingham proceeded to involve themselves in war with both France and Spain at virtually the same time by actions which involved a disastrous naval attack on Cadiz and an equally amateurish naval attempt to relieve the French Huguenot town of La Rochelle. By what alchemy, even if successful, either of these expeditions would help the beleaguered Protestants in Europe was not clear. The only direct action consisted of a small, ill-equipped, ill-paid force of largely pressed men under a soldier of fortune, most of whom perished miserably. The only honour achieved was by a handful of volunteers who sought in vain to help the cause in which they believed.

However inept, Charles's enterprises, like those of his father, required money. His first two Parliaments of 1625 and 1626 had granted only the most meagre supply, and even the customary customs duties, the 'tonnage and poundage' normally granted to a sovereign for life, had been offered to Charles for one year only. The impassioned speeches of orators like Sir John Eliot made it clear enough why supply was witheld. Charles attempted to raise money from his subjects. Those who refused to make the 'forced loans' were imprisoned – Sir John Eliot, Sir Thomas Wentworth and no less than four Cromwell relations – Sir Francis Barrington, Sir William Masham, Sir Edmund Hampden, and Cromwell's cousin, John Hampden, as well as close family friends Richard Knightley and Sir John Trevor who would later, by marriage, come closer within the Cromwell circle. There was also talk of a 'ship money' tax to be levied on London, the shires, and the coastal towns. The idea was dropped then but it was enough to spread alarm in the Eastern seaboard towns and their hinterland.

Finally, in order to finance a further attempt on La Rochelle, Charles called another Parliament. To this third Parliament of the reign, summoned in 1628, Oliver Cromwell and James Montagu, third son of the Earl of Manchester, were elected for the town of Huntingdon. For the county Sir Capel Bedell of Hamerton and Sir Robert Payne of St Neots were returned. There was no longer a Sir Oliver Cromwell of Hinchingbrooke in the House: the family was represented by young Oliver – a not so young Oliver, for he was just on thirty years old when he made his first appearance on the national stage.

The preparations for the journey to London, the farewells, the instructions concerning the farmland and the animals can only be imagined. Then the ride to the capital in the early spring, the river Ouse still swollen from the winter rains, the corn on the arable already carpeting the dark earth. Perhaps sufficient exhilaration to throw off any depression; nervousness allayed by the friends and relatives gathered at Westminster; a consciousness of tradition springing from the knowledge that his grandfather and his uncle and his father had all served as Members of Parliament. Above all, a sense of purpose was evident then as it would always be in everything he undertook.

He made contact with his relations – Oliver St John, John

Hampden, Edmund Dench, Sir Francis Barrington and his two sons; with Richard Knightley, Sir Miles Hobart, Sir Robert Pye, who would join the Cromwell family later. He met others of like mind, foremost among them in vigour, in bulk and in personality John Pym, the Member for Tavistock, who invited Oliver to his lodgings behind the Parliament House; the sardonic Lord Saye and Sele, whose colonizing activities in the New World were famous; the lawyer Sir Edward Coke, cool and caustic, whose reverence for statute law and in particular *Magna Carta* could convert him into a blazing firebrand in debate; Sir Thomas Wentworth, 'Black Tom of the North', a man of whose strength one might stand in awe without clearly understanding whither he was leading; Sir John Eliot, kind, approachable, normally a gentle man but fanatical when his sense of injustice was aroused, when he could rise to heights of oratory hitherto unknown to Oliver. There was William Laud, Bishop of Bath and Wells, chosen by Charles to preach the opening sermon to Parliament – an affront, some considered it, that such an exponent of Arminianism should be so singled out. And the memorable scene at the opening of Parliament, with the Duke of Buckingham sitting by the King in the House of Lords. Surely the eyes of the roughly clad squire from Huntingdon, standing below the bar with fellow Members of the Commons, would have gazed with curiosity, even amazement, at this gorgeous figure, handsome and haughty, carelessly smiling as though about to enjoy a stage play. The King beside him looked almost insignificant. Perhaps Cromwell compared himself with the small, delicately formed monarch.

More importantly he saw and heard something of the King's method of procedure: the cold, formal opening of Parliament – 'I mean not to spend much time in words ...' If the Parliament men did not do their duty he would use 'other means'. And the conclusion: 'Take not this as threatening for I scorn to threaten any but my equals.' Cromwell would have preferred King James's homely scolding.

The duty which the King expected of the Parliament was the supply of money for a further attempt to relieve La Rochelle. The Commons were angry and indignant. They remembered the humiliation of the previous year – '. . . since England was England it received not so dishonourable a blow'. They remembered the forced loans of 1627 and the imprisonment of those who refused to pay. The emphasis in debate was upon the theme 'no taxation without consent of Parliament' and the danger to property if this principle were ignored. They were one and all property-owners and the point struck home to them all. As the dispute broadened Cromwell heard Members cite the ancient laws of the realm, in particular *Magna Carta*, in a context that held up for enforcement the 'ancient rights' and 'freedoms' won in earlier times but now disregarded by the King. When Charles insisted that a monarch must retain a certain 'sovereign power' even if only to use in emergency, the Members rounded on him: '*Magna Carta* knows no sovereign', thundered Coke. 'There is no sovereign power but the law', asserted Pym. Cromwell heard the attack upon Buckingham rising in a crescendo: '... the Duke of Buckingham is the cause of all our miseries ... that man is the grievance of grievances'. He listened as the age-old, basic assumption of no supply without redress of grievances was voiced from all parts of the House of Commons. He was there when John Selden on May 8 emerged from Committee with a paper in his hand which he proceeded to read to the Members: no direct taxation without consent of Parliament; no imprisonment without cause shown; no billeting of soldiers or sailors against the householder's will; no martial law except for military offences. This *Petition of Right*, which amounted almost to a statutory limitation of the powers of the sovereign, was passed by both Houses on May 26, in spite of some resistance by the House of Lords. Cromwell noted the firmness of the Commons, the King's manoeuvring to try to prevent the Petition's final passage. He saw the bonfires in the streets of London and heard the church bells ring after the *Petition* became law; he no doubt collected some of the broadsheets scattered about London streets and heard the ballads chanted in hatred and derision against the Duke of Buckingham.

Then, in common with most other Members of Parliament, he returned home for the recess. He had been away for three months: few farmers could afford to be absent from their fields for longer during the spring and summer. While in Huntingdon he heard of the assassination of the Duke of Buckingham at Portsmouth on August 23 when he was preparing to sail once more for La Rochelle. Perhaps Cromwell had some sense of satisfaction that he had at least seen the magnificent Duke before he was struck down by a twopenny knife in the hand of a half-crazed soldier. There was much to think about in the quiet fields of Huntingdon but he could not find enough peace to eradicate the tension and excitement of his first, momentous Parliament. He tried taking the waters at Wellingborough, a spa visited by the King and Queen and only a few miles from Huntingdon. A month after Buckingham's assassination he was back in London seeking the advice of the eminent physician, Theodore Mayerne, probably recommended to him by one of his Parliamentary connections. His troubles were not unlike those for which he had consulted Dr Simcott. Second advice resulted in a similar diagnosis: he was *valde melancholicus* – extremely melancholy – reported Dr Mayerne. The physical symptoms that the doctor noted accord with those which are commonly described as 'psychosomatic' – a pain in the left side and stomach pains some hours after eating. A dryness of the skin could have been a mild eczema, perhaps associated with the 'pimples' of which Dr Simcott spoke, or the famous warts of later years, or may merely have been the result of long hours in the saddle riding against the strong winds of his native county.[1]

The fact that his farming was not going well at this time was a further cause of depression. Oliver turned for help to his uncle, his mother's brother, Sir Thomas Steward, who was rich and whose heir he was assumed to be. But Sir Thomas was unwilling to make an advance to his nephew. Cromwell's conduct at this point was questionable. He put forward a legal claim to his uncle's estate on the grounds that Sir Thomas was of failing mind and unable to manage it. Though details are uncertain it seems that Cromwell's claim reached the King and was personally turned down by him. It was claimed later that Cromwell bore a grudge against Charles for this reason. In the family, however, the episode appears to have left no rancour. At all events, when Oliver's father's brother, Richard, died without issue in 1628 he left a small bequest to his nephew of property around Huntingdon and this, for the time being, saved the situation.[2]

On 23 January 1629, after a seven-month recess, Cromwell once more rode up from Huntingdon to the capital for the second session of his first Parliament. In the interval the King had continued to levy the tonnage and poundage denied him by Parliament and merchants who refused to pay were in prison, their merchandise impounded. A conciliatory opening speech by Charles was nevertheless applauded by the Members, though they now had their teeth into the religious issue. For the King had been consistently advancing Arminians or authoritarian High Churchmen to positions of influence in the Church. The Sees of Winchester, Durham, Oxford, York, and Cromwell's own Ely, were now held by such men, while William

Laud himself had been promoted during the recess and in July 1628 had become Bishop of London. The spread of their influence by writing and preaching was of the highest concern. The House of Commons had resolved itself into a Committee on Religion, of which Pym was chairman, and was angrily discussing the way in which divines, censored by Parliament for preaching 'popery', had been subsequently pardoned, when on 11 February 1629 Oliver Cromwell rose to make his first contribution to the debates of the House. He had first-hand experience, he said, of the matter. He made a rough speech, probably not prepared, somewhat confused, but brief and personal.

First he cited Mainwaring, who had been censured by Parliament for his sermons but had nevertheless been raised to a rich church living: 'If these be the steps to preferment, what may we not expect?' Then he became personal. Dr Alablaster, in a sermon at Paul's Cross, had preached flat popery. Dr Beard, Cromwell's one-time tutor, was to have refuted him, but Dr Neile, the Bishop of Winchester, had forbidden him to do so. When he persisted he was 'exceedingly rated', and he recounted his experience to Cromwell.[3]

Parliament then had only three weeks to run. Members were so firmly exercised by the religious issue that they had done nothing about supply. Popery, they declared, was on the increase, the mass was celebrated with impunity not only in the Queen's household but in public places; Arminians were equally objectionable: 'An Arminian is the spawn of a Papist.' Amid such cries Charles adjourned the House for a week, begging it in vain to consider supply. On March 2 he ordered a further adjournment, and the Speaker accordingly rose to leave the chair. As he did so two young men strode forward – Denzil Holles and Benjamin Valentine – and held him down. Privy Councillors helped him to break away but he was pushed back into the Speaker's chair: 'God's wounds! You shall sit till we please to rise!' cried Holles. Sir Miles Hobart clinched the matter by locking the door of the Chamber and putting the key in his pocket. With Black Rod, sent by the King to dissolve the House, knocking on the locked door and the Speaker held firmly in the chair, Holles briefly made the four points on which the House was bent: no innovations in religion, no tonnage and poundage against the wishes of Parliament; innovators in religion, those who counselled, gave or took tonnage and poundage against the wishes of Parliament to be pronounced enemies of the state. When he called for approval of these resolutions the response was overwhelming. 'Aye!, Aye!, Aye!' came, it seemed from every throat, Cromwell's among them. The Commons then voted their own adjournment, the doors were flung open and the Members poured from the House in an excited, chattering, gesticulating stream. Cromwell had, indeed, entered well and truly upon the stage of national politics. He had not found much to calm his spirit or to ease his melancholy, though the memory of what Parliaments could do, or what could be done with Parliaments, remained with him.

4

'Fresh fields and pastures new'

Cromwell's experience of national politics had given him an appetite for local affairs. Shortly after his return from Westminster he became, together with Dr Beard, involved in the politics of Huntingdon. The existing government of the town consisted of two bailiffs and a common council of twenty-four persons, freely elected each year by the burgesses. This degree of democracy was being challenged by a local barrister named Robert Bernard who was himself intent on gaining control of the town and who had little sympathy with Puritans. In 1630 Bernard and his supporters successfully appealed to the King for a new town charter. This vested the government of Huntingdon in twelve Aldermen and a Recorder appointed for life by the King, and in a Mayor chosen each year by and from the Aldermen. The first Mayor, as well as the twelve Aldermen, were named in the charter.

It was no surprise that the Mayor was none other than Robert Bernard, though Beard and Cromwell were named as Aldermen. In spite of this sop Oliver protested against what he saw as the alienation of the rights of the citizens of Huntingdon. In particular he feared that the members of the new, self-perpetuating town Council were bent on alienating to themselves the rights in the common fields held by humbler citizens. He made no secret of his views, spreading them abroad with some vehemence, with the result that he was called before the Privy Council in London and examined by that very Earl of Manchester who now owned Hinchingbrooke – a double indignity. Cromwell won his point insofar as Manchester ordered the Mayor and Aldermen of Huntingdon to guard against any injustice to the people of the town, but he nevertheless acknowledged that he had 'spoken in heat and passion' and begged that the words be not remembered against him.[1]

He was not personally punished but it was apparent that Cromwell's influence in Huntingdon was diminished, just as his family's influence in the county was declining before the rise of the Montagues. To a man of his temperament there was a sense of humiliation. More practical was the realization that his election to another Parliament as Member for Huntingdon was now extremely unlikely. It is possible that his strongly developed Puritan beliefs led him to contemplate emigration to New England, whither many of his friends and family connections had already gone. The idea was reinforced by trouble in another direction. He had not come forward to be knighted on Charles's accession, as was required of all freeholders holding lands worth £40 a year or more. Nor did he take up the honour in 1631 when the King was raising money by instituting a 'knighthood fine' as the compulsory alternative. He was again with six others brought before a Royal Commission on which, once more, sat the Earl of Manchester. Oliver's name heads the list of those who compounded, though it has obviously been written in later, after the others. Whether this implies a late and reluctant conformity, whether the fine was, perhaps, paid for him, is uncertain. At all events he did not suffer imprisonment.[2]

And all the time he was seeking, probing, searching his soul for guidance on the path to righteousness. In such a tangle of the practical and the spiritual did he speak to his wife or other members of his family? Did they wrestle together for the elusive truth? A decision had to be made and, early in 1631, it came in the form of the quite remarkable determination to sell the family holdings at Huntingdon and the house where he was born and move down river to St Ives. On 7 May 1631 the sale was agreed and Oliver with his mother, his sisters and his wife jointly sold the Huntingdon property for £1,800.[3] In its place Cromwell rented grazing land from the estate of Slepe Hall five miles to the east but still on the banks of the river Ouse to the south-east of the ancient cattle market of St Ives. The surprising decision to cease to be landowner but merely a leaseholder may well reflect Cromwell's spiritual indecision at this time and possibly imply that he still had emigration in mind. But he also had had two brushes with Royal Commissions, two confrontations with the Earl of Manchester; he now held what he might consider a humiliating position in Huntingdon with little chance of again becoming its Member of Parliament; his capitulation over knighthood fines – should he have gone to prison rather than pay? – possibly rankled.

And overall his straitened financial circumstances may have added to his decision to leave his native town. Why he should have been financially insecure is not clear, for the lands he farmed round Huntingdon were fertile and his father had managed well enough. Perhaps, as later gossip-writers alleged, he was profligate or, at least, a bad manager.

At all events the move gave him temporary peace and a quiet life free from responsibilities. He had at least one close friend there for Henry Downhall, godfather to his son Richard, became vicar of the church of St Ives at about the time the Cromwell family moved. With Henry Lawrence, from whom he rented his land, Oliver soon formed close ties which endured throughout the difficulties of later years. St Ives was a pleasant little town among the meadows, dominated visually by the high slender spire of the church which rose through the willows on the river bank and was visible for miles. Grazing land was probably less demanding than arable, though Cromwell also kept a few ploughs and a ploughman or two. He took a responsible though not very demanding interest in local affairs. He attended church regularly – with a red flannel round his neck because of an inflammation of the throat; he enjoined upon his work-people attendance at his house for long prayers with his family each morning and evening. He thought much of his past misdemeanours and resolved to make such restitution as he could, actually paying back to a Mr Calton the sum of £30 which he had won from him at cards years before. He was much concerned with the 'silenced' ministers for whom he had spoken in Parliament and invited many of them to lectures and services at his house.[4]

Preaching, as opposed to ceremony, was one of the marks of Protestantism and many congregations or groupings of like-minded people had joined together to finance 'lecturers' either resident or visiting. Thomas Beard, for example, was resident lecturer at Huntingdon. Beard died in 1633 while Cromwell was at St Ives and Laud immediately suppressed his lectureship. A new lecturer was appointed by the Mercer's Company but he was likewise dismissed. It was typical Laudian policy and particularly saddening to Cromwell since his friend's memory was involved, and particularly galling since, no longer resident at Huntingdon, he could do little to help. He did, however, two years later write to a friend in London begging him to see that the endowment for a lectureship in some unspecified part of Huntingdonshire be continued: 'Building of hospitals', he wrote, 'provides for men's bodies; to build material temples is judged a work of piety; but they that procure spiritual food, they that build up spiritual temples, they are the men truly charitable, truly pious.'[5]

Few relics remain of Cromwell's farming in St Ives. It is not even certain where the Cromwell family lived; old branding irons for marking sheep with the initials O.C. which were said to be in existence in the eighteenth century have long since disappeared. An old barn still bears his name, a few local records testify to his interest in local affairs. The baby who was born there in January 1632 was taken for baptism as James to the family church of St John in Huntingdon on January 8 and he was buried in the churchyard the following day.[6] But Cromwell's stay in St Ives was not long. In 1636 came a momentous change in fortune. Sir Thomas Steward, Oliver's uncle, was childless and, after the death of his wife in 1636, and hearing accounts of his nephew's Puritan devoutness, he made Oliver his heir. Clearly he felt no animosity at whatever had previously passed between them, and when he died shortly afterwards his entire estate in the Isle of Ely, including his house in the town of Ely, came to Oliver.

The Isle of Ely was an area some seven miles by four, consisting of several islands of slightly higher ground intercepted by the Ouse, Nen, Welland and other rivers. For six years Hereward the Wake had defied William the Norman from within its watery protection. The name 'Ely' perhaps derived from the eels which flourished in these waters; possibly it came from a word meaning 'marsh' or from the British word which signified 'willow' or 'sallow'; for willows were, indeed, the only trees that flourished in the area where, if they did not grow wild, they were planted on the banks of rivers in an effort to prevent overflowing. Being frequently cut, they came again 'with a numerous offspring', which were particularly useful for basket-making, being pliable as well as strong. It was not unfamiliar country to the Cromwells. The town of Ely itself stood on the left bank of the river Ouse, seventeen miles downstream to the north-west of Huntingdon. Cambridge was sixteen miles to the south-east, London seventy miles away. A short ride from his home could bring Oliver to the 'great solitude' of marsh and sky which had brought hither the monks and hermits of earlier generations and resulted in the imposing churches at Crowland, Thorney, Peterborough, Ramsay, Chatteris, and Ely itself. This great cathedral, 537 feet long, 189 feet across the great transepts, which had been begun at the end of the eleventh century and completed three centuries later, could be seen for miles around over the flat open country, the only artefact that interfered with the otherwise boundless views of marsh and sky.

The air was less healthy here than at Huntingdon or St Ives, the soil was marshy and fenlike, the roads round the town of Ely perpetually flooded. But there were good pastures, fresh and pleasant, somewhat hollow and spongy yet famous for their richness. The town of Ely itself was unremarkable. The house to which the Cromwells moved was a substantial, handsome, half-timbered building next to the fourteenth-century church of St Mary, close by the great cathedral and adjoining the famous Sextry barn. In this long fifteenth-century barn the monks had stored the grain gathered from various monastic centres and brought by water to Ely. Nearby was the horse-driven mill for grinding corn, while the west end of the barn included stalls and stables. Across Palace Green stood the old Bishops' Palace, the Prior's house was nearby, while on the slight rise of Mill Hill were the remains of a Norman Castle. The plague of 1630–1 had struck the city severely; nevertheless the population was increasing, especially along the Lynn Road, which was referred to as 'Little London'.[7]

Cromwell's legacy had not made him a great landowner but he was well up in the middle range. He now owned ninety acres of arable land, eight of pasture, he was the lessee of many Cathedral properties and farmer of the tythes.[8] His mother, who had been born in the Ely house and lived much of her life in nearby Stuntney, with his two sisters, Elizabeth and Robina, who had stayed with her in Huntingdon while the rest went to St Ives, joined him and his wife and six children, and the eleven of them all transferred happily into the big, old family home. Oliver's sister Jane – a good augury for a good year – married the attractive and highly eligible John Desborough, a lawyer and second son of the squire of Eltisley.

In Ely, backed by the security of land and income, Cromwell's life was calmer and more settled than it had been. He rode the familiar, willow-banked countryside, attended to his land and enjoyed his enlarged sphere of interests and obligations. His health and spirits improved. Daughters were born to him in 1637 and 1638, he sent his sons to school at Felsted in Essex, a school with a good Puritan reputation. It was also near to his wife's family and the Barringtons, with the Puritan Earl of Warwick and his son, Lord Rich, as neighbours. There were visits to friends and relations. Oliver and one of his sons visited Otes, the home of Sir William Masham and his family, where Oliver's cousin, who had married Oliver St John as his second wife, was staying with her husband. The boy was probably on his way to school at Felsted and Cromwell was grateful that the influential and strongly Puritan Mashams showed kindness to him. Among these Puritan families there was, indeed, much interchange, much visiting. Cromwell was closely involved, not only in talking and preaching among the elect but in endeavouring to teach and to convert the ungodly. Bishop Williams of Lincoln, another kinsman, reported to the King that Cromwell was 'a common spokesman for the sectaries and maintained their part with great stubborness'.[9] In this crusading period of his life he was filled with a great thankfulness that God had shown mercy to him, had picked him out for favour – presumably in the form of worldly prosperity. 'Truly no poor creature hath more cause to put forth himself in the cause of his God than I. I have had plentiful wages beforehand, and I am sure I shall never earn the least mite', he wrote to Mrs St John from Ely on 13 October 1636 when she was still staying with the Mashams. He reveals in this letter how he has come through his periods of doubt and despair, of profligacy, of sinfulness, and through God's mercy has seen the light; 'blessed be His Name for shining upon so dark a heart as mine! You know what my manner of life hath been. Oh, I lived in and loved darkness, and hated the light; I was a chief, the chief of sinners. This is true; I hated godliness, yet God had mercy on me.'[10]

Whether this letter refers to actual incidents of Cromwell's youth and substantiates the stories of a dissolute young man, or whether it is referring to Cromwell's inner struggles and his morbid belief in his own unworthiness is not clear. But it is evident that shortly after his arrival in Ely he had emerged as the true, devout Puritan, feeling himself close to God, believing in the destiny that God would reveal to him.

A basic kindness and a desire to help the poor and the underdog became apparent in the role he now played in the affairs of his town and parish. Various factors had combined to make important the problem of poor relief: the population of the town was growing, particularly with the influx of people from London; the plague, only a few years earlier, had left its mark in distress and poverty; municipal and monastic aid had fallen into disuse and some of the private charities which existed to help the poor were ill-administered or had lapsed. Cromwell concerned himself particularly with one charity, known after its fifteenth-century founder as Thomas Parsons' Charity, whose almshouses still testified to his benevolence, though they did not now, in the seventeenth century, provide all the care that Parsons had intended. Cromwell did what he could to reverse the decline, coming down on the side of liberality to the poor. There were also personal interventions, as a note in his handwriting indicates: 'To Mr Hand, at Ely', he wrote

> I doubt not but I shall be as good as my word for your money. I desire you to deliver forty shillings of the Town money to this bearer to pay for the physic for Benson's cure. If the gentlemen will not allow it at the time of account, keep this note, and I will pay it out of my own purse. Sept. 13, 1638[11]

He was following in the footsteps of his grandfather and of his uncle who had both shown care for the poor by dealing with grain speculators in the famine years at the end of the previous century. His uncle had also acted for the fenmen in the long disputes concerning drainage which had continued over the years. Oliver himself had presented a petition against fen drainage to James I in 1623.[12] But there were strong interests on the other side and James had consulted the Dutch drainage engineer, Cornelius Vermuyden, with a view to recovering the English fenland for profitable agriculture.

In 1634 the Duke of Bedford, who owned large areas of the southern fen, revived the idea of drainage. With the authority of King Charles a group of 'adventurers' headed by the Duke were authorized to drain an area of fenland round Ely known as the Great Level – the area upon which Cromwell's father had pronounced. In return for their work they were to receive a share of the reclaimed land. In 1637 drainage was declared finished though, in fact, it had improved only summer pasturage and in winter it remained much as before. But the fenmen had lost their accustomed way of life with many of the rights of pasturage and fishing they had previously enjoyed. 'Tell the fenmen', said Thomas Fuller, 'of the large benefit to the public of fattening a bullock or sheep where formerly a pike or duck fed, and they will reply that if they be taken in taking that bullock or sheep, the rich owner inditeth them for felons; whereas

37

that pike or duck were their own foods only for their pains of catching them.'[13]

The fenland riots that ensued in May and June 1638 were incipiently dangerous. Forty or fifty men gathered at Whelpmore fen on June 4 to fill in the ditches which encroached upon the common lands of Littleport, Ely and Downham. They arranged a so-called 'football match' for the following day when they expected some 600 people to gather at a place they called 'Anderson's camp'. But the weather joined with the authorities to suppress them. The rain deluged, few people turned up and their leaders were arrested. Nevertheless 200 men of Ely and Lakenheath came out on the next day, throwing down many of the Undertakers' ditches but not hurting any man's person or goods, as the JP's for the area testified. Four men were committed to gaol at Ely, the others dispersed. Brave speeches were made in Ely declaring that the gaols would be opened and the prisoners released, some of the warrants sent out in the King's name were resisted or neglected. Cromwell, who had been resident in Ely for a couple of years, was closely concerned. The flooded roads round his home in Ely indicated that a certain amount of drainage was necessary, but his spirit rose in protest against any lord or king riding roughshod over the rights of the fenmen. He swung into the conflict, putting himself at the head of some of the riots. More practically he guaranteed that, if the fenmen would pay him a groat towards his legal expenses for every cow they had upon the commons, he would 'hold the drainers in suit of law for five years, and that in the meantime they should enjoy every foot of their commons'. Not surprisingly they chose him to be their spokesman before the Commissioners of Sewers at Huntingdon.[14]

Later in the year, in the midst of these clamorous protests, the King intervened in a double-edged Proclamation. The work was incomplete, he said, he would make the area fit for winter as well as summer grazing and meanwhile the inhabitants should continue to exercise their customary rights. It seemed that Cromwell and the fenmen had won – at least partially and for the time being.

But the decade ended tragically for the Cromwell family. In May 1639 their eldest son, Robert, died at school in Felsted at the age of seventeen. The cause of his death is unrecorded but he was regarded as an intelligent, God-fearing boy of great promise. He was very dear to his father and the fact that early death was not uncommon in the seventeenth century did not soften the blow: it 'went as a dagger to my heart', Cromwell later recounted. They buried the boy at Felsted. There is no evidence to show why he was not brought home to Ely. But his family would have been there with the many friends and kinsmen who lived in the area. The entry in the Felsted parish register referred to him simply as a boy of exceptional promise, fearing God in all things. Cromwell's only comfort was in the Scriptures and he turned to a passage from St Paul: 'I have learned in whatsoever state I am, therewith to be content; I know both how to be debased, and how to abound ... I can do all things through Christ that strengtheneth me.' 'This Scripture', he later said, 'did ... save my life.'[15] As he continued that life with his many interests and responsibilities in the Isle of Ely he was drawn more surely into national affairs as the effects of the King's rule reached out to all parts of the kingdom.

Part II

*'... while indefatigable
Cromwell hyes
And cuts his way still
nearer to the Skyes'*

5

Member for Cambridge

There had been no Parliament since the dramatic break-up of 1629. For the King the period was one of domestic happiness and a growing tranquillity reflected in a meticulously ordered life and a Court of some decorum enlivened with expensive pleasures like Court masques. Riding and hunting gave him physical exercise, picture-collecting satisfied his aesthetic needs. Above all, an ordered religion brought security and solace. While Cromwell was living in torment, endeavouring to come to terms with his God, Charles had already found Him in the beauty and security of his Church. To preserve intact that purity of worship he was steadily advancing the forms of Anglicanism and promoting the churchmen who would practice them. William Laud, who had become successively Bishop of St David's, of Bath and Wells, and of London, was promoted in 1633 to the See of Canterbury. His steps up the ladder of Church preferment were accompanied by an increasing emphasis on the outward show that marked the 'seemliness' and 'decency' of his religion, by a greater emphasis on uniformity, and by an unquenchable zeal to suppress unorthodoxy. What comprised 'unorthodocy' was not always easy to determine. The altar controversy was still unsettled; bowing, the sign of the cross, the giving of the ring in marriage, the presence of images in churches, the wearing of vestments, were all still in question. So was the relation of the sermon to the service and to the Prayer Book itself.

The position was worse confounded by the 'dumb mouths' who could barely read or write or understand the church service they were expected to conduct. With absenteeism and pluralism practised on a wide scale even such ministration as they could offer was frequently missing. The *Visitations* which Laud set on foot in 1633 revealed cases of parishes, often miles apart, in the charge of the same priest; they told of broken-down church fabric, of images defaced, altars used as hatstands or seats, gossip, ribaldry during services, the mustering of trained bands in churchyards.[1] Such Reports fuelled Laud's zeal for reform; the altar must be at the east end of the church, decently railed; communicants should kneel when taking the sacrament; services should follow the Prayer Book with the inclusion of a short, prepared sermon, if any, with no extempore preaching; though he did not prescribe it, Laud himself set the example of reverence by crossing himself and bowing towards the east when entering a church and when he heard the name of Jesus. Example and, if necessary, punishment would rest with the hierarchy of priests and bishops that led up to the Archbishop and the ecclesiastical Court of High Commission.

To a generation nurtured on the newly translated Bible the words of condemnation came easily: Bull of Bashan, Whore of Babylon, Worke of the Beaste, were roared from pulpit, at market cross, even from a man's own doorstep by established clergy, itinerant preacher or by some simple soul convinced of his own righteousness. Illegal pamphlets that defied the licensing laws called for the extirpation of bishops and the end of all ceremonial in worship. Culprits were brought before the High Commission or the King's own Star Chamber and punished for their defiance. Thus the Puritan movement produced its martyrs.

On an unseasonably hot day in April 1638, one of these was a handsome young apprentice named John Lilburne who stood in Palace Yard, Westminster, his neck clamped in a pillory that was too small for him, his back bleeding from the whipping he had received on his two-mile walk from the Fleet prison in the City of London. Lilburne's showmanship surpassed any that had gone before as he first hurled defiance at the bishops and then, when he was gagged, succeeded in throwing pamphlets from his pockets among the crowd.[2] It cannot be doubted that Oliver Cromwell heard the Puritan preachers either in London, in Cambridge or nearer home, or that the pamphlets which the clandestine presses were now widely distributing reached him in Ely.

Religion was only one of the King's problems. He had shaken himself free of Continental commitments with the Treaty of Madrid in November 1630. In so doing he had abandoned the Protestant cause and his own sister while the Thirty Years War dragged on towards its end with the Treaty of Westphalia in 1648. At his Court in Whitehall, meanwhile, Van Dyck succeeded Rubens, more pictures were hung in his galleries, while the masques and the royal Progresses continued. With a rising population, which reached about 5,500,000, and an improving economic situation helped by good harvests and the end of war the country was not unprosperous. Farmers like Oliver Cromwell were doing well and corn from the Sextry Barn helped to swell the East Anglian grain that went by ship to London; more calves, more geese trod the London road.

Yet there was uneasiness. The King required money for both public purposes and to cover his own personal expenditure. His private income was small and pledged to the hilt. He had tried by Knighthood fines to bring money into the Exchequer – Oliver had himself experienced the indignity of having to compound for the non-receipt of an honour he had neither wanted nor asked for[3] – but the amount received was small. The King raised a little money by granting monopolies for various industrial and commercial enterprises which were regarded as scandalous means of rewarding Court favourites. He instituted fines on all landowners who, over the centuries, had encroached upon or taken into their own possession land that, as royal forest, had anciently been reserved for the King's hunting. The fines imposed on the big landowners were heavy, even if not always collected in full, and a class solidarity included the Cromwells in the opposition. The King was also continuing to levy the customs duties denied him by Parliament and they were enhanced by higher rates introduced by his Chancellor of the Exchequer in 1634. The Cromwell family were hit both through their merchant connections and through the higher price of imports.

The tax which hit Cromwell hardest and came closest to him was the ship money tax, partly because of its very nature, partly because his near kinsman, John Hampden, was a principal actor in the outcry against it. Ship money was an ancient tax levied upon the ports in times of danger in order to provide ships for national defence. It had fallen into disuse in spite of attempts by James and Charles to revive it. Now, however, Charles returned to the idea and in October 1634 ordered the cities, port towns, and maritime counties of England to provide ships, or money instead, on the plea of general defence and the safeguard of the seas. The money raised was actually spent on ships and a small ship-money fleet put to sea. A year later, in August 1635, encouraged by this partial success, a second writ of ship money was issued which included inland coun-

45

ties as well as maritime on the justifiable plea that defence concerned the whole country. Further writs followed in 1636, 1637 and 1638. Now, indeed, what might possibly have been accepted as a necessary tax in time of national emergency was violently opposed as being a new and permanent tax in an old guise.

The Earl of Warwick spoke to the King himself on behalf of his Essex tenants. They could not consent, he said, to such a tax which was a prejudice to the 'liberties of the kingdom': pregnant words which doubtless Warwick had uttered elsewhere and which Cromwell had heard, for Essex was the home of his wife's family, of the Barringtons and the Mashams, and the school where his sons were being educated. No taxation without consent of Parliament was the second rallying cry of the growing and increasingly vocal opposition to the King. As Lord Saye and Sele put it, 'he knew no law besides Parliament to persuade men to give away their own goods'. Cromwell himself spoke strongly against ship money. He was, it was said, 'a great stickler' against the tax, but there is no evidence of his refusal to pay.[4]

The numbers who did refuse, however, became larger and it was upon the ship-money issue that the growing opposition to the King took its stand. Of all who refused payment it selected as a test case that of John Hampden, a large and prosperous Buckinghamshire landowner, reputedly one of the richest commoners in England. It was demonstrably not upon grounds of hardship that he refused to pay the sum of 20 shillings levied upon his manor of Stoke Mandeville, it was clearly a matter of principle. Hampden's trial came up on 6 October 1637 before the court of Exchequer. His Council were Robert Holborn and Cromwell's cousin Oliver St John. These defence lawyers took their stand not on the King's right to decide when ships were needed but on his right to levy any tax to provide those ships other than through Parliament. The judges' verdict mattered less than the enunciation of the principle. In the event it was a narrow victory for the Crown – seven judges for the King, three for Hampden, and two for Hampden on technical grounds – and the collection of ship money continued.

Hampden was not imprisoned but some whom Charles had detained after the break-up of the 1629 Parliament were still held in custody. Sir Edmund Hampden, kinsman of John Hampden and Cromwell, died in prison. Cromwell also heard of the King's callous refusal to grant Sir John Eliot liberty when he was dangerously ill or to allow him burial among his own people. Eliot's daughter married Nathaniel Fiennes, the son of Lord Saye and Sele, who was a close associate of John Pym and Oliver St John, and so another link was forged in the chain of opposition to the King. The propertied classes all over the country, indeed, were at one in fearing encroachment upon their wealth, whether it consisted of land, trade, investment, or manufacture. The sanctity of 'property' was deeply ingrained in the make-up of seventeenth-century Englishmen and in none more so than in those of Puritan belief. The Puritan ethic of hard work followed by just reward if the Lord approved was bound up with their belief in predestination. If God had so ordained a man would be successful in his worldly pursuits and no arbitrary government could be allowed to rob him of the fruits of Divine favour.

The desire for religious freedom and economic gain, free from the shackles of arbitrary government, had sent many of Oliver's contemporaries to the New World and Oliver himself and his family had been rumoured to be among later emigrants. Two leading Puritans, Lord Saye and Sele and Lord Brooke, had given their names – Saybrook – to a Puritan colony founded on the shores of Long Island Sound in 1632. At the same time economic enterprise in the New World had been developed from England more specifically in the Massachusetts Bay Company of 1629 and the Providence Island Company of 1636. The latter, in particular, was a veritable opposition cell of leading Puritans which included many of Cromwell's family connections: John Hampden, Sir Thomas Barrington, Oliver St John, Richard Knightley of Fawsley in Northamptonshire who married John Hampden's daughter, Lord Saye and Sele, the powerful and immensely rich Earl of Bedford whose wealth, like Oliver's more modest inheritance, was founded upon Abbey lands, and who had been a leading spirit in the drainage operations in the fenland, and Bedford's protégé, the physically and mentally powerful John Pym, whom Cromwell had met in the Parliament of 1629.

One other tie bound together the men who were in opposition. They were 'Country' as opposed to 'Court'. This was not a class division. Wealth, social standing, aristocratic connections lay on both sides of the divide. On the Court side lay the path to preferment, to influence, power and greater wealth. The ear of a favourite, of the King himself, was more easily obtained at Court than in the country. But life at Court was expensive, extravagant, ostentatious. Fortunes were as often lost as gained at Court. To many a country gentleman the frivolities of Court were reprehensible if not scandalous. He had no wish to bring himself or his family to the capital. At home in the country his fortune depended on his land, the weather and possibly merchant interests which were more stable even if they did not yield such glittering gains as the Court might offer. He fulfilled his duties as Justice of the Peace or Sheriff and looked after the interests of the less fortunate members of the community. He was roused to anger when called upon to pay in higher taxation for the ineptitude of Royal policy or when his property rights were in any way threatened. He resented any interference with his religion. He was legally minded and he sought for the sanction of law for any policy that would affect him. 'Arbitrary government' was his bane, a term he used to cover most of the evils emanating from a monarch who ruled without a Parliament. He sometimes suffered a sense of exclusion from the favours and prizes accumulated by courtiers and found it easy to think in terms of 'them' and 'us', so emphasizing the difference between 'Court' and 'Country'. But it was not easy to build a country 'party' in any sense of the term for purely geographical reasons. Meetings required planning and journeys could be long and even hazardous. When a Parliament was in session contact came more naturally and country gentlemen were united in feeling themselves 'representative' – a term increasingly used – of country interests. Yet they were not self-consciously a 'party'. They were a prosperous group of aristocracy and gentry, their mutual interests reinforced by many ties of kinship. They had more 'mere gentry' in their ranks than would be found around the Court, yet this did not affect a social conservatism that was as strong among them as among the King's courtiers.[5]

Cromwell and his friends and relations were typical of the most vocal section of the opposition and a glance at their names makes it clear that there was no class conflict between them and those who supported the King – the Earl of Warwick, owner of sixty-five manors in Essex; the Earl of Bedford, owner of much London property as well as large stretches of fenland he hoped he was turning into profitable enterprise; Lord Saye and Sele and his sons of Broughton Castle in Warwickshire; the Earl of Clare, whose younger son, Denzil Holles, was particularly active in opposition affairs; wealthy commoners like the Hampdens, the Barringtons, the Mashams; the Montagues of Cromwell's native Huntingdonshire including the Earl of Manchester whose rivalry with Cromwell did not at this time affect their common opposition to the King; well-off landowners like Henry Lawrence, who rescued Cromwell from Huntingdon after his clash with Barnard by renting him land at St Ives.

The group had not broken the links it forged at the time of the 1628 Parliament and meetings continued throughout Charles's years of Personal Rule. Broughton Castle was one of their meeting places, conveniently situated geographically, with a well-hidden entrance to a private room and the protection of a moat. At nearby Fawsley, the home of the Knightleys, a printing press was hidden. The opposition was well aware of the new weapon, the printed sheet or pamphlet, and prepared itself to make full use of it.

So matters might have continued but for the religious zeal of Charles and his Archbishop. In Scotland the Reformed Church had followed the teaching of Calvin at Geneva and Knox at Edinburgh and in place of the episcopal hierarchy had adopted a form of church government based on presbyters, lay-elders, and deacons elected by their congregations. James I had re-established bishops in 1612, restored some ceremonies and appointed a group of Scottish bishops to prepare a Prayer Book for Scotland on the lines of the English Book of Common Prayer. The result was a Book more Puritan in character than Charles or Laud could stomach. Charles's coronation in Scotland in 1633, in which Laud played a prominent part, together with the ritual he practised in England, swung to the other extreme, and amid rising Scottish anger a new Prayer Book was again considered. Scottish bishops played a part in drawing it up but Charles and Laud were known to be closely concerned and when it was published in 1637 it was with the authority of the King himself. It was found to be basically the English Prayer Book with canons of uniformity prescribing the English form of worship, the only concession to the Scots being the substitution of the word 'presbyter' for 'priest'. Its introduction on 25 July 1637 in St Giles's Cathedral in Edinburgh was greeted with cries of 'the mass is come amongst us!' Even if its rowdy reception was somewhat contrived it sparked off such opposition as had not been heard for a century. Charles's typical response was to order all magistrates in Scotland to accept the new Prayer Book. The peoples' retort was to covenant one with another, as the Bible had taught them, to hold faith and preserve the true, reformed religion. They proceeded to abolish episcopacy and to establish full Presbyterianism in its place, while enjoining all people to take the Covenant. Their defiance was complete and now involved the whole question of sovereignty as well as of religion. So, after nearly ten years of peace, Charles prepared for war – not with a foreign foe, not with a Roman Catholic enemy, but with Protestants within his own kingdom.

In the Bishops' wars that followed he had difficulty in mustering support from even his northern subjects to whom the Scots over the border were the traditional enemy. He mistakenly pressed men from the strongly Puritan eastern counties of England. Even more mistakenly some of these were billeted at Cromwell's house at Ely on their march northwards, and this gave Oliver the opportunity to air his views. Whatever he said only served to make him more popular and more of a leader among his neighbours and to spread his fame as a good opposition man.[6]

The King exhausted the money he had saved in the years of peace and gained nothing. There was no battle. Though the Scottish army was demonstrably superior it lacked the will to cross the border and fight on English soil. In the uneasy peace that followed the Treaty of Berwick Charles turned to the strongest man in his kingdom – Baron Wentworth, Lord Lieutenant of Ireland. But Wentworth's advice was 'Call a Parliament!' Only so could the King raise money to continue the war. At first Charles refused. He feared the 'hydra-headed monster' that had blocked his earlier attempts at financial solvency; and after eleven years without one it was difficult to give way now. But with his Privy Council ranged behind Wentworth he yielded. In February 1640 the writs went out and a Parliament was summoned to meet on 13 April 1640.

The opposition were prepared. Hampden and Pym rode to Scotland on opposition business. Oliver's friends and relations accelerated their campaigning from Broughton and Fawsley. It would be strange, indeed, if a similar enclave of like-minded people were not operating in Essex. With his sons at school at Felsted Oliver had every reason for visiting the area. He knew what he must do. He could not be returned to Parliament for Huntingdon but he was now a Cambridgeshire man and he made his preparations in the city of Cambridge, only twenty miles from Ely, using to the full his Puritan and family connections. To be elected to Parliament it was necessary first to become a freeman of the city and this required residential qualification. His inspired preaching helped to this end, for Richard Timbs of Cambridge would customarily come to Ely to hear Cromwell preach in various conventicles and was so impressed that he enlisted support for Cromwell in Cambridge. This was not difficult, for Cromwell's championship of the fenmen, his opposition to ship money and to the Scottish war were well known. In Cambridge connections with a draper named Wildbore, another distant kinsman, led upward through various channels to the Mayor himself, Thomas French, probably related to the Dr Peter French who later married Cromwell's sister. And so the wheels began to turn and Cromwell lived for a while early in 1640 in the yard of the White Bull Inn in Bridge Street in Cambridge. No matter that the lodgings were 'mean'; they served their purpose. Cromwell was duly entered as a freeman of the city on 7 January 1640 and in due course elected to the Parliament of April 1640 amid the usual junketings of beer and sweetmeats.[7] It was slightly deflating that his fellow Member was Sir Thomas Meautys, a King's man who owed his election to the influence of Lord Keeper Finch, who was Steward of the Borough of Cambridge. But it is significant that this Court influence was not strong enough to counter that of Oliver's sponsors. In spite of his elation Oliver may have cast a wry look at Huntingdon, his 'own' town, where two Montagues were returned. It was satisfactory that his brother-in-law Valentine Walton was returned for the county, though he had to share that honour with another Montague.

In the eastern counties the opposition were making sure that the electorate voted the right way. The Earl of Warwick was threatening voters on his Essex estates with the levy if they failed to support his candidates. Propaganda leaflets in the form of petitions were circulated, mostly outlining grievances but sometimes suggesting remedies such as annual Parliaments. As the results came in Warwick, Barrington, Harbottle Grimston and other opposition men waited in Warwick's London lodgings. They need not have worried. The King had little support in the Parliament which met on 13 April 1640. Cromwell was among those who had already experienced a Parliament. He had no need of the hurriedly prepared pamphlet on election procedure issued for the benefit of new voters and their Members. The ride to London was familiar. Apart from Essex and Cambridge, how many times in the past decade had he ridden to London or Banbury or Fawsley or to Hampden's home in Buckinghamshire on opposition business! It is obvious that he was already considered a man to be reckoned with, one whose presence in Parliament was an asset to the opposition. He had been summoned to the 1628 Parliament as a local man, with his roots in the area he represented. He was called to the Parliament of 1640 by an opposition of which he was part to resist the arbitrary government of a King without a Parliament. The business in hand was too important for a fenland spring to hinder him.

Oliver Cromwell was sworn in by the Clerk of the Court on the morning of April 13. It was not a good omen that the King had chosen the Bishop of Ely to preach the opening sermon in Westminster Abbey at noon and it is unlikely that Cromwell attended. But later he stood with other Members below the bar of the House of Lords for the official opening of the fourth Parliament of the reign. Charles spoke briefly of the 'great and weighty Cause' that had led him to call his people together. His ten-year-old son, Charles, Prince of Wales, sat by him – the same age as Cromwell's second son, Henry. Lord Keeper Finch followed the King with a tedious speech whose substance was a request for supply and the retrospective granting of tonnage and poundage to the King. The Members were unheedful. The Scottish war meant nothing to them. They soon threw off the slight uncertainty and diffidence of their unaccustomed role and began to read aloud the petitions for redress of grievances which, conveniently, had been coming in from all over the country: petitions had already become an opposition tactic. The appointment of committees was another. Cromwell, already marked out as a religious zealot, was appointed to the Committee on Religion of which John Pym was chairman. Pym, the tacitly accepted leader of the House, stated the opposition case in a two-hour speech on April 15 which asserted that their grievances concerned the liberties and privileges of Parliament, innovations in religion, and the sanctity of property, making it clear that without satisfaction on these points there would be no supply. Cromwell heard his own religious convictions put into words: the condemnation of 'altars, images, crucifixes, bowings and other gestures' which had 'put upon the churches a shape and face of popery'; heard from Pym's lips the long tale of arbitrary fine and taxation from ship money to coat and conduct money, from knighthood fines to penalties for afforestation; of impressment, imprisonment, the granting of monopolies, the levying of tonnage and poundage without consent of Parliament; heard the assertation that regular and frequent Parliaments were the best form of redress; heard the Members shout of 'A good oration!' as Pym sat down.

Thereafter there was deadlock. If the Scots had not been so nearly of their religion supply might have been forthcoming. But to vote money to fight their fellow-religionists and inflict on the Scots a Prayer Book which they themselves abhorred was unthinkable. Charles never had a chance. The 'Short' Parliament lasted for only three weeks and was dissolved on May 5.

And so the drama unfolded. Rioting spread over the country, most of it concerned with religion. Churches were desecrated, Laud fled for protection from his Palace at Lambeth to Whitehall. Roman Catholics, and in particular the Irish, the Queen and her priests were the targets. It was rumoured that Wentworth, who had become the Earl of Strafford in 1639, was about to bring over Catholic Irish to subdue not only the Scots but the English as well. Efforts by the King to raise men and money yielded little. Even the trained bands were reluctant and pressed men ran away. In Hampden's Buckinghamshire, of £2,000 demanded as coat and conduct money only a fraction came in. The Scots demanded the extension of the Covenant to England and on August 20 crossed the border at Coldstream with 25,000 men. Charles had no alternative. Writs went out for a new Parliament to assemble on November 3. The 'shuffling' for nomination and election began again. King's Lynn was sufficiently conscious of its Puritan connections to refuse the nomination of the Royalist peer, Lord Arundel. Again the opposition used its influence to the full – Saye and Sele in Oxfordshire, Bedford in East Anglia, Warwick in Essex, Hampden in Buckinghamshire, and it is unlikely that Cromwell was attending only to his fields. Pym rode round the country gathering support. Again Hampden rode to Scotland, again Broughton and Fawsley were centres of intrigue, again Cromwell was returned for the City of Cambridge, but this time with a good opposition man, John Lowry, as his fellow Member. The poet, John Cleveland, who was then a tutor at St John's, said that Cromwell was elected by a single vote. Even if true, which is unlikely, this made no difference at the time but it opens some interesting historical speculation.[8]

Few of those returned for either side were not connected with the land. Most of them were wealthy or at least comfortably off. Lawyers formed a large group; trading and other commercial interests were prominent; generally speaking, family, legal, financial, commercial and landed interest interlocked in a way that was bewildering to any but themselves. They were on the whole experienced – about sixty per cent of them, like Oliver, had sat in the Parliament of 1629 and most, again like himself, had experience of local government.

Some of them were personally and traditionally devoted to the King, religious zeal burned strongly in most, as it did in Oliver. There were few who did not regard the end of 'arbitrary government' as the chief reason for being there at all.[9] And overall there was an increasing sense of obligation to the electors who had sent them there. The provinces, even distant provinces, were becoming aware of the reciprocal relationship between themselves and the government at Westminster, and their representatives brought their wide-ranging grievances to Parliament in the form of petitions for redress.

6

The Long Parliament

Parliament met on 3 November 1640 amid wild rumours that Strafford would accuse their leaders of treason. The Bishop of Bristol preached in the Abbey, Charles cut down ceremony to the minimum but still had his son at his side as he opened what would be his last Parliament. He stated the obvious: that he needed money to pay the Scots according to the terms of the Treaty of Ripon, and to pay the English soldiers who still waited, undisbanded, in the north of England. But, he promised, he would consider Parliament's grievances at the same time, and he begged them to 'lay aside all suspicions one of another'.

The Commons paid no heed. With a sense of their own power they proceeded to arrange their own business in their own way. On the 6th, even before the inevitable well-organized petitions were read, they appointed committees to consider religion, 'privileges' and grievances and, even in the emotional and abnormal conditions in which they met, they were hard-headed enough to consider trade, the life-blood of their prosperity, without which other reforms would falter. On the third day they re-appointed the Standing Committee on trade and industry, arranging for it to meet each Tuesday. But even before that, on the opening day, the first committee to be appointed was one to consider the outstanding disputes in the fenland. To this, appropriately, Cromwell was appointed. The apparent urgency of the matter was no doubt due to disturbances in the area and also to the interests of big landowners like the Duke of Bedford and the Montague family who had a great deal of capital locked up in the drainage enterprises.

On the 7th, while the committees began their work, the petitions were read, many of them being printed and widely distributed as part of the opposition tactic. On the following day motions for the release of the 'Puritan martyrs' – men who had been punished for their religion – were heard. On the 9th Oliver Cromwell rose to make his first speech in the Long Parliament. He spoke on behalf of John Lilburne, presenting a petition for release from the young man who, since his whipping and pillorying in 1638, had been held in solitary confinement in the Fleet prison. Cromwell spoke with great passion, thumping the table before him, the blood rising to his face as he did so. To some he appeared to be magnifying the case beyond all proportion. But to Cromwell this was the essence of what he had come to put right: religious persecution by an arbitrary court. He was an uncouth figure as he stood there, his face red, his nose somewhat swollen, the veins standing out on his neck. He was never a stickler for dress and had brought no special clothes for Westminster; the rough country suit he wore did not fit very well. Without his wife's care his linen was not over clean and there was a little blood upon the collar of his shirt. He had lost his hat band and had not troubled to replace it. He had not, however, forgotten his sword, which stuck closely to his side. He was a burly man, quite tall, and the high-pitched, nasal voice was unexpected. A courtier who came that morning late to the House, carefully dressed like most of the Members, was astounded by what he saw and heard. He was equally amazed at the 'eloquence full of fervour' with which the provincial voice, 'harsh and untuneable', pushed its case and, above all, by the attention it received from the House. For they immediately ordered Lilburne's release. For Cromwell it was a good beginning to his Parliamentary career.[1]

Why was it Cromwell who rose to speak for Lilburne in the House of Commons in 1640? Was he moved by what he had heard of the young man? Had Cromwell on a visit to London witnessed his punishment? It is likely he had read some of Lilburne's prison pamphlets. Moreover Lilburne was not much older than Cromwell's eldest son who so tragically died in 1638 in the very year of Lilburne's punishment; there may have been some association in Cromwell's mind between the two young men. His extraordinary and uncharacteristic patience with Lilburne over the years was, indeed, almost that of a father to his son. Three days after he spoke in the House Lilburne and other prisoners of conscience were released from prison and Cromwell sat on a committee to consider the compensation to be made to them for unjust imprisonment.

In the long-drawn-out proceedings against Strafford Cromwell played no recorded part. There is no evidence of his attitude towards Strafford's trial, no indication that he joined in any of the heated discussions or wild scenes that led to the minister's condemnation and execution. It is just possible that Pym deliberately excluded him, fearing that his ungovernable temper, or even a misplaced admiration for the strength of Strafford, so like Cromwell's own, might jeopardize a sequence of events that had been carefully planned. But there was plenty more to be done and the House of Commons was almost frenzied as it turned from one idea to another. The cutting off of extra-Parliamentary sources of supply was urgent: tonnage and poundage, ship money, forest fines, distraint of knighthood were all violently denounced early in the session but in that hustling, jostling, bustling Parliament they had to wait until the middle of 1641 for their final passage into law. The 'arbitrary' courts of Star Chamber and High Commission were abolished and, while the props of arbitrary rule were being destroyed, the foundations of constitutional government were being laid. Cromwell moved the Second Reading of a Bill for annual Parliaments at the end of 1640 and this was more realistically converted into one for triennial Parliaments to which the King sadly gave his assent on 16 February 1641. He had, he said, yielded up one of the fairest flowers of his garland. Early in May the Commons passed a complementary Bill against dissolution without its own consent. The King signed it on the 12th at the same time as he accepted the Bill for Strafford's attainder. The Bill for 'perpetual Parliaments' was passed with no more struggle than that for Strafford's execution, but the tragedy of abandoning his friend perhaps overcame the full significance of abandoning his prerogative.

John Pym was continuing where he had left off in the Short Parliament as the unchallenged leader of the House, and in the numerous committees with which he conducted much of his work – committees were Pym's speciality[2] – he made full use of Cromwell, who served on at least eighteen of them, apart from those which specially concerned his constituency.[3] Cromwell considered the removal of 'scandalous ministers', the shortage of 'preaching ministers', an Act for abolishing superstition and idolatry and for the better advancing of the true worship and service of God. He considered the breach of privilege that had occurred in the 1628 Parliament: as a participant in that fatal clash it was an appropriate appointment. He served on a committee to deal with an issue that might not seem to have had a high priority – complaints against the inland post concerning both cost and 'abuses'. At a time when communication for official and propaganda purposes, as well as for private and social reasons, was becoming important a speedy and well-organized postal service was essential. Very important to Cromwell was the committee that considered complaints against Matthew Wren, Bishop of Ely. Wren was a Laudian who had helped prepare the unfortunate Scottish Prayer Book. Even more reprehensible in Cromwell's eyes had been his conduct when he was Bishop of Norwich when 'passionately and furiously' he had persecuted the immigrant Puritan communities of East Anglia. It took only eight months from the opening of Parliament for the Bishop, largely at Cromwell's instigation, to be voted unfit to hold office in church or Commonwealth.

Issues concerning the fens, too, Cromwell pushed on with a furious zeal and authority. There is no record of the proceedings of the committee on the fens to which he had already been appointed but since then rioting had become more serious and another committee was appointed to consider the lands in the fens granted to the Queen by Charles and sold by her to Lord Mandeville. Mandeville was endeavouring to enclose this land, the fenmen were beating down his fences on the grounds that an agreement had been made that the lands should remain common until drainage was complete. The commoners appealed to the House of Commons, Lord Mandeville to the House of Lords, who made an Order in his favour on the strength of which his father, the Earl of Manchester, sent out writs against the inhabitants of Huntingdonshire for pulling down enclosures. Cromwell protested vigorously to the House of Commons that the Lords had made their Order in favour of Mandeville while the commoners' petition was before the House of Commons, thereby bringing into question the privilege of the House: Cromwell was learning quickly! On his insistence the matter was referred to the committee on the fens already appointed. At the end of June 1641 Edward Hyde took his place as chairman, plaintiffs and defendants before him. Lord Mandeville and his witnesses sat calmly, remaining covered, while the fenmen and the many supporters who had accompanied them on the unaccustomed and long journey to London were ill at ease, possibly dressed in their best clothes but quite likely 'outlandish' in the eyes of the court. To Cromwell they were familiar enough and he understood their feelings. He moved among them, instructing them as to procedure, seconding and enlarging upon their possibly incoherent statements, working himself up as he did so into

a great passion. This gave the fenmen courage to interrupt the counsel
and witnesses for the other side and to make great clamour when
anything was said with which they disagreed. When the chairman
attempted to call them to order Cromwell, in great fury, accused
him of bias and of threatening witnesses. The rest of the committee
sided with Hyde which further inflamed Cromwell who then vented
his anger on Mandeville who was one of the family who had bought
Hinchingbrooke and, in Cromwell's eyes, usurped the place of the
Cromwells in Huntingdonshire. Cromwell now used a great deal
of offensive language against him and was altogether so insolent and
tempestuous that Hyde threatened to adjourn the committee and to
complain of Cromwell to the House of Commons. Cromwell did
not get his way this time but he was instrumental in getting a clause
inserted into the *Grand Remonstrance* in favour of the fenmen.[4]

Towards the beginning of this Parliament a petition had been received
from the City of London and several counties for the extirpation
of Bishops, 'root and branch'. It had been laid aside in the stress
of other business but similar petitions continued to arrive at Westminster and evidence accumulated of congregations who refused the
Prayer Book, broke down altar rails, brought the altar to the body
of the church, defaced images and broke stained-glass windows. It
was nevertheless not at all clear that a majority of people, or a majority
of Members of Parliament, wished to wipe out the ecclesiastical hierarchy. It was rather reform that was in many minds and a petition
from a group of church ministers to this effect came before the House.
When the question was debated early in February 1641 it was these
two petitions – the 'root and branch' and the 'reform' – that were
under consideration. To many, like Cromwell, they went to the heart
of the matter and the discussion was of high quality, wide-ranging,
with strong arguments on both sides. Sir John Strangeways made
a point which was not unlike that of King James's 'No bishop no
King' and which expressed the underlying fears of many Members:
'If we make a parity in the Church, we must come to a parity in
the Commonwealth'. Cromwell, too, was a property-owner. He,
too, would discountenance any threat to property. But this was a
different issue. The bishops could not shelter behind such specious
argument. He rushed into the fray, his temper blazing: he did not

59

understand why the gentleman that last spoke should make an inference of parity from the Church to the Commonwealth; nor that
there was any necessity of the great revenue of bishops. He clearly
spoke with great violence – quite unlike the fumbling newcomer
who had made his halting contribution to the debates of the 1629
Parliament. But he was too heated. He was reproved for unparliamen-
tary language and the Speaker made to call him to the bar of the
House to apologize. But Denzil Holles and John Pym himself came
to his defence. If he had said anything to offend he could explain
from his place and need not be called to the bar. Cromwell apparently
spoke words of conciliation and there the matter ended. But he had
served notice both in committee and in the House of Commons
itself that here was a force to be reckoned with, a character not easily
silenced. On the main issue a compromise was reached and the petitions were referred to a committee on which, yet again, Cromwell
served.[5]

Committees were a convenient way of dealing with unfinished
business. But this business would not remain unfinished for long.
Cromwell, with young Sir Harry Vane, who had come back from
the New World with his religious views strengthened, drew up a
Bill based on the Root and Branch petition and handed it to the
influential Sir Arthur Haselrig who set the right wheels turning, with
the result that a Bill for the Abolition of Bishops Root and Branch
was introduced in the Commons by Sir Edward Dering on 21 May
1641. Meanwhile the very root and branch of Episcopacy, Archbishop
Laud himself, had been imprisoned in the Tower for nearly three
months and lay, almost forgotten, while the House of Commons
feverishly turned from one thing to another. There were rumours
that the King was intriguing with the Northern army. He was certainly planning to visit Scotland. Pym drew up a *Protestation*, a form
of Covenant, which would be signed by Members of Parliament
and their constituents promising to maintain the true and reformed
Protestant religion, His Majesty's person and estate, the power and
privileges of Parliaments and the lawful rights and liberties of the
subject. It did not envisage a clash between these interests. Cromwell
was enthusiastic. Besides signing it himself he sent a copy immediately to his Cambridge constituents with a covering note encouraging
them to sign 'with alacrity and willingness' as 'a right honourable
and necessary act'. 'Combination carries strength', he said.[6]

Cromwell's presence was constantly felt. When negotiations with the Merchant Adventurers for a loan faltered he was for breaking off negotiations immediately. He 'diligently attended' a committee to clear Henry Burton who was being attacked for a pamphlet supporting the *Protestation*. As the summer wore on he was appointed to committee after committee: to confer with persons who might lend money to the army; to clear up abuses in Cambridgeshire; to consider an Act for the better enabling Members of Parliament to discharge their consciences in the proceedings of Parliament; to consider explaining an Act to raise money speedily. He joined in the debate against the King going to Scotland. On what necessity, he pertinently asked. On what occasion? He would not trust the King among his Scottish subjects. He was also concerned about the Prince of Wales and moved in the House that the Duke of Bedford and Lord Saye and Sele – both good Puritans – should join the Marquis of Hertford as Governor to the Prince. The motion was not seconded but it attested his good common sense and the confidence with which he now rose to speak in Parliament. He was, indeed, somewhat apt to intervene with slightly offbeat or not immediately relevant contributions to debate. In the midst of vital national considerations he presented in August 1641 a petition from prisoners in the Fleet that they might go to the country upon bail in times of plague. When an army plot was being discussed in March Cromwell moved 'to remove the Bishops of the Lords' House before we proceed in this'. Three days before Strafford's execution in May he moved that 'we might take some course to turn the Papists out of Dublin'! In September the House was debating an Ordinance against innovations in the worship of God when Cromwell directed the discussion to the Prayer Book 'shewing that there were many passages in it which divers learned and wise Divines could not submit unto and practice'.[7]

But though idiosyncratic and at times over-forceful, Cromwell was clearly regarded as a good committee man. Perhaps his tenacity was the reason, his ability to go to the heart of the matter and not be fobbed off by compromise. He was not a great talker and would not waste time with more words than were necessary to his purpose. Above all, he was already showing a power, a gift of command that brought men to his way of thinking and to the action he recommended. It was doubtless for these qualities that he began to be used as messenger from the House of Commons to the House of Lords in the spring and summer of 1641 and helped to arrange the sending of money collected from counties and towns to York for payment of the English army that had been raised to fight the Scots.[8]

The Root and Branch Bill had been tacitly laid aside, but Cromwell was one of a committee appointed on February 13 to consider an Act for the Abolishing of Superstitution and Idolatry and for the Better Advancing of the True Worship and Service of God. Bishops must remain for the time being but the House agreed to abolish Laud's 'innovations' and return to the simplicity of Puritan worship. They also prohibited dancing and sports on the Lord's Day and Cromwell moved for sermons to be preached in the afternoons. Thus people's minds might be improved (though not their bodies) and rowdy and seditious gatherings be avoided.[9]

Cromwell was striking out right and left. When in February 1641 he heard that the Scots were urging a uniformity in religion between the two countries he felt this was a step in the right direction and wrote to a friend with whom he had apparently been discussing the matter of notes or a pamphlet which he could consult before the expected Parliamentary debate. When he heard that the Earl of Arundel had written a recommendatory letter for a candidate in Arundel he demanded that it should be a free election and was granted a committee to consider the case.[10]

But the House was thin. Plague had been raging since the summer of 1641 and many MPs returned home, both to cleaner air and to attend to their own business. The country generally was not happy. Saddled with even heavier demands for money than the King had imposed, it made little difference who had instituted the taxes or to what purpose: six subsidies and a poll tax had been raised in a session. But the Scots, having been paid in accordance with the Treaty of Ripon, had returned home at the end of August and the English armies which had been raised to resist them were being paid prior to disbandment. With the King safely in Scotland, and no sign from either the Scottish or the English armies, the Houses felt they could safely adjourn. They did so on September 8. Cromwell remained until the end.

The opposition leaders had won a breathing space but it was merely that they could continue to plan their future strategy. It is not known whether Cromwell was one of those who met during the six weeks' recess in Lord Mandeville's house in Chelsea to prepare for the new session, but it would not be a wild assumption that he was at work on one or some of the committees that continued to meet throughout the recess. When the House reassembled on

October 20 it seemed the right moment to bring forward a so-called *Grand Remonstrance* on which various committees had been working since the beginning of the year. Parliament's activities had been so diverse, so incohate, even to itself, so shot through with anger and passion, that a reasoned account of its work would be salutary both to itself and to the country at large. More importantly, if a substantial majority were won for the *Remonstrance* it would be a public mark of approval for Parliament's activities since its inauguration. So the document set out all the evils from which the country had suffered in the years of Personal Rule and all the measures that Parliament had taken to alleviate them. It was a condemnation, a justification and an appeal for support. As such, Cromwell attached great importance to it. Moreover, an omnibus approval in black and white would make backsliding less likely.

But the *Grand Remonstrance* was a hodge-podge, a crude cobbling together of grievances and remedies, great and small, as though every Member of Parliament had insisted upon the insertion of his own particular interest: Cromwell, most likely, would have put forward the section on the fens. It amounted, all in all, to a potted history of the reign. It asked now that the King should 'advise' with Parliament over the appointment of ministers, while on religion it appeared to offer a compromise. The 'root and branch' ejection of bishops was no longer required but instead a synod of 'grave, pious, learned and judicious divines' would work out a system of church government.

It was soon apparent that the *Remonstrance* was far from winning the approval of all Members of Parliament: in general it was an unnecessary attempt at justification which did them harm, indicating not success but a growing apprehension; in particular it went too far with both constitutional and religious innovation. Committee after committee wrestled with the details. But to Cromwell the virtues of the *Grand Remonstrance* were self-evident and he was all impatience to get it debated and passed, which he thought could be done in an hour or two. The Bill was several times amended in committee after the House had reassembled and the delay angered him. Of the judicious Falkland, who was serving on this committee, Cromwell impatiently asked why it was again being postponed? To Falkland's cautious reply that the day was far gone, that they needed more time, for it would be a long debate, Cromwell replied sarcastically, 'A very sorry one!' But Falkland was right. The debate, when the *Remonstrance* came before the House at last on November 22, lasted from noon far into the night of November 23, the Members becoming more and more excited and vehement. All their underlying interests and allegiances, all their antagonisms one to another, came to the fore. It was the great divide. 'I thought we had all sat in the valley of the shadow of death, ready to catch each other's locks and sheath our swords in each other's bowels,' wrote a Member. At midnight the *Remonstrance* was carried by only eleven votes. It took a further three hours of furious wrangling to pass a resolution to have it printed and circulated to the country. 'If the Bill had not been passed,' whispered Cromwell to Falkland as they left the House in the grey hours between night and day, 'If the Bill had not been passed, I would have sold up all I had and left the country.' The Lord had been with him, but only just.[11]

Behind the preparation of the *Remonstrance* and the determination of Pym and men like Cromwell to get it passed without delay lay the realization that support in Parliament for the opposition was dwindling. When Parliament assembled in November 1640 the King had few supporters. But the very measures enumerated in the *Remonstrance* had satisfied many of them. An able group had already coalesced round the four intellectuals – Hyde, Falkland, Culpepper and Dering – who were ready to support Charles against further innovation. They strongly opposed the passages in the *Remonstrance* that required the King to 'advise' with Parliament over the appointment of ministers and those that would subject the form of religion to the findings of a specially appointed synod. In short, the revolt, the revolution, if such it was, had gone far enough and they cried 'halt!'. The constitution as it now stood satisfied them, and the ecclesiastical hierarchy and the Prayer Book, as Dering had already made clear, must remain intact in order to preserve the social order.

By their stand in Parliament they had gained constitutional government with its arbitrary overtones removed, freedom from arrest or punishment outside the law, protection for their property by the abolition of old feudal obligations like the Court of Wards and certain inheritance dues, relief from feudal practices like the levying of knighthood fines or forest fines, freedom for their business interests by the ending of monopolies. It was a sound achievement. They were satisfied with religion and the church settlement as it stood and, but for the gnawing uncertainty of whether the King would keep his word, they were generally content.

Cromwell had benefited with the rest of them, but he was not as willing as some to trust the King's word and he would not desist until the Church of Charles and Laud was torn down and freedom of worship established. His determination was reinforced by news that reached England on November 1 of rebellion in Ireland accompanied by hideous massacres of English and Scottish Protestants by Irish Catholics. The news was a trump card for Pym, about to launch the *Grand Remonstrance*, and stories of Irish atrocities lost nothing in the telling. He also exaggerated an army plot which allegedly the King had been hatching in Scotland. But neither episode appeared to affect the voting on the *Grand Remonstrance*. On the contrary it was clear that, on his return from Scotland on the day the *Remonstrance* was passed, the King had much support. His family met him in the City of London and they all returned to Whitehall amid great enthusiasm. But Charles could not let well alone. He was as rash and impetuous as Cromwell but without his homely common sense. The Irish rebellion told heavily against him with rumours, avidly embroidered by Pym, that the Catholics and the Queen were responsible and that they intended to establish Papacy in England. Elections to the Common Council of London dispossessed the royalist majority. With demonstrations against the Bishops and the Queen becoming more violent, Charles sought to get control of London by putting his own man in charge of the Tower and ejecting the parliamentarian Lieutenant. Bishops were prevented from sitting in the House of Lords and as confusion grew at the beginning of 1642 Charles made one of the biggest mistakes of his career in coming himself to the House of Commons and seeking to arrest five of its Members, including Pym and Hampden. They were forewarned and escaped, and the King withdrew, baffled. Shortly afterwards he left London with his family. The words 'To Let' appeared on the door of his palace in Whitehall.

In a little over a year Oliver Cromwell had learned much of Parliamentary procedure. He had also seen that a dramatic *coup* against Parliament or any of its Members must be attempted only if success was certain.

Part III

'Now he began to appear in the world'

7

'War without an enemy?'

In the aftermath of the alarm occasioned by the King's attempt on the five Members the House of Commons adjourned to the protection of the City of London. On January 14, three days after they had returned to Westminster, Cromwell moved in the House of Commons for a committee to consider the means to put the country into a posture of defence.[1] It was noteworthy that it should be Cromwell who both foresaw the end and was willing to accept the means. The motion was carried, but not until March did the House of Lords join the Commons with its own vote to the same effect. But by that time Parliament was already issuing Militia Ordinances which they claimed had the force of law to recruit men to arms and to organize the counties into a war posture. Cromwell was working on a committee which in March organized the raising of loans amounting to £1,000,000 on the security of 2,500,000 acres of Irish land. A public subscription list was opened and he himself lent £500 on the security of nearly 1,000 acres of good, fertile land in Leinster. His friends and relations followed him: £2,000 from Sir Gilbert Gerard, £1,200 from Sir Thomas Barrington, £1,000 from John Hampden, £600 each from Oliver St John and Sir William Masham.[2]

But Cromwell still had time and energy to get himself worked up about other matters. When Sir Edward Dering published a collection of the speeches he had delivered, or contemplated delivering, in the House of Commons, they were seen to contain views concerning religion and the monarchy which were contrary to those intended or laid down by the House. Cromwell was incensed, particularly since he himself appeared to be referred to in outrageous terms by his initials 'O.C.'. On February 2 he stood up in the Commons in a furious rage demanding that Dering's book be voted 'scandalous'. It was 'full of impertinences', he said. Others supported him. It was 'vainglorious', it 'overvalued himself', as D'Ewes put it. In short, it was a piece of self-advertisement. Cromwell's motion was carried, Dering was deprived of his seat in the Commons and sent to the Tower for what amounted to temporary imprisonment.[3]

Equally typical of Cromwell was his attention to smaller matters and less prominent people even in the midst of demanding public business. On February 7, five days after the heated debate about Dering, he presented a petition to the House from some Monmouth men who were in danger of being prosecuted because on a Sunday they had travelled away from their parish where there was no sermon in order to hear one in another place.[4]

But more and more his energy was engaged by war. Not only was he among the first to realize the inevitability of armed conflict and the necessity of preparing for it, but he seemed to know by instinct the steps that needed to be taken. No one could be further from the truth than Carlyle when he asked, a couple of centuries later, how 'a staid, most pacific, solid Farmer of three-and-forty decides on girding himself with warlike iron, and fighting, he and his, against principalities and powers'.[5] Cromwell was three-and-forty, but he was neither staid, pacific nor solid. His whole life was evidence to the contrary, though his appetite for war, his strategical instinct, his rapport with fighting men, may have surprised even himself – until he attributed all to God's purpose, and himself a mere instrument. But he would certainly have heard stories of his grandfather haranguing his men as they prepared to fight the Spaniard. He was probably well-versed in the actions of the Thirty Years' War and of the career of Gustavus Adolphus. Pictures of his home life are lacking but it is easy to see Oliver Cromwell after a day's work on his estate settling down with *The Swedish Intelligencer* or *The Swedish Soldier* or one of the *courantos* dealing with the war in Europe. There is no evidence that, like the King, he enjoyed himself with model soldiers and fortifications, playing mock battles, considering strategy in the confines of his study; but it is more than likely that he had routed out old drill manuals and maps in his father's house or among his grandfather's library at Hinchingbrooke. There does, indeed, exist an Elizabethan manual by John Polemon containing descriptions of sixteenth-century continental battles and signed 'O. Cromwell' on the recto of B.1.[6] The survival of this book opens speculation as to Oliver's further reading and the extent of his interest in war. But at what period of his life? There is no date to go on.

It can only be surmised that he consulted books like Gervaise Markham's *Souldiers' Grammar* or John Cruse's *Militarie Instructions for the Cavalry*. Predictably he supported Parliament's Militia Ordinance of March 3 which denied the King the power of raising troops and vested it in Parliament instead, and the appointment of the Puritan Earl of Warwick, with whom he was well acquainted, to the command of the fleet. At the beginning of June he saw *The Nineteen Propositions* sent to the King at York ostensibly as a negotiating document but knowing full well it was merely a statement of Parliament's position. No one was surprised when it was treated as such.[7] But with men of the intellectual calibre of Hyde, Culpepper and Falkland with him it gave the King the opportunity of scoring in the paper war which was in full swing on both sides. Cromwell played no active part in this.

But the committees proliferated. One looked into the numbers and quality of any persons who had not signed the *Protestation*. Cromwell's practical interest in the Prince of Wales took him on to a committee to consider Hertford's refusal to promise that the young man should not leave the kingdom. Many dealt with Ireland, more with the raising of money. Most of Cromwell's actions had a practical turn. When he heard that quantities of saddles and warlike materials were being carried out of London he put through a motion in the House of Commons that the Wardens and Company of Armourers should enquire into what store of saddles, arms and muskets were being made where, and to whom they were being sold. With his brother-in-law, Valentine Walton, he reported to the Commons words spoken by Mr Ravenscroft, a JP of Huntingdon, who allegedly said that if the King and Parliament should disagree most gentry would be for the King and that he himself had 1,000 men ready to assert their royalist allegiance.[8]

Increasingly Oliver's work concerned recruitment. On July 1 he carried a message to the House of Lords that touched him closely for it requested that the counties of Norfolk, Suffolk, Cambridge, Hertford, Dorset and Derby put the Militia Ordinance in execution and hasten their declarations against the King's Commissions of Array. Four days later he was conferring with six others and the Lieutenant of the Tower on measures for the safety of that bastion of the City. A few days after that he was considering which counties should be urged to bring in money, plate and horses; and what measures should be taken to prevent horses being sent to the King, who was recruiting at York. The importance of horses both for cavalry and for draught was evident and they were being requisitioned from farms and private houses with or without their owners' consent.

On July 9 Charles appointed Robert Bertie, Lord Willoughby de Eresby, Earl of Lindsey, his Commander-in-Chief. Three days later Parliament named the Earl of Essex Captain-General of all its forces. With tension growing Cromwell moved in the House of Commons on July 15 that the townsmen of Cambridge be permitted to raise two Companies of volunteers and to appoint Captains over them. He himself arranged and paid for arms to be sent into the county for its defence. The Commons ordered that the money should be repaid to him. It was typical that he would not wait for the machinery of supply to proceed but set things going himself. A month later he acted even more emphatically on his own initiative. He seized the county magazine in the Castle at Cambridge and, with Valentine Walton and John Desborough, raised enough men to intercept the valuable plate which the loyal University was about to send to the King. Shortly afterwards he secured also the county plate, valued at £20,000, for Parliament's use. When Charles had the temerity to send a Commission of Array to Cambridge Cromwell, the elected Member of Parliament for the city, rushed in 'in a terrible fury' with what force he could hastily muster. He surrounded several colleges while their Fellows were at devotions in their college chapels, seized several Doctors of Divinity and Heads of Houses and carried them with him in triumph to London where they were imprisoned in the Tower.[9]

Predictably, Oliver Cromwell was among those commissioned at the end of August to raise a troop of horse probably in Cambridge, with the rank of Captain and £1,104 mounting money. His brother-in-law, John Desborough, was his Quarter-master, the officers and men under him were mostly from Cambridge and Huntingdonshire. John Hampden, Nathaniel Fiennes, son of Lord Saye and Sele, Lord St John, Sir Philip Stapleton, were among those commissioned Colonels. Cromwell's son, another Oliver, left St Catherine's College, Cambridge, and enlisted as cornet in the troop of Lord St John. Valentine Walton was Captain of another troop of horse in which his own son, Cromwell's godson, another Valentine, was an officer.

The speed with which men adapted themselves to the situation and to Cromwell's leadership is well illustrated by what must have been the first action of Cromwell's troop. Two sons of Judge Bramston, the ship-money Judge, were returning in mid-August 1642 from the King's headquarters at York to their home at Skreens in Essex when, between Huntingdon and Cambridge, several armed men started up out of a cornfield commanding them to stand. They told us we must be searched, recounted one of the sons, 'and to that end must go before Mr Cromwell, and give account from whence we came and whither we were going. I asked, where Mr Cromwell was? A soldier told us, He was four miles off. I said, it was unreasonable to carry us out of our way: if Mr Cromwell had been there, I should have willingly given him all the satisfaction he could desire.' Twelve pence reinforced this argument and the soldiers let the young men pass: it was conduct for which Cromwell would later have hanged them from the nearest tree. But the lesson learned by John Bramston and his brother was that their father would never be allowed to get to the King at York.[10] A little later the young Earl of Carlisle, who headed the Essex and Cambridgeshire Commissions of Array for the King, had the temerity to attempt recruitment in Cromwell's own territory only to find himself arrested by that firebrand with a force of London dragoons.

Both sides were waiting, in the spring and summer of 1642, for the decisive step they felt to be inevitable. The King acted first when, on August 22, he raised his standard at Nottingham and proceeded to march westward recruiting men as he went – Derby, Shrewsbury, Chester and towards Wales. A week after the royal standard flew over Nottingham Cromwell was recruiting in his native Huntingdon, clearly feeling strong enough to tackle any obstruction from Barnard. Here he could enlist more of the men he wanted – honest yeoman farmers and their sons, most of them freeholders with all the independence which that implied; men he had known all his life, whom he had been to school with, who with him had been part of the Puritan congregations; who knew of his fight for the men of the fenland, of his stand against enclosure; men of whose sincerity and intelligence he had ample proof; men who would not fight merely for money or worldly gain but for conscience' sake. He told them he sought nothing but their welfare and desired nothing but to stand with them for the liberty of the Gospel and the laws of the land. Or, as he would put it a couple of years later when the war was in full swing, for the maintenance of their liberties as men and their religious liberties as Christians.

As he stood at the window of the Falcon in the market place at Huntingdon on August 29, speaking straightly and simply to men he still regarded as his fellow-citizens, he cut through the euphemisms with which many Parliamentarians had tried to hide the enormity of their action in raising arms against an anointed King. He would not deceive or cozen them, said Cromwell, by the perplexed and involved expression in his commission of fighting for 'King and Parliament'. Nor would he shelter behind the fiction that they were fighting not the King but his evil counsellors. If the King chanced to be in the body of the enemy that he was to charge he would discharge his pistol upon him as at any other private person, and if their conscience would not permit them to do the like, he advised them not to list themselves in his troop or under his command.[11]

As the country dissolved into civil war both Parliament and nation were divided. After the vehemence of denunciation and the unanimity with which the props of the King's government had been torn down, at the moment of war the numbers on either side were fairly evenly matched: the *Grand Remonstrance* was the true indication of ultimate allegiance. Falkland, who had perceived this, tried to solve his own inner conflict by going with the King when words became weapons. So did some 235 others – about forty per cent of the House of Commons – most of whom joined the royalist army. A little more than 300 were for Parliament of whom most joined the fighting forces while the rest remained at Westminster controlling both the affairs of the nation and the armies in the field. Fighting MPs like Cromwell returned to the House to report, to receive instructions, to speak or vote on urgent business. They generally found Pym or young Sir Harry Vane in charge. Of the House of Lords about eighty supported the King, thirty the Parliament, while twenty remained uncommitted.

So far as it was possible to make a division over the country as a whole the North and the South-West, including Wales, and Cornwall, were for the King, the East and South-East, including London, for Parliament. The Midlands were debatable territory. Most of the ports and wealthy industrial towns were for Parliament, the Cathedral cities for the King. But everywhere there was divided allegiance, pockets of conflicting loyalty, country houses fortified and holding out for one side or the other, generally for the King. On a balance of wealth Parliament held the advantage with London and the commercial interests on its side; but tradition, loyalty and the divinity hedging a King, were powerful on the other side. On both sides there were many of tortured conscience, pulled both ways in the conflict. Cromwell's family was with him in his allegiance with the exception of his now aged uncle, Sir Oliver, and his cousin, Henry Cromwell, who were for the King. He was spared any deeper rift such as separated fathers and sons like the Verneys or close friends like Sir William Waller, who became a notable Parliamentary commander, and Sir Ralph Hopton who became Charles's best commander in the West. Waller's tragic, bitter words written to his friend just before they met in battle had no echo in the mind of Oliver Cromwell: 'The great God, who is the searcher of my heart, knows with what reluctance I go upon this service, and with what perfect hatred I look upon a war without an enemy.'[12] Cromwell had no reluctance, no hatred except for the enemy – and he knew well enough who that was. In that single-mindedness lay a great part of his success. He was also more simplistic than many others in that his reasons for fighting were concrete and he did not seek to clothe them in abstract concepts of freedom or liberty but in the reality of worship as a Puritan and secure government as a citizen. This was the sense in which Cromwell spoke and he easily gathered together the sixty men of his troop, most of them substantial enough to come with their own horses and well-equipped.

Whatever the questions, whatever the answers, there was an inevitability about it all as marching began: a core of professional soldiers including the King's nephews Princes Rupert and Maurice from Germany; courtiers and Parliament men, tradesmen and farmers, gentry and labouring men, masters and servants – ragtag and bobtail armies with their accoutrements and possessions. The secretariat; the commissariat (one pound of biscuit, one pound of cheese per person per day), guns, mortars and ammunition dragged by horses over execrable roads in foul winter weather; few or no tents, the armies being expected to quarter in the villages or homesteads in their path for which vouchers were issued to householders for redemption later. The biggest headache was horses, required sometimes as mounts but mostly for haulage. Farms and villages were scoured for miles around an army to secure them.

Cromwell returned to London from Huntingdon at the end of August 1642. On September 6 he was with a committee of eight men to meet delegates from the House of Lords and the City of

London to consider subscriptions of money and plate from supporters. The following day he was at Ely raising money there. The next day, September 8, his Quartermaster received a month's pay for Cromwell's troop of horse. The first step was accomplished. Captain Oliver Cromwell and his troop of horse were a reality.

On September 13 they were ordered by the Committee appointed to settle the affairs of the Kingdom to join Lord General Essex, Captain-General of Parliament's forces, at Northampton. William, Earl of Bedford commanded the cavalry with 75 troops of horse. No. 67 was that of Captain Oliver Cromwell which was put into the Lord General's own regiment of horse under Sir Philip Stapleton. Young Cornet Oliver Cromwell, now twenty-one years old, was in troop no. 8.[13]

The desultory preliminaries of war reached a reluctant climax on 23 October 1642. Both armies had been marching round the Midlands enlisting support, sometimes within shouting distance of each other, yet so immature was the Intelligence on either side that they were frequently unaware of each other's presence. A clash had been narrowly averted at Worcester when Rupert abandoned the town in face of an advancing Parliamentarian force of greater strength. But on September 23 occurred the first real encounter of the war when Rupert routed a line of unsuspecting Parliamentarian horsemen, ill-advised by their scouts, who were riding unguardedly in single file up a narrow path with high hedges on either side near Powicke Bridge. The opportunity was too good to miss, the little force was scattered, the horsemen not drawing rein until they reached the main Parliamentarian army many miles away. This amateurish approach to war was continued as the two armies marched eastwards sometimes on a nearly parallel course within a few miles of each other. The King was trying to reach London and was at Edgcott, four miles from Banbury, on the evening of October 22. During the night Essex reached Kineton some seven miles to the west of the King's position. Unwilling to continue his march towards London with Essex so firmly on his heels, Charles, on Rupert's advice, decided on battle and drew up his forces on the ridge of Edgehill, in full view of Essex. When the Parliamentarian leader became aware of the King's intention to fight he brought his own men into a large open field. He knew that Charles had 4,000 cavalry to his 3,000; his full force was not yet with him, two regiments of foot and one of horse being

a day's march behind. So he prudently waited. It was not until
3 o'clock in the afternoon of the 23rd that the battle began. Rupert
was the first to charge, sweeping down the hill on the King's right
wing with his seasoned horsemen who swept the Parliament's left
wing before them, scattering it as far as Kineton, where the baggage
trains were, but themselves sweeping beyond the main line of battle.
The Royalist left wing made a similar, if not so devastating, attack
on Parliament's right, where Cromwell with his troop were stationed
as part of the regiment of Sir Philip Stapleton. Stapleton did heroic
work that day. When he had repelled the first Royalist attack he
turned upon their infantry in the centre and wreaked heavy damage.
Cromwell was there. When Colonel Nathaniel Fiennes made his
report on the battle to Parliament he specially mentioned Cromwell
who, he said, never stirred from his troops but fought until the last.
But there is no detail of this, Cromwell's baptism of fire, nor of
his own emotions. That he was impressed with Rupert's charge and
the Royalist cavalry in general is evident from his later conversation
with his cousin Hampden; that he had his first practical lesson in
tactics is certain, for maintaining a reserve, restraining his cavalry,
and turning upon the enemy's foot in the centre was a tactic he would
frequently use.[14]

The inconclusive battle where father fought against son, brother
against brother, friend against friend, the scene in the bitter cold
of a winter morning with Englishmen slaughtered by Englishmen
piled indiscriminately upon the ground regardless of 'side' or 'cause',
the shrieks of the wounded, the groans of the dying, sapped the
will of the survivors. Charles made no decisive effort to reach London,
Essex made no strong move to hinder him. There is no evidence
that Cromwell was affected by his first experience of large-scale
slaughter. Rather the contrary. What most impressed him was the
lesson to be drawn for future battles. The indecisive confrontation
following upon the desultory marching and the humiliation of Powicke Bridge led him soon after to speak to his cousin. 'Your troopers',
he said, 'are most of them old decayed servingmen and tapsters,
and such kind of fellows; ... do you think that the spirits of such
base and mean fellows will ever be able to encounter gentlemen that
have honor and courage and resolution in them? ... You must get
men ... of a spirit that is likely to go on as far as gentlemen will
go, or ... you will be beaten still.'[15] It was not his own troop of
horse to whom he was referring, who formed, after all, but a small

part of the whole, but more likely those of the left wing who were swept away by Rupert. His words express the despair and humiliation he felt and his determination to match his own carefully recruited men with others in Parliament's army as a whole. But for the time being he remained with his regiment and marched with Stapleton and Essex to Warwick and London to take his place in the House of Commons and receive official thanks for the battle of Edgehill, which both sides were claiming as a victory. It is probable that he was already irked by the dilatoriness of Essex and wished that Parliament's army had taken greater advantage of the King's uncertainty. As it was, Charles made for Oxford where he was firmly entrenched with his army and his Court by the end of the year. It would be his headquarters for the rest of the war.

With the King in winter quarters at Oxford and the weather precluding any large-scale campaigning, Parliament turned its attention to organization and to uniting counties into groups or associations that would give greater strength to the scattered Parliamentarian forces within each county. Association began with the Midland Association on December 15 – Leicester, Derby, Nottinghamshire, Rutland, Northamptonshire, Buckinghamshire, Bedfordshire. The second, on December 20, was Cromwell's own, the Eastern Association, comprising Essex, Suffolk, Norfolk, Cambridgeshire and Hertfordshire. Lord Grey of Groby was appointed Commander of the Midland Association, Lord Grey of Wark of the Eastern Association, under whom Cromwell served. He was, however, named to the Committees of both Associations, thus achieving considerable influence which he used to the full, riding round each Association and from one to the other, making use of his unsurpassed local knowledge, furthering plans for the increased recruitment he was intent on carrying out. When, early in 1643, he was commissioned Colonel of a regiment of horse there was nothing to stop him. On January 26 he was being referred to as 'Colonel Cromwell' and was on his way to the Eastern Association with a few troopers 'to raise such men as had the fear of God before them' when he came upon the High Sheriff of Hertfordshire, protected by a *posse comitatas*, proclaiming the King's Commission of Array in the market place of St Albans. This was rivalry, indeed, not to be stomached by Colonel Oliver Cromwell! There was a considerable struggle between his men and the Royalists but the Sheriff was taken prisoner and sent to London and to imprisonment in the Tower.[16]

Cromwell's recruiting was meanwhile doing well. As a contemporary put it, 'he had special care to get religious men into his troop; these men were of greater understanding than common soldiers... and making not money but that which they took for public felicity to be their end, they were the more engaged to be valiant.' By March 1643 he had five troops, the nucleus of an excellent regiment. His son Oliver, his nephew Valentine Walton, his cousin Edward Whalley, his brother-in-law Desborough, and his friend James Berry were all Captains of troops. By September he had ten troops under him, as full of religious men as he could get.[17]

There was an alarm early in the year when, in January, Rupert was rumoured to be at Wellingborough in Northamptonshire and Cromwell, with the Cambridge Committee of the Eastern Association, sent to the Deputy Lieutenant of Norfolk for a force of horse and foot. The rumour was groundless but in March it seemed possible that the Royalists had designs upon Cambridge itself, especially when Lord Capel appeared in the area. Cromwell, as member of Parliament for the town, as member of the County Committee, and as Colonel of a regiment of horse, was the head of resistance. Men not only from Cambridgeshire but from the surrounding counties flocked into him in such numbers that he had some 12,000 men at his disposal. Under his guidance Cambridge was fortified and garrisoned, ordnance and ammunition brought in. Cambridge was saved without a struggle and Cromwell proceeded to Croyland where a Royalist garrison was in possession. In compelling its surrender at the end of April Cromwell had his first experience of siege warfare.

He continued with other enterprises, sending out men to take delinquents and to bring in prisoners and money, which they did from all over the area – Norwich, King's Lynn, Lowestoft, where in March a Royalist rising was nipped in the bud. Cromwell himself was at Norwich where he interviewed the prisoners taken at Lowestoft before sending them to Cambridge. At King's Lynn he seized a small barque laden with arms from Dunkirk, apparently intended for the Royalists. In ten days he had ridden from Cambridge to Norwich, to Yarmouth and Lowestoft, back to Norwich and thence to King's Lynn and back to Cambridge, crushing incipient Royalist resistance as he went, bringing in Royalist gentry as prisoners, seizing their plate for Parliament's war chest, collecting contributions from both supporters and opponents. He no doubt derived satisfaction from sending men into Huntingdon to investigate the activities of his old enemy, Robert Bernard. 'I know you have been wary in your carriages', he wrote maliciously, but 'I heard you reported active against the proceedings of Parliament.' If Bernard did not mend his ways Cromwell would act accordingly. Bernard did not comply and Cromwell wrote again in April with a certain amount of satisfaction to tell him he had been found out and would be subject to the full assessment to Parliament's funds.[18] He visited church congregations seeking for subscriptions. He put the needs of the cause before loyalty to family or age and sought out his aged uncle, Sir Oliver Cromwell, who had declared for the King and retired to Ramsay after the sale of Hinchingbrooke, and took away all his silver plate.[19] He made himself responsible for seeing that needy officers were supplied with money. When, for example, Captain Nelson was being sent into Norfolk to round up delinquents, Cromwell himself lent him the money to pay his accounts in Cambridge before leaving. 'It's a pity a gentleman of his affections should be discouraged,' he asserted to the Committee, 'I earnestly beseech you to consider him and the cause. It's honourable that you do so.' The Committee repaid Cromwell the following day. It was a help to him when in May Huntingdonshire was added to the Eastern Association.

In the first six months of war Cromwell had galvanized into a veritable rocket of energy – strong, mobile, speedy, determined. His mind was always open to new necessities. He had the ability to learn quickly and was impatient of those who did not realize the immediate need, whether it concerned recruitment, money, strategy or the need to strike – when, where and how. He allowed his men a certain amount of licence. He did not, for example, stop them from burning books and shattering the great glass window in Peterborough Cathedral. But this was common policy. At about the same time the House of Commons was ordering the stained glass and the images of Westminster Abbey and St Margaret's church to be destroyed and the City Fathers were tearing down Cheapside Cross. In other respects Cromwell's discipline was tight, reinforced by his own personality as he developed into an army officer to be obeyed and a leader of men. Plunder was not permitted, 'no man swears but he pays his twelve pence; if he be drunk he is set in the stocks or worse'. His arms and his mount must be kept in tip-top condition. 'Cromwell used them daily to look after, feed, and dress their horses, and, when it was needful, to lie together on the ground; and besides he taught them to clean and keep their arms bright and to have them ready for service.'[20] However good the quality of the men he enlisted, ceaseless energy, a strong will, his own example, and officers ready to act for him, were all necessary to maintain the standards he required.

8

'Lay not too much upon the back of a poor gentleman'

The war began to assume a pattern. In the extreme South-West Sir Ralph Hopton was advancing through Cornwall and Devon, and in the North the Duke of Newcastle had secured Newcastle for the King, overrun much of Yorkshire, and set up winter quarters at York. The joining of these two armies was clearly the Royalist intent. To place a wedge between them was Parliament's objective. In the North Ferdinand, Lord Fairfax of Cameron, and his son, Sir Thomas, though severely outnumbered, were checking the Royalists, though for how long they could hold them was uncertain. To reinforce the Fairfaxes and drive back Newcastle was an obvious strategy but Lincolnshire, which was virtually a buffer zone between Cavalier and Roundhead, stood in the way. Not only had Newark been occupied by contingents of Newcastle's army, but the area was subject to constant incursions from raiding Royalists, in particular the 'Camdeners' from Rutlandshire, followers of Noel, Viscount Camden, who kept up a constant and lively harassment of the population, driving cattle and plundering indiscriminately; they captured Stamford and occupied Croyland. An added humiliation to the Parliamentarians was the knowledge that the Queen, who had been purchasing arms and ammunition on the Continent with the proceeds of the sale of the Crown jewels, had landed at Bridlington in February 1643 and was making a triumphal journey southwards to meet her husband.

In May 1643 Essex ordered the Eastern counties to unite with those of the East Midlands and relieve Lincolnshire as a preliminary to giving aid to the Fairfaxes across the Humber in Hull and to restraining Newcastle's cavaliers. Cromwell was all eagerness but found local commanders unwilling to leave their localities undefended – a familiar feature of the fighting where local problems and local loyalties were more real and urgent than national. Cromwell was one of the few and one of the earliest to view the war as a whole, but as yet his appeals fell on deaf ears. Time and time again his fellow-commanders failed him at promised rendezvous. He wrote despairingly on May 3 to the Committee at Lincoln: 'My Lord Grey hath now again failed me', being unable to meet Cromwell at Stamford according to their agreement 'fearing the exposing of Leicester' to enemy attack. 'Believe it', thundered Cromwell, 'it were better, in my poor opinion, Leicester were not, than that there should not be an immediate taking of the field by your forces to accomplish the common end, wherein I shall deal as freely with him when I meet him as you can desire.' Let us try once more, he urges, to get our scattered forces to meet at a general rendezvous 'and then you shall receive full satisfaction concerning my integrity; and if no man shall help you, yet will not I be wanting to do my duty, God assisting me.' Practical as ever, he suggests Grantham as the meeting place. His letter was read in the House of Commons on May 8 and Lord Grey and others were commanded to join him at once. Cromwell's determination and vigour had paid off.[1]

It was only ten days later, two miles from Grantham, on the Newark road, that with twelve troops of his own Cromwell met a Royalist force twice that size. Both sides halted and looked at each other. War was not yet an accustomed exercise. For half an hour there was a little desultory shooting. Cromwell was the first to move. We 'came on with our troops a pretty round trot, they standing firm to receive us', he reported, 'and our men charging fiercely upon them, by God's providence they were immediately routed, and ran all away, and we had the execution of them two or three miles.' He took forty-five prisoners, some horses and arms, and rescued many Parliamentarians recently taken. 'God hath given us, this evening, a glorious victory over our enemies', wrote Cromwell to the Committee of Lincolnshire. It was not with the picked force he intended to have and was steadily building up. Some of his men, he said, were 'so poor and broken, that you shall seldom see worse'. Yet with 'this handful it pleased God to cast the scale'. This was the first of Cromwell's 'battle' letters; it was also the first to be published in the news-sheets which were now giving news from both sides. In it there was already the mature Cromwell: the exultation, the belief in Divine intention, even the denigrating of his men to make the victory, and God's intervention, the more remarkable.[2]

Ten days after the skirmish near Grantham Cromwell was at Nottingham with twenty-four troops of horse and dragoons. Newark was still in Royalist hands, the weather was execrable with thirteen days of unbroken rain, his troops were mutinous through lack of supplies. A glimmer of light came from the North where the Fairfaxes had achieved a victory over Newcastle at Wakefield. But they had only 3,000 foot to Newcastle's 6,000 and nine troops of horse to his sixty. They could not hold out for long and their pressing needs were added to Cromwell's own. Desperately he wrote to the Committee at Colchester on May 28, his broken sentences testifying urgency and near despair:

> Why you should not strengthen us to make us subsist! Judge you the danger of the neglect, and how inconvenient this improvidence, or unthrifty, may be to you!... The enemy draws more to the Lord Fairfax. Our motion and yours must be exceedingly speedy, or else it will do you no good at all.
>
> I beseech you, hasten the supply to us; forget not money... the foot and dragooners are ready to mutiny. Lay not too much upon the back of a poor gentleman, who desires, without much noise, to lay down his life, and bleed the last drop to serve the Cause and you. I ask not your money for myself; if that were my end and hope I would not open my mouth at this time. I desire to deny myself; but others will not be satisfied. I beseech you hasten supplies...[3]

Supplies were not forthcoming. Cromwell got no further than Nottingham although he was joined briefly there by Lord Grey and other Parliamentarian commanders from Lincolnshire and Derby. These, however, after a few skirmishes with the garrison at Newark, decided to withdraw fearing an attack upon Lincoln. The Fairfaxes were left helpless and Cromwell with no alternative but to fall back into the Eastern Association. The Fairfaxes were defeated a month later at Adwalton Moor and retreated into Hull.

The cavaliers had dominated much of Lincolnshire in raids and skirmishes from Newark. Now Newcastle's cavalry under his nephew Charles Cavendish began to press southwards with determination. Peterborough and Stamford were threatened. Lord Willoughby, the commander of Parliament's forces in Lincolnshire, was besieged in Gainsborough. Cromwell pushed northwards once more. He captured Stamford and drove the groups of Royalists who were trying to hinder him into nearby Burleigh House which the Countess of Exeter was holding for the King. He successfully laid siege to the mansion which surrendered on July 24 in an encounter free from slaughter, although Cromwell took 200 cavaliers prisoner. He later sent the Countess a portrait of himself by Robert Walker, which still hangs in Burleigh House. It may have been an indication of his respect for the lady or of the high regard he found it easy to develop for the opposite sex; it may have been an indication of the regard she showed for him, and she may herself have requested it; it may commemorate some unrecorded episode in Cromwell's life. But one wonders at the arrogance of the gift.

Cromwell left his infantry behind and made all speed to Gainsborough with 600 horse and dragoons. He was met at Grantham by Meldrum from Nottingham and at Newton Searle by troops from Lincoln. Meldrum took command and on the morning of the 28th they came upon Cavendish and his horse on the Gainsborough road just north of Lea. The Royalists were already gathered on the edge of a sandy plateau which sloped sharply down to the road up which Parliament's forces were advancing. The Parliamentarians attacked immediately. Though severely hampered by rabbit burrows in the side of the hill they pushed upward. Not only did they get to the top, they forced the enemy to fly and the bulk of their forces set off after them. Here, however, was a lesson Cromwell had already learned. He held his own troops back from the pursuit and, perceiving that Cavendish had done likewise and was now advancing, Cromwell waited and let him pass before turning his men and attacking the cavaliers from the rear. The startled Royalists continued their forward march in a panic, rushing down hill and into a bog at the bottom into which the unfortunate young Cavendish was precipitated and where Captain Berry killed him with a thrust under the short rib.

Gainsborough, it seemed, was safe for the Parliament. Food and supplies were being sent in to the town when what appeared to be a small Royalist force was seen approaching from the North. The Parliamentary commanders almost casually marched out to meet it with 400 of Willoughby's foot and some of Meldrum's cavalry when they found themselves faced with Newcastle himself and his complete army coming up in serried ranks. Willoughby's foot fled. Meldrum's cavalry remained and Cromwell, who was in command of the main body, immediately set in motion an operation which was one of the most remarkable of the whole war. He sent forward two parties of horse under Captain Ayscough and Major Whalley ordering them to fire and retire alternately. This they did with astonishing control and regularity. They 'with this handful faced the enemy so, and dared them to their teeth, in the least eight or nine several removes, the enemy following at their heels, and they, though their horses were exceedingly tired, retreated in this order near carbine shot of the enemy.' They reached Gainsborough with the loss of only two men. Now, wrote the lawyer and politician Bulstrode Whitelocke of Cromwell after Gainsborough, '. . . he began to appear in the world'.[4]

On July 24 Parliament appointed Cromwell Governor of the Isle of Ely,[5] his home territory; a week later he received £3,000 for his men and the thanks of the House of Commons for himself. On August 10 Manchester was appointed to command the forces of the Eastern Association and to raise 10,000 foot and 5,000 horse, with four Colonels of horse of whom Cromwell was one; he rapidly became virtually Manchester's second-in-command. But the Royalists were on the offensive. Gainsborough surrendered to them, they occupied Lincoln and King's Lynn. Manchester besieged King's Lynn with all his foot and sent Cromwell on September 5 to assist Willoughby who was defending Boston and the fens with his cavalry. Fortunately Newcastle turned back to besiege Hull, where the Fairfaxes were still entrenched, and Willoughby and Cromwell followed with their cavalry. A daring and imaginative co-operation then began between these two leaders and the Fairfaxes. On September 18 the sorely pressed garrison of Hull was cheered by the sight of Cromwell's troopers on the south bank of the Humber. On September 22 Cromwell himself crossed the Humber and was in Hull, meeting Sir Thomas Fairfax for the first time and bringing with him supplies of muskets and powder. He returned the same day but Willoughby followed on the 23rd when plans were completed. The Fairfaxes had been doing all they could to protect Hull, among other enterprises opening the sluices and so flooding the land for miles around. But cavalry was of little use to them within a beleaguered city and they were stabling their horses in the open outside the city walls. Now, as plans materialized, men and horses were being ferried down the Humber estuary on each tide and so down the coast to Saltfleet under the protection of Cromwell's men. Lincolnshire cavaliers tried to prevent their landing but, reported Cromwell, 'we marched up to their landing place, and the Lincolnshire horse retreated'. The sight of Cromwell's disciplined troops was clearly too much for the Royalists. When the operation was completed on the 26th the Parliamentarian forces had been augmented by twenty-one troops of horse and dragoons from Hull. Sir Thomas Fairfax himself slipped out of the city and joined Cromwell and Willoughby at Boston.[6]

The operation had worked admirably, but it was typical of this stage of the war that when he came to Boston Cromwell found no money for his troops. He wept. But after conferring with Manchester at King's Lynn he pushed on with Fairfax to besiege Bolingbroke Castle. The Royalist Governor of Newark, Sir John Henderson, was, however, advancing to its relief through Horncastle. The two forces met near the little hamlet of Winceby on a ridge south of Horncastle. Winceby was, again, a cavalry action which was typical of the development of Cromwell and his men, between forces of about equal numbers. This time Cromwell did not wait. But with his troops 'pealing forth a battle hymn as they rode', he led the charge. His horse was immediately shot from under him and he was thrown violently to the ground. He freed himself from his mount, seized another and was again in the thick of the fight. The cavaliers were forced by the onrush back on to their second line, a charge from Fairfax completed the rout, and the whole enemy force fled, some to be drowned in the waters of the fens, some to be taken prisoner, some to reach Horncastle, a few to get back to Newark. Thirty-five colours were taken and nearly 1,000 prisoners. The day after Winceby Newcastle abandoned the siege of Hull. On October 20 Lincoln surrendered to Manchester. Gainsborough gave in shortly afterwards and the whole of Lincolnshire was in Parliament's hands.[7]

As winter set in and campaigning slowed down Cromwell, as Governor of Ely, was able to spend more time in his own town and even in his own house with his family. He had completed a year of active campaigning including recruiting, raising money, and actual fighting. He had learned much and was already a match for more seasoned veterans. While he waited impatiently for the next campaign which might well put an end to the war, there was much to do in stirring up committees, encouraging contributions to Parliament's funds, checking the forms of Puritan worship, and still recruiting.

Strangely enough his own Ely Cathedral, under whose shadow he lived and whose tythes he farmed, had been sluggish concerning the removal of images and the abandonment of ritual. When Crom-

well found the Reverend Henry Hitch, Vicar Choral of the Cathedral
and Headmaster of the Cathedral school, conducting a choir service
in the Cathedral his anger was roused. On 10 January 1644, he wrote
a short letter to Mr Hitch which was both offensive and to the
point:

> Lest the soldiers should in any tumultuary or disorderly way attempt
> the reformation of your Cathedral Church, I require you to forbear
> altogether your choir-service, so unedifying and offensive: and this
> as you will answer it, if any disorder should arise thereupon.

He signed himself 'Your loving friend'.

When Mr Hitch failed to respond, 'his loving friend' stormed
into the Cathedral with what was described as 'a rabble at his heels',
strode up to the choir and announced: 'I am a man under authority;
and am commanded to dismiss this assembly.' Mr Hitch paused for
a moment but then started again. 'Leave off your fooling and come
down, Sir!' commanded Cromwell. This was enough. The Reverend
Henry must have heard that harsh, commanding voice many times
before. He reluctantly complied.[8]

More satisfactory to Cromwell was his official appointment in
January as Lieutenant-General to Manchester with particular responsibility for the cavalry, thus making official what had been a virtual
fact since Manchester's appointment. He continued his recruitment
of what was probably a double regiment of fourteen full troops of
eighty harquebusiers each. Manchester was surprised and somewhat
affronted at the kind of officers he chose: 'not such as weare souldiers
or men of estate, but such as were common men, pore and of mean
parentage, onely he would given them the title of godly, pretious
men'. They were the very words Cromwell used in writing to the
Committee of Suffolk in September 1643:

> I beseech you be careful what captains of Horse you choose, what
> men be mounted; a few honest men are better than numbers...
> If you choose godly honest men to be captains of Horse, honest
> men will follow them.

But the Committee of Suffolk was dragging its feet and in recruiting
his thirteenth troop Cromwell chose his own man, Captain Ralph
Margery, to command it. Margery, however, was not acceptable
to the Suffolk worthies because he was not a 'gentleman'. 'Gentleman!' retorted Cromwell, 'I had rather have a plain russet-coated

captain that knows what he fights for and loves what he knows, than that which you call a gentleman and is nothing else.'

'It may be', he continued with rising anger and some sarcasm,

> it may be it provokes some spirits to see such plain men made captains of horse. It had been well that men of honour and birth had entered into these employments, but why do they not appear? Who would have hindered them? But seeing it was necessary the work must go on, better plain men than none, but best to have men patient of wants, faithful and conscientious . . .

He was writing in the midst of campaigning in Lincolnshire. Fairfax had just escaped from Hull and they were contemplating their next move. If Margery and his men are troublesome, he writes, 'Send them all to me! I'll bid them welcome!' A pregnant contrast between the armchair critic and the soldier in the field.[9]

Another side of Cromwell's character was shown when the 'young men and maids of Norwich' raised twelve score pounds hoping to provide a troop of horse for him. He was kind and tactful in thanking them but explained that the money was not sufficient in itself to provide a troop. But, he says, 'I thank God for stirring up the youth to cast in their mite.' If they would buy pistols and saddles with the money he would provide four score horses. As for the volunteers to ride them: 'Pray raise honest godly men', he urged, 'and I will have them of my regiment.' They did so and he was as good as his word. 'The Maiden Troop' became a reality.[10]

The raising of men was one thing, the raising of money another. As Cromwell wrote to St John, he had a 'lovely company' but they needed to be treated as men with adequate supplies and wages. His energy in writing to Committee after Committee for money throughout 1643 is as remarkable as his energy in marching from place to place to fight or to raise a siege.

The overall direction of the war, as well as the government of the country, remained meanwhile with the truncated body that remained at Westminster. It was hardly less aware than Cromwell of the financial problem. Gifts of money and plate were a drop in the ocean. The pretence of 'borrowing' from sympathizers was abandoned early in the war, though the City of London continued to lend to Parliament upon good security. But, as Pym said, 'as the burthen is universal, the aid must be universal too' and Ordinances of increasing stringency raised money compulsorily from property-owners all over the country where Parliament had control: on 29 November 1642 a tax on all who had not contributed voluntarily; on December 8 a similar tax on all persons within the areas controlled by Parliament; on 24 February 1643 the tax took the form of a weekly payment imposed on every county in England with Commissioners to assess property owners at their discretion. On May 27 an Ordinance sequestered the estates of all who supported the King, and on the following day Pym suggested an excise on all commodities bought or sold. Opposition was vehement. There had been furious denunciation of such a tax when suggested by the King; it was no different now. Excise would hit small men and large enterprises, buying and selling, the private individual, the corporation, the home trade and overseas markets. Pym toned down the proposal to cover 'superfluous commodities' only, but his motion was lost at the time though, under stress of necessity, renewed and passed as an Ordinance on 22 July 1643. When in the same month the Eastern Association was enlarged to include Lincolnshire it was also empowered to raise taxes from the Associated Counties.

Increasingly valuable was the growing practice of compounding with delinquents for part of their estates in return for permission to live peacefully outside the conflict, the sum aimed at being about equal to two years' purchase of their estates. This was begun on a regular basis in January 1644 and made general in October 1645 by the establishment of a Committee for Compounding with Delinquents. A Sequestration Committee managed the estates of Royalists who would not, or were not allowed to compound. There were also Committees for the Advance of Money (called, from the place where it met, the Committee of Haberdashers' Hall), the Committee for Plundered Ministers, the Committee for Irish Affairs, and various county committees all of which had the question of raising money high on their agendas. The most important of these committees, which had started as a Committee of Safety even before the war started, was enlarged in February 1644 by the inclusion of the Scots and became the Committee of Both Kingdoms. To this Committee Cromwell was appointed on its inception. It was government by committee, indeed, but there was also a war to win and directing operations by committees of civilians from Westminster was neither efficient nor acceptable to the soldiers in the field. The fact that serving soldiers like Cromwell also served on committees of civilians at Westminster was not a satisfactory solution to the problem.

In general, by the end of 1643 the war was going badly for Parliament. Royalist forces had advanced through Devonshire defeating Parliament's forces at Roundway Down. In July Bristol was captured by Rupert from Colonel Nathaniel Fiennes. In the North the Royalists were in the ascendant, apart from the efforts of the Fairfaxes, and in June a shattering blow was dealt to Parliament's morale and to Cromwell personally when on one of Rupert's forays from Oxford into the Chiltern hills John Hampden was mortally wounded in a small skirmish near Chalgrove on the Watlington Road and died four days later at Thame. In December, probably a greater blow to Parliament's cause in general, John Pym died. A few months before his death he had been instrumental in appealing for help to the Scots who were, after all, Parliament's allies in religion. And religion did, indeed, prove to be the bond of the agreement reached between the two countries when, in September 1643, they agreed to unite with England for the reformation of religion 'according to the word of God and the example of the best reformed churches'. The Solemn League and Covenant was to be signed by all officers of the army.

With the army mostly in winter quarters Cromwell spent much of January in Westminster, though he did not neglect the Eastern counties and by March was operating round Newport Pagnell, guarding ammunition on its way to Gloucester, and capturing Hillesden House, an advanced post of the Oxford Royalists. He was slow to sign the Covenant, probably fearful already of the strict Presbyterianism which he knew was intended. When he did sign, on February 3, he no doubt took refuge in the ambiguous phrase 'according to the word of God'. He was already having trouble with some of his more rigid Presbyterian officers. Major-General Crawford, in particular, a Scot of narrow Presbyterian beliefs, was objecting to some of Cromwell's Independent officers. Cromwell spoke to him, pointing out that it was service in the war that counted, not the form of a man's worship — so long as it was not popery or prelacy. Nevertheless, back in Cambridge briefly on March 10, he had to deal again with the problem. Crawford had sent Lieutenant Packer to him under guard for disciplining because allegedly he was an 'Anabaptist'. Cromwell immediately released Packer. He spoke to him, as he had spoken to Crawford, emphasizing that service to the cause was paramount and that he must keep his particular religious beliefs under restraint. Then he sent him back to Crawford with a letter. Cromwell was angry that a good soldier should be disciplined and should be kept idle when his regiment had been called to action merely because of his religious beliefs. 'Surely', he wrote, 'you are not well advised thus to turn off one so faithful to the Cause, and so able to serve you as this man is.' He continued with a little homily:

> Sir, the State, in choosing men to serve them, takes no notice of their opinions, if they be willing faithfully to serve them, that satisfies. I advised you formerly to bear with men of different minds from yourself; if you had done it when I advised you to it, I think you would not have had so many stumbling-blocks in your way... I desire you would receive this man into your favour and good opinion. I believe, if he follow my counsel, he will deserve no other but respect from you. Take heed of being sharp, or too easily sharpened by others, against those to whom you can object little but that they square not with you in every opinion concerning matters of religion...[11]

There were Presbyterian officers and Presbyterian chaplains in other regiments and there seems little doubt that Cromwell consciously tried to leaven them with men of Independent views. He had, for example, continued his friendship with John Lilburne. Lilburne had enlisted at the beginning of the war, been captured at Brentford and imprisoned by the Royalists in Oxford castle. When he was released on an exchange Cromwell at once recruited him and they were sufficiently close for Lilburne to speak of Cromwell as 'my then most intimate and familiar bosome friend'. When he was commissioned Major of Foot on 7 October 1643, it was in the regiment of Colonel King, a noted Presbyterian. Lilburne believed Cromwell had posted him thus in order to keep an eye on King, and this may not be far from the truth. Lilburne was certainly to the fore in substantiating the charges which later were brought against King and he was appointed on May 16, probably on Cromwell's instigation, to Manchester's regiment as Lieutenant-Colonel of Dragoons.[12]

While Cromwell was tackling these problems he learned of the death from smallpox at the garrison at Newport Pagnell of his son Oliver, who had served at Edgehill. But his father had no time to indulge his grief. Battle was imminent in the north.

Part IV

Ironsides

9

'Is Cromwell there?'

As their part of the agreement the Scots raised 21,000 men to assist their English co-religionists, and in January 1644 Alexander Leslie, who had been created Earl of Leven by Charles I, crossed the border with David Leslie, in the winter snows and joined the Fairfaxes before York. The Earl of Newcastle was now beleaguered in the city with Scots to the North and the Fairfaxes in control of the surrounding Yorkshire. But Prince Rupert was coming to the rescue. He was a long time coming for he had other work to do and Lincolnshire was hotly debatable land where fortunes swung from one side to the other. The armies of the Eastern Association meanwhile arrived before York at the beginning of June with 9,000 men, of whom 3,000 were Cromwell's cavalry. It was a month before Rupert, responding to the King's urgent demand, reached the area 'pouring over the hills from Lancashire with 14 or 15,000 men'. To the besieging armies it was an unnerving sight, particularly since it opened them to a pincer movement from the Royalists in York and Rupert's relieving army. The allied commanders therefore decided to give battle to Rupert before he reached York and to that intent they raised the siege intending to draw up on the moor of Long Marston some six miles due west of York. But Rupert outwitted them, crossing to the north bank of the river Swale while they were concentrating their forces to the south. He entered York without opposition while Parliament's commanders, red-faced, were slowly marching away, Cromwell, Fairfax and Leslie guarding their rear. Rupert was determined on battle though his forces numbered no more than 18,000 to Parliament's 27,000, and he began a series of sniping attacks on Cromwell's rear. This was not a tactic to employ when Cromwell was involved and his counsel was strong in urging Manchester to stop and fight. They chose as their battle ground the long ridge of open land which stretches down to Marston Moor. All might have been well for Rupert but he chose to insist that the reluctant Earl of Newcastle join him in the fight, and with Lord Eythin, Newcastle's second, he was not on good terms.

On Tuesday July 2 Parliament's armies drew up on the ridge. Their left wing was in good corn country, their right was impeded by rough ground pitted with holes and covered with furze. In front of the whole army ran a line of hedges and ditches. Rupert's men began to gather on the moor itself shortly afterwards. But Rupert was without Newcastle who, probably deliberately, was slow in responding to the younger man's peremptory demands, while Eythin's men demanded their pay before they moved. So the day wore away. Parliament's commanders made their dispositions, but it was not until four in the afternoon that Rupert was joined by the rest of the Royalist forces and it was not until six or seven in the evening that all was ready. Too late for an attack that night, they thought. Rupert and other officers started their supper, while Newcastle, still apparently out of humour, retired to his carriage to smoke a pipe. Meanwhile Cromwell's men 'in Marston corn fields fall to singing psalms'. Rupert heard them. 'Is Cromwell there?' was his anxious question. He did not have to wait for the answer. Parliament's forces attacked while Rupert and his officers were at supper and Newcastle was with his pipe. Rupert had lost the initiative upon which he relied for the force of his cavalry charge. Instead it was Cromwell's horsemen who, between 7 and 8 pm, fell on Lord Byron and the Royalist right wing. They were Cromwell's own men, horse and dragoons of the Eastern Association, together with some Scottish dragoons. Not less than 3,000 strong they rode 'in the bravest order and with the greatest resolution that ever was seen', according to Scoutmaster-general Watson. 'In a moment we were past the ditch into the Moor, upon equal ground with the enemy.' Cromwell himself was wounded in the neck by a pistol shot which narrowly missed his eye. He remained to organize a second charge before retiring to have his wound dressed. A desperate conflict continued. Rupert vainly tried to stem the unaccustomed rout of his cavalry but Cromwell had a reserve of three regiments of Scottish cavalry which completed the rout and the Royalist right wing broke, flying 'as fast and as thick as could be'. When Cromwell returned from the field hospital he quickly assessed the situation and, finding the Parliamentarian centre and right wing in poor shape, he immediately combined with

Leslie and Crawford and swept round behind the Royalist centre to their assistance. The fighting was still fierce but the Royalists were broken. The last to remain was a group of Newcastle's White Coats who fought with the utmost bravery to the end. Three thousand Royalists fell, 1,600 were taken prisoner together with a hundred colours, ten guns, and 6,000 muskets. Rupert escaped by hiding in a beanfield. But he had seen enough of Cromwell and his men to assess their worth. It was Rupert who first dubbed Cromwell and his men 'Ironside' or 'Ironsides'.[1]

For Cromwell there remained the sad task of writing to Valentine Walton, whose son had been killed in the battle. In the opening sentence Cromwell prepares him for the worst:

> It's our duty to sympathise in all mercies; that we may praise the Lord together in chastisements or trials, that so we may sorrow together.

To let the purport of that opening sentence sink in he then turns to a short account of the battle:

> 'this great victory given unto us, such as the like never was since this war began ... We never charged but we routed the enemy. The left wing, which I commanded, being our own horse, saving a few Scots in our rear, beat all the Prince's horse. God made them as stubble to our swords ... of twenty-thousand the Prince hath not four-thousand left. Give glory, all the glory, to God'.

Then, abruptly,

> Sir, god hath taken away your eldest son by a cannon-shot. It brake his leg. We were necessitated to have it cut off, whereof he died.
>
> Sir, you know my trials this way: but the Lord supported me with this, That the Lord took him into the happiness we all pant after and live for. There is your precious child full of glory, to know sin nor sorrow any more. He was a gallant young man, exceeding gracious.

Cromwell stayed with the boy to the end and recounted his last words to his father. There follows a short account of the young man's bravery in the battle and then Cromwell speaks of the high regard in which he was held:

> Truly he was exceedingly beloved in the Army, of all that knew him ... he was a precious young man, fit for God. You have cause

to bless the Lord. He is a glorious saint in Heaven ... Let this drink up your sorrow ... The Lord be your strength.[2]

After the battle of Marston Moor the armies divided with a good campaigning season still before them. Leven went north to besiege Newcastle, the Fairfaxes remained in Yorkshire operating round Scarborough, Pontefract and Helmsley; Manchester and Cromwell returned into the Eastern Association. Manchester took Welbeck Abbey, Newcastle's mansion near Worksop in Nottinghamshire, but refused to secure the nearby Belvoir Castle or to make any attempt upon Newark, much less to follow Rupert into Lancashire. Cromwell, more than ever dissatisfied with his Commander-in-Chief, directed Lilburne to quarter at Tickhill on the Nottingham-Yorkshire border. That fiery young man not only did so but carried out with his men what he conceived to be Cromwell's underlying wish by taking Tickhill Castle about a week after Marston Moor. Lilburne was probably correct in his interpretation of Cromwell's instructions but Manchester had not agreed to the exercise – Tickhill was 'only a little hole', 'he valued ten men more than the castle', to summon it might break up his whole army. The castle, however, without a fight yielded to Lilburne eighty horses, 120 muskets and much valuable gunpowder and provender. Despite this – perhaps even because of it – Manchester was threatening to hang Lilburne when Cromwell appeared on the scene in time to save him. Cromwell countered Lilburne's impetuous desire to leave the army then and there by advising him to stay and work from within. The advice he gave Lilburne he himself followed.[3]

Manchester lingered at Lincoln while Rupert took Chester and with it control of much of North Wales, while Charles marched through Devon, and boxed up Essex in Cornwall. The Committee of Both Kingdoms wanted Manchester to march to the assistance of Essex: 'My army was raised to guard the Eastern Association' was all that he would say. The poor condition of his troops did, indeed, constitute some reason for delay but Cromwell was bitter. He linked Manchester's inertia with the influence of the Presbyterian Crawford, whose dismissal he demanded, and threatened the resignation of all his own colonels if Crawford were not dealt with. To Cromwell Crawford personified the evils of Presbyterianism, in spite of valiant fighting at Marston Moor; perhaps he attributed the failure of a mortar attempt on York, which was under Crawford's control, to deliberate sabotage. Religious antagonisms were becoming wild enough for any accusation to be levied. Cromwell himself allegedly proclaimed of the Scots that 'in the way they now carry themselves, pressing for their discipline, I could as soon draw my sword against them as against any in the King's army'. For their part Manchester's officers jeered at the 'godly, precious men' in Cromwell's regiment who 'had filled dung carts before they were captains of horse and since', who had turned the Isle of Ely into 'a mere Amsterdam' and who included men who professed 'to have seen visions and had revelations'. Cromwell's retort was simple and exasperating: 'I will not deny, but that I desire to have none in my army but such as are of Independent judgment.'[4]

Apart from gibes the serious aspect of the religious situation had been indicated by a joint letter sent two days after Marston Moor by Manchester, Leven and Fairfax to the Committee of Both Kingdoms. It implied both their desire for peace with the King and the establishment of Presbyterianism, and was therefore a threat on both fronts to Cromwell and the Independents. The House of Commons was divided. As a whole it knew it had to keep on good terms with the Presbyterian Scots but a strong and vociferous group, led by Sir Harry Vane the younger and including St John and Henry Marten, were Independent in religion and against an accommodation with the King.

The victory at Marston Moor might have induced the allied commanders to sink their religious differences, at least for the time being, and concentrate on winning the war; for militarily the condition of their Commander-in-Chief, Essex, was critical. At the beginning of September Cromwell expressed his bitterness to his brother-in-law whose son had been killed at Marston Moor:

We do with grief of heart resent the sad condition of our Army in the West, and of affairs there ... So soon as ever my Lord ... set me loose, there shall be no want in me to hasten what I can to that service ... We hope to forget our wants, which are exceeding great ... Indeed we find our men never so cheerful as when there is work to do ... We have some amongst us much slow in action: if we could all intend our own ends less, and our ease too, our business in this Army would go on wheels for expedition ... Pardon

99

me that I am thus troublesome. I write but seldom; it gives me a little ease to pour my mind . . . into the bosom of a friend.[5]

He was obviously very troubled. He had to be content with writing but a personal contact would have helped.

Only a day or two after, on September 8, the news of the King's victory at Lostwithiel reached them. Essex had escaped with much of his cavalry but virtually his entire force of infantry with all his guns and ammunition had been captured and the King was slowly marching back towards Oxford in considerable triumph. The urgency of reconciliation between quarrelling armies was apparent. Cromwell, in a mood of temporary tolerance, agreed to drop his charges against Crawford if the Committee of Both Kingdoms would instruct Manchester, and Manchester would agree, to march westward to intercept the King. But Manchester still had misgivings on several grounds. The report that Cromwell's men at Huntingdon were as joyful at the defeat of the Presbyterian Earl of Essex 'as though it had been a victory gained to themselves' did nothing to pour balm into an open wound. Apart from the religious issue he would have heard the rumour that Vane had a plan for dethroning Charles and putting either the Prince of Wales or the Elector Palatine, Charles's nephew, on the throne – an unthinkable proposition to a man who, although he was fighting the King's armies, yet maintained that if you beat the King ninety-nine times he would be King still. He had to ask himself whether his allies were not more distasteful to him than the men he was fighting? Another suspicion was, moreover, slowly taking shape in his mind. He had heard strange rumours of Cromwell's aims, apart from the religious: Cromwell had, it was said, spoken against the nobility and said he hoped to see never a nobleman in England. . . . He had indicated that the army might be used to further the ends that he and his friends stood for – that if there should be proposals for a peace that did not accord with their views 'this army might prevent such a mischief'. Or, again, as he had said to Manchester himself 'My Lord, if you will stick firm to honest men, you shall find yourself at the head of an army that shall give the law to King and Parliament.' Edward Hyde, Lord Clarendon, who recounted the incident years later, remarked that Cromwell's statement 'startled those who had always an aversion to Cromwell and had observed the fierceness of his nature, and the language he commonly used when there was any mention of peace.'[6]

Manchester also had to deal with the innate chivalry of his own nature which was alien to the idea of winning a war against men and women of his own class. His refusal to take Belvoir Castle when the family of the Duke of Newcastle was in residence illustrates his dilemma. Altogether he had little stomach for marching away from his command in the Eastern Association to fight a King he had little enthusiasm for defeating.

On September 13 Cromwell contrived a solution that he hoped would quieten the religious accusations that were being hurled from one side to the other. The occasion was auspicious. He was in his place in the House of Commons after an interval of seven months to receive the thanks of the House for the victory of Marston Moor 'where God made him a special instrument in obtaining that great victory' when he joined with St John to frame an Order for toleration or, as it was expressed, for the 'accommodation' of tender consciences which could not in all things submit to the common rule. The 'Accommodation Order' was approved by the House without a division. It gave Cromwell at least a breathing space. Even if powerful interests favoured the establishment of Presbyterianism there would at least be a respite for those of Independent views.

There remained the serious military situation and the charges which Cromwell was pressing against Crawford. These came before the Committee of Both Kingdoms on the following day, September 14, when Manchester had so far exerted himself as to be present. Cromwell, who was not in fact at the time concerned either with political change such as Vane was considering or social change such as Manchester was saddling him with, was intent on only one thing (apart from the religious issue to which he believed he had given an at least temporary *quietas*) and that was the use of the army to defeat the King. With Charles on his way to Oxford Cromwell was eager for the army to march westward to challenge him. Such an order could only come from the Committee of Both Kingdoms to Manchester. With the partial security for toleration provided by the Accommodation Order he proposed to drop his charges against the Presbyterian Crawford if the Committee would order, and Manchester would consent, to a march westward to intercept the King. He got his way. The Committee so ordered and Manchester, after making one excuse after another and with constant prodding, reluctantly obeyed. It was a piece of shrewd bargaining on Cromwell's part. He was not only learning how to become a general but how to subject temporarily one desired end in order to achieve a greater. Crawford could wait. The King's advance could not.

Manchester with the army of the Eastern Association, including Cromwell and his Ironsides, reached Thatcham three miles east of Newbury on October 26. There they were joined by the remnant of Essex's army which had come up from Cornwall, though Essex absented himself on the plea of sickness, and by Waller and his men who had been operating in the Midlands. They were even joined by a brigade of the trained bands, so determined was Parliament to make an end of the King's army once and for all. They had a combined force of 19,000 against the King's 9,000 – a numerical superiority of two to one. There seemed every reason why they should inflict a crushing defeat on the Royalists. But the overall command was divided. Aware of most of the difficulties the Committee of Both Kingdoms had placed overall command in the hands of a Council of War consisting of Essex, Manchester and Waller, with the co-operation of senior officers. It is not certain how far co-operation with senior officers extended or whether Cromwell played any significant role in the deliberations.

Charles had entrenched himself within a rough triangle north of the river Kennet whose strong points were Shaw House to the east, Speen village to the west, and Donnington Castle to the north forming the apex of the triangle. The Parliamentary commanders determined on a simultaneous attack on Shaw House, under Manchester, and Speen village, under Waller. On Waller's right was a cavalry force under Balfour, on his left Cromwell with his Ironsides, who would be fighting between Speen and the Royalist force in Donnington Castle. Waller took Speen village but Manchester, though numbers were three to one in his favour, was driven back from Shaw House in a fierce and spirited defence by the Royalists. At about 4 o'clock in the afternoon of the 27th Cromwell led his cavalry charge on the other side of the battle ground. He had against him Lord Goring and a cavalry brigade which had been told that the King personally was in danger and which charged consequently with such fervour, assisted by the guns from Donnington Castle, that the Ironsides were driven back in confusion. The general nature of the battleground, widespread territorially and not integrated, different from anything Cromwell had yet experienced, may have affected the outcome. Cromwell perhaps resented serving under Manchester and Waller and possibly his advice had not been sought, or not taken, in spite of his experience and success. Perhaps he had little heart in the whole battle. It has even been said that he 'sulked'. This is hardly possible. He had worked hard to get Manchester there with the express purpose of stopping the King and he was far too much of a realist to let personalities intervene. It is more likely that Manchester, getting his own back on Cromwell for compelling him to be there at all, ignored the Lieutenant-General, planned the battle without his co-operation, relegating him to a difficult position and failing to support him. Nothing is certain except that Manchester was dilatory and Cromwell ineffective and exasperated. But Charles did not win and it could have been a victory for Parliament if Manchester had been whole-hearted in his participation. As it was the King left stores, ammunition, and heavy guns in Donnington Castle, sent 500 horse to Bath to reinforce Rupert, and with his main army marched unhindered away during the night towards Wallingford on his way to his headquarters at Oxford. Manchester's army lay nearest to the King's and it remains a mystery how they could have passed by in the night without anyone being aware of their passage. A willingness to be finished with the whole episode is a likely explanation. As it was, Waller and Cromwell set off immediately the news reached them at daybreak, but their forces were tired and ill-equipped and they were compelled to give up the pursuit. It remained for Rupert to secure Donnington Castle and its stores. Cromwell was ordered to check him. For once Cromwell refused a 'try', and it was his horses not himself he had in mind. 'My Lord', he told Manchester, 'your horse are so spent, so harassed out by hard duty, that they will fall down under their riders if you thus command them; you may have their skins but you can have no service.'[7] Cromwell had learned to draw the line between the possible and the impossible and Manchester had been paid in his own coin.

10

'Ironsides is come!'

The exhilaration of Marston Moor had been dissipated in the humiliation of the second battle of Newbury. The Report to the Committee of Both Kingdoms delivered on November 15 was signed by Manchester, Waller and Balfour but drawn up by Cromwell.

> The horse are so tired out with hard duty in such extremity of weather as hath seldom been seen, that if much more service be required of them you will quickly see your cavalry ruined without fighting. The foot are not in better case, besides the lessening of their numbers through cold and hard duty; sickness also is much on the increase, which we dare not conceal from you, daily regarding their extreme sufferings with not a little sorrow. The places we are in do not afford firing, food, or covering for them, nor is the condition of the people less to be pitied, who both within our horse and foot quarters are so exhausted that we may justly fear a famine will fall upon them.[1]

To Cromwell the fault for the sad condition of the army as well as their lack of military success lay with Manchester. The Earl represented all that Cromwell disliked. In character he was dilatory, unsure of himself, incapable of taking action; as a Presbyterian his religion was suspect; as a courtier his allegiance was suspect; and – dare it be said – as a landowner his family had usurped the property and place in Huntingdonshire which might have been Cromwell's. He was altogether unfit to command the forces of the Eastern Association and was incapable of the action needed to organize and command a fighting army. Whatever personal animus activated the quarrel between Cromwell and Manchester the second battle of Newbury underlined the need for reorganization. Sir William Waller had already experienced the impossibility of trying to command an army com-

posed of local contingents raised to protect their own localities who
would return home as soon as they had accomplished the immediate
task – the old song of 'Home! Home!', as he put it. 'My Lords',
he wrote to the Committee of Both Kingdoms on 2 July 1644, 'an
army compounded of these men will never go through with your
service, and till you have an army merely your own, that you may
command, it is in a manner impossible to do anything of importance.'[2]

Petitions from the Eastern Association to Parliament complaining
that they could no longer bear the cost of maintaining their troops
emphasized the need for speed. On November 23 Parliament
instructed the Committee of Both Kingdoms to consider the reorganization of the whole army. On the same day Cromwell was back
in Parliament and two days later he and Waller gave their report
on the battle of Newbury. Cromwell coupled his account with a
renewed attack on Manchester, the basic charge of which was that
Manchester acted 'from some principle of unwillingness to have the
war prosecuted to a full victory; and a desire to have it ended by
an accommodation on some such terms to which it might be disad-
vantageous to bring the King too low.'[3] The Commons referred the
matter to a committee of which Zouche Tate was chairman. Thus
committees on the reorganization of the army and on Manchester's
ability to command were proceeding simultaneously in the closing
weeks of 1644.

Manchester made his reply to the charges against him in the House
of Lords on November 28, and on December 2 put his case in writing.
He not only vindicated his own conduct but made counter-charges
against Cromwell. As the bitter quarrel became open the House of
Lords and the Scots sided with Manchester, the Scots even proposing
to bring charges against Cromwell as an 'incendiary'. But this would
have implied impeachment and the English lawyers advised against
it. It was evident that the whole affair threatened to rip the Parliament's forces wide open. Cromwell, realist that he was, drew back
and began to relate Manchester's conduct to the wider issue of army
reorganization already being considered by the Committee of Both
Kingdoms: how could a largely amateur committee at Westminster
direct armies all over the country? How could local forces whose
first loyalty was to their home territory be expected to operate with
decision in distant places? How could men whose pay was in arrear,
who were badly fed, clothed, quartered, be restored to keenness and

vigour? How could the civilian population upon whom fell the burden of free quarter be reconciled to further war if they were not paid and recompensed? It was not that he dropped his case against Manchester. But he saw a better way of achieving his aim. So, on December 9, when Zouche Tate's committee on Cromwell's quarrel with Manchester reported to the House of Commons, Cromwell had changed tack.

Characteristically he resolved the smaller problem into the greater, envisaging a solution which, while reorganizing the army, which was generally agreed to be essential, would also rid it of Manchester. He realized that there was some danger to himself in the solution he contemplated but he was prepared to relinquish for a time his own position in the army in order to achieve his ends. He had sufficient confidence in himself and in other people's assessment of his ability as a cavalry officer to feel certain that ultimately he would be called upon to play his part in the continuing conflict. There was nevertheless an element of risk in the solution he suggested. Cromwell was not basically or characteristically a gambler and that he should hazard so much on this throw indicates both its importance to him and his willingness to subject himself to the public good as he saw it.

When Zouche Tate reported to the House of Commons on December 9 he did not enter into details of the rights and wrongs of the quarrel between Cromwell and Manchester he had been appointed to investigate, but asserted 'that the chief causes of our division are pride and covetousness'. Cromwell immediately rose in his place. Either he sensed the feeling of the Committee or, more likely, he had come to some arrangement with its chairman, for he immediately declared that unless the war were more vigorously prosecuted people would be weary of Parliament and army. And, he asserted, they were already saying that Members of Parliament were prolonging the war for their own interests. 'I hope', he said, 'we have such true English hearts, and zealous affections towards the general weal of our Mother Country, as no Members of either House will scruple to deny themselves, and their own private interests, for the public good; nor account it to be a dishonour done to them, whatever the Parliament shall resolve upon in this weighty matter.'

As though responding to his cue, Tate then moved 'That during the time of this war no member of either House shall have or execute any office or command, military or civil, granted or conferred by both or either of the Houses of Parliament, or any authority derived from both or either of the Houses of Parliament.' That he was seconded by Sir Henry Vane the younger at once signalled the interest of the Independents in the motion and indicated a collaboration with Cromwell. This, the Self-Denying Ordinance, which took its name from Cromwell's words, passed through all its stages in the House of Commons in ten days and was sent to the Lords on December 19, only to be laid aside by their lordships. On 13 January 1645, they threw it out.

The opposition of the Lords was due in large measure to what appeared to be an attack upon their Members. Their ranks had traditionally supplied the leadership of the armed forces and many peers had followed careers of honour and profit in the Services. In the present struggle the Commander-in-Chief was the Earl of Essex, with Manchester, Fairfax, Denby, Warwick and other peers among the serving officers. Nor were they all unpopular. Even Essex, in spite of his laconic manner, was popular with his men and the London populace.

The Commons were meanwhile considering the Report of the Committee of Both Kingdoms which had been instructed both to consider the state and condition of all Parliament's armies and to suggest a plan for re-modelling that army. This Committee, of which Cromwell was a member, was dilatory and Cromwell's impatience had undoubtedly added to his resolve to get rid of Manchester by means of a self-denying Ordinance. On December 9, the day he suggested the Ordinance, he announced in the House of Commons that it was more needful to 'put the army into a new method' than to examine the faults of its generals. But it was not until a month later, on January 9, that the Committee reported to the House. Thereafter events moved rapidly. By the 18th a plan for a new army had been agreed upon, the Ordinance establishing it was read a third time on January 27, and the Lords passed it on February 15. It was not, however, until April that the organization of the new army was completed and not until May that it was ready to take the field.

Although the Lords had thrown out the Self-Denying Ordinance the Commons were proceeding as though it was already law. Not only were they approving plans for re-modelling the army but they considered, and actually appointed, the General who would lead it. Under the terms of the Self-Denying Ordinance this could not be Cromwell and the choice fell on Sir Thomas Fairfax who was actually

107

appointed on 21 January 1645 with Philip Skippon as his Major-General in charge of the foot. The post of Lieutenant-General, which carried with it the command of the cavalry, was left unfilled. When the House of Commons authorized the appointment of Fairfax, Cromwell and Vane were tellers for the 'Ayes'. Fairfax was not a Member of Parliament, his experience in war ranged from service in the Low Countries to campaigning in the North of England since the beginning of the civil war. He had siege experience, he was capable of daring enterprises like extricating himself and his horsemen from Hull; he was personally brave and not violently partisan, although a Presbyterian. At thirty-three – eight years younger than Cromwell – he was, perhaps, a little young for such responsibility, but his gravity of manner and calmness in crisis earned him respect; his lack of ostentation, his affection for his men, earned him their affection too. Cromwell was satisfied. He had worked with Fairfax; he respected him and liked him. The omission of the cavalry appointment suited him well. He would have found it hard to see another man appointed as Lieutenant-General. As it was he knew, and he knew that others knew, that he was the best cavalry officer in the country; and his time would come. It is possible he had more directly influenced the omission of this appointment. It is also possible that he believed that, as Whitelocke put it, 'Cromwell was to have the power, Sir Thomas Fairfax only the name, of general: he to be the figure, the other the cypher.'[4]

The new army was to consist of ten regiments each of 600 horse; twelve regiments of foot of 1,200 each; a regiment of dragoons of 1,000 men. A week later another regiment of horse was added, making 22,000 in all. An assessment of £56,000 a month on districts controlled by Parliament was made to support them. Besides this New Model Army there were also, on Parliament's side, some 20,000 Scots under Leven, 10,000 men under Major-General Poyntz in and about Nottingham; another 10,000 under Massey in the West; 5,000 horse and foot still in the Eastern Association, and a few local levies in the Midlands and in Wales, making some 80–90,000 men in all. Overall control would still rest with Parliament through the Committee of Both Kingdoms.[5]

The winter season when the Self-Denying Ordinance and the New Model Army were being planned was necessarily one of modified military activity. But in the West, Goring was having some success for the King while Blake for the Parliament was holding Taunton against Royalist forces. Waller, in one of his last commands, was sent westward. He was to be reinforced by Cromwell's old regiment which was to accompany him. The men protested, grew mutinous, but on March 3 Cromwell was ordered to go with them and the protests at once ceased. Cromwell made no objection to serving under Waller and, as usual, lost no time. At Andover they captured a small party of cavaliers under Henry, Lord Percy. Waller desired Cromwell to entertain the prisoners 'with civility'. There were about thirty of them, one 'a youth so fair of countenance' that Cromwell suspected his sex and desired him to sing, which he did with so much 'daintiness' that Cromwell remarked to Lord Percy that, being a warrior, he did wisely to be accompanied by Amazons.[6]

The Parliamentarians had a limited success in relieving part of the large garrison in Taunton but inadequate supplies forced them back. There was, wrote Waller to Lenthall on March 27, 'a great smoke of discontent rising among the officers. I pray God no flame break out. The ground of all is the extremity of want that is among them, indeed, in an insupportable measure.' So worried was Waller at the condition of his men that he almost welcomed the opportunity given him by the Self-Denying Ordinance to lay down his commission. He wrote again to the House of Commons on April 16. He would rather 'give his Yea and No in the House of Commons than ... remain among his troops so slighted and disesteemed by them'. Waller's resignation took effect on 17 April 1645 and he served thereafter as a Member of Parliament.[7] Cromwell rode to Windsor on April 19 to do likewise and to take leave of Fairfax. But the Committee of Both Kingdoms was now alarmed at Royalist activity round Oxford. The forty days allowed after the passage of the Self-Denying Ordinance by the Lords was not yet up so Cromwell was technically a serving officer still and he was ordered to prevent a junction between Charles issuing from Oxford and Rupert who was operating round Hereford and Worcester. Cromwell responded immediately with his usual energy. On Monday the 21st he was crossing Caversham Bridge near Reading, two days later he was at Watlington and marched to Wheatley Bridge whence he sent ahead for intelligence – it being market day at Oxford – hoping to gain some information about the enemy from the country people. He learned from some Oxford scholars of carriages and wagons that were being made ready near the town to transport the King's ordnance; he put them out of action by the simple expedient of removing the horses. On the 24th he scattered three regiments of the King's horse and drove the fugitives into Bletchingdon House which he then forced to surrender. Two days later, at Bampton in the Bush, he intercepted a regiment of foot marching from Faringdon to Oxford. Most importantly, by sweeping up all the draught horses in the area, he successfully delayed the King's move from Oxford.[8]

But on May 11 the King, in spite of Cromwell, eluded Parliament's men and marched out of Oxford with a force of 11,000 to join a Council of War at Stow. For the next few weeks Charles was never far from Oxford for the town was poorly victualled and in no fit condition to withstand a siege without substantial assistance from the main Royalist army. That army, nevertheless, was moving sufficiently freely to constitute a threat to Parliament's troops in the Midlands. Disregarding this, a contingent under Fairfax had been sent by the amateur strategists at Westminster to the West, but it now became clear that either the King's marching army should be stopped or that Oxford, weak and short of food, should be invested. So Fairfax was recalled and joined Cromwell at Islip on May 22.

But the Royalists made mistakes, too. Their army separated, Rupert and the King marching North, Goring going West to confront Fairfax. Goring had no success but the main Royalist army captured Leicester on May 31. The danger of a free-moving Royalist army was sufficient to induce Parliament to raise the siege of Oxford and concentrate their forces against the armies of the King and Rupert. Both sides began manoeuvring for position. There were rumours of a Royalist incursion into the Eastern Association and even a threat to Cambridge; Cromwell rode eastward to stop them. The Royalists, however, meandered inconclusively round the Midlands while waiting for Goring's return from the West. The Parliamentarians were equally aware that Cromwell was some distance away near Ely or Cambridge.

On June 12 Charles was hunting in Fawsley Park, with his army in scattered villages round Daventry, when an urgent summons from Rupert informed him that enemy horse were nearby. The first instinct of the Royalists was to gather their forces and depart towards Harborough, for without the army from the West they were heavily outnumbered. But Fairfax had reached Kislingbury, only eight miles from Daventry. His numbers were adequate, though he was short of cavalry. More important, there was still no Lieutenant-General in the New Model army to take charge of the horse and Cromwell was miles away. There had been petitions to Parliament from London for the reappointment of Cromwell. Fairfax himself and his Council of War had begged them to appoint Cromwell to the vacant post immediately. With a major confrontation ahead that could win or lose the war, it was no time to stand on the niceties of the Self-Denying Ordinance. Still Parliament was grudging. The House of Lords offered no answer. The House of Commons renewed Cromwell's appointment for only so long as he was 'needed' by the army. But that was enough. Cromwell was not a man to stand upon punctilios or to nurse injured pride. He lost no time. Leaving his main body of horse behind he rode hot-paced with 600 horse to Fairfax's camp at Kislingbury, which he reached on June 13. 'Ironsides is come!' went up the mighty shout from the soldiers as he rode in among them.

He had not long to wait before again proving his worth. That evening a party of horse under Commissary-General Henry Ireton came upon a group of Rupert's cavalry casually amusing themselves at Naseby, and that very night manoeuvring for position began. The Committee of Both Kingdoms had given Fairfax freedom of operation without reference to them. With this freedom, with Cromwell in command of the cavalry, and with superior numbers, they prepared for battle.

The alignment for the battle was conventional. The armies faced one another each from slightly rising ground with a little declivity between them. As so often the case the ground was littered with furze, scrub, and rabbit warrens. Cavalry was on the wings, infantry in the centre, musketeers lined the hedges on either side. The Commanders of both armies were up early making their dispositions. It was a bright June day and Cromwell looked across the little valley at the men he would have to fight, the sun glittering on their armour and on the colours of their commanders. Through his perspective glass he could even see the peak of perfection to which they had groomed their horses. There was no mistaking the figure of the King himself as he rode before his army in full armour, his sword held high. Involuntary words of admiration rose to Cromwell's lips and he laughed aloud in the conviction that the Lord had chosen him to humble that glittering army. 'I could not', he wrote later, 'but smile out to God in praises in assurance of victory, because God

111

would by things that are not, bring to naught things that are, of which I had great assurance – and God did it!'

Henry Ireton, soon to be Cromwell's son-in-law, was at Cromwell's request in charge of the cavalry of Parliament's left. He was no match for Rupert who swept forward on the Royalist right with his usual force. Ireton was nevertheless having some partial success when inexperience and a desire to help the Parliamentarian foot, who were sore pressed in the centre, caused him to turn aside instead of following through. He himself was unhorsed and wounded in the side and face before being taken, temporarily, a prisoner. Rupert followed his usual tactic and continued the rout as far as Naseby. Cromwell on Parliament's right, though much hampered by the rough ground and the rabbit burrows 'which put them somewhat out of order', broke the Royalist left, sent four regiments to complete the follow-through, and turned the rest against the Royalist foot in the centre who were pressing Parliament hard. The King, it seems, was preparing to counter-attack when the bridle of his horse was seized by a courtier to restrain him from courting personal danger. The action was interpreted as a command to turn, which the whole of the Royalist reserve did while the execution of their foot continued. Fairfax, who had been riding bareheaded round the whole field of battle, encouraging and supervising, now joined with Cromwell and together they received the capitulation of the bulk of the Royalist infantry while the rest of Charles's army streamed away towards Leicester to be joined by Rupert who had, indeed, restrained his men from looting or lingering at Naseby but who nevertheless returned to the battlefield too late to make an effective contribution to the fighting. It was victory for Parliament, indeed. But, as at Marston Moor, though the odds were not as great, they had the benefit of superior numbers – 13,400 to 10,000.

Naseby was the decisive battle of the civil war. Militarily the King was broken.[9]

For Cromwell it was not just the victory of Naseby but the fact that he had been reappointed Lieutenant-General that was important. His tactics, if tactics they were, had been triumphantly vindicated: an army re-modelled, Manchester, Crawford and other lukewarm Presbyterians ejected, a Commander who was a good soldier but not concerned to cross swords with Cromwell on most matters. Could Cromwell have foreseen all this? Perhaps not exactly, but he doubtless envisaged some such outcome when he first abandoned his direct attack upon Manchester and suggested that the Self-Denying Ordinance go forward with the re-modelling of the army. To his prophesying soul the sequence of events showed clearly that the Lord was with him.

The King was beaten. He had a little support still in the South-West, and Bristol was in Royalist hands, but there was no Royalist army that could take the field with the exception of the small force under Montrose which was fighting for the King in Scotland. With a remnant of his cavalry Charles wandered dejectedly, taking refuge once more in Raglan Castle, suffering great hardship as he marched up through Wales over desperately difficult country in abominable weather with some notion of receiving help from Irish forces at Chester and subsequently joining Montrose in Scotland. Parliament's armies, meantime, were dealing with Royalist support in the South-West. At the battle of Langport on July 10 Goring's forces were scattered by Fairfax and Cromwell; Bridgewater was reduced on July 23 after a siege, and by the end of the month Parliament had a line of garrisons, extending from Lyme to Bridgewater, south-west of which the Royalist remnant was contained. Bath and Sherborne Castle were taken by Parliament and Fairfax and Cromwell together laid siege to Bristol where Rupert was holding out. It took from August 22 to September 10 to reduce the city. One of the fullest accounts of the siege is from Cromwell himself in the report to Parliament which Fairfax had asked him to write.[10] When he knew the position was hopeless Rupert surrendered in order to save the city and its inhabitants, but for Charles the loss of Bristol was as deep a wound as any he had received. Rupert was deprived of his rank and ordered to leave the country. At Rowton Heath, two miles from Chester, on September 24 Charles's hopes finally perished with the defeat of the remnant of his cavalry. With his resolution shattered, travelling mostly at night to escape detection, utterly exhausted, Charles reached Oxford with a small party of his own horse on November 5. His friends and supporters were leaving the country or compounding with the victors, some were in prison, others already executed.

The House of Lords had confirmed Cromwell's position as Lieutenant-General for three months from June 16, and thereafter

113

the command was renewed from time to time so as to make it more or less permanent. After the fall of Bristol he was employed in mopping up operations in Wiltshire and Hampshire. One of his last operations in 1645 was the reduction in October of the strongly fortified Basing House which had withstood many sieges. Its Catholic defenders were determined and strongly entrenched but Cromwell rapidly overcame their resistance, killing some 500, taking 300 more prisoners and giving his soldiers free play in sacking and burning the house to the ground. Here, at Basing, there emerged more strongly than before the frenzied hatred aroused in Cromwell by papists who resolutely opposed him. 'I thank God', he wrote to the Speaker, 'I can give you a good account of Basing.'[11] For the last two months of the year he was with Fairfax, blockading Exeter.

In January 1646 Cromwell's command was extended for a further six months. Military operations started early, and the finishing touches were put on the Cornish campaign with the capitulation of Hopton's army in March. Exeter surrendered in April and the Prince of Wales, on his father's instructions, left the country for the Channel Islands. At the beginning of May Fairfax turned to Oxford, the lingering remnant of Charles's rule. Cromwell joined him from the West just before Oxford capitulated on June 24. No damage was done to the city and the terms were lenient. The King had already left. He had had time to ponder the situation and had come to the conclusion that he must play off his opponents one against the other. He was aware that there were sufficient divisions in Parliament's ranks to make this feasible: the strongly Independent army, the Presbyterian majority in the Houses of Parliament, the Scots, who eyed both Parliament and army with suspicion. He knew they would make a deal with him if he would guarantee their religion. A period of secret negotiations came to an end when Charles left Oxford with only two attendants in the night of April 25/26 and turned up at the Scottish camp outside Newark ten days later.[12]

Part V

'The inglorious arts of peace'

11

'We are full of faction and worse'

There was no reason to believe that Cromwell's army command would again be renewed and he was beginning to think in terms of Parliament and of his family. Early in 1646 his daughter, Elizabeth, had married John Claypole, a Nottinghamshire squire, and on June 15 he had seen his eldest daughter, Bridget, married to Henry Ireton at Lady Whorwood's house at Holton outside Oxford, which was probably his headquarters during the siege. Ireton, like John Claypole, was a Nottinghamshire landowner; he had graduated from Trinity College, Oxford and studied law at the Middle Temple. At Edgehill he led the troop of horse he had raised in his native county. He was with Cromwell at Gainsborough, and in 1643 had become Cromwell's deputy at the Isle of Ely. He was handsome but, according to Clarendon, 'was of a melancholic, reserved, dark nature, who communicated his thoughts to very few.' He and Bridget were well suited. Both were uncompromising Puritans, Ireton not only stern and rigid but of a sharp and penetrating intellect – a good man for Cromwell's son-in-law, perhaps a little forbidding as a family man. He and Bridget had met at Ely when he was acting as Cromwell's deputy, and the handsome officer, as devoted as her father to the Puritan cause, was a welcome suitor.

Cromwell also had time to help his friends and on August 26 wrote to John Rushworth, Secretary to Fairfax, on behalf of Henry Lilburne, younger brother to John. Robert, the eldest Lilburne, was already serving as Colonel in the Parliamentarian army. Henry, it seems, had reached major's rank but had recently been wanting employment. 'As for his honesty and courage, I need not speak much of that, seeing he is so well known both to the General and yourself,' wrote Cromwell.[1] It was probably in consequence of this letter that Henry Lilburne was appointed Governor of Tynemouth

Castle. But for once Cromwell's trust was ill-founded. Henry Lilburne abandoned the castle to the Royalists in the second civil war and was slain by his own soldiers for doing so.

Earlier in the year 1646 Parliament had voted to Cromwell an income of £2,500 a year to come from the estates of the Marquis of Winchester in Hampshire. Abbotston and Itchin, clear title lands, were readily assigned and in the summer of 1646, after the fall of Oxford, Cromwell moved to Drury Lane in London with his wife, his mother, and four children, Richard, Henry, Mary and Frances. Of the rest of his family his two eldest sons were dead, the eldest at school before the war, the second while campaigning; his two eldest daughters and his sisters, with the exception of Elizabeth who stayed at Ely with a friend, were all married.

Parliament, to make up its dwindling numbers, was recruiting new Members. Ireton, Skippon, Fleetwood, Ludlow, Henry Lawrence the friend and one-time landlord of Cromwell at St Ives, Sir John Harington, a family connection, were among the 200 Independents who took their places in the House of Commons on the basis of 'recruiter' elections which were taking place from the middle of 1645. The voting was sufficiently supervised to ensure that no Royalist was returned. Cromwell himself contrived once more to serve on many committees, including one which considered the disaffected of London and Westminster and a very important one on arrears of pay for the army. He successfully opposed the use of the ballot in selection for office fearing, probably, that merit might be obscured by factional feeling.

He was deeply perturbed about religion. In March 1646 an Ordinance for the Establishment of Presbyterianism, with no allowance for tender consciences, became law. Episcopacy was at last formally abolished by both Houses of Parliament in the autumn, and at the end of the year the use of the old Prayer Book was proscribed. But the Directory of Public Worship introduced in its place was not to his liking, being purely Presbyterian in form, while the new Articles of Belief and the new Catechism which were in preparation would be no more acceptable. On the very last day of the year he lost to the Presbyterian majority in the House of Commons when a resolution was passed 'to proceed against all who preach or expound the Scriptures . . . except they be ordained either here or in some reformed church'. With Sir Arthur Haselrig Cromwell protested vainly against a resolution which would silence the lecturers of the Independent

118

congregations as well as the more unorthodox sectarian preachers. It was small comfort that the Scots were as disgusted with the English Presbyterian system as he was, though for different reasons. To them it was an Erastian Presbyterianism, dependent upon the state, whereas in their country the Presbyterian hierarchy was independent of state control: apart from the interference of certain powerful nobles it virtually *was* the state. Without allowance for tender consciences there was no practical difference to Cromwell between the two. He was not happy. 'Sir', he had written to Thomas Knyvett in July, 'this is a quarrelsome age; and the anger seems to me to be the worse, where the ground is things of difference in opinion.' 'We are full of faction and worse', he told Fairfax in August.[2]

But in the midst of these anxieties Cromwell had the time and inclination to write one of his most charming letters to Bridget, shortly after her marriage to Henry Ireton:

> I write not to thy husband; partly to avoid trouble, for one line of mine begets many of his, which I doubt makes him sit up too late. . . .

He speaks of Bridget's younger sister, Elizabeth, also recently married. She is

> exercised with some perplexed thoughts. She sees her own vanity and carnal mind, bewailing it; she seeks after . . . that which will satisfy. And thus to be a seeker is to be of the best sect next to a finder; and such an one shall every faithful humble seeker be at the end. Happy seeker, happy finder! . . . Dear Heart, press on; let not husband, let not anything cool thy affections after Christ. . . .[3]

Since the spring of 1646, however, the most immediate problem had concerned the King. For eight months he remained with the Scottish army accompanying them when they moved north to Newcastle. He would not consent to the full Presbyterianism they wanted as the price of their support and endless negotiations continued between Charles, the Scots, the Queen (in secret communications with her husband), the Presbyterians, the Independents, Parliament and Army. Such negotiations between King and Parliament had been going on throughout the War and there was little to add to the interminable discussions which ended only when the Scots reached agreement concerning their pay with the English Parliament. Cromwell's signature was one of those by which the Committee of Derby House agreed on December 23 to the payment of £400,000 to the Scottish army on condition that it returned to Scotland leaving the King in Parliament's hands, and his vote was given to the appointment of Sir James Harrington, Member of Parliament for Rutland, as Commissioner to receive the King on Parliament's behalf. At the beginning of 1647 the Scots were on the move northward and on February 3 a cheerful King was escorted by Parliamentary Commissioners and a detachment of the army to Holmby House in Northamptonshire, a small property belonging to the Queen. By the middle of the month the last Scottish soldier was over the border.

In these last events Cromwell played no part. He had been serving on several committees in January but shortly afterwards gave out that he was seriously ill with what was described as 'an imposthume in the head', although no evidence suggests medical treatment. A Royalist letter of Intelligence to Hyde merely says Cromwell was ill. More substantial is Cromwell's own letter to Fairfax written on March 7 when he was back in action. 'It hath pleased God', he said, 'to raise me out of a dangerous sickness.'[4] But the whole complaint, and Cromwell's own assessment of it, may have been similar to his earlier disorders as a young man, as much in the mind as in the body, brought on by worry and frustration, emphasized by overwork and physical debility. It is even possible that Cromwell's absence from affairs at this time was deliberate, some slight indisposition being used as an excuse. To observe and then to act with decision was Cromwell's policy in battle. In the same way he needed now a period of observation and consideration or, as he would say, of consultation with the Lord, to tell him where his path lay. He had played his part in sending the Scots home and bringing the King to the Army. What next? The King, the Parliament, the Army, the Scots, Presbyterians, Independents, sectaries, the soldiers, the populace, Ireland, Scotland – all were entangled in a web whose unravelling would tax the cleverest. And if unravelling were impossible there was always the Gordian knot as example!

Cromwell knew already the quarter from which immediate trouble would arise. When he returned to public life after his illness the New Model Army was restless. The troops of Colonel Edward Massey, who had never been part of the New Model, had already been disbanded, but their arrears of wages remained unpaid. The same was true of other local armies, and unemployed soldiers were becoming a menace in the streets of London and Westminster. Parliament considered the words it heard uttered 'that a Victorious army, out of imployment, is very inclinable to assume power over their Principals' and while Cromwell was ill it was much exercised to find a solution. Disbandment or service in Ireland seemed the best alternatives. In Ireland Royalist and Roman Catholic factions were still in arms and force was required to subdue both them and the numerous warring groups that threatened the stability of English rule. But neither disbandment nor the Irish service would be considered by the veterans of the English civil war until their wages had been paid and freedom of worship guaranteed.

On the formation of the New Model Cromwell's Ironsides had been divided among several regiments of the new army, and they carried their religious convictions with them. Independency in religion spread to independency in politics, as Richard Baxter, chaplain to Colonel Whalley's regiment, found when he visited the army after Naseby. He confirmed that the most fractious were in Major Bethel's troop who had formed part of the original Ironsides. He also noted that they were egged on by the pamphlets 'abundantly dispersed' of John Lilburne which they took to read in their quarters when there was none to contradict. These pamphlets put Lilburne's case strongly but linked it with that of the soldiers: they were all suffering from the tyranny of a Parliament that had used them for its own advantage, made promises it did not keep, and now was about to post them to Ireland or send them back to their homes without meeting their just demands. There is no doubt that the practical grievances of the soldiers concerning pay, arrears, free-quarter, indemnity and religion, which were felt by all ranks in the army, were at the bottom of the unprecedented role which the army was about to play in national affairs. But it was the voice of John Lilburne, himself a soldier, suffering the same grievances as they, who first gave substance to their protests. Lilburne had a power of words, remarkable even in that age of evocative prose, and he had, moreover, an active party growing round him both in the army and in the City of London. When the army began to march towards London from its headquarters in the Eastern Association it was not only responding to Lilburne's appeal but to its own basic needs.

121

While the army had become strongly Independent in religion and radical in politics Parliament continued to be dominated by the Presbyterians whose objectives were to come to terms with the King, establish firmly the Presbyterian worship, and maintain the constitutional position they had won by 1640. Cromwell, more than anyone else, was caught up in the antagonism of these two bodies. Independency in religion, which to him implied a wide toleration, was paramount for him; he knew and loved his soldiers and resented their neglect by Parliament; but also he feared the radicalism that was sweeping the ranks. He remained a man of property in the sense that he believed that property was the lynchpin of civil society without which stability and order would crumble. Representing and underpinning this ordered society must be a constitutional, representative body like Parliament.

A bitter struggle ensued. The Commons fixed the numbers of men required for the Irish service, the numbers to be disbanded. In a provocative vote on March 8 they stipulated that in the new army there should be no officer, apart from Fairfax, above the rank of Colonel, that all officers should conform to the church government established by Parliament, and that no Member of the House of Commons should hold any command in England. The clauses seemed aimed at Cromwell. It was bitter medicine to be proffered on his return to Parliament. He expressed his feelings to Fairfax. 'Never', he wrote on March 11, 'were the spirits of men more embittered than now.' And 'It is a miserable thing', he said to Ludlow, 'to serve a Parliament, to which let a man be never so faithful, if one pragmatical fellow amongst them rise and asperse him, he shall never wipe it off.' He let it be known that he thought of leaving the country for service in the European wars which the Elector Palatine was fighting for the Protestant cause in Germany. In previous crises before the war he had intimated similar possibilities. There is no evidence, in spite of conversations with the Elector, that he really intended leaving the country. His attitude was a natural reaction when frustrated, showing a petulant, even childish, side to his character and giving a little credence to the suggestion that he had sulked at Newbury. On the other hand, he might reasonably have felt that since fighting was the thing he did best, he might reasonably go and do it!

In the event he stayed, though the role he chose for himself was the most difficult he had yet played. He had to bring both sides with him as far as he could and only then, when further co-operation was impossible, would he take the final step. It is not a far-fetched guess that when he was ill he was seeking the Lord in his usual practical way and that he was in touch with both Ireton and Lilburne; or that, before any of the various deputations from Parliament and from the Committee for Irish Affairs had reached army headquarters at Saffron Walden, he had already sounded out the men for himself. In Cromwell's story there are too many examples of illness preceding action for the sequence to be mere coincidence.

In March, after one of these meetings, the soldiers drew up a petition embodying their five simple demands which covered pay and arrears and indemnity for acts committed during the war. Cromwell was one of the officers who toned it down. Nevertheless the panic that ensued when it was produced in the House of Commons on March 27 was out of proportion. The fear of officers and men being in collusion, the knowledge that the army was on the move towards London, Leveller activity in the City, Lilburne's contacts with the army, added to the consternation. Cromwell apparently tried to put the affair in perspective. It is not clear what he said but he gained little credit from either side. Some Members of Parliament accused him of fomenting army unrest and called for his arrest. Lilburne accused him of betraying the rank and file by assuring the House that the army would disband peacefully. When, two days later, Ireton, Robert Lilburne, Thomas Pride and the two Hammonds, all of the higher command, were called to the bar of the House of Commons to explain the petition, Cromwell was not named. On the same day, in a thin House, late at night, a resolution by Denzil Holles was passed by the Commons and accepted the following morning by the Lords expressing Parliament's dislike of the soldiers' 'dangerous petition' and pronouncing all who supported it 'enemies of the state' and 'disturbers of the public peace'. Holles and Ireton quarrelled violently and a duel was only narrowly averted by startled Members of Parliament.

The Commons now proceeded to snub Cromwell. It named two officers for the Irish command – Skippon as Field Marshal, who would be virtually Commander-in-Chief; Massey as Lieutenant-General with command of the horse. Cromwell's name had been put forward but he had not been chosen. The soldiers added a further grievance to their list. At yet another meeting in Saffron Walden church to enlist men for the Irish service someone shouted out 'Why

not our old Generals?' The cry was taken up: 'Fairfax and Cromwell
and we all go!' The officers signed a petition to Parliament to this
effect and immediately afterwards Fairfax posted from the army to
London on the grounds of illness. Certainly he was not in good
health, but how genuine was this need to visit the capital? Holles
maintained that Cromwell, Fairfax, Ireton, Fleetwood and Rainsborough deliberately kept away from the army at this time in order
that disorders might increase without any embarrassment to them.

The pay of the foot soldiers was now eighteen weeks in arrears,
that of the horse forty-three weeks. Parliament offered a paltry six
weeks' arrears. Under Lilburne's guidance eight regiments of horse
now chose two representatives from every troop – agents or agitators
they called them – to push their case. Parliament advanced its offer
to eight weeks. There were further meetings in Saffron Walden with
Cromwell and Skippon in charge. It was rumoured that Ireton told
his men they need not disband till justice had been done. 'Justice'
now included a lengthening list of demands embodied in a *Declaration
of the Army* signed by 223 Commissioned Officers on May 16. But
when Cromwell reported to the House on May 21 he was trying
to be conciliatory: 'We found the army under a deep sense of some
suffering, and the common soldiers much unsettled', he said. Perhaps
Cromwell again said or implied more than he intended for the report
again gained credence that he told the House that the army would
disband. It is likely that he merely said that, given the right treatment,
the army would disband.

But army organization had gathered a momentum of its own.
The foot soldiers were now following the example of the horse, choosing committees for every troop and company and electing their own
agitators. There was a Council of Agitators representing horse and
foot, a subscription to meet expenses, a printing press at their disposal.
To cap all, strange rumours were circulating. The Cambridgeshire
foot and Ireton's regiment at Ipswich were, it was being said, ready
'to fetch' the King from Holmby. Whence, when, and to what purpose was not clear.

The extraordinary obtuseness of Parliament caused them to rush
headlong into plans for disbandment. To keep disturbance to a minimum they announced on May 25 that this would be carried out
in separate rendezvous, one regiment at a time. 'I doubt the disoblig-
ing of so faithful an army will be repented of,' wrote Ireton to Cromwell on the 27th. 'They may as well send them among so many

bears to take away their whelps', wrote a correspondent. Even Fairfax was roused. On the 29th his Council of War substituted a general rendezvous of the whole army for the piecemeal gatherings ordered by Parliament. When the Parliamentary Commissioners arrived on June 1 they went to the wrong place, they found no regiment to disband and returned sheepishly to Westminster on the 2nd.

Fairfax was now with the army, drawn both ways by sympathy with his men but also by an inborn respect for the only legally constituted authority that existed – Parliament. Cromwell had remained quiet since his unavailing attempts at reconciliation in May. Like Fairfax, he feared the use of force against political authority – even an unjust political authority – for where would the end be? But there was another factor that had to be taken into account: Parliament was predominantly Presbyterian and had refused the toleration which he had repeatedly urged.

The next two days were of the utmost importance but are shrouded in uncertainty and confusion. Lilburne, still in the Tower, was stridently urging the soldiers to oppose the Parliament making use of messengers who eluded his captors. The agitators were riding between the army and the Tower, to the Northern forces, to the navy. Some of the agitators, like Edward Sexby, appeared to be running ahead of their creator and envisaging a general anarchy. A vociferous Leveller group in the City of London was opposed by a strong Presbyterian party. The Scots were dissatisfied at their lack of success in establishing their kind of Presbyterianism in England. Parliament was increasingly aware of its own internal division between Presbyterian and Independent. The King, at Holmby, was detached, certain he could play off each of these slightly amusing and incompetent groups against each other to his own advantage.

Cromwell was as near as anyone to comprehending the play of these diverse forces. With his son-in-law Ireton at his elbow he began to think that the King was an important and recently somewhat neglected piece in the game. But until he was certain he was loath to thrust himself forward. In accordance with his usual policy in such circumstances he did as little as possible. He was, he would have said, 'waiting on the Lord'. As usual, he found good cover for what he was doing. His son Richard, now nearly twenty-one years old, had been admitted to Lincoln's Inn under the patronage of John Thurloe. There were, naturally, various meetings of the Cromwell family and it was not unnatural that matters of public concern should also be discussed: a man of Cromwell's importance could not live in London, however quietly, without attracting like-minded people to the small beer and bread and butter that the thrifty housewife, Mrs Elizabeth Cromwell, served to her husband's friends – much as Oliver and others had gathered round John Pym's board nearly ten years before. The King was spoken of, the belief gained ground that Parliament was intending to remove him from Holmby to a place under their direct control. It was rumoured that, to serve their ends, they also had designs on the army's store of ordnance at Oxford. They might even be planning to put the King at the head of another army ... Once such a train of thought was lit in Cromwell's mind he could not fail to act. Not frontal action but a more delicate manoeuvre was called for. There were many present who would understand Cromwell. But why it should be Cornet Joyce who acted, why, indeed, Cornet Joyce was there at all, is puzzling. He was an agitator, though otherwise obscure. Perhaps his very obscurity lent him to the purpose, perhaps the agitators were the only ones whose co-operation could be assured. There is no evidence that Cromwell and Cornet Joyce had any previous contacts save as soldiers in the same army. At all events, Joyce reached Oxford on June 1, satisfied himself that the train of artillery was secure, and then made his way to Holmby. It is clear that the soldiers who were guarding Charles already had an inkling of what was afoot. Travelling agitators had worked on the garrison at Holmby and they now greeted Joyce and his men as comrades and showed little surprise at seeing them there. Their commander, Colonel Graves, made off and Joyce was left in charge of the King – a tricky situation for a subordinate officer. He was understandably nervous, there were rumours that Graves would return with a relieving force, and Joyce took the step which led to so much speculation and recrimination.

On the morning of June 4, indicating his little force of well-turned out troopers as his authority, he requested King Charles to accompany him. Now that it was done all the parties concerned except the King himself appeared at a loss. Joyce had written to Cromwell immediately after his arrival at Holmby: 'Sir, we have secured the King. Graves is run away ... lett us know what we shall doe.' But there was no answer. Cromwell, at daybreak on the 4th, was posting from Westminster to the army having heard of threats by Parliament to send him to the Tower. The troubled agitators naturally also made for the army where they might deliver up the burden of a captive

King. Charles himself eased their dilemma by announcing that he would like to be escorted to Newmarket where he had a hunting lodge. Newmarket was close to army headquarters so thither the little company made its way. They reached Huntingdon, stopped at Hinchingbrooke and proceeded to Childersley, four miles from Cambridge. Fairfax, having heard of the King's departure from Holmby, had already ridden to Leicester to kiss his hand. Cromwell and Ireton came to Childersley – not, presumably, to kiss the King's hand. Here, for the first time, in the garden of Sir John Coutt's house, Cromwell and the King came face to face. It was a tense moment for defeated King and victorious General. Although, according to Clarendon, Charles was in great doubt how to carry himself, he appeared the more confident of the two. When Fairfax and Cromwell disavowed Joyce's action in bringing him there the King laughed: 'Hang him up and I will believe what you say!' There was some embarrassment. Ireton said Joyce had orders only to 'secure' the King. Colonel Whalley was instructed to take Charles back to Holmby. But Charles himself, urbane and unperturbed, declined to go. He preferred Newmarket and his hunting lodge. He stayed for four days at Childersley, made much of by the local people and by the students, masters and Fellows of the University of Cambridge who flocked out to see him. He moved to Newmarket on the 8th. So far, Joyce's action had merely given a further twist to a tangled situation. In particular it opened speculation concerning Cromwell's relation to the agitators: if he intended Joyce to go to Holmby he must also have known that the garrison there had been prepared for the Cornet's coming. And if in these respects he and the agitators were working together, why not in other respects also? And what does this imply for Cromwell's relationship with Lilburne at this time?[5]

12

'Overturn, overturn, overturn!'

The army was meanwhile developing its own momentum, playing its part in the drama that was being enacted on the heathlands of East Anglia. As the King arrived at Childersley and Cromwell reached Newmarket on his flight from Westminster, the army was gathering on Kentford Heath, four miles away, for rendezvous. Seven regiments of foot and four of horse were drawn up to present to their General an *Humble Representation of the Dissatisfaction of the Army*, which was unanimously agreed to and subscribed by both officers and men. The following day when the army was again drawn up on the Heath Cromwell rode out to it and saw *The Solemn Engagement of the Army* unanimously agreed to. Besides justifying the soldiers' organization and pledging themselves not to disband until their grievances had been righted, the *Solemn Engagement* replaced the Council of War, the governing body of the army, which consisted of officers, by a Council of the Army which would consist of two commissioned officers and two private soldiers elected from each regiment with those general officers who stood by the *Engagement*. That this would be no paper organization was demonstrated when Skippon led yet another group of Commissioners to the army, this time drawn up on Triploe Heath on June 10, to read Parliament's latest concessions. They gave the soldiers much that they had demanded – full arrears, a more complete indemnity, and a promise to expunge from the Journals of the House of Commons the 'enemies of the state' resolution. The Commissioners might have expected grateful acclaim. Instead, an officer stepped forward. The propositions, he said, would be referred to the Council of the Army. 'Is this the wish of the whole regiment?' asked the startled Commissioners. 'All, All, All!' they cried in thunderous unanimity. The Commissioners hastily withdrew. It was not what Cromwell would have wished. He liked neither the Council of the Army nor the reception given to Parliament's votes. What of his carefully imposed discipline? What of his respect for authority? Had he hatched a cockatrice which had grown beyond his control? And what of the King, who was now in the hands of this army?[1]

This army certainly now had the bit between its teeth and, with the agitators setting the pace, it continued its march towards London. The City was alarmed. When it showed signs of opposition Cromwell threw in his lot more decisively with the soldiers and on the Army Council 'spake as gallantly and as heroic as if he had been charging his enemies in the field'.

In their approach to the City the rank and file were undoubtedly influenced by Lilburne and the agitators who had been telling them for some time in pamphlets and *Declarations* that if Parliament did not accede to their demands they must coerce or change the Parliament. The influence of the agitators in the spring of 1647 was, indeed, generally recognized. Even Fairfax was in no doubt. 'The power I once had,' he admitted, 'was usurped by the agitators.' Sir John Berkeley, a Royalist who was allowed to join the King, asserted that 'though Cromwell and Ireton and their faction were strong, yet the agitators were even more powerful'. And a letter of Intelligence to Hyde put the matter succinctly: though the army ruled all, yet the agitators ruled the army. But, although the agitators were strong, there was subtlety in Cromwell's handling of them. John Rushworth, the secretary to the army, made no bones about what they were doing. It was prudent, he said, to admit the agitators to debate; it was 'the singularest part of wisdom in the General and the officers so to carry themselves . . . as to be unanimous in Councills, including the new persons into their number'. Lilburne was aware of what was happening. They packed the Army Council with their own nominees, he asserted, and bribed soldiers with promises of promotion to vote their way.[2]

The army nevertheless continued marching, Cromwell and the Higher Command with it. On July 1 it was at Wycombe. On July 6 a formal charge against the eleven Presbyterian Members most hostile to it was presented to Parliament. On July 20 the eleven obtained leave to go abroad. Fears of Royalist risings combined with fears of a Scottish invasion. Agitators were posting round the country demanding the dissolution of Parliament. Lilburne's letters to Cromwell became more vehement and accusatory. He told the soldiers they were dissolved into the original law of nature and absolved from all obedience to Parliament and could advance against it with their swords in their hands for their own preservation and safety. He was echoing the philosophical discussion of pre-war days and turning it against Parliament. Cromwell appeared to heed him for he did nothing to stem the advance of the soldiers.

As the army marched towards London the King came too on a nearly parallel course – Newmarket, Richmond, Windsor, Caversham, Oatlands (his wife's house, the birthplace of his third son, Henry). Cromwell was dealing with Levellers and agitators on the one hand, with Parliament and Presbyterians on the other. Like an experienced juggler he was at the same time dealing with the King as though he had a third hand as well. Ireton was to some extent that third hand and together the two men led the groups of army officers who were endeavouring to come to terms with Charles. The need for a treaty was, indeed, the chief reason for bringing him there at all and he was allowed his old advisers, Sir John Berkeley and John Ashburnham, to assist him, Berkeley having been specially chosen by the Army Command as a suitable negotiator who could be trusted. The French Ambassador, Bellievre, was also allowed to visit the King and his own chaplains were in attendance. It was, therefore, by no means a one-sided series of negotiations which were in train.

Cromwell had courtier blood in his veins and though he did not kneel or kiss the King's hand it is probable that something of the age-old relationship of sovereign and subject had rubbed off on him. The tight-lipped Ireton held more aloof, and Charles could make nothing of him or his proposals. With Cromwell he had a more immediate *rapport*. Cromwell was basically a warmer man than his son-in-law and came to know the King personally in a way that Ireton never could. He was present when the King's children visited their father at Lord Craven's house at Caversham and he came away with tears in his eyes. He had just seen, he told Berkeley, 'the tenderest sight that ever his eyes beheld, which was the interview between the King and his children'. Such incidents inclined Cromwell to think well of the King and he told Berkeley that Charles 'was the uprightest and most conscientious man of his three kingdoms', though sometimes, he conceded, he could wish the King to be more frank. Since, according to Berkeley, the King never really trusted Cromwell, it seems that the two men were wary of each other in spite of moments of mutual understanding. Cromwell felt that Ireton was partly responsible. There were times, he admitted, when he wished that his son-in-law would make things a little easier for him.

It was inevitable that the rank and file of the soldiery should regard this coming and going with the King with suspicion. They resented the presence of Berkeley and Ashburnham at army head-quarters, the presence of the King's 'deceiptful clergy'. Why did their officers now make an idol of the King? Why do they 'kneele and kisse, and fawne upon him?' Cromwell felt the force of this reaction but he was also aware of the need for a treaty. He had a deep-seated belief that strong, constitutional authority, fully representative of the chief interests in the kingdom, was necessary if either anarchy or the rule of the sword was to be averted. As he told Berkeley at this time he thought 'no men could enjoy their lives and estates quietly without the King had his rights' and unless the Presbyterian and Independent interests were also provided for. Constitution-making with the King was absolutely necessary, and Cromwell, in spite of his soft heart and ready tears, was not the man to allow the social graces to affect the issue. Nor were either he or Ireton affected by suggestions of worldly advantage for themselves. This failure to fit into the accepted mould puzzled the King, and the French Ambassador went so far as to mention the matter to Cromwell who replied with the cryptic remark that 'No one climbs so high as he who knows not whither he is going.' To Berkeley he was more explicit. 'Whatever the world might judge of them', he said, 'they would be found no seekers of themselves further than to have leave to live as subjects ought to do, and to preserve their consciences.'[3]

The rough document upon which they were working had been prepared by Ireton and other officers and was called simply *The Heads of the Proposals*.[4] Its modest title belied its ambitious design, for it was intended not only as the basis of a treaty with the King but as the foundation for a new constitution restrictive of Parliament as well as monarch. As soldiers and Royalists went over and over the draft the rank and file grew more and more restless, accusing the High Command of allowing the King to alter it 'in material points'. Ireton attempted to break the deadlock by printing the document as it stood and on July 17 submitted it to the Army Council. Fairfax then appointed a committee of twelve officers and twelve agitators, with Cromwell to join them when he could, to consider it. At the end of the month an amended version was presented to the King. But Charles by this time was even less prepared to accept what the army offered, for he was again intriguing with the Scots and was encouraged by Presbyterian discontent in the City to hope for better terms.

The army's resumed march to London was all that Cromwell could have wished. On August 2 the army was on Hounslow Heath – 20,000 strong. Along the mile and a half of the spreading battalions rode the General and the Lieutenant-General and they were joined by some hundred Independent Members of the House of Commons, by the Speaker, and by fourteen Members of the House of Lords. 'Lords and Commons and a free Parliament!' was the cry. On the 5th the army was at Hammersmith, on the 6th it entered Westminster, each soldier wearing a laurel leaf in his hat. On the 7th it marched through the City. Fairfax went to the Tower, called for Magna Carta and declared, 'This is that which we have fought for, and by God's help we must maintain.' On the 18th the Army Council, supporting a motion of the agitators, agreed that it was necessary to purge the House of Commons of what was still a majority of Presbyterian Members. On the 20th Cromwell had a regiment of cavalry drawn up in Hyde Park and himself, with those army officers who were MPs, went to the House. The threat was sufficient. The most prominent Presbyterians quit the House leaving control to the Independents. By August 24 Army headquarters had been established at Putney and the King had been brought to his Palace at Hampton Court where Cromwell and Ireton and their families were among his visitors. Not only Cromwell's daughter, Bridget, Ireton's wife, but his daughter Elizabeth Claypole, even Mrs Cromwell, came to pay their respects together with friends from Charles's happier days. The situation was worrying to many of the soldiers, and not least to John Lilburne, still imprisoned in the Tower in spite of the army's occupation of London.

At this point the relationship of Cromwell and Lilburne became of crucial importance. Lilburne was loudly accusing Cromwell and Ireton of perfidy in not releasing him and was already working on the soldiery to take further action by changing their original agitators and electing new. He had also turned his guns against Cromwell by sending to a contact in the army, and threatening to publish, a list of Cromwell's relations for whom, he alleged, Cromwell had found positions of profit in the army. Cromwell, fully aware of the justice of Lilburne's demands, was held back by the cold logic of Ireton and by his own deep-seated instincts. It was largely owing to Lilburne's work in the army that the soldiers had proceeded to occupy London and Cromwell had been happy enough to ride with them. Now, with a House of Commons purged of Presbyterians, he could hope to proceed constitutionally. Lilburne's way would entail more force. Whether Lilburne in the Tower was less danger than Lilburne at liberty deprived of his main grievance was a nice question.

From the time when Cromwell spoke for Lilburne in the early days of the Long Parliament a substantial friendship had developed between the two men. Cromwell had used Lilburne in his campaigns against Manchester, he had helped Lilburne's brother, Henry, he made a 'large token of friendship', as Lilburne termed it, when the Leveller leader was in prison. There were intimate meetings in London and elsewhere where Lilburne brought his wife, probably meeting Mrs Cromwell at the Cromwell house. Cromwell formed a high regard for Elizabeth Lilburne. It was Elizabeth whom her husband sent from the Tower to Cromwell at the end of March 1647 to beg him to support the army and turn away from those who were trying to persuade him to compromise. As the army approached London, Elizabeth haunted its headquarters endeavouring to secure her husband's release.

Perhaps partly as a result of her solicitations Cromwell made one of his characteristic gestures of goodwill towards his friends and visited Lilburne in the Tower on September 6 under pretence of coming to inspect the ordnance. Their greetings were friendly and courteous according to the Royalist prisoner, Sir Lewis Dyve, who occupied a nearby apartment. Lilburne had a strong personal case: sentenced for illegal writing and publishing, kept in prison by a ruling of the House of Lords, he was right in saying that the situation was no different from that obtaining under the King.

But, said Cromwell gently, the King's reign was a *habit* of oppression and tyranny. Parliament had been driven by factors outside its control to seem to swerve from what was just and right. Be patient, give us a little more time, he said. What he meant, and Lilburne knew this, was that Lilburne's influence with the soldiers was so strong that, at a time of delicate negotiations with King and Parliament, they dare not let Lilburne loose. He made enough trouble

133

when in prison. Would he promise, if freed, not to go down to the army and 'make new hurley-burleys there?' as Cromwell put it. Lilburne would not promise, but the interview nevertheless finished on a friendly note. 'Well', said Cromwell, 'though you have given me little encouragement, yet such is the affection I beare you, as you shall see I will not be wanting in my best endeavours to procure your liberty of the Parliament whereof I hope you shall find the effects in a very short time.'

They talked of Lilburne's arrears of army pay, of the compensation, still unpaid, for his Star Chamber ordeal. Lilburne also repeatedly insisted that the House of Commons should deny the jurisdiction of the House of Lords over a commoner. He drew up a paper embodying his demands with which Cromwell appeared in agreement. They then dined amicably with the Lieutenant of the Tower, discussed the hard conditions under which many of the prisoners existed, and Cromwell with ready sympathy talked with several of them after the meal.

Lilburne expected immediate action. But it was not until September 14, over a week later, that his case came before the House of Commons. On Cromwell's motion it was immediately recommitted in order that search should be made for precedents concerning the Lords' jurisdiction over commoners. Was this the logical way forward? Or was it an example of Cromwell's double-dealing? Lilburne had no doubt. It was Cromwell's intention 'to keep the poore people everlastingly . . . in bondage and slaverie, with a rotten and putrified Parliament'. He had even undermined the work of the agitators in the army so that they were merely tools of his own desires. Nor did he hesitate to use force when that suited his purpose – 'a just and moral act done by a troop of Horse', exclaimed Lilburne with biting sarcasm, referring to the recent purge of Presbyterian Members from the House of Commons, 'being as good law as now I can see executed by any Judge in England!' He had no conception of the distaste Cromwell himself felt for that action. He was right, however, in his belief that the agitators would no longer serve his purpose. They had been the driving force behind the occupation of London and the purging of the House of Commons and had been accepted and used by Cromwell for these purposes. But with his own hopes dashed, Lilburne wanted more. He had already made one appeal to the soldiers to call their representatives to account. He now repeated that advice. The agitators must be recalled by their regiments and replaced by new representatives who had not been corrupted by the army command. To assist them, Lilburne appealed over the head of the army to 'the hobnails and clouted shoes', the ordinary working people of England.[5]

The soldiers heeded Lilburne, showing how well founded were Cromwell's fears. Before October was out the men had recalled their original agitators and chosen new. Moreover, to counter Ireton's *Heads of the Proposals* they had drawn up, in close collaboration with representatives of the hobnails and clouted shoes, their own constitutional document – the *Agreement of the People*. Since Lilburne was obviously handicapped by imprisonment a young lawyer named John Wildman was called in to help draft it. The new agitators submitted the document to the Army Council as their scheme for settling the Kingdom and it came up for debate at the meeting on October 28 which was held at Putney, with Cromwell in the chair, Fairfax being absent allegedly through ill-health.[6]

The *Agreement of the People* marked the progression of the Levellers from general opposition to constitutional reform, a step already taken by Cromwell and Ireton and expressed in the *Heads of the Proposals*. Both documents called for the dissolution of the existing Parliament and thereafter for Parliaments of two years' duration. The *Agreement* proposed to ensure freedom of conscience by specifically 'reserving' religion from any compulsion by Parliament. There were other specific 'reserves' and the general statement that as the laws ought to be equal, so ought they to be good. The basic difference between the *Proposals* and the *Agreement*, and the one round which the most heated discussion ranged at Putney, concerned the suffrage. The *Proposals* envisaged a continuance of the existing electoral qualifications which, apart from the mixed suffrage of the towns, confined the vote to the 40/- freeholder. The *Agreement* reached out to a much wider suffrage based on equal electoral districts according to the number of inhabitants. When questioned specifically by Ireton the Levellers alleged that their intention was manhood suffrage. Women were not even thought of. And even within the male category there were to be exceptions, for servants and beggars would be excluded on the grounds that their interest was comprised in that of their masters. Nevertheless, the extension of the suffrage would be wide enough to include many who had hitherto been excluded.

The standard of debate at Putney was high. Cromwell and Ireton carried the weight of the argument for the High Command. Of the agitators and their civilian allies only John Wildman was a match for Ireton in debate. But the soldiers, speaking from the heart, simply and often emotionally, kept the discussion to the basic principles for which they had fought. All in all the Putney debates revealed men crudely in their fundamental beliefs and attitudes.

Cromwell throughout, though speaking less than Ireton, was tenacious, worrying like a terrier at his argument, seeking to get it right, obviously thinking as he went along, fumbling for the correct phrase, the apt word. Here was the General standing up among his men, the scars of battle upon them all, all of them less at ease in framing a constitutional settlement than in seeking victory in the field. The voice, still 'harsh and untuneable', though accustomed now to command, was conciliatory and cautious.

He had had little time to consider the *Agreement*, he said. This was the first time it had come before the Officers. The paper was plausible. But it contained 'very great alterations of the very government of the kingdom, alterations from that government that it hath been under, I believe I may almost say, since it was a nation'. And what would be the consequences? How did they know that other people would not suggest other changes? 'And not only another, and another but many of this kind.' 'Would it not be confusion? Would it not be utter confusion?'

Later in the debate he went on to consider how far they were bound by the statements and promises made in their own Army *Declarations*. He had a sly dig at the civilians present – '. . . you reckon yourselves at a loose and at a liberty, as men that have no obligation upon you.' He admitted there were many good things in the paper, but to him it all depended upon how far he was free to adopt them.

Lieutenant-Colonel William Rainsborough, old soldier, son of a sea-captain, the only one of the High Command to side with the agitators, interpreted this as concern with the 'difficulties' of implementing the proposals of the *Agreement*.

'Difficulties!', exclaimed Rainsborough. 'If ever we had looked upon difficulties I do not know that ever we should have looked an enemy in the face!'

This stung Cromwell. 'I do not think that any man here wants courage to do that which becomes an honest man and an Englishman to do,' he retorted.

Ireton, clipped of speech, versed in political theory, more used than his father-in-law to talking in political and philosophical terms, widened the issue. For him it was not only the Army *Declarations* but the very obligations inherent in organized society that must be taken into account.

'What right hath any man to anything if you lay not down that principle, that we are to keep covenant?' he asked. Wildman had spoken of the Law of Nature. 'If you will resort only to the Law of Nature', responded Ireton, 'by the Law of Nature you have no more right to this land, or anything else, than I have. I have as much right to take hold of anything that is for my sustenance, to take hold of anything that I have a desire to for my satisfaction, as you.' It is the law which entitles a man to hold what he has received from his ancestors. It is the law which 'does fence me from the right which another man may claim by the Law of Nature; it is the law', concluded Ireton, 'which makes it mine really and civilly.'

The talk of 'obligations', 'commitments', 'covenants', went on interminably during the first day's debates at Putney with scarcely a reference to that which had sparked it all off – the proposed extension of the suffrage. It was left to the stern Puritan, Major Goffe, to announce that they had had enough and to propose that they seek the Lord more concretely by beginning the next day's proceedings with a Prayer Meeting. The atmosphere at once lightened. Here was something they could come to grips with. Even Ireton was moved to enthusiasm. To Cromwell, communing with God was the way out of any difficulty. He had also resorted to another of his panaceas and had suggested a committee to consider the various *Engagements* made by the army, particularly those of Newmarket and Triploe Heaths. The suggestion was reasonable enough considering the turn the debate had taken but it was not necessarily relevant to the *Agreement of the People*. Had there been a deliberate side-stepping of the main issue?

The prayer meeting was held the following morning and in the afternoon they got down to worldly business with a discussion of the first Article of the *Agreement of the People* concerning the suffrage. This was when Ireton asked if it implied universal manhood suffrage and was told that it did.

'We judge,' said Petty, 'that all inhabitants that have not lost their birthright should have an equal voice in elections.' Or, as

Rainsborough put it, '. . . I think that the poorest he that is in England hath a life to live, as the greatest he; and therefore truly, sir, I think it's clear, that every man that is to live under a government ought first by his own consent to put himself under that government.'

Ireton could see no justice in this argument. A birthright, living under a government – this gave no entitlement to choosing a government, to deciding which laws to live under. 'No person hath a right to this, that hath not a permanent fixed interest in this kingdom.'

The debate developed hotly between Ireton and Rainsborough. When Ireton declared 'All the main thing that I speak for, is because I would have an eye to Property', Rainsborough wanted to know 'how it comes to be the property of some men, and not of others?' and Sexby exclaimed that it didn't seem to matter how the property had been acquired.

'If it is property by law', cried out Rainsborough, 'that law is the most tyrannical under heaven!'

It was left to Colonel Nathaniel Rich to underline Ireton's point:

> If the master and servant shall be equal electors, then clearly those that have no interest [i.e. no property] in the kingdom will make it their interest to choose those that have no interest. It may happen, that the majority may by law, not in a confusion, destroy property; there may be a law enacted, that there shall be an equality of goods and estate.

Ireton and his friends had enunciated, simply and clearly, the issues for which they had gone to war and which they would defend against Leveller incursion. Cromwell was with them – but only up to a point. When Rainsborough cried out that Ireton should not make the world believe they were for anarchy, Cromwell intervened gently – Rainsborough was a good soldier. 'No man says that you have a mind to anarchy, but that the consequence of this rule tends to anarchy, must end in anarchy; for where is there any bound or limit set if you take away this limit, that men that have no interest but the interest of breathing shall have no voice in elections? . . . We should not be so hot with one another', he concluded.

But passions were roused and the debate went on, Ireton at ever greater length. Only Wildman, the civilian, seemed capable of putting the issue in a nutshell: 'I conceive that's an undeniable maxim of government that all government is in the free consent of the people.'

More realistically, voices were raised for moderation, for bringing the debates to an end. Someone reminded them that external dangers still threatened. Again it was Wildman who put the matter succinctly: 'If we tarry long, the King will come and say who is to be hanged first.'[7]

There were several more days of discussion ahead, of which no record has been found. But a letter of the Leveller agents to their regiments of November 11 indicates that they won, or thought they had won, their demand for the suffrage. It 'being long debated', they wrote, 'it was concluded by vote in the affirmative ... and there were but three voices against.'[8] What is more certain is that while the debates at Putney were in full swing the new agitators were planning a general rendezvous of the army, like the already famous gatherings at Newmarket and Triploe Heaths. None of this is what Cromwell wanted. Edward Sexby at Putney had asked the bitter question: 'What have we fought for all this time?' Cromwell could ask it too. He had fought for liberty of conscience and he had fought for stability of government. The preservation of property would not interfere with the former and was necessary to maintain the latter. The extension of the franchise to the unpropertied would destroy everything in ever-lengthening steps towards anarchy. The army debates at Putney had revealed more starkly than he had realized the social divisions in his army, deep fissures of which he had been unaware, not only bringing to the surface men's basic social and political beliefs but causing him to question his own deeply held beliefs. That he could not countenance the extension of the vote to the unpropertied was certain. But what then of the soldiers in his army, many of whom had risen to high rank? Would he deprive the men who commanded his armies of the civilian vote in time of peace? He thought of Thomas Harrison, the butcher's son, of Colonel Ewer the serving man, Hewson the shoemaker, Kelsey the button maker, Colonel Pride the drayman, Okey the tallow chandler, and many more with rank and without.

Angrily his thoughts turned to the agitators and the rendezvous they were planning. He would not permit it. On November 8 he carried a motion on the Army Council sending the agitators back to their regiments and thus virtually dismissing them, and he dismissed the Council of the Army bringing authority back to the Council of Officers. He lessened the impact of the forthcoming rendezvous of the army by commanding that it be held in three parts. On November 15 the first of these rendezvous was held on

Corkbush Field, near Ware. The Leveller soldiers arrived with the sea-green ribbons of their party on their tunics and copies of the *Agreement of the People* in their hats. In the presence of General Fairfax they were somewhat overawed, uneasy at their defiance. When Lieutenant-General Cromwell appeared, obviously in one of his towering rages, angrily riding among them, striking the offending papers from their hats, they were cowed. This was the General who had so often led them to victory, who had supported their stand against Parliament. Could he be wrong now? All but a few submitted. Some who did not were tried on the spot for mutiny, three sentenced to death, and Richard Arnold, on whom the lot fell, was shot then and there on the field at Ware.[9]

13

'A net of such a scope'?

While first principles were being debated at Putney events were moving at Hampton Court. The King had shown some interest in the debates. But whatever slight amusement he may have felt at what he considered the army's antics had given way first to puzzlement and then to some fear at Leveller diatribes against himself, coupled with the feeling that he might do better somewhere else, away from the immediate influence of the army. On November 11, as the debates were drawing to a close, the King was slipping away from the Palace with Ashburnham and Berkeley in attendance. On November 15 when the armies were drawn up at Ware Charles arrived at Carisbrooke on the Isle of Wight for what he expected to be no more than a token restraint while he intrigued with the Scots and with his Royalist friends and made arrangements to sail for the Continent if necessary.

It is just possible that the escape was connived at. The exit from his rooms was ridiculously easy – down a back stair, horses at Thames Ditton. Reasons for his departure had been planted in his mind by fears of an assassination attempt by agitators. Cromwell had written to Whalley, who was in charge at Hampton Court, a note of warning which might have been intended for Charles's eyes. A more direct letter warning him of a plot by agitators arrived on the 9th, when his plans were probably already laid. But could there be any certainty of Charles's destination? So far as can be gathered from their later accounts neither the King nor his two friends had any definite plan. This, however, seems a little odd. To plan an escape on which so much depended with nothing fixed except the first step seems unlikely. Ashburnham mentioned the Isle of Wight. The King showed no enthusiasm for anywhere else. This in itself makes it likely that the Island was already in their minds. It had obvious advantages of remoteness from the army; it was near the Continent if escape should be necessary; there were many Royalists both there and in the south of England.

It is possible, however, though not proven, that more sinister forces were at work. The Governor of the Island, in whose charge Charles would be, was Robert (Robin) Hammond, recently appointed, a youngish man married to one of John Hampden's daughters and therefore a kinsman of Cromwell – though Whalley, in charge at Hampton Court, was a cousin. Cromwell visited Hammond in the Isle of Wight in September. Another Hammond, Dr Henry Hammond, uncle to the Governor of the Isle of Wight, had introduced his nephew to the King in the autumn of 1647 as sympathetic to the royal cause, and not without loyalty, and this could have been construed as an open invitation to Charles to proceed to the Isle of Wight.

It was Cromwell who received first official news of the King's departure late on the night of the flight. He made all speed to Hampton Court: the King was missed 'at supper' – he had obviously left by the back stairs to the waterside – and had left letters on the table. Many hours had passed. Charles was by then at the house of the Earl of Southampton, who also had recently visited him at Hampton Court. Could not Whalley have put two and two together and sent immediately to Southampton's house in the New Forest if he had seriously wanted the King? Southampton was a friend of the King. If there had been more to the King's flight than met the eye he, too, would have been duped.

What Cromwell or the army leaders would have gained by having the King in the Isle of Wight rather than in Hampton Court is not very clear. Undoubtedly the relationship between Charles and the officers had become strained. A place where they had access to him when they wanted with less opportunity for comment, a place far enough away to relieve them of the embarrassment of his presence so near the army and Parliament, was very desirable. But at first it was the King who appeared to gain from the change.[1]

The army rendezvous had gone off well and Fairfax, as well as Cromwell, had asserted his authority over the men. Officers who had been arrested were pardoned, imprisoned soldiers released. Nothing could be done about young Arnold but Cromwell arranged a reconciliation with Rainsborough and there were three days of prayer meetings towards the end of December. But the King had made fresh overtures to Parliament from Carisbrooke immediately after Corkbush Field asking for a Personal Treaty. After all his efforts with *The Heads of the Proposals* and the long weeks of negotiation, Ireton was particularly bitter. Scowling before the fire at his quarters at Kingston he said he hoped that the proposals would be such that the army might fight vigorously against them.[2] It looked as though it might turn out this way, for a few days later a spy at Carisbrooke gave Cromwell and Ireton the sight of a letter from the Queen to Charles which implied that he was intriguing with the Scots and indicating that his reply would be carried by a man with a saddle on his head who would stop on a certain day at the Blue Boar tavern in Holborn in the City of London. Cromwell and Ireton were there and found Charles's letter sewn up in the saddle carried by the spy. It indicated all too clearly that the King would make terms with the Scots.[3] When Commissioners from Parliament visited him he turned down their offer. Shortly afterwards it became known that he had secretly signed a treaty with the Scots which promised them Presbyterianism for three years while they promised to raise another army for him, and that he was planning to escape from Carisbrooke. Cromwell alerted Hammond and the escape was prevented but what was considered the King's perfidy remained. Ludlow and Vane were stridently calling for a Republic, other Independent leaders were discussing a scheme for deposing Charles and substituting either the Prince of Wales or the Duke of York. The Presbyterians remained discontented because their form of worship had failed to take root outside London and parts of Lancashire. There was defiance from sectaries who clamoured for full liberty of prophesying. On January 3 Parliament proposed a vote of No More Addresses to the King. Cromwell supported the motion. Would Presbyterians and Independents come together and suffer the inconveniences of each other's friendship for fear of worse – as a Royalist letter to Hyde put it? Cromwell would not commit himself. Any form of government could be good 'according as Providence should direct'. He must still wait upon Providence. Whether he could help Providence along was another matter.

It did not help that Lilburne, presenting his own case at the bar of the House of Lords on January 19, repeated the charge of high treason against Cromwell. At the same time pockets of Royalism were coming to life – in Kent, in the Eastern counties (too near his own shires), in Lancashire, in South Wales. Presbyterians in the

City of London were drawing closer to Parliament. Over the country as a whole discontent in one form or another was rising. It was like a gigantic bonfire in one of his own fields. Damp it down. It would remain hot to the touch. And then a flame would burst through – here, there, one place after another – igniting the whole field unless drastic action were taken.

There were meetings early in 1648. Cromwell gave a dinner party for leading Presbyterians and Independents followed by a conference between the leaders of the House of Commons and of the Army. Cromwell and his supporters spoke and acted as might have been expected; they 'kept themselves in the clouds, and would not declare their judgments either for a monarchical, aristocratical, or democratical government, maintaining that any of them might be good in themselves, or for us, according as Providence should direct us', while the Commonwealth men argued strongly against monarchy, saying that the King had broken his Coronation Oath and should be brought to account for the blood shed.

Cromwell, despairing of a solution, resorted to the horse-play that came natural to him in times of stress and threw a cushion at Ludlow's head, running off downstairs afterwards. 'But', recounted Ludlow, 'I overtook him with another which made him hasten down faster than he desired.'[4]

Shortly after this Cromwell became ill. It was even said his life was despaired of. It could have been again psychosomatic. Perhaps the cushion-throwing presaged such a development. On March 7, when he was recovering, he wrote to Fairfax on the same note of pessimism that had accompanied his recovery from an earlier sickness: 'I find this only to be good – to love the Lord and His poor despised people; to do for them, and to be ready to suffer with them.'[5] Pessimism was not his alone. With trouble brewing on every side the uncertainties of the situation led to orgies of self-recrimination among the soldiers, and at further great prayer meetings of the army held at Windsor at the end of April Lieutenant-Colonel Goffe preached to the text 'Turn ye at my reproof' and they all prayed and wept very fervently.[6] To this meeting came news that fighting had broken out in Wales where Colonel Poyer had declared for the King and the Book of Common Prayer, and was heading a strong Royalist reaction fired off among the soldiers by lack of pay and among the populace by taxation and deprivation. In Kent and in Essex Royalist plans at the same time were coming to fruition, while in the North parties of English Royalists with Scottish help seized Berwick and Carlisle. Fairfax sent Cromwell to Wales, himself marching south to Maidstone in Kent, while it fell to Lambert, who was already in the North, to hold the situation there. It was not so much a second civil war as a series of local outbreaks engendered by particular sources of friction.

Cromwell left for Wales at the beginning of May with three regiments of foot and two of horse. On May 8 he was at Gloucester telling his men as of old that he was willing to live and die with them. As they marched the fleet mutinied, declared for the King and captured the castles defending the Channel coast while the Prince of Wales with a Dutch fleet reached the mouth of the Thames. Colonels Horton and Ewer were already in Wales and Poyer had been defeated at St Fagans before Cromwell arrived. By the end of the month Chepstow and Tenby had fallen to them and Cromwell was laying siege to Pembroke Castle. He had only a few guns and no heavy artillery; provisions were scarce and the local people hostile. It took him six weeks to subdue the castle, though why he should have stayed there so long with Horton and Ewer on the scene is not clear. When he wrote to the Speaker on July 11 announcing the fall of the town and castle he struck a new note in the retribution he exacted. Those he had excepted from mercy, he wrote, were 'such as have formerly served you in a very good cause, but, being now apostatised I did rather make election of them than of those who had always been for the King, judging their iniquity double, because they have sinned against so much light.'[7]

Fairfax meanwhile, having successfully dealt with the Kentish insurrection and secured London and Westminster from attack, had invested Colchester. The siege of Colchester lasted ten weeks. Long before it was over the Scots had crossed the border and Royalists in the north of England were joining them. Cromwell, even before Pembroke fell, had sent some of his horse northward and was now hastening thither himself. His men were ill-equipped being without shoes or stockings and this may have been one reason for his delay. We could not replace them, wrote one of his soldiers, except by plunder and that 'was never heard of by any under the Lieutenant-General's conduct'. But replacements came in more orthodox fashion

– 2,500 pairs of shoes from Northampton, 2,500 pairs of stockings from Coventry – and the army marched on.[8]

Major-General Lambert, Commander-in-Chief of the Northern Counties, had been holding the English Royalists at bay but was compelled to draw back into North Yorkshire as Hamilton advanced from Scotland to join them. Cromwell, however, was marching rapidly through Gloucester, Leicester, Nottingham, to Knaresborough in the West Riding where he joined Lambert on August 12 and caught a glimpse of his son, Henry, who was a Captain in Hewson's regiment of Lambert's army. Pontefract and Scarborough had been taken by Royalists and after leaving troops to invest these towns Cromwell and Lambert had 8,500 men with them of whom three-quarters were horse and many were experienced veterans. Cromwell now learned that Hamilton was advancing, not through Yorkshire but through Lancashire. Without hesitation he crossed the intervening hills. Setting out on Sunday August 13 he was at Skipton on the 14th, Gisburn on the 15th and on Wednesday the 16th was marching down the valley of the Ribble towards Preston. He thought it likely that Hamilton would make a stand at Preston and he intended to put himself between Hamilton and his line of retreat into Scotland. He might have considered driving Hamilton back into Scotland whence he came. But instead he took the more daring decision to fight him on English soil and prevent his retreat into friendly country.

Cromwell camped for the night at Stoneyhurst about nine miles from Preston on the northern bank of the Ribble. Hamilton's forces were divided, the van being far in advance of the rest, which made Cromwell's task easier. The following morning he fell upon the main body irresistibly, gained Preston and bridges over the Ribble and the Darwen, annihilated a good part of the Scottish army, took 4,000 prisoners and stood solidly between Hamilton and Scotland. Pursuit southward finally ended at Warrington and Cromwell turned north leaving mopping-up operations to Lambert who accepted Hamilton's final surrender at Uttoxeter on August 25. Three days before that Colchester at last surrendered to Fairfax.[9]

Cromwell now needed to secure the Scottish border and to render the Scottish Royalists powerless. By early October Berwick and Carlisle had surrendered and he reached Edinburgh on October 4. Three days later, having secured the submission of Hamilton's party, he was on his way south again reaching Carlisle in a week. A few days after that he took up his quarters at Knottingly intent on subduing

Pontefract and Scarborough, which still held out for the King. The cavaliers in Pontefract were well-provisioned, well-equipped with arms, the castle and town were strongly fortified, the surrounding countryside was inhospitable to any besieging force, the men themselves were daring and devoted to their cause. One of their exploits was into the nearby town of Doncaster where Colonel Rainsborough had recently arrived with a small force. The cavaliers were particularly incensed against Rainsborough because of his reported diatribes against the King and one evening they broke into his quarters, demanded that he accompany them as their prisoner and, when he refused, they shot him dead. Cromwell was particularly outraged and distressed and the murder reinforced his determination to take Pontefract.

Parliament, in the absence of Cromwell and Fairfax, had begun, yet again, its own negotiations with the King, sending Commissioners to the Isle of Wight who met him at Newport on September 18 when Cromwell was marching towards Scotland intent on defeating the King's supporters. It was a bizarre situation and wearisome enough for Parliament and King as the stale discussions began once more – Presbyterianism for three years, the militia for ten, for twenty – but was Charles sincere? The seemingly endless negotiations were leading nowhere, rumours circulated of the King's attempts to escape. The discussions were still proceeding when Hammond learned definitely that Charles was planning to leave the Island. The talks halted. A week later a *Remonstrance*, again prepared by Ireton, demanded the ending of negotiations and the trial of the King.

Cromwell was still at Knottingly, laying siege to Pontefract. His men were restless and Cromwell sent to Fairfax several of the petitions in which they demanded justice against the King. But what induced their General to stay away so long? He said later that they in the North were 'in a waiting posture'. Certainly it was difficult enough to take Pontefract, but it was not beyond Cromwell's powers; or he might have delegated his command in view of the business of no common importance that was brewing in the South. But he waited.

In previous times of crisis Cromwell had become ill, absented himself from public affairs until he had made up his mind, or until something had occurred that made up his mind for him, 'seeking the Lord' as he would have said. Now, though well aware of the developments in Westminster and Carisbrooke, he waited for six weeks before Pontefract seeking the Lord or, in this case, unburdening his soul in long letters to Robert (Robin) Hammond, 'the ingenuous young man whom Oliver much loves'. And while he waited he watched developments in London and Westminster and the Army in the South. Hammond was in command in the Isle of Wight when the King arrived there and had been forced, willy-nilly, to constitute himself the gaoler of the King. He had written to Cromwell complaining of his 'sad and heavy burden'. Cromwell chides him: '. . . call not your burden sad or heavy. If your Father laid it upon you, He intended neither'. He cannot resist a sly dig at Hammond:

> Dear Robin, our fleshly reasonings ensnare us. These make us say, heavy, sad, pleasant, easy. Was there not a little of this when Robert Hammond, through dissatisfaction too, desired retirement from the Army, and thought of quiet in the Isle of Wight? Did not God find him out there? . . . seek to know the mind of God in all that chain of Providence, whereby God brought thee thither, and that person to thee.

Hammond had argued that authority lay in the Parliament and that therefore, in their dealings with the King (he was thinking of the negotiations which were proceeding at Newport), however much one disagreed with them, they should be obeyed. But Cromwell urged, using the standard arguments that had been used before the war, that there are cases when it is lawful to resist. The question is, he says, 'whether ours be such a case?'

Again he uses the language of political obligation. Is not *salus populi suprema lex* – the safety of the people the supreme law? If it had been lawful to oppose the King in their interest is it not also lawful to oppose the Parliament for the same reason? But who would lead this opposition? Somewhat diffidently he asks whether the army was not a lawful power 'called by God to oppose and fight against the King' and is it not therefore fit to use force against the Parliament?

Then he pulls himself up – '. . . these kinds of reasonings may be but fleshly' – and he reverts to arguments which are more familiar to him. 'My dear Friend, let us look into providences; surely they mean somewhat. They hang so together; have been so constant, so clear and unclouded . . . . Thinkest thou in thy heart that the glorious dispensations of God', he asks, could be set aside? As 'a poor looker-on', he concludes, he had rather live in the hope that those dispensations had taught him, expecting a good issue, than be led away

John Lilburne the Leveller

Cromwell's son-in-law, Henry
Ireton – politician and soldier
(Fitzwilliam Museum)

The strain of battle shows on Cromwell's face in Gaywood's engraving of the
painting by Robert Walker, c. 1649 (Cromwell Museum)

Sir Thomas Fairfax, Commander-in-Chief of the New Model Army (Cromwell Museum)

Samuel Cooper's evocative miniature of Cromwell. 'Il me fait peur' exclaimed
King Christian VII of Denmark when he saw the portrait in 1768 (Sidney Sussex
College)

Major-General John Lambert, soldier and politician

Dobson's poignant portrait of King Charles I, painted during the Civil Wars
(National Portrait Gallery)

Top: Charles I's death warrant, which includes Cromwell's signature
Above: The Seal of the Commonwealth, c. 1651, emphasizing the power of
Parliament (British Museum)

Secretary of State, John Thurloe, Cromwell's friend and chief Intelligence Officer
(the Chequers Trust)

by other considerations. Meanwhile, he says, he was 'in a waiting posture'.

He finishes his letter, 'This trouble I have been at, because my soul loves thee, and I would not have thee swerve, nor lose any glorious opportunity the Lord puts into thy hand. The Lord be thy counsellor. Dear Robin, I rest thine . . .'[10]

When Cromwell at last left Pontefract it was not of his own volition but because he was summoned home by Fairfax 'with all convenient speed' to give 'a merciful furtherance . . . to the very great business now in agitation'. Cromwell responded immediately, leaving Lambert in charge. Even so, he did not hurry. On December 1, with Cromwell marching slowly southward, officers sent by Fairfax removed Charles from the Isle of Wight to the isolated stronghold of Hurst Castle off the Hampshire coast. Fairfax himself and his troops re-entered London the following day. The House of Commons nevertheless persisted in considering its treaty with the King. On December 6 Colonel Pride, backed by a force of soldiers, stood outside the House of Commons with a list in his hand. By his side stood Lord Grey of Groby who identified the Members as they appeared. One by one those, mostly Presbyterians, who were unfavourable to the Army or favoured a treaty with the King were turned back or arrested. In the evening of the same day Cromwell reached Westminster. He had not been acquainted, he said, with the design 'but since it was done he was glad of it, and would endeavour to maintain it'. He entered the House the following day with Henry Marten, the outspoken Republican, who had long since urged the breaking off of all negotiations with the King. He and Cromwell had been opponents rather than friends which made their present amity more remarkable, particularly when Marten moved the vote of thanks to Cromwell for his services in the second Civil War. The next day the process of exclusion continued until about 143 Members had been forcibly kept from taking their seats in the House.[11] Perhaps it was not precisely what Cromwell would have chosen to do. Possibly he had envisaged a dissolution of the existing Parliament, of somehow securing a majority of Members to vote their own demise and the election of a new Parliament in accordance with one of the political schemes that had been brought forward. This would have had the advantage of being constitutional and not dependent upon even a show of force. But could it have been done? Those nearer the scene thought otherwise and Cromwell is certain to have been kept in touch with their reasoning. In any case, as he said, he was glad it was done and, perhaps, not sorry to be free of the responsibility of doing it. It left him free to open his mind to the basic, underlying issue with which he had been wrestling for so long: what to do with the King.

14

'A man against whom the Lord hath witnessed'

Events now moved briskly. On December 15 the Council of Officers moved to bring the King from Hurst Castle to Windsor with the object of bringing him 'speedily to justice'. Cromwell was not present at this meeting. A small committee was then appointed to consider how this should be done and at this meeting Cromwell presided, Ireton was present, Fairfax absent. They brought him to Windsor three days later, on the 19th. His old home was now a prison as well as a castle, with Hamilton and other Royalist prisoners held there. The soldier Members of Parliament were now very powerful. In the rooms and offices of Whitehall, close to the Houses of Parliament, they conducted the urgent business now in hand, army contingents billeted round them in case of trouble. Cromwell, working late, would occupy one of the old state bedrooms when, as Whitelocke disapprovingly remarked, 'he slept in one of the King's rich beds'.

There is little evidence of Cromwell's actions or of his intentions at this time. He interviewed Hamilton but no help was forthcoming from that loyal and devoted Royalist. He appeared anxious that leading Royalist prisoners should come to trial before the King. He attempted compromise in meetings with Lenthall, Whitelocke, Widdrington and a few others. He instructed Whitelocke to draw up a paper summarizing their findings and calling for the restitution of some of the secluded Members. The attempted compromise failed and the Army Council issued a Declaration insisting that the King be brought speedily to justice. Cromwell did not sign. The King certainly stood convicted of being 'a man of blood', responsible for the Second Civil War, of intriguing with the Scots and with the Irish to bring in what was seen as a foreign army, of negotiating with the Presbyterians behind the Army's back. As Cromwell had written to Hammond, the King was 'a man against whom the Lord hath witnessed'. What more did he want? Perhaps he was aware that these were charges that would look thin in a Court of Law. Perhaps, also, it was a stumbling block that he had known the King as a man and as a father and was reluctant, when it came to the point, to condemn him on generalities. Overall was the knowledge that they were about to do what had never been done before – bring a reigning monarch to trial, condemn him and execute him. For neither Cromwell nor any of his close associates had any doubt of the outcome once the King was brought before the Court of Justice that they would institute. Legal procedure began to occupy his mind. In the depleted House of Commons, becoming daily even thinner, the lawyers were absent. Cromwell summoned them to meetings with himself and the Speaker. When on December 23 the House of Commons appointed a Committee to consider the King's trial not only the lawyers but the Clerk to the House, Henry Elsyng, were not there. Even Sir Henry Vane was absent.

On the same day Cromwell spoke to the Army Council advising a last attempt to come to terms with the King. He was more aware than anyone of the necessity of removing the King, yet more aware than anyone of the danger of loosening the structure that held society together. He expressed his views as nearly as he could in the House of Commons on the 26th: If any man had suggested the trial of the King for worldly calculations only, he said, 'he should think him the greatest traitor in the world, but since providence and necessity had cast them upon it, he should pray God to bless their counsels ... though he were not provided on the sudden to given them counsel.' He supported, even if he did not instigate, a last-minute attempt at negotiation when the Earl of Denbigh was sent to the King at Windsor. But Charles also could seek his God and had accepted the inevitability of a trial, even if he had not envisaged the outcome. He refused to see Denbigh.

Since there was nothing now to do but accept the inevitable the Council of Officers and the almost empty House of Commons turned their attention to procedure. On 1 January 1649, an Ordinance presented by Henry Marten for the trial of the King passed the Commons without a division. One hundred and fifty Commissioners were to act as jury of whom twenty would form a quorum. Chief Baron Wilde with Chief Justices St John and Rolle would be the judges. The charge was that 'by the fundamental laws of this kingdom, it is treason in the King of England ... to levy war against the

152

Parliament and Kingdom of England'.

No voice was raised in the almost empty House of Commons for the King. In the equally empty House of Lords three Peers protested. He would rather be torn in pieces than sit as a Commissioner, declared Denbigh. It was in contradiction to the law to declare the King a traitor, asserted Manchester. Northumberland maintained with justification that 'not one in twenty of the people in England are yet satisfied whether the King did levy war against the Houses first, or the Houses against him; and, besides, if the King did levy war first, we have no law extant that can be produced to make it treason in him to do so'. Pembroke uneasily declared that he liked not to meddle with matters of life and death. The Ordinance was rejected by the House of Lords.

This was not the only setback, for not one of the judges named by the Commons agreed to sit – not even St John, the defender of Hampden in the Ship Money case, the kinsman of Cromwell. It mattered little. The 135 Commissioners would assume the functions of both Judge and Jury. The force of law was given to proceedings by three resolutions passed on January 4:

> That the people are, under God, the original of all just power; that the Commons of England, in Parliament assembled, being chosen by and representing the people, have the supreme power in this nation; that whatsoever is enacted or declared for law by the Commons in Parliament assembled, hath the force of law, and all the people of the nation are concluded thereby, although the consent and concurrence of King or House of Peers be not had thereto.

The constitutional position being now established an Act for the bringing of Charles Stuart to trial was passed by the House of Commons on January 6. Since they could not use the Great Seal inscribed in the name of Charles I they made their own inscribed 'In the first year of freedom, by God's blessing restored'. It seemed that neither the King's acquittal nor his Restoration had entered into their calculations. But they could not control those who still had their doubts and fears. When the High Court of Justice met for the first time in the Painted Chamber at Westminster on January 8 only fifty-two Commissioners were present. Fairfax was there but never came again. On the Court's second sitting on the 10th only forty-five appeared and they chose as their President the virtually unknown Sergeant

Bradshaw. Lawyers of greater note, including Bulstrode Whitelocke and John Selden, had left the capital.

Cromwell, having expressed his doubts and emphasized the difficulties before them, had accepted the voice of 'Providence and Necessity' and produced no more arguments against a trial. But his nerves were at breaking point. When Algernon Sydney made the valid point that the King could be tried by no Court and no man by that Court, Oliver shouted out, 'I tell you we will cut off his head with the crown upon it!' Circumstances had at least quieted his own doubts. Sydney was among those who never put in another appearance. But they still had a number of Commissioners, a very low quorum protected them, and they had a President of the Court. But who would present the charge? The Attorney General withdrew on the plea of illness and a fanatical lawyer named John Cook was brought in. He was helped in drawing up the indictment by Dr Isaac Dorislaus, a Dutch lawyer who taught at Cambridge University.

On January 9 Proclamation was made in three places by the Sergeant at Arms – in Westminster Hall, at Cheapside, and at the Old Exchange – that Charles Stuart, King of England, would be brought to trial. This was a momentous announcement in itself. Meanwhile work was going on in Westminster Hall where the trial would be held. It was cleared of the stalls, of the hawkers, the newsmongers, the gossiping public, the courts of law which sat in various parts of the great Hall. Careful provision was made for positioning the King and his accusers. The public would be allowed in but would be separated from the King by a wooden partition which would stretch the width of the Hall and be high enough to keep him from view except when he stood up. Soldiers would stand behind the partition, between him and the public. His entry would be as unobtrusive as possible by a short flight of stairs beneath the Hall that led straight to the dock where the King would sit. At the south end of the Hall were the tiered benches for the men who would be his judge and jury, with John Bradshaw, the President of the Court, a little raised in the middle.

How much of this was planned by Cromwell, with how much of it he was familiar, can only be surmised. It is unlikely that it would have gone forward without his approval, though what evidence exists of Cromwell at this time shows him as highly emotional, intent on the main issue only. On the day of the trial the Commissioners had a last meeting in the Painted Chamber adjoining the Hall.

Here, so runs the story, Cromwell saw through the window the King as he came through the gardens from Cotton House where he had spent the night. Cromwell turned 'as white as a wall'. What should they say, he asked, if the King should demand by what authority they brought him to trial? Harry Marten was equal to the occasion: 'In the name of the Commons in Parliament assembled and all the good people of England', he said. The story, if not apochryphal, can only mean that Cromwell needed reassurance, for the charge, in similar terms, was about to be presented by John Cook:

> ... in behalf of the Commons of England and of all the people thereof I do accuse Charles Stuart here present of high treason and high misdemeanours, and I do, in the name of the Commons of England, desire the charge to be read unto him.

Cromwell took his place in one of the back rows of the tiered seats to the right of the King as he faced them. Just behind Cromwell was Valentine Walton. Not so long ago young Valentine had come courting to the Cromwell home in Huntingdon. Less than five years had passed since his son, the fruit of that union had perished on the field of Marston Moor. Cromwell's son – Captain Oliver of his father's own troop – had likewise given his life in the wars. Their fathers, and other fathers, sat there now regarding the King, serene and untroubled, as he sat before them. He had never known the dagger at his breast as these men had, whose sons had perished. The youth had gone from them. Grim-faced men, battle-scarred and weather-beaten, they had come to render justice on their King.

The sixty-eight Commissioners who were present answered to their names. Fairfax was not among them. When his name was called a woman's voice from the public galleries, said to be that of Lady Fairfax, cried out that he was not there, nor would be. As had been expected the King refused to plead to the indictment. By what lawful power had he been brought there, he asked? But the charge stood. He was accused of conceiving 'a wicked design to erect and uphold in himself an unlimited and tyrannical power to rule according to his will and to overthrow the Rights and Liberties of the People'. He had 'traiterously and maliciously levied war against the present Parliament and the people therein represented'. He was responsible for 'all the treasons, murders, rapines, burnings, spoils, desolations, damages and mischiefs to this nation' committed in the wars.

Still the King refused to plead, coming out well from the

exchanges with Bradshaw and Cook. There were conferences in the Painted Chamber between sessions in the Hall but by the third day the Court was uneasy. Charles himself opened proceedings by asking to make a statement. Bradshaw brushed him aside 'in the name of the people of England . . .'

'Not half, not a quarter of the people of England. Oliver Cromwell is a traitor!' came the same woman's voice from the gallery. She was hustled out by friends as Colonel Axtell's men levied their muskets. Cromwell must have known it was Lady Fairfax. Later that day a further unsettling incident occurred. John Downes, one of the Commissioners sitting just behind Cromwell, was moved to anguish by the King's plea to be heard. 'Have we hearts of stone? Are we men?' he was asking as he stumbled to his feet. Valentine Walton and William Cawley who were sitting next to him tried to pull him down. 'If I die for it, I must do it', he persisted. Cromwell turned round. 'What ails thee? Art thou mad? Canst thou not sit still and be quiet?' With infinite courage, but shaking and tremulous, Downes remained on his feet. 'Sir, no, I cannot be quiet.' There was a general shuffling as others made to rise, whispers of concern, even of approbation. Bradshaw adjourned the court.

In the Painted Chamber, though others may have wished to protest, Downes was the only one who spoke out, begging them to hear the King who might be about to suggest something they could entertain. But Cromwell would not halt now. As rage took over he called Charles 'the hardest hearted man on earth' and Downes 'a peevish troublesome fellow'. Downes, until then courageous in standing up to Cromwell, collapsed in tears at the futility of it all. They went back to the Hall and left him alone, though he later returned to his place.

Cromwell was shaken by the interruptions of Lady Fairfax, by Downes and by the attitude of others who were seen to be wavering. But his ferocious determination swept aside any doubts. The trial continued to its inevitable end, the King's proposal was never heard by the Court, he was denied the last word he had been promised, and the sentence was read on Saturday January 27 'that Charles Stuart, as a Tyrant, Traitor, Murderer and a public enemy, shall be put to death, by the severing his head from his body'.

More preparations: the place of execution to be decided, the executioner appointed, the selection and deployment of the regiments who would be on duty; the scaffold, the platform, the railings to keep back the crowd, the axe itself ... Most immediate was the death warrant, without which nothing legal could be done. It is possible, indeed likely, that this was already in existence awaiting signatures, even with some names on it already. Others were collected in the Painted Chamber on the 29th. Cromwell was rowdy and unseemly, as he often was in times of emotion. The story goes that he dragged Richard Ingoldsby to the table, guiding his hand as he forced his signature; that he dipped his pen in the ink and daubed Marten's face with it; that Marten retaliated in kind; that Cromwell then went straight to the door of the House of Commons, catching Commissioners for their signatures as they went in; that he followed into the House itself to secure any that had eluded him crying 'Those that are gone in shall set their hands! I will have their hands now!'

Fifty-nine names in all were appended to the death warrant of Charles I. The day was to be Tuesday, January 30, the place the public street outside the Banqueting Hall that Inigo Jones had built for his father. There were rumours that an executioner was difficult to find but it is likely that Richard Brandon, the public hangman, was not unwilling. There also had to be signatures to the actual order of execution which would need to be handed to the executioner by the three men who had been guarding the King. On the very morning of the execution one of these, Colonel Huncks, refused to sign. Cromwell, Ireton and Harrison confronted him in a small room in Whitehall, Cromwell shouting at the unfortunate Huncks that he was 'a forward, peevish fellow', but he still refused to sign and the execution went forward without his signature. One final, essential act which had been unaccountably overlooked in the excitement – perhaps in the absence of so many lawyers – was hurriedly performed by the House of Commons on the very morning of the execution when they passed an Act making it illegal for anyone to proclaim a new King. New for old was not what they had envisaged.

Herbert, who had been the King's companion to the end, met Cromwell in the Long Gallery of Whitehall immediately after the execution and Cromwell promised him the orders for the King's burial. Though there is no direct evidence of his presence it is inconceivable that Cromwell had not witnessed the beheading. He had seen too many violent deaths to have been affected by the sight except to ask whether it was the Lord's will? And as to that he had no doubts. His feelings were most likely expressed by the story that he visited the dead monarch where he lay in St James's Palace before his funeral and murmured 'Cruel necessity!'.[1]

The King left behind him a potent piece of propaganda in the form of a book which was published on February 9, the day of his interment. The *Eikon Basilike* embodied his meditations while in captivity and painted the picture of the martyred King, devoted to his God, his country, his people, his family. It is likely that he wrote it himself but it was probably edited by Bishop Gauden who published it. As edition after edition appeared with illustrations showing King Charles at prayer, noble and serene, and translations into French, German, Dutch, Italian, Danish, Latin, Greek rapidly followed, a reply in kind was sought by the men who themselves must now form a government.

A fortnight after the King's execution John Milton published *The Tenure of Kings and Magistrates*, a work which justified the trial and execution of the King and which must have been in preparation for some time, 'proving that it is lawful ... to call to account A Tyrant or wicked King, and after due Conviction to depose and put him to Death'. Cromwell had wanted the lawyer, John Selden, to make a more direct reply to the *Eikon* but in the event it was again Milton who published *Eikonoklastes* the following October. There was too long a gap in time for it to be really effective, but in any case it in no way matched the appeal of the *Eikon* and the legend of the martyred King grew. Milton's two publications, however, added lustre to his own reputation and a month after the publication of *The Tenure* he was appointed Secretary for Foreign Tongues, or Latin Secretary as it came to be called since most foreign correspondence was in Latin.

A few days after the King's execution a new High Court of Justice was established. Several judges had retired but enough remained to bring the Royalist prisoners to trial. The trials opened with the leading Royalists on February 10 and went relentlessly forward. Cromwell was opposed to mercy.[2] These were 'men of blood' and on March 9 Hamilton, Holland, Capel and others were executed. By that time the forms of the old order had been abolished. It is likely that Cromwell would have retained the House of Lords as a purely consultative body. Nevertheless on February 6 and 7 resolutions were carried in the House of Commons without a division 'that the House of

Peers in Parliament is useless and dangerous and ought to be abolished' and that the office of Kingship in a single person is 'unnecessary, burdensome, and dangerous to the Liberty, safety and public interests of the people of this nation, and therefore ought to be abolished'. Acts embodying these resolutions were passed on March 17 and 19.

The only legally constituted authority that remained – apart from the newly established High Court of Justice – was the truncated rump of the House of Commons that had been elected in 1640 and which had, in one way or another, lost about 400 of its Members so that whole areas of the country were unrepresented, and where the average attendance was well below 100. This body had recently had two proposals for reform before it, both going by the revived name of *Agreement of the People*. In the Mews on December 28 Lilburne and others had presented to Cromwell their version, while Ireton and the officers presented theirs direct to Parliament on January 20. Both were laid aside under pressure of other business. The Act of 1641 laying down that Parliament could not be adjourned, prorogued, or dissolved except by its own consent was still in force and it seemed that little could be done. Cromwell spoke in disapproval of 'a perpetual Parliament, always sitting', but he took no action. He was again waiting for circumstances to reveal his next step. As was becoming usual with him, he was making of private matters a protective covering while he waited upon events. This time it was the marriage negotiations for his son, Richard, and Dorothy, daughter of Richard Mayor of Merdon Manor, Hursley, near Winchester, that was occupying his attention.

But an executive organ of government was essential to the existence of the new régime and Cromwell played an important part in the committee work that preceded the formation of a Council of State. Its powers would be wide but it was to be ultimately responsible to Parliament. Its composition would obviously be important and its place in the constitution carefully circumscribed. In particular, it would need to be subject to recall by Parliament. It was finally agreed that such a Council of State would consist of forty-one Members nominated by a committee and approved by the House of Commons. It would have full executive authority in the management of home and foreign affairs and it would sit for a year only unless otherwise ordered by Parliament. Specifically it was directed to oppose the pretensions of Charles Stuart to the throne of England; to reduce Ireland; the Channel Islands and the Scillies; to secure all magazines of arms and stores; to direct overseas trade and foreign affairs. It was a far-reaching brief. Cromwell was one of the original members of the Council of State together with Fairfax, St John, Bradshaw, and Whitelocke. Ireton was turned down by Parliament. It was originally intended that members of the Council of State should take an Engagement signifying their approval of the High Court of Justice and the execution of the King, the abolition of the monarchy and the House of Lords. Cromwell in the chair wrestled with members through many committee meetings but the opposition to one or other section of the oath was strong and the idea of the Engagement in this form was dropped. The Council of State, however, came formally into existence on February 15. Not until May 19 did an Act of Parliament establish England as a 'free Commonwealth ... to be governed by the representatives of the people in Parliament ... without any King or House of Lords'. A new great seal bearing a picture of Parliament was then inscribed 'in the first year of freedom by God's blessing restored'. They even had time to consider with some care the execution of this device, bearing in mind the excellent workmanship of Nicholas Briot, engraver to Charles I. The man they chose, Thomas Simon, was a not unworthy successor to Briot.

Europe watched events in England with a range of emotions which included astonishment, incredulity, horror and alarm. But there was no positive threat of any significance to the new Commonwealth. Prince Rupert, who had transferred his fighting skill from land to sea, harassed her shipping in the Mediterranean and was a menace in the Irish Sea. The Queen was in her native France but received little more than sympathy. The Prince sought help from his mother's family and made plans with his most able adviser, Edward Hyde. William II of Protestant Holland, who might have been expected to offer support, stood aloof with his wife, the daughter of the dead King.

Isaac Dorislaus, who had helped draw up the indictment against King Charles, was murdered in the Hague and the assassins escaped. A year later Ascham, a Commonwealth agent, was murdered in Madrid. English merchants were imprisoned in Russia. States which shrunk from direct action allowed their pulpits to be used to denounce the regicides.

Cromwell continued to sit on various committees. An important one on which Ireton also served considered an Act for abolishing Deans and Chapters and appropriating their property – a significant consideration in view of the financial difficulties of the young Commonwealth. The question of the sale of the Crown jewels, which had been bandied about so freely by the King and Queen during the wars, was referred to the Navy Committee. Also under consideration was the sale of Charles's art collections – his library, the statues and pictures at St James's and Whitehall. Cromwell had been working on this with Ireton and Whitelocke when they supped one evening long and late at Whitelocke's house. After which, as Whitelocke relates, being 'very cheerful' and 'extremely well pleased; we discoursed together till twelve o'clock at Night and they told me wonderful Observations of God's Providence in the Affairs of the War, and in the Business of the Army's coming to London, and seizing the Members of the House, in all of which were miraculous Passages .... As they went home from my House', Whitelock continues, 'their Coach was stopped, and they examined by the Guards, to whom they told their names, but the Captain of the Guards would not believe them, and threatened to carry these two great Officers to the Court of Guard'.

Typically, Ireton 'grew a little angry' but Cromwell 'was cheerful with the soldiers, gave them twenty shillings, and commended them to their Captain for doing their Duty'. The guard later confessed that they knew Cromwell and Ireton well enough but were intending to demonstrate their strict adherence to duty. Besides, they said, they suspected that the affair might have been intended to test them![3]

Cromwell also showed himself interested, as Charles I had been, in the history of his country. But whereas Charles had wanted a comprehensive work from early times Cromwell wanted a history, which would also be a justification, of the civil wars. Through a lawyer of Gray's Inn named Greaves he made an unlikely approach to Meric Casaubon, a classical scholar born at Geneva but educated in England who had received preferment at the hands of Laud but had been deprived of his offices in 1644. Casaubon, adhering more to his principles than Cromwell had done, and in spite of considerable pressure, steadfastly refused the task. There were many accounts of the wars, but not the one that Cromwell would have liked to see.

But there were more important problems to attend to in the spring of 1649. Lilburne, disillusioned and near despair, watched the scene from his lodgings in Winchester House. He was seeking employment and the means to support his family and not only constitutional but immediate practical affairs engaged his attention. He found that he was still hampered by the very obstacles to freedom that he had campaigned against in the King's time – tythes, customs, excise, monopolies, imprisonment for debt, Ordinances against printing, impressment, a High Court of Justice. He may have had some justice on his side but he gave the new régime little time. On February 26 he was at the door of the House of Commons with a pamphlet that expressed in its title only too clearly what he felt: *England's New Chains*. He was followed to the door of the Commons a few days later by eight troopers representing the soldiers who were once more sadly in arrears of pay. 'We were before ruled by King, Lords and Commons; now by a General, a Court Martial, and House of Commons; and we pray you what is the difference?' they asked.

Three weeks later *England's New Chains Part II* was read aloud by Lilburne at the door of his house to a large crowd before being presented to Parliament. This time the army leaders were the particular target: 'everything is good and just only, as it is conducing to their corrupt and ambitious interests' and 'the most hopefull opportunity that ever England had for recovery of her freedoms was spent and consumed'. Lilburne, Richard Overton, Thomas Walwyn and Thomas Prince, all leading Levellers, were committed to the Tower by sentence of the much-derided Council of State while John Milton, the newly appointed Secretary for Foreign Tongues, was instructed to reply to the pamphlet. While the four prisoners were waiting in an ante-room Lilburne put his ear to the keyhole and heard Cromwell thumping upon the Council table until it rung again shouting out

> I tel you Sir, you have no other way to deale with these men, but to break them in pieces ... if you do not break them, they will break you! ... you are necessitated to break them [otherwise they will] make void all that work that, with so many years' industry, toil, and pains you have done.

This was Cromwell's case. The Levellers' case was that the 'many years' industry, toil, and pains' had not been followed by the promised 'freedoms'.

The imprisonment of the civilian Leveller leaders was complemented by the cashiering of five of the soldiers who had presented the army petition to the House of Commons. This was only two

162

months after the execution of the King and before the new Common-wealth had been even nominally established.[4]

While unrest in England was expressed in a multiplication of petitions and processions from both the army and from civilians, the affairs of Ireland were becoming increasingly important.

Part VI

'Still keep thy sword erect'

15

'An Irish interest . . . is most dangerous'

Of all the problems which beset Oliver Cromwell in 1649 after the execution of the King that of Ireland might well have seemed the least immediate. With so many imponderables there could have been justification for postponing the Irish question. It might have seemed the wrong time to commit troops and money and resources to Ireland and deplete the English base of commanders and men whose speedy return would be jeopardized by the stretch of hazardous Irish Sea.

Yet neither geographically nor historically could Ireland be ignored. Geographically, in spite of the Irish Sea, Ireland was a convenient base for attacking England's vulnerable western flank and there were signs that it might be from Ireland that the Royalists would strike. How far the Irish would make common cause with the Royalists, whether they would support the young Commonwealth, or even stand aloof, were difficult questions to answer; the kind of questions which had, indeed, been asked by Charles I and which were raised now both by his son and by Cromwell. The answers were entangled in Irish history, bound up with religion and with the land, and were as imponderable as everything else in that torn and bleeding country.

Leader of the forces opposing Parliament was the charismatic James Butler, Earl of Ormonde, a Protestant who had supported the Royalists throughout the civil wars and who had been appointed Lord Lieutenant of Ireland in 1644. A group of Catholic landowners who condemned regicide (the Confederate Catholics) provided unlikely support. English settlers in Munster under Murrough O'Brien, Earl of Inchiquin, violently anti-Catholic and guilty of many atrocities ('Murrough of the Burnings'), were another unreliable ally. So was Owen Roe O'Neill, Earl of Tyrone, ancient Catholic Irish chief.

Dublin and the territory immediately round it (the Pale) remained the bastion of English rule and the residence of the Lord Lieutenant. Michael Jones, the Parliamentary Commander, had driven Ormonde out in June 1647 and now held the city for the Commonwealth. In the north the command was under Colonel George Monck, a professional soldier who had fought for Charles I but later taken the Covenant and had been in Ireland since 1647 with the title of Adjutant General and Commander of all the Parliament forces in Ulster. Drogheda, north of Dublin, was held by a Parliamentary garrison, Sir William Cole held Sligo for the Parliament, and Sir Charles Coote controlled Londonderry. In the south Cork and Youghal were Protestant and for the Parliament, Waterford was strongly Catholic, Wexford with a thriving business in piracy was more or less indifferent. All over Ireland, where land had been taken over or assigned to English settlers, the dispossessed formed a largely Catholic and discontented population more inclined to favour the Royalist cause than Parliament's. The big landowners themselves were likely to support Ormonde though not to the extent of fighting for him.

It is useless to speculate as to how much Cromwell knew of Ireland's tragic and turbulent history. Like most of his countrymen he saw Ireland, as he did the Americas, as territory open to settlement by God-fearing Englishmen of his own religious persuasion. He approved the Protestant Plantations of Munster and Ulster by Elizabeth and James without worrying about the fate or the present condition of the Roman Catholic chiefs and peasants who had been displaced. He had no hesitation in assuming that large tracts of Irish land could be traded as security to English creditors. The uprising of 1641 had come as a shock, though its impact had been lessened by the fact that the *Grand Remonstrance* was at that time being debated in Parliament. He had nevertheless heard Pym in the House of Commons reading the despatches from the Justices in Ireland with their accounts of the massacre of Protestants of all ages and both sexes by what were painted as the bloodthirsty Irish. The news-sheets had confirmed the stories and added crude woodcuts of victims spurting blood and babies being butchered. Thirty thousand, they said, had been massacred in Ulster alone. The impression on an already impressionable Puritan like Oliver Cromwell was indelible. On the other hand, he had not paid much attention to the seeming threat of Irish troops being brought over by Strafford – whether against Scotland or against England was merely a debating point, as he realized at the time, which Strafford had lost. The danger was now more real.

Cromwell was not the first choice of a commander to deal with the situation, nor was he altogether anxious for the Irish command. But Fairfax was unwilling to undertake the task, Waller and Fleetwood were talked of but neither they nor the Council of State showed much enthusiasm. To the name of Cromwell, it was reported by their Secretary, Whitelocke, 'a silent consent was given', a large majority of the Council supporting, the rest afraid to oppose. Motives all round were probably mixed. There were those of the Council and elsewhere who would be glad to have Cromwell out of the way for a time. Others might not be averse to seeing the Lieutenant-General scorch his fingers in the Irish fire or sink himself both actually and metaphorically in the Irish bog. Some, maybe, were reluctant to contemplate the glory that would attach to his person after a successful campaign. Others simply felt that he was needed in England and could not be spared on the western perimeter. But, however they regarded him – in friendship or admiration, with jealousy or with fear – the majority considered that Cromwell was the only person who could restore order to Ireland and free England from a dangerous Royalist threat. So, with a majority in favour and with the authority of Parliament, the Council of State on 15 March 1649, offered the Irish command to Cromwell.

Cromwell would not immediately commit himself. 'Whether I go or stay is as God shall incline my heart,' he said. He expected no joy of campaigning in an unknown, difficult countryside notorious for its boggy and mountainous terrain, execrable communications, bandits in the wild hinterland and a native population fierce and bitterly hostile. Nor was he unaware of the opportunities his absence would give to his enemies, with the Commonwealth not yet formally established and a wide range of conflicting views clamouring to be heard. He might, on his return, find himself of less importance than before. More importantly, action might be taken in his absence that would jeopardize all that had been gained in the previous seven years.

On the other hand, part of him spoiled for action. The negotiations with the King, the final decisive, irreversible act, the ending of the struggle, the climax of his personal relationship with Charles, had sapped him. He yearned for the field of battle, for the rough soldier's life where action followed swiftly on decision, where the wrong decision, or the lack of decision, was immediately apparent and the price was paid or the gain harvested without the endless words of the Council Chamber.

There were other considerations. His soldiers were restless, partly through arrears of pay but also because an army needs action. In Ireland he could give them action and he could raise money to pay them on the security of Irish lands – a device already used and to honour which the conquest of Ireland was all the more necessary. Above all, militarily and strategically the conquest of Ireland was essential and he knew he was the one to do it. On March 23 he spoke to his fellow-officers on the subject. Truly, he said,

> ... if we do not endeavour to make good our interest there, and that timely, we shall not only have ... our interest rooted out there, but they will in a very short time be able to land forces in England and to put us to trouble here. I confess I have had these thoughts with myself, that perhaps may be carnal and foolish. I had rather be overrun with a Cavalierish interest than a Scotch interest; I had rather be overrun with a Scotch interest, than an Irish interest; and I think of all this is most dangerous. If they shall be able to carry on their work, they will make this the most miserable people in the earth, for all the world knows their barbarism – not of any religion almost any of them, but in a manner as bad as Papists – and truly it is thus far that the quarrel is brought to this state, that we can hardly return unto that tyranny that formerly we were under the yoke of ... but we must at the same time be subject to the kingdom of Scotland or the kingdom of Ireland, for the bringing in of the King.[1]

It took him another week to make up his mind. The practical turn which his communing with the Lord so often took was demonstrated when he made his acceptance of the Irish command dependent on cast-iron assurances of an adequate number of troops fully paid respecting arrears and current wages, with a guaranteed back-up of ships, supplies and equipment. The Council of State on March 6 assigned 12,000 men for Ireland to be chosen by lot; although no decision had been taken as to the actual sources of money to pay them Cromwell was satisfied with the Council's guarantee. So, with the support of Fairfax and the Council of Officers, Cromwell on March 30 accepted the Irish command subject to money being available to equip, supply and pay the army in his charge. He would not move until he was sure that the men, the money and the backing were actually there. Two days later he preached at Whitehall and on April 13 the selection of the regiments for the Irish service began.

Immediately there was trouble. About sixty men of Captain Savage's troop of Colonel Whalley's regiment seized the regimental colours and barricaded themselves in the Bull Inn in Bishopsgate Street. Cromwell and Fairfax were swiftly on the scene, fifteen men were taken into custody, the rest dispersed. A court martial on April 26 sentenced six men to death; five were reprieved, but Robert Lockier, who appeared to have been the leader of the mutiny, was shot. His death sparked off widespread unrest. His funeral procession, which included women wearing the sea-green colours of the Levellers, was long and emotional. To objection to the Irish service were added the points of Leveller propaganda. It seemed as though the events of 1647 were repeating themselves. Cromwell could hardly have selected for execution a trooper with more friends and a wider appeal than young Lockier. He was, indeed, after Cromwell's own heart. He was only twenty-three years old, had joined the army at the beginning of the wars when he was only sixteen, and throughout his seven years' service had been known for his piety and devotion to the cause. Cromwell could be hard, but Lockier was one of his own.

But he had to turn his attention immediately to more substantial troubles. Troops at Salisbury and at Banbury were in open mutiny. There was unrest at Aylesbury and in the West. Leveller leaflets were widely dispersed in the Midlands. From the Levellers in the Tower came a timely reissue of the *Agreement of the People*. There was serious unrest among the London populace with long processions of people wearing the Leveller emblem and bringing petitions to Parliament for the release of their leaders. To cap all, some people in Surrey were out digging the common land saying that it belonged to everyone and they should work together, eat bread together.

Mutiny was obviously the most immediate threat. Cromwell called a rendezvous in Hyde Park of men from his own and Fairfax's regiments. The men came but many wore the Leveller badges; some bravely displayed the placard 'For a New Parliament By the Agreement of the People'. There were murmurings that they would not fight their fellow-soldiers. But Cromwell's power was still there. He was the General whom they had followed to many a victory – the same voice, the same stance – he had always been right. Could he be wrong now? The only Leveller who could have counteracted that influence, John Lilburne, was fast held in the Tower. And Cromwell was clever. He not only roughly commanded them to remove their Leveller colours but he spoke more softly, reminding them of the many difficulties against which he and Parliament were wrestling, assuring them of the great care and pains which he and Parliament were exercising on their behalf. And, he concluded, those who wished could receive their arrears and leave the army forthwith. It was a good speech. Once more he had them in the palm of his hand and even before he had finished the sea-green emblems were blowing in the wind over the grass of the Park. The following day, May 10, Cromwell and Fairfax marched against the Leveller mutineers, having ordered 400 troops of Pride's and Hewson's regiments, unsympathetic to the Levellers, to secure the Tower where Lilburne and his friends lay.

It was a masterly march by the two Generals. Fairfax put himself between the main body of mutineers at Salisbury and the Levellers of Buckinghamshire so depriving them of support from Aylesbury. In all three places – Salisbury, Aylesbury, and Banbury – there was serious defection from the rebel ranks and their hope now lay to the west. With about 1,200 men and twelve colours they made westwards towards Newbridge on the Thames. They forded the river near Faringdon and, wet and weary, but thinking themselves safe from attack, they turned in for the night at Burford. But their pursuers, with Cromwell in command, knew how to march with speed and only a few hours after the weary Levellers had turned in Cromwell fell upon them. They were taken by surprise, their arms laid by and there was little resistance. Only one man was killed, many escaped, about 400 were taken prisoner and secured in Burford church while a court martial considered their case. For three days and nights they were held in the church, long enough for the majority to sign a petition of repentance; four were chosen for execution and three of these were shot against the churchyard wall on May 17 while the rest of the prisoners were herded onto the roof of the church to watch. Smaller areas of discontent and incipient revolt continued for some time but this was virtually the end and Cromwell was free to concentrate on Irish affairs.[2]

16

'. . . but the instrument . . '?[1]

Cromwell was familiar enough with the financial situation and what would be entailed in raising money for the Irish enterprise. When Parliament proceeded to tax the counties further with an Act for a general assessment of £90,000 a month for six months on all property save that of charitable institutions and the Universities he was appointed Assessor for his native Huntingdonshire and Ely, for Cambridgeshire, and for Hampshire and Glamorgan where he had more recently acquired property. With Vane and others he approached the City for an advance of £120,000 as a loan on the security of two months' assessment. The City complied after some hard bargaining. Another £30,000 was raised from previously unsold Deans' and Chapters' lands. On June 27 the excise was charged with £400,000 and on that security Cromwell attempted to raise an immediate £150,000 but at first to no avail. In the City they were offering a wager of twenty to one that Cromwell would not leave England. But he knew how to press a case and by July 12 they had agreed to lend the £150,000. Cromwell was working with the energy and the frenetic determination he had shown at the outbreak of the civil war, forcing others to do what he knew was necessary. His further requirement was the backing of a fleet both to deal with Rupert and to ensure supplies for the English army. Coastal shipping had been useful during the civil wars but this would be a campaign totally dependent upon shipping for supplies. Rupert, now Admiral of the Royalist fleet, had sailed from Holland with eight ships and a convoy of three Dutch East Indiamen and on January 3 was at Kinsale on the coast of Munster, south-west of Cork, where the Bandon river flows into the sea providing excellent protective harbours. The English Parliament responded by increasing the strength of the navy by thirty merchantmen and reorganizing its command. It was hardly politic to retain the services of the Earl of Warwick whose brother, Lord Holland, had been executed as a Royalist on March 9. It appointed instead Sir George Ayscue as Admiral on the Irish coast, but the men on whom the work would fall were three Colonels – Popham, Blake, and Deane – the three 'Generals at Sea' – who were officially named as Commissioners. Ships and Generals at Sea needed men no less than land armies and the Council of State, mindful of the dismal and tragic experiences of Cadiz and the Isle of Rhé, set about recruitment in a way which was in salutary contrast to the haphazard and unfeeling methods of Charles and Buckingham. Impressment was considered necessary but in conjunction with the Impressment Act of February 22 the distribution of prize money was authorized and £10 was promised for every gun captured. Twenty additional merchant ships were put under contract for Ireland and £80 was voted for surgeon's chests to accompany them.

Blake arrived at Kinsale with his English ships on May 22 successfully containing Rupert who still patrolled the south Irish coast. On land Colonel Jones still held Dublin for Parliament though Ormonde with his Confederate army had broken camp at Kilkenny on May 30 and with 6,000 foot and 2,000 horse had reached Finglass, north-east of Dublin.

For Cromwell waiting in England until he was assured of money, supplies, and ships, the news was not good. But he assessed the perilous situation of Jones in Dublin and organized ships and men to relieve him from the sea side, the only side open to a relieving force. He won over influential support in Munster by enlisting the services of Lord Broghill, son of the Earl of Cork, who was bitterly hostile to the Catholic Irish but who would have served Prince Charles but for Cromwell's intervention. Cromwell put out feelers to the garrison at Cork; he made secret advances to the unstable Inchiquin. At last, reasonably satisfied on most counts, with a warrant for £30,000 in his pocket, Cromwell gave a farewell dinner in London on July 5 and sent the bulk of his troops ahead to embark from Milford Haven. Three regiments of foot and one of horse embarked from Chester to help Jones in Dublin. They were at first defeated by the weather and driven back on to the Welsh coast but finally reached the hard-pressed city in detachments between July 22 and 26.

Cromwell, meantime, had set off from London at 5 o'clock in the evening of July 12 in considerable state. The bright summer evening was full of sound and colour spilling over the green verges of the roads between hedges of wild roses and early blackberries, the pervasive scent of elderberry over all. Six Flanders mares of whiteish-grey drew his coach, possibly his wife was at his side. Many of the Army High Command rode with him, well-wishers and friends accompanied him, an impressive life-guard of eighty high-ranking officers, splendidly accoutred, protected the Lord-Lieutenant of Ireland on his way to the coast. With trumpets sounding they took him as far as Brentford whence he proceeded with a more modest train through Windsor, Reading, Newbury, Marlborough and Bath to Bristol which he reached on July 14. He stayed there for some time with his wife and some of his family while supplies were being sent to the coast for shipment.[2]

Cromwell would not have known, as he set out for the coast with his splendid entourage, that the previous day, July 11, Drogheda had surrendered to Inchiquin with its entire garrison of 600 foot and 220 horse, or that Dundalk, where Monck himself was in charge, had similarly been taken. Jones, in Dublin, was now caught in a pincer movement from North and South. Ormonde brought the bulk of his army to Rathmines on the south side of Dublin. Rather than a frontal attack on the city he took Rathfarnham, a fortified house in the rear of his new position on July 28 and then occupied the old castle of Bagotrath, which commanded the mouth of the Liffey and the meadows where Jones's cavalry foraged. But the strategy foundered. The newly arrived troops from England were making good their landing and Jones broke out of Dublin on the morning of August 3. Together they took Bagotrath and then pushed on to Ormonde's main position at Rathmines where the bulk of his army lay unprepared. Jones's victory was decisive. Ormonde's men fled or threw down their arms. How many were killed in battle is uncertain. Ormonde alleged that Jones butchered in cold blood the prisoners who had surrendered and the accusation was not denied. It was the end of Ormonde's diligently gathered army, and he himself retreated to Drogheda. An attempt by Jones to take it was unsuccessful.

Cromwell left Milford Haven on August 13 with thirty-five sail, 3,000 men, artillery and general stores, a vast quantity of scythes to cut the standing corn and to deal with bush and bramble, 'an immense supply of bibles' – and money. He had just embarked when the news of Jones's victory at Rathmines reached him. For the first

175

day they were becalmed. When they got away on the second day Cromwell, on shipboard for the first time and on the turbulent Irish Sea, was violently sea-sick. But on the 15th they were at Ringsend on the southern side of Dublin's harbour where the lush meadows stretched that so recently had been the scene of skirmishes between Jones and Ormonde. Three thousand men with their stores and equipment needed to disembark and set up camp. Cromwell himself saw for the first time the wide stretch of Dublin Bay from Howth to Dalkey with its green and gold hinterland, at its best now in August, with the Wicklow mountains to the south and low hills and plains enclosing it closely to the north. His practised eye assessed the military situation. It was satisfactory to know that Blake would keep Rupert from entering the Bay and that Dublin itself was in English hands. That would enable him to go north, beyond the shores of the Bay, to assert his presence there and to control the northern approach to the city. The south would need a little further consideration.

Cromwell immediately took carriage from Ringsend to the centre of Dublin. He halted his coach where the the throng was thickest and, hat in hand, rose in his seat. The words came easily. The Irish were the 'barbarous and bloodthirsty Irish'. Dublin had been delivered from 'the rage and cruelty of a bloody enemy'. He would restore the country to its 'former happiness and tranquility' and would put rigorously into execution laws against 'profane swearing, cursing and drunkenness'. Rewards were promised to those who supported him. In a way the words were conventional. He himself had recently been described as 'the bloody brewer, Cromwell' and the English news-sheets in general did not mince their words. But this was his first visit to Ireland, he had little contact with Irish people, and his understanding of the Irish situation was blocked by his own religious views and the colonizing mentality which considered the Irish no more than it considered the natives of North America.[3]

His speech was accounted 'sweet and plausible' and was predictably applauded by the mainly Protestant, English inhabitants of Dublin, joyous after their recent relief from siege, and Cromwell proceeded to the lodgings where he would stay until Dublin Castle was ready to receive its new Lord Lieutenant. Shortly afterwards Ireton reached Dublin, having changed his plans either because of a change in wind or because he had not been admitted to either Cork or Youghal, as he had hoped. With him came seventy-seven vessels and others followed. In all 130 ships were anchored off Dublin, filling the Bay with their sails. Ten thousand men and more were accommodated in and round the city. The cavalry had no compunction in stabling their horses in St Parick's Cathedral. The house of the Archbishop of Dublin was turned into a hospital, its upkeep charged against church income.

Time was not on the side of the English. Dublin was safe but the north and the northern ports, with the exception of Londonderry, which was closely besieged, were in Royalist hands. To control Dublin's northern approaches Cromwell needed Drogheda. He sent 1,000 foot and 500 horse under Venables to relieve Coote in Londonderry and on August 31 himself set out from Dublin towards Drogheda thirty-two miles to the north. Ormonde had put Sir Arthur Aston, an English Catholic who had fought for the King and been Governor of Oxford, in charge of Drogheda with 2,200 foot and 320 horse, mostly Catholic, Ormonde himself moved to Tetroghan, a few miles to the west. Most of Inchiquin's men had deserted after Rathmines but they held a few scattered posts at Trim and Newry to the north. Aston was confident. He who could take Drogheda could take hell, he boasted. This was indeed Cromwell's main reason for marching against it. Once in his hands he could feel confident of controlling the whole of the northern route from Dublin to Londonderry.

His instinct for planning did not desert him and he arranged for arms and supplies to go by sea up the coast to Drogheda. This was all the more important since he would be in unknown country of unpredictable difficulty and it would relieve him of the cumbersome business of dragging gun-carriages and procuring draught horses, so making for speed. The usual strict discipline was emphasized with orders against plunder or straggling from the colours. Two of his men who disobeyed were without compunction hanged on September 7. With such discipline there were few or no camp followers. His army made a brave sight as some 10–12,000 men crossed the Liffey and encamped on the estate of Nicholas, Lord Barnewell before stretching out along the coastal plain on their march northward. They marched through a comfortable landscape of fields greener than Oliver commonly saw in England, apart from the Fenland in the spring, with the supporting ships accompanying them to their right. The next night they were very close to the sea at Ballygrath where they were joined by some of Inchiquin's deserters. On September 2 the advance guard was outside Drogheda, on the 3rd the whole

177

army and the supporting vessels were there; unloading began immediately, unhampered from the town which was woefully short of artillery.

Drogheda rose steeply from the banks of the river Boyne, the river and the sea saving it from being surrounded, but at the same time giving to a besieging army which controlled the sea the great advantage of safe anchorage. Another double-edged geographical quirk was the fact that the town was cut in two by the river, each half rising steeply from its banks. A drawbridge connected the northern or main part of the city with the southern section, on which stood an artificial mound called Mill Mount which served as the bulwark of defence for the town. At the south-east corner of this southern section stood St Mary's church, which was used as an observation point and for sniping. Surrounding the whole built-up area of the town, an area of some sixty-four acres, was a massive wall, $1\frac{1}{2}$ miles in circumference, 22 feet high, 6 feet thick at the base, $4\frac{1}{2}$ feet wide at the top, part of it running through St Mary's churchyard. Aston was not far out in his boast of impregnability. But he had reckoned without Cromwell.

Cromwell's attack must be from the south, for he had not enough troops for a pincer movement from both south and north. It took him a week to land and assemble his guns and siege equipment, to dig trenches and deploy his forces. Then, at eight in the morning of September 10, he summoned Drogheda. He had 10,000 men to Aston's 2,500 and was well supplied with stores and equipment while Aston was virtually without cannon or gunners to fire them. But the rejection of Cromwell's summons was a formality and the garrison opened fire with what weapons they had. Cromwell's reply was to attack the city wall and by nightfall two breaches had been made in the section that ran through St Mary's church, while the steeple of the church itself had been partly destroyed. The defenders meanwhile had been feverishly throwing up earthworks on their side of the wall and when Cromwell in the afternoon of the 11th gave word to attack his men were driven back, once, twice, until Cromwell himself leapt to the attack and carried his men with him through the breached wall, over the defensive earthworks. Some of Aston's men fled down the slope to the river, across the drawbridge into the northern section of the town. Aston himself with some 300 soldiers climbed Mill Mount. It had been erected for defence and there is no reason to believe that they did not intend to carry on the fight.

178

Cromwell's soldiers followed, breaking down the defences of the Mound and offering quarter, as was customary, to all who surrendered. But Cromwell was incensed. The heat of battle was upon him. The ferocity of the fighting that had gone before, the dearly-bought victory paid for in the blood of his own men, was not to be challenged by a few hundred Catholics on Mill Mount. He gave the order to kill them all. His command was carried out. Aston's head was beaten in with his own wooden leg which was thought to contain his money. Even this was not enough. Cromwell and his men followed the rest of the defending army across the river and into the northern section of the town slaying, on Cromwell's command, all who were in arms. About eighty men had taken refuge in St Peter's church at the top of the northern hill. On Cromwell's orders the wooden pews were dragged beneath the steeple and set on fire to burn them out. No one escaped. 'I burn!, I burn!' was the agonized cry from the steeple. From the whole engagement there were few prisoners, and these were sent as slaves to the Barbadoes. Every priest in the town was killed. Even civilians perished, though immune by the rules of war. Cromwell may not have known it but included in the massacre were the English Protestant troops of Colonel Byrne's regiment. But he knew the slaughter was complete. 'I do not believe', he wrote to the Speaker, 'that any officer escaped with his life, save only one lieutenant.' After describing the horrific scenes in some detail he continues

> I am persuaded that this is a righteous judgment of God upon these barbarous wretches, who have imbued their hands in so much innocent blood; and that it will tend to prevent the effusion of blood for the future, which are the satisfactory grounds for such actions, which otherwise cannot but work remorse and regret.

The slaughtered officers and soldiers of Drogheda, he adds, 'were the flower of all their army.'[4]

By the time Speaker Lenthall read these words Cromwell was back in Dublin preparing to march south with his spirit in no way disturbed nor his outlook changed by the carnage of Drogheda.

Cromwell was obviously expecting that he would be in Ireland for some time and that Dublin Castle would be his official residence,

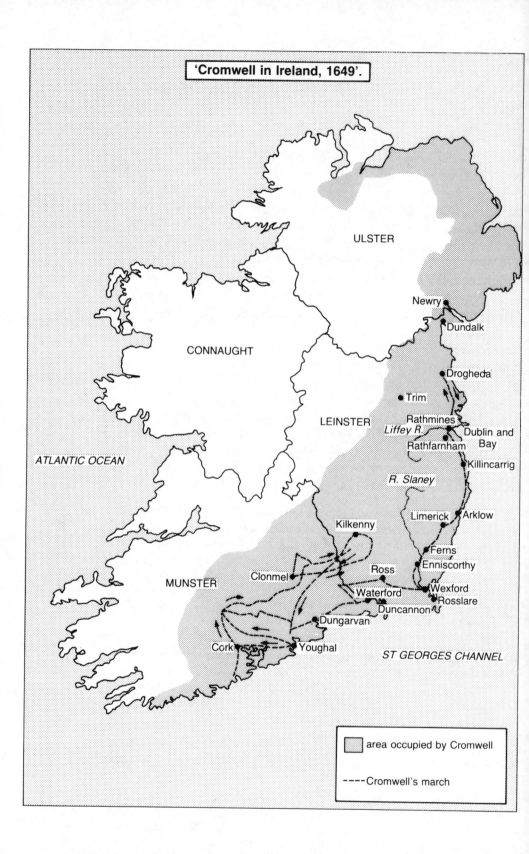

'Cromwell in Ireland, 1649'.

ULSTER

CONNAUGHT

LEINSTER

MUNSTER

ATLANTIC OCEAN

Newry
Dundalk
Drogheda
Trim
Rathmines
Liffey R.
Rathfarnham
Dublin and Bay
Killincarrig
R. Slaney
Limerick
Arklow
Kilkenny
Ferns
Enniscorthy
Clonmel
Ross
Wexford
Waterford
Rosslare
Duncannon
Dungarvan
Cork
Youghal

ST GEORGES CHANNEL

☐ area occupied by Cromwell

---- Cromwell's march

for he had arranged that his wife would follow him with some of their household goods. The news-sheets were surmising that Mrs Cromwell would be not averse to her role as Vicereine. Perhaps she would not be sorry to leave England, expecting a simpler life in Dublin. More likely she simply did as her husband requested and was happy to come to him. At all events she had been at Milford Haven to see him off and by the middle of September was reported to be on the Irish Sea in the *Concorde* – for her, as for Oliver, a new and probably daunting experience. When she arrived she was allowed only a few days to recover before accompanying him on his march to the south.

For speed was essential to Cromwell. He had to follow up his advantage before Ormonde, who was darting about somewhere between Trim and Wexford in country he knew well, could realign his scattered forces; it was vital to secure the ports of Munster for in the wrong hands they could undo much of what had already been done; above all, there was the weather, already worsening with rain and wind. At the same time events in England remained unpredictable: he could better deal with whatever might arise if he had finished his work in Ireland.

Before setting out for the south he did what he could to secure his rear. In the north the position was satisfactory with sufficient forces and Parliamentary garrisons to hold the position. He made a characteristically diplomatic gesture to English Protestants living in and about Dublin by substantially reducing their taxes with the result that many joined him at their own charge.

He sent his main army off to the south by the coast route on September 23. He himself left on the 27th, perhaps to give his wife a little more respite, for she was to accompany him. Colonel Hewson was left in charge of Dublin while Jones, with the rank of Lieutenant-Colonel, marched with Cromwell. The main army drove out the Royalists and established a Parliamentary garrison at Killincarig, fourteen miles south of Dublin. It then proceeded to Arklow, the site of one of Ormonde's castles, where the river Avoca flows into the sea. The garrison fled, some of them being caught up in a bog where they were surrounded and slain. The town of Arklow surrendered on the 28th as Cromwell joined the main force.

Thereafter it was not an easy march. His main objective was Wexford, but there were strong points, garrisons and small towns to secure on the way, so he turned inland, marching through the lower slopes of the Wicklow mountains where the way was wet and boggy and the mountain passes treacherous. He came to the Darragh river, a branch of the Avoca – 'almost a desolated country', as he reported – but wild and beautiful with rushing streams whose waters joined in narrow tree-lined valleys. It was not good marching country. He lost many horses in the treacherous passes, he was attacked by bandits who swept down from the higher mountains and carried off his own horse and some of his personal belongings. Limbrick (Limerick) Castle he found burnt and deserted by the Esmond family who had fled; he took Rosseminoge and Ferns Castle, the mighty, moated fortress built upon solid rock with the ancient ruined Cathedral by its side and the land, green and productive, stretching round it. He forded the river Slaney at Slane Passage and came into the village of Enniscorthy where the army camped in the surrounding fields under the shadow of Vinegar Hill. The country people, on the strength of Cromwell's promise of payment, brought in corn and barley from the fertile land around. The castle at Enniscorthy was strong and stubborn but finally surrendered with guns, ammunition and supplies. Next day Cromwell and an advance guard, crossing the river again, continued along the right bank of the Slaney through Muchwood and Ardandrisk to the north-west corner of Wexford. There they set up camp and were heartened by the sight of Admiral Deane in the harbour, where he had arrived two days earlier with twenty ships, food, supplies, ammunition, equipment and men. Storms and the protective fort of Rosslare prevented their immediate landing but it was a comfort to know they were there. On October 2 Cromwell was joined by the main army – 7,000 foot and 2,000 horse – and he opened negotiations with Colonel Sinnot, the Governor of Wexford.

The river Slaney flows into the sea at Wexford forming a secure harbour protected by Raven Point to the north and Rosslare Point to the south. The town itself lies on the southern side of the estuary running in a narrow line from north to south along the coast. It was connected to the northern side of the estuary by a ferry, its chief defences were the town walls, the fort of Rosslare which stood on Rosslare Point, and a castle which guarded its southern edge. Northward it relied on the protective waters of the estuary but on the landward side there was little apart from the town itself.

Sinnot had been instructed by Ormonde not to surrender, though the population, in spite of being mainly Catholic, would probably have done so. Cromwell, for his part, was suffering from incessant rain, the ground on which he had encamped was becoming ever more wet and soggy, and dysentery was prevalent among his men. So, while still negotiating with Sinnot, he moved his army to the rocky ground on the south-east of the town, beyond Wexford Castle. Here he had the advantage of firmer ground, he was in a favourable position to attack the castle, and he would be able to proceed against Fort Rosslare. He needed contact with his fleet both to take off his sick and to land supplies but this could not be done until the fort was put out of action. It proved an easy task. At the approach of Lieutenant-Colonel Jones on the 2nd it yielded without a blow and Deane's ships sailed into Wexford harbour.

Feeling secure, Cromwell on the 3rd summoned the town. Sinnot still procrastinated. On the 11th Cromwell opened fire on the castle. The Commander, Captain Stafford, lowered his defences and Cromwell turned the guns of the castle upon the town. The defenders of Wexford fled in panic, some to beg quarter of the conquerors, others to seek escape by sea. Cromwell's men poured into the town. With few defenders on the walls nothing was needed but scaling ladders and even these were dispensed with by some of the eager invaders who stuck their pikes into crannies in the walls to make footholds. Without protective ships in the harbour, with Fort Rosslare out of action, with no relieving force in sight, there was no defence for the town save the city walls and these, undefended, were useless.

The carnage resembled that of Drogheda. Cromwell's men poured into the market place which was defended only by ropes and cables stretched across the narrow streets that led to it. Soldiers, civilians, churchmen, were slaughtered indiscriminately. Our forces, wrote Cromwell, 'put all to the sword that came their way.' Those who sought refuge in the church were struck down with the friars who worshipped there. Those who sought escape by sea were drowned when the overcrowded boats capsized.[5]

Cromwell's next objectives were the port towns of Munster, and primarily Waterford. He advanced first to Ross, a fortified town commanding a ferry over the river Barrow, which it was essential to cross. Ross surrendered on the 19th, two days after it was summoned. The soldiers were spared but their cannon and ammunition were left behind and 500 men of English birth came in to serve Cromwell. The building of a bridge over the Barrow was essential to allow the passage of his troops and while it was building Cromwell sent

Jones with 2,000 men to lay siege to Duncannon, the fort which protected Waterford, some twelve miles south of Ross. Waterford lay on the west side of the wide estuary formed by the confluence of the rivers Barrow and Suir. Duncannon faced it from the eastern shore of the estuary in a virtually impregnable position high on a rocky promontory, protected on the land side by a deep ditch and by a massive and precipitous rampart hollowed out of the rock. Cromwell himself, too impatient to wait inactive at Ross while the bridge was building, followed Jones to Duncannon. He had some reason for optimism for by this time he had heard that Cork had declared for the English Parliament on October 16.

But the fort of Duncannon was a hard nut to crack. As winter set in the condition of Cromwell's troops became more difficult, debilitated by dysentery, reduced in numbers by sickness and death and the necessity of leaving garrisons in the towns and fortresses they had subdued. On November 5 he raised the siege of Duncannon and returned to Ross. The bridge had been completed but Cromwell was ill. He sent Jones and Ireton to seek out Ormonde but they found the Royalist leader in an impregnable position at Thomastown. But on the credit side a Parliamentary force captured Carrick, which gave them a bridge over the Suir and enabled them to approach Waterford from the land side. Cromwell lost no time and on November 24 was outside Waterford. But sickness and winter conditions were still against him. On soggy, muddy roads men could barely pass, let alone horses and guns which sank into the soft earth when they were mounted. Men slept in wet and mud, provisions were short for the country people here were not bringing in supplies. December 2 was, as Cromwell wrote, 'as terrible a day as ever I marched in my life'. On that day he raised the siege of Waterford and marched away to seek winter quarters. For Jones the order came too late. He was sick with fever and had to be left at Dungarvon. There he died on 10 December 1649. They took him to Youghal where he was buried in St Mary's church in the chapel belonging to the Earl of Cork. The weather, as Owen Roe O'Neill had prophesied, was defeating the invaders.

The winning of Cork was the greatest blessing of that bleak winter. Blake and Deane sailed into the harbour, Ireton joined Cromwell in the town and they all spent Christmas at the house of Mr Coppinger in South Main Street. There was some reason for cheer. In spite of their failure before Waterford, Dungarvon, Bandon, Kinsale,

184

Baltimore and Castlehaven had declared for Parliament and most of Inchiquin's foot had come in to Cromwell. Ormonde retired to Kilkenny. His forces had dwindled, Owen Roe O'Neill was dead, Inchiquin had proved a broken reed, everywhere his strongholds were surrendering. He had neither men, money nor supplies.

On the other hand the rest for Cromwell and his men though short, was invigorating. Fresh troops and supplies arrived from England and the campaigning season started early with Kilkenny and Clonmel the main objectives. With Monck coming down from the North and Hewson advancing from Dublin the customary war of attrition began. Grennan, Gowran, Cantwell Castle all surrendered. Broghill advanced from Cork, Cook from Wexford, Cromwell himself from Youghal. With Broghill protecting his rear he crossed the Nore at Bennett's Bridge and halted at Black Quarry, about a mile south of Kilkenny. On March 23 Kilkenny was summoned. It took five days to subdue Ormonde's proud castle and town. On the 25th a breach was made in the city wall, St Patrick's church near the west gate was seized and three pieces of ordnance placed there. Meanwhile Colonel Ewer had taken Irishtown on the north and entered the city proper by Dean's Gate, occupying both town and cathedral. On March 28 Kilkenny capitulated. There was no bloodbath. The soldiers evacuated the town, the citizens were fined, there was no looting, though Cromwell's men could not be kept from smashing the signs of 'idolatory'. Crosses, crucifixes, fonts, altars and stained glass were destroyed or damaged.

There remained only Clonmel.

On 27 April Cromwell appeared before the town. The garrison of 1,200 Ulster Celts under Hugh O'Neill, the nephew of Owen Roe, fought with unparalleled bravery and the place was strongly fortified. A breach was effected but on May 9 the assault was driven back with the heaviest loss Parliament's troops had yet suffered. One authority said 2,500 men were lost. But the defenders could do no more. Hugh O'Neill and his remaining men slipped away in the night of the 9th leaving the town to Cromwell. There was no massacre or destruction of property.[6]

Little more than a fortnight later Cromwell left Ireland. He had already heard rumours of his recall but had determined to finish his work before he left. When the summons actually came he was ready. He knew well enough the nature of the 'urgent affairs' he was summoned to deal with. He left Ireton as his Lord Deputy and

Commander-in-Chief to take Duncannon and Waterford and little more than a fortnight after the fall of Clonmel he left Youghal for Bristol, where he landed on June 1. He was only slightly sea-sick.

After a three-gun salute at Bristol he came on to Windsor with only a small personal retinue and was met by members of the Council, officers of the army, Members of Parliament who had adjourned their House for a long weekend, and by members of his family, including his wife. Part of Colonel Rich's regiment of horse came to Windsor and many ordinary people, intent on escorting him home, filled the inns to bursting point. Cromwell was 'very affable' and courteous, allowing many to speak to him on business as well as to congratulate him. The route to London was lined with cheering crowds. On the Saturday afternoon he made a call on Fairfax in Queen Street that was both personal and politic: any idea that Fairfax and Cromwell were not on the best of terms must be scotched. The Lord Mayor and Aldermen of the city waited on him at his lodgings in Whitehall; when Parliament met on the following Tuesday Lenthall offered an address of thanks on behalf of them all. Cromwell remained humble throughout. He was but the 'instrument' of 'those great and strange works' which the Lord had effected.

The Irish campaign had been a war of sieges, not battles. Cromwell's experience of siege warfare in a hostile environment was now unparalleled. But he left behind him a legacy of hate which endured for centuries.

17

'Let God arise and His enemies shall be scattered'

Cromwell's success in Ireland had assured him of the approval of the Almighty for his actions. His welcome home demonstrated the affection and gratitude of his countrymen. If confirmation of his powers were needed it was this recall to deal with the menace on the northern frontier. He might well begin to regard himself as indispensable.

Scotland was now the focal point of activity against the Commonwealth and all eyes were turned to the young Prince whom the Scottish Parliament had already recognized as Charles II, subject to his taking the Covenant. The Presbyterian Scots had fought for Parliament during the civil wars but the Commonwealth had remained lukewarm in fulfilling its part of the deal and had established in England but 'a lame Erastian Presbytery' with full allowance for Independents and for even less orthodox sects. The terms upon which the Scots were willing to support Charles included, therefore, the full establishment of Presbyterianism in England. Reluctantly Charles agreed and a considerable Scottish force under the same Leslie who had fought side by side with Cromwell at Marston Moor was massing in Scotland ready to take action against the English Commonwealth. But a more welcome ally to the young Prince was the Scottish Laird, James Graham, Earl of Montrose, who had fought for Charles I and been defeated by Leslie at Philliphaugh in September 1645. He had escaped to Europe where he managed to raise a few troops and a little money for the Royalist cause and landed on the Scottish coast at Caithness in March 1650. He was no Presbyterian and was met by Leslie and his Presbyterian army at Invercarron (Carbisdale) on April 27 when his little force was heavily defeated. When Cromwell landed in England from Ireland on May 25 Montrose's mutilated corpse was hanging in the Grassmarket in Edinburgh.

Negotiations with the Scots proved fruitless and the English Parliament voted that Fairfax, with Cromwell as his Lieutenant-General, should command the northern forces that would march against them. Fairfax, who had no quarrel with Presbyterians, laid down his commission when he understood that his command would entail invading Scotland. He would protect England but he would not invade another country. It is likely that he was seeking an excuse to retire, but his resignation was not accepted lightly. On June 24 he met a committee which had been specially appointed to dissuade him. Cromwell, Lambert, St John, Whitelocke, were there and Whitelocke wrote in his report of the meeting that none were so earnest as Cromwell and the soldiers in trying to dissuade Fairfax. He added, however, that 'there was cause enough to believe they did not over much desire it.'[1] Cromwell was pulled both ways. He liked, respected and admired Fairfax; they had successfully campaigned together; yet the freedom that overall command would give him was no light consideration. But whatever his inner feelings and desires Cromwell seems genuinely to have tried to persuade Fairfax to stay, begging him to consider whether it was not 'better to have this war in the bowels of another country than our own'. When it was all over and Fairfax had laid down his commission Cromwell was appointed by Act of Parliament of 26 June 1650 Captain-General and Commander-in-Chief of all the armed forces of the Commonwealth of England.[2] For the man of forty-nine, who had been only eight years a soldier, the rise to supreme command had been spectacular.

Parliament in a printed paper put on record the justice and necessity of an invasion of Scotland,[3] and the reliable Skippon was appointed to command in London where Presbyterian interests in the City might cause trouble. Cromwell pondered a little over the fanatical sectarian Major-General Harrison who would not regard Cromwell's elevation favourably. But Harrison, Cromwell judged, was so far committed to keeping Royalist and Presbyterian elements in check that he would not be a danger. So Harrison remained as Major-General in command of the troops left in England. Ireland also had to be considered. The army there was without Cromwell's leadership and without the services of the gallant Colonel Jones, to say nothing of the other soldiers who had perished in the difficult campaigning. But with Ireton in command Cromwell was satisfied that the general direction of affairs would not be halted, and on June 26 the Council of State confirmed Ireton as Lord Deputy assisted by two (later four) Commissioners. When Monck joined Cromwell in England it was necessary to find a second-in-command to Ireton. Cromwell's choice fell on Edmund Ludlow who he wanted to act both as Commissioner under Ireton and as Lieutenant-General, which carried with it the command of the horse which had been vacant since the death of Jones. Ludlow would also be a welcome absentee during Cromwell's campaigning in Scotland.

Ludlow was reluctant. He was dissatisfied with many aspects of affairs, particularly those which concerned Cromwell and himself, and was suspicious of promotion that entailed absence from England. Cromwell listened to Ludlow. Even in the heat of preparations to march into Scotland he listened. He knew the importance of placating old friends. His innate sense of justice told him that a man must be heard, particularly when he had the root of the matter in him. His common sense told him that Ludlow was too influential to leave behind in England, unmollified, too dangerous to be consigned to Ireland with his grievances rankling. So he listened as Ludlow raked up the old charge that he was too familiar with the King in the old days when Charles I was a captive guest among them; he listened to the heavy indictment of killing young Arnold at the Ware rendez-vous; he listened to the accusations of unfair preferment and reward – was this perhaps a personal grudge? – of undue severity against some who had formerly been their friends – probably a reference to the Levellers.

In reply Cromwell admitted there were good reasons to be dis-satisfied with the Army while it was endeavouring to come to an understanding with the King; he excused the execution of Arnold at Ware as 'absolutely necessary to keep things from falling into confu-sion'. He spoke of what he aimed at – a thorough reformation of the clergy and of the law – and the difficulty in achieving it. The law 'as it is now constituted', he said, 'serves only to maintain the lawyers, and to encourage the rich to oppress the poor'. But when reform is mentioned the lawyers, he said, 'cry out we desire to destroy property'. He professed to desire nothing more than that the govern-ment of the nation might be settled in a free and equal Commonwealth as the only way of preventing a return to the old régime. He said he was accomplishing what was prophesied in the 110th Psalm – and he spent an hour explaining it to Ludlow. Ludlow went to Ire-land. It was rarely possible to resist the combination of Cromwell and the Lord.[4]

Parliament had already, while Cromwell was still in Ireland, faced up to the need to provide yet more money if the Scottish campaign was to succeed. The sale of Royalist and Ecclesiastical lands and those of other delinquents which had not yet passed through the hands of the Sequestration or Compounding Committees was speeded up and loans raised on the security of these sales provided money more quickly. Cromwell also saw in train before he left for Scotland the reorganization of the militia, so essential to guard against any Royalist rising or invasion by Charles or the Scots. The Militia Act, which was passed on July 11 when Cromwell was before Edinburgh, included a system of taxation based upon means: those with income from land amounting to at least £200 a year were charged with providing the horse and arms of a cavalry officer; those with about £133 a year with the horse and arms of a dragoon; those with at least £20 with the arms of a foot soldier. No one with less than £10 a year income would be charged at all.[5]

Cromwell, having done all that he could to secure the situation in England concentrated, as he had done for Ireland, on securing adequate men with supplies and backing for the Scottish enterprise itself. He and the Parliament had the experience of the Irish campaign to draw on and they had learned a great deal. Ships were ready to sail up the coast with supplies of all kinds. Horses were commandeered (there were six for Cromwell's personal use), ammunition, guns, siege pieces, clothing, boots, bread and beer were conveyed over the long land route but mainly by the ships at sea. Surgeons were appointed and surgeons' chests provided. Godly ministers attended to the army's less material needs. When Cromwell left London on June 28, having given himself only two days of preparation after his official appointment, he had under his command 5,000 horse, 10,000 foot and 700 in the artillery train. Most of the men were seasoned campaigners. The experienced and trusted Lambert and Fleetwood were there as Major-Generals, Whalley was in Ireton's old post as Commissary-General. It was an experienced and highly disciplined force, well versed in the art of war, spiritually compact, well aware of the issues for which it would soon be fighting, full of confidence in its leader, in his generals, and never doubting its own success. In the whole of Europe there was no better fighting force, and Cromwell had every reason to be proud.

Parliament prepared a *Declaration* justifying the enterprise ahead:

the invasion of Scotland could not be taken lightly. When it was issued on July 4 the army was well on its way marching through Ware to Cambridge with enthusiastic crowds showering it with blessings. Some, including John Lilburne, accompanied them on the first stage of their march. Lilburne was grateful to Cromwell who, in the short time between his return from Ireland and his departure for Scotland, had been influential in obtaining a grant of Deans' and Chapters' lands to help the Leveller leader set up in trade as a soap-boiler in London.

Cromwell stopped at the Beare in Northampton amid enthusiastic crowds. At Leicester he was entertained by the mayor and aldermen with 'wyne, biskits, sugar, beare and tobacco'. York was equally enthusiastic.[6] At Durham they were met by Haselrig, now Governor of Newcastle. In Northumberland another ten regiments provided reinforcements with Colonels Pride and Hacker and other experienced commanders. From Alnwick on July 17 Cromwell made his own personal testament in a letter to Richard Mayor, father-in-law to his son Richard.

> ... you see now I am employed. I need pity ... I have not sought these things', truly I have been called unto them by the Lord ...

But he still had time to be worried about Richard:

> I hope you give my son good counsel; I believe he needs it. He is in the dangerous time of his age, and it's a very vain world ... I know my son is idle.

More happily he speaks of his little granddaughter born four months before to Richard and Dorothy: 'I should be glad to hear how the little brat doth.' But the young parents had little time even for a grandfather as famous as Oliver. 'I could chide both father and mother for their neglects of me,' he wrote: 'If I had as good leisure as they, I should write sometimes.'[7]

Two days later the Army issued its own justification for the enterprise it was embarking upon in the *Declaration of the Army of England*, possibly printed by a press that accompanied the army. Five hundred copies were sent to Scotland, 300 to Carlisle for English consumption.[8] The English army was by this time on the banks of the Tweed and rumours were circulating in Scotland based, no doubt, on stories

of Irish atrocities, that they would 'put all men to the sword, and
... thrust hot irons through the women's breasts'. Cromwell himself
wrote the reply, to be distributed among the Scottish people, assuring
them of his protection:

> Did you not see us, and try us, what kind of men we were, when
> we came among you two years ago? Did you find us plunderers,
> murderers, monsters of the world? Whose ox have we stolen?[9]

For any with first-hand knowledge of Drogheda or Wexford it would
not have been convincing. But the Scottish kirk would have appre-
ciated the difference between themselves and the Irish Catholics.

The Scots answered *Declaration* with *Declaration* but their practical
reply was seen as the English army left Berwick, Cromwell with
his regiment of horse and Pride's regiment of foot being the first
to cross the Tweed on July 22 and encamp at Mordington just across
the border. It was a scene of desolation. The men had fled, driving
away their cattle, and that night the Scottish beacons were set on
fire consuming all the crops and fodder that remained. While Leslie
had his native Scotland behind him for supplies, Cromwell was
dependent upon his ships. The strange thing was that some of the
women had remained and, as reported by Whitelocke who was
accompanying the army as its secretary, 'do bake and brew, to provide
bread and drink for the English army', presumably from stores
brought by the fleet.[10] Perhaps the pay was good. They were probably
reassured by Cromwell's customary orders which were always rigidly
carried out: nothing to be taken without payment, no straying from
their regiments, no 'straggling' for more than half a mile. Before
they moved on a little light relief was provided by some of the men
and enjoyed by Cromwell: 'Oliver loved an innocent jest', as the
man said who recounted the incident. Some of the men in foraging
found a forgotten churn filled with cream. When most of it had
been used a soldier lifted the churn to his mouth hoping to catch
the few drops that remained but the heavy churn tipped up over
his head and stuck fast, the cream trickling down over his apparel.
Hearing the shouts and the laughter Oliver and his staff officers looked

out of their window and joined in the merriment.[11]

But he spoke to his men soberly now that they were across the border. He spoke 'as a Christian and a soldier' telling them to be

> doubly and trebly diligent, to be wary and worthy, for sure enough we have work before us! But have we not had God's blessing hitherto? Let us go on faithfully and hope for the like still![12]

They pushed on to Musselburgh on the coast some four or five miles from Edinburgh, still in touch with their fleet. Several brief encounters with the enemy gave them no advantage. On July 31 they were still there and the pattern had been more or less set for the next five months. The Scots were playing a tactical game. They hindered Cromwell's supply ships from coming into Leith, they organized a guerilla resistance to the invaders in which even the camp at Musselburgh was temporarily occupied by Scotsmen. The weather was atrocious – 'so sore a day and night of rain as I have seldom seen', as Cromwell wrote to the Council of State on July 30.[13] The attempt to take Edinburgh was abandoned amid the downpour. 'The men eat nothing but bread and cheese, drink ill water and lie on the ground without huts', as Lieutenant Hodgson of Lambert's regiment wrote.[14] Cromwell sent home for supplies, particularly clothing and blankets – 'the enemy having enough to cover them, and we nothing at all considerable' – as well as for medicines and surgical supplies. Even the supplies brought with them by land and sea were inadequate in these taxing conditions.

For five weeks the Scots kept up a guerilla warfare while the sick and wounded from Cromwell's army were taken to Berwick, the harbour at Musselburgh proving barely adequate even for the landing of supplies. Efforts to engage Leslie failed because of the difficult boggy ground and, as Fleetwood wrote, because the passes were 'so many and so great that as soon as we go on the one side, they go on the other'.[15] Cromwell's army was unused to these typical tactics by an enemy on familiar home ground. On August 6 he was compelled to make a partial and temporary retreat to Dunbar where supplies could more easily be landed. The population here, in the path of the invading army, had been reduced to near starvation and Cromwell stopped to give them food before returning to Musselburgh with his own supplies. Here he found that the women who had baked and brewed had been forced away by Leslie and the condition of the men left behind that much the worse.

An accompaniment to this strange half-war of guerilla tactics and attrition was a constant exchange of *Declarations*, *Manifestoes* and *Letters*. On August 3 Cromwell himself wrote to the General Assembly of the Kirk of Scotland with a powerful plea for toleration:

> Is it ... infallibly agreeable to the Word of God, all that you say?
> I beseech you, in the bowels of Christ, think it possible you may
> be mistaken.[16]

This was not a word known to the stern Scottish kirk and Cromwell's plea had no discernible effect. The guerilla warfare continued throughout August with every advantage going to Leslie. For five weeks Cromwell manoeuvred in vain round Edinburgh. With difficulties of supply, without the Scots familiarity with the terrain, with increasing illness among his men, he shipped his sick as best he could from Musselburgh and began to withdraw towards Dunbar which he reached on September 1 with his 'poor, shattered, hungry, discouraged army' amounting to no more than 11,000 men. Leslie followed with his 22,000 men, comparatively fresh, but made no attempt to engage on that day because it was a Sunday and the Scots had been told by their kirk not to stain the Lord's day with blood. But Leslie occupied Doon Hill overlooking Dunbar and seized the passes to the south so cutting Cromwell off from Berwick. It seemed that the English army was well and truly trapped. Oliver knew that his position was desperate. It was not only that defeat stared him in the face but that the confidence which he and others had built upon his success was most likely about to be shattered. Going into Dunbar for a little refreshment about 4 o'clock in the afternoon of the 2nd he wrote a hurried note to Haselrig to be conveyed to him with 'haste, haste', as he wrote at the top. For Haselrig at Newcastle or thereabouts would be the first to be affected by a rout of the English army. Cromwell knew that Haselrig had few troops at his command and his chief concern was that the English could get together sufficient men to hold the position in England. Meanwhile, he wrote, 'our spirits are comfortable ... And indeed we have much hope in the Lord; of whose mercy we have had large experience.'[17] This fortitude in the face of superior numbers and what appeared to be certain defeat, if not annihilation, throws as much light on Cromwell's character as do any of his victories. It also shows that his dependence on the Lord was a real and living part of his being and not just an adjunct of success. For he knew that defeat would destroy the confidence that he and others had built upon his success; that, to himself, it would undermine the justification for all that he had done.

Most people would have agreed that only the Lord could save him now. And it might well have seemed that the orders which the Scottish Parliamentary Committee now issued to Leslie came

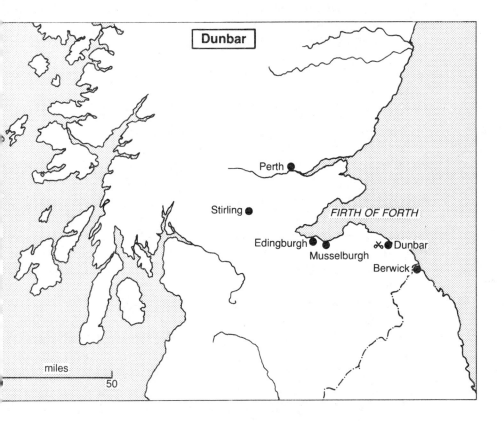

straight from the Lord on Cromwell's behalf. That civilian Committee ordered Leslie to come down from his position of strength on the hill and block Cromwell's path south with his whole army.

Cromwell, who had been watching Leslie's movements all day, was walking with Lambert in the gardens of Brooksmouth House after his return from Dunbar when he saw clearly the intentions of Leslie. 'The Lord hath delivered them into our hands!' he exclaimed.

When Leslie had taken up his new position his centre stood with its back to Doon Hill. In front and on its left was a steep ravine formed by the Brook Burn. On the right, where the ground was level and open, Leslie had deployed the bulk of his cavalry. Cromwell's strategy, agreed with Lambert, was simple. The Scottish left was shut in by the hill and the ravine, its centre, with its back to Doon Hill, had little room for manoeuvre. If the Scottish right, on the open ground, could be routed the battle would be more than half won for the English. Throughout a dark and stormy night Cromwell deliberately gave the impression that he would stand upon the defensive. But he was worried. He 'rid all the night ... through the several regiments by torchlight, upon a little Scots nag, biting his lips till the blood ran down his chin without his perceiving it, his thoughts being busily employed to be ready for the action now in hand.'[18] Then, towards dawn of September 3, he made a feint attack upon the enemy's left and while they were dealing with this, to the battle cry of 'The Lord of Hosts!', he hurled all the force he could muster against their right and centre. At first Leslie's superior numbers told, but finally the attack on their right flank became so strong that the Scottish centre was rolled up from right to left and penned in between the hill and the ravine. As the sun rose over the sea one of Cromwell's officers heard him exclaim 'Now let God arise and his enemies shall be scattered!' And shortly afterwards he was heard to shout in exultation 'I profess they run!'

The battle had lasted less than three hours. Cromwell halted his pursuing troops and they all sang the 117th psalm: 'O give ye praise unto the Lord!' The Scots, as Cromwell wrote to the Speaker, were made by the Lord of Hosts as stubble to their swords. Or, as he expressed it more soberly, Dunbar was 'one of the most signal mercies God hath done for England and his people, this war'. Three thousand of Leslie's men fell in battle, 10,000 were taken prisoner together with 15,000 swords, pikes, shot-guns and arms of various kinds, artillery trains, baggage trains, and 200 colours. Not more than twenty of the English army were lost. Cromwell wrote at length, obviously both elated and deeply aware of a Providence outside himself and his soldiers. 'The Lord hath done this', he repeated. 'We that serve you beg of you not to own us, but God alone . . .'[19] Cromwell knew the odds against him. Nothing but a miracle could have saved him. And that miracle God had vouchsafed on his behalf. But not everyone could have seized the opportunity offered as Cromwell did. The tactics were all his, the perception of the enemy's weakness, the relentless force against the chosen place. For the miracle to have worked a general of no uncommon ability was needed.

The support he received from Parliament and the backing provided by the ships which sailed unhindered up the coast were of the greatest importance. Parliament not only sent him off initially with the supplies and materials he needed but continued to meet his constant demands as the war proceeded. True, he was the initiator and the urgency he gave to his demands made it difficult to refuse them, but Parliament might easily have been less responsive, more niggardly, and the result would have affected Cromwell's campaign: in four days alone, between August 9 and August 13, two shallops and four provision ships came in to the Firth of Forth, and the supply continued with arms and ammunition, siege artillery, battering rams, bread, beer, even reinforcements of men and godly ministers for their spiritual needs. Provisions were low, sickness was rife in Cromwell's army. But without support from Westminster it would have been decimated.

In his thankfulness for victory Cromwell's thoughts turned to reform and he begged Parliament to regard the power which victory had given them not as their due but as a means 'to curb the proud and the insolent'. He exhorted them to 'relieve the oppressed, hear the groans of poor prisoners in England; be pleased to reform the abuses of all professions; and if there be any one that makes many poor to make a few rich, that suits not a Commonwealth.'[20]

On the day after Dunbar, the day he sent his despatch to the Speaker, he wrote also to his wife. The letter was of great delicacy, surprising from the rough and somewhat uncouth soldier with the heat of battle upon him still. It makes clear the love and understanding between them, indicates that she writes to him frequently. He does not give details of the battle. These, he says, she will get from Harry Vane or Gil Pickering – an indication that these are family friends. He starts instead in the playful, personal style he sometimes uses to his family and friends and continues with a reassertion of his faith.

But the physical, mental and emotional strain of the past weeks proves too much and he ends on an almost despairing note:

> My Dearest,
>
> I have not leisure to write much, but I could chide thee that in many of thy letters thou writest to me, that I should not be unmindful of thee and thy little ones. Truly, if I love thee not too well, I think I err not on the other hand much. Thou art dearer to me than any creature; let that suffice.
>
> The Lord hath showed us an exceeding mercy: who can tell how great it is. My weak faith hath been upheld. I have been in my inward man marvellously supported; though I assure thee, I grow an old man, and feel infirmities of age marvellously stealing upon me. Would my corruptions did as fast decrease. Pray on my behalf in the latter respect ... My love to all dear friends. I rest thine,
>
> Oliver Cromwell[21]

He wrote also to Henry Ireton in Ireland:

> 'Though I hear not often from you, yet I know you forget me not. Think so of me, for I often remember you at the Throne of Grace.[22]

He had kept in touch with his son-in-law and had heard from Scoutmaster William Rowe as recently as August 30 of Ireton's 'pen, tongue, head, hand, or both or all, being incessantly at work'. As the news of Ireton's successes at Waterford and Duncannon had rejoiced and stimulated the forces in Scotland, he says, so he hopes that the news of Dunbar will do likewise to Ireton and his men.

Still on the same day after Dunbar he wrote a short note to Richard Mayor telling him of the victory – 'the Lord's doing, and it is marvellous in our eyes'. He added a personal postscript almost as long as the letter itself.

> I pray tell Doll [Dorothy, his daughter-in-law] I do not forget her nor her little brat. She writes very cunningly and complimentally to me; I expect a letter of plain dealing from her. She is too modest to tell me whether she breeds or no. I wish a blessing upon her and her husband. The Lord make them fruitful in all that's good. They are at leisure to write often – but indeed they are both idle, and worthy of blame.[23]

In the midst of campaigning Cromwell still receives and writes personal letters and, indeed, hungers for more. The few that survive show clearly the affectionate, family man who, but for circumstances, might still have been farming his land and collecting his tythes at Ely.

18

'I am wearied . . .'

After Dunbar Cromwell occupied Edinburgh and Leith. He controlled the Firth of Forth and the Eastern Lowlands but the South-West still held out, Edinburgh Castle resisted stubbornly, and Leslie was firmly entrenched in Stirling. While continuing his efforts at reconciliation with the Scots on both religious and political grounds, Cromwell sent to Haselrig for reinforcements. 'Surely its probable', he wrote, 'the Kirk has done their do. I believe their King will set up upon his own score now.' The truth of the prognosis was demonstrated by the story that Charles and his supporting Scotsmen flung their caps in the air with joy upon news of the defeat of Leslie's Presbyterian forces at Dunbar. Cromwell also asked Haselrig for some three or four masons to fortify the places he expected to take. And, added Cromwell, constantly with an eye for detail, 'I think it will be very fit that you should bake hard bread again, considering you increase our numbers.'[1]

The taking of Edinburgh Castle was no easy task. Mining proved ineffective because of the hardness of the rock upon which it was built and Cromwell sent for heavy guns from England. Meanwhile, 'because I am at some reasonable good leisure', as he wrote, he indulged in a series of remarkable exchanges with Walter Dundas, the Governor of the Castle. When Dundas regretted that men of civil employment should preach, Cromwell asked, 'Are you troubled that Christ is preached?'

Is preaching so inclusive in your function? ... Is it against the Covenant? Away with the Covenant, if this be so! ...

Approbation, he says,

is an act of conveniency in respect of order, not of necessity ...

200

Your pretended fear lest error should step in, is like the man who would keep all the wine out of the country lest men should be drunk. It will be found an unjust and unwise jealousy, to deny a man the liberty he has by nature upon a supposition he may abuse it. When he doth abuse it, judge,

He was particularly annoyed by an assertion made by Dundas on September 9. They had been discussing the manifestations of Providence, in which Cromwell so devoutly believed, when Dundas wrote that the Scottish Presbyterians 'have not so learned Christ as to hang the equity of their cause upon events'. 'We could wish', exclaimed Cromwell in reply

blindness hath not been upon your eyes to all those marvellous dispensations which God hath wrought lately in England. But did not you solemnly appeal and pray? Did not we do so too? And ought not you and we to think, with fear and trembling, of the hand of the Great God in this mighty and strange appearance of His; but can slightly call it an 'event'! Were not both yours and our expectations renewed from time to time, whilst we waited upon God, to see which way He would manifest Himself upon our appeals? And shall we, after all these our prayers, fastings, tears, expectations, and solemn appeals, call these bare events?

Oliver never put his belief in the justification of actions by results more clearly than in this remarkable communication sent in the middle of a military campaign to a military opponent at whom he might well be directing his arms the next day. It was accompanied by an equally remarkable set of queries including that which asked whether the Scots had not been in error in making the Covenant 'which, in the main intention, was spiritual, to serve politics and carnal ends?' and whether their religion required 'such carnal politics, such fleshly mixtures, such unsincere actings as to pretend to cry down all malignants, and yet to receive and set up the Head of them [i.e. Charles Stuart] and so act for the Kingdom of Christ in his name?'[2]

The exchange with Dundas illustrates the extraordinary make-up of Oliver, pouring out his soul in theological argument in the middle of a battle campaign as if his only desire was to convert the Scotsman. Even though the composition of the letters was sometimes dreadful, 'the meaning struggling, like a strong swimmer, in an element very viscous',[3] the intention was always apparent.

Cromwell formally summoned Edinburgh Castle on 12 December 1650. It surrendered peaceably on December 24. If it had not done so, Cromwell wrote to the Speaker of the English Parliament, much blood would have been spilt, for it was very strongly defended and the army would have been tied up for a considerable time. It was not any skill or wisdom of theirs but 'the good hand of God' that had given them the place. It looked as though Cromwell's point had been made; and it almost seemed that Cromwell's arguments had influenced Dundas for there was certainly no shortage of defensive weapons in the castle. The brass ordnance, arms and ammunition it contained amazed Cromwell.

Winter quarters for Cromwell and his staff were in the Earl of Murray's house in the Canongate in Edinburgh and Cromwell spent a great deal of time in continuing his arguments with the Scottish Kirk, much as Charles I had done during his sojourn in the Scottish camp in 1644. Cromwell had opportunity enough to observe the inhabitants at close quarters. 'I thought I should have found in Scotland', he wrote to the Council of State from Edinburgh on September 25, 'a conscientious people, and a barren country; about Edinburgh it is as fertile for corn as any part of England, but the people generally given to the most impudent lying, and frequent swearing as is incredible to be believed.'[4]

He was by no means isolated in Edinburgh. Directives from Parliament, and documents to sign, poured in. He began to use John Thurloe as a personal agent to gather intelligence for him. Links with home and family were established. Letters from his wife reached him. One, dated 27 December 1650, indicated that he had not failed to write to her, though not as often as she would have liked:

> My Dearest,
> I wonder you should blame me for writing no oftener, when I have sent three for one . . .
> I should rejoice to hear your desire in seeing me, but I desire to submit to the Providence of God; hoping the Lord, who hath separated us, and hath often brought us together again, will in His good time bring us again, to the praise of His name . . . Truly my life is but half a life in your absence . . .[5]

In February 1651 Thomas Simon, the medallist who had already struck several medals and seals including the two Great Seals of the Commonwealth, arrived in Edinburgh on the instructions of the

Committee of the Army in London to take the likeness of Oliver for a commemorative medal of the battle of Dunbar. A picture of Parliament was to figure on one side and a portrait of Cromwell on the other – which indicated a very fair apportionment of the credit. Cromwell was touched and flattered but modestly protested. 'It was not a little wonder to me to see that you should send Mr Symonds so great a journey, about a business importing so little, as far as it relates to me . . .' He approved the idea of Parliament being represented on one side but suggested that instead of his head there should be engraved on the reverse an army with the inscription over it *The Lord of Hosts*, which was their battle cry on that victorious day. 'I most earnestly beseech you', he said, 'if I may do it without offence, that it may be so.' And, to make his wishes quite clear, 'it will be very thankfully acknowledged by me', he said, 'if you will spare the having my effigies in it'. Whatever the Army Committee thought of Cromwell's proposal they would not abandon their original idea and Cromwell allowed Simon to proceed with the work which, indeed, gave him great satisfaction. '. . . the man is ingenious', he wrote with enthusiasm, 'and worthy of encouragement', and he recommended that he be appointed to the place that Nicholas Briot formerly held under Charles I.[6] Simon, for his part, tried to please Cromwell by depicting both a small battle scene and the battle cry on the medal as well as Cromwell's head in profile. It was a nice gesture but the head alone, or the head with just the words round it, would have been more effective.

For much of the life of the Rump Cromwell was absent. He did not see the Parliament at first hand though contacts were made, letters and reports reached him, and leading Members of Parliament made the long journey northwards to consult him on one thing or another. Thomas Scot, for example, braved the winter snows of 1650 and reached him in December picking up Haselrig from his northern Empire on the way; he had been specially briefed by Challoner to speak to Cromwell of trade and the sea where lay 'our main business now.'[7]

Among others who arrived in Edinburgh to see Cromwell were delegates from Oxford University to request him to become their Chancellor, a position held by Archbishop Laud in the far-off days before the wars and, more recently, by the Earl of Pembroke who had just died. Oxford, the home of the Court, headquarters of the Royalist army during the civil wars, had accepted the Commonwealth early in February 1651 and was offering its highest accolade not to a statesman or churchman but to the country's most successful general. Cromwell accepted the honour with a certain pride and dignity, while pointing out the extent of his other commitments.

> The known esteem and honour of this place is such that I should wrong it and your favour very much, and your freedom in choosing me, if, either by pretended modesty or in any unbenign way, I should dispute the acceptance of it. Only I hope it will not be imputed to me as a neglect towards you, that I cannot serve you in the measure I desire.

Consider my position, he says, and be 'most free to mend your choice'.[8]

Anthony Wood described it as 'a canting letter', but when it was read in Convocation the House resounded with the 'cheerful acclamations' of the Members and Cromwell's appointment was confirmed. He made good use of his position for only ten days later he sought the degree of Doctor from the University for a physician who had rendered good service in Ireland and now wanted to consolidate his professional standing.[9] Three weeks after that he was writing to the Speaker of the House of Commons on behalf of Colonel Robert Lilburne, brother of John but a devoted officer in Cromwell's army, asking for the intervention of the House in securing some property in county Durham.[10] So Oliver, as was customary with him, mixed private and personal affairs with the business of war and the state. And, though his thoughts were turning to the coming campaign, there was still one other project on his mind which was no less than the founding of a College at Durham. 'The Sheriff and Gentlemen' of the county had the previous April petitioned the House of Commons to allow the conversion of some of the buildings of the late Dean and Chapter into a College or School of Literature. The business had lagged and in the spring of 1651 a deputation from Durham rode, not to Westminster, but to the Lord-General at Edinburgh. Cromwell had acquainted himself with the findings of the Committee and on his march northward had been impressed by the magnificent location proposed for the College. To the Committee's findings that the property concerned would 'be a fit place to erect a College or

School for all the Sciences and Literature' and that it would be 'a pious and laudable work and of great use to the Northern parts' he added his supporting voice. The project, he wrote, 'by the blessing of God, may much conduce to the promoting of learning and piety in those poor rude and ignorant parts; there being also many concurring advantages to this place, as pleasantness and aptness of situation, healthful air, and plenty of provisions . . .'[11]

But while reaching out to other enterprises Cromwell never lost sight of his main task. The atrocious weather precluded a major campaign, though a couple of castles were captured and in February Cromwell himself headed an attempt to drive Leslie from Stirling. His little force was driven back and, shortly after, the 'infirmities' of which he had written to his wife after Dunbar took firm hold of him. From February until the end of June he suffered debilitating bouts of fever and ague with three serious relapses when his life was despaired of. The Council of State sent urgently to enquire after his health but on March 18 he was reported to be in his dining room with his officers 'very cheerful and pleasant' though with Dr Goddard in attendance. At the end of the month he even took part in various small sieges. But he was obviously weak and his thoughts were much with his family. A letter to his wife of April 12 reveals all the anxiety of a sick man struggling with physical disability and mental fatigue. To his constant worry over the idle and spendthrift Richard had been added an only partly disclosed anxiety for his daughter Elizabeth (Bettie) Claypole. 'Mind poor Bettie of the Lord's great mercy', he now wrote to his wife:

> Oh, I desire her not only to seek the Lord in her necessity, but in deed and in truth turn to the Lord; and to keep close to Him; and to take heed of a departing heart, and of being cozened with worldly vanities and worldly company, which I doubt she is too subject to. I earnestly and frequently pray for her and for him. Truly they are dear to me, very dear; and I am in fear lest Satan should deceive them – knowing how weak our hearts are, and how subtle the adversary is, and what way the deceiptfulness of our hearts and the vain world make for his temptations. The Lord give them truth of heart to Him. Let them seek him in truth and they shall find Him.

'My love to the dear little ones', he continues, referring to his two youngest children, Mary and Frances, born at Ely, now aged fourteen and thirteen. 'I pray for grace for them. I thank them for their Letters; let me have them often.' Then, on an enigmatic note he counsels his wife to 'Beware of my Lord Herbert, his resort to your house. If he do so, it may occasion scandal, as if I were bargaining with him. Indeed, be wise, you know my meaning.'

Lord Herbert was the son of Lord Glamorgan, now Marquis of Worcester, one of Charles I's most ardent supporters, a large part of whose confiscated lands had been given to Cromwell. Whether Cromwell suspected that Herbert had designs on one of his unmarried daughters as a way of re-acquiring some of his property, whether, as an early annotator of the letter suggests, there was some kind of intrigue between Bettie and Herbert, Cromwell obviously trusted his wife: '. . . be wise, you know my meaning'. He also counsels her to contact Sir Henry Vane and Mr Floyd concerning his estate.

As, wearily, he concludes his letter his thoughts turn once more to his eldest surviving son:

> If Dick Cromwell and his wife be with you, my dear love to them. I pray for them; they shall, God willing, hear from me. I love them very dearly. Truly I am not able as yet to write much. I am wearied; and rest,
>
> Thine[12]

In spite of his weariness Cromwell attended a muster of the army on Musselborough Links on Wednesday April 16 when he was greeted with shouts of welcome and acclaim. He marched to Glasgow, no mean enterprise, where he visited a couple of kirks and called for theological discussions. It was probably when returning to Edinburgh, seeking a guide through desolate country in Lanarkshire, that he came upon the house called Allertoun, the property of Sir Walter Stewart and his family who were open supporters of Charles II. Sir Walter was absent, probably with the young King, but a glass of canary was proferred by his wife which Oliver accepted after offering a long grace which asked for a blessing on the house. He was pleased to say that his mother was a Stewart and in the affable exchanges that took place one of the sons of the house, a backward boy of ten years old, ventured near enough to the great general to handle the hilt of his sword. Oliver stroked the boy's head; 'You are my little Captain', he said. Cromwell and his officers dined at Allertoun, he offered his own wines to the lady and made a long grace of thanks after the meal. It was said that after this episode the Lady Stewart abated much of her zeal for the Royalist cause while the little boy was known throughout his life as the Captain of Allertoun.[13]

But the ride to and from Glasgow had been taxing in the extreme and on his return to Edinburgh Cromwell suffered the most severe of his relapses. High fever shook him, and that he survived was largely through the efforts of his faithful French servant, Duval, who himself became ill and died. Cromwell, when he returned to England, asked his wife to take Duval's family into her service. Parliament, in alarm, sent two of the best physicians in the country to attend Cromwell, at the same time imploring him to return to the kinder climate of England. Fairfax lent his own coach to convey the doctors to Scotland. In his weakness Cromwell's thoughts were again with his family, and while the doctors were still on their way he wrote on May 3 another loving letter to his wife – the simple, loving words of a strong man who needed comfort in his physical weakness – which, again, revealed her as counsellor and guide to the family in her husband's absence; a pillar upon which he knew they could all lean.

> I could not satisfy myself to omit this post, although I have not much to write; yet indeed I love to write to my dear, who is very much in my heart ... The Lord bless all thy good counsel and example to all those about thee ...

He sends his duty to his mother and once again the profligate Richard occupies his thoughts: 'I hope thou wilt have some good opportunity of good advice to him.'[14]

Though some of the wives were now joining their husbands in Scotland – for example Mrs Lambert and Mrs Deane – Mrs Cromwell did not come, in spite of her husband's illness and the fact that she had followed him to Ireland. Ireland might have been different, for Oliver, as Lord-Lieutenant, would have expected a long stay with an official residence in Dublin if other affairs had not called him home. With her family commitments and caring for Oliver's property she would have had little time for travelling and Oliver would not have much cared to see his wife participating in the social life of Edinburgh for which other wives were ordering special clothes from England and France, nor mixing with the Scottish families for whom he had little regard.

Dr Wright and Dr Bates arrived on May 30. Less than a week

later Cromwell was out in his coach but looking, according to one report, old and weary. He himself admitted the severity of the last bout of sickness: 'it was so violent that indeed my nature was not able to bear the weight thereof.' He paid tribute to the two physicians from whom, he wrote, he had 'received much encouragement, and good directions for recovery of health and strength'.[15] But at the end of the year when he was back in London with the Scottish campaign behind him, it was Dr Goddard whom he rewarded with £100 and preferment to the Wardenship of Merton College in Oxford.

The physical hardships of campaigning in Ireland and Scotland, the atrocious weather in both countries, the shortness of the respite between the two campaigns had drained him physically. The frustration of the five months before the battle of Dunbar followed by the elation of victory, the religious and spiritual exchanges with the Scots, the letters, the reports to Westminster, the constant harrying of Parliament for supplies had exhausted him further. There is no evidence to suggest what remedies his physicians prescribed to bring him back to health.

19

'Crowning mercy'

When at last Cromwell was restored to something like his old vigour he found Leslie still so firmly entrenched in Stirling that direct assault was useless. Instead, he mounted an attack across the Firth of Forth sending Lambert into Fife with 4,000 men, protected by the fleet which still patrolled the coast. Lambert wiped out the Scottish force sent against him at Inverkeithing on July 20. Cromwell followed with 14,000 men and marched on Perth which capitulated after a twenty-four hour siege on August 2. Leslie was now cut off from communication with the north of Scotland but Cromwell had left open the route to England down the west coast. To Charles this was a heaven-sent opportunity, for he expected considerable support from English Royalists and Catholics once he was among them. His Scottish followers were divided but many were as impetuous and as ardent for action as the young King himself and by the end of July they were on the move. On August 5 the first contingents were over the border.

Cromwell realized the danger. But he had allowed the situation to develop with his eyes open and was prepared to take what many would consider an audacious and dangerous gamble – not unlike that which had lured Hamilton to defeat in 1648. '... how God succeeded then', he wrote to Parliament on the 4th, 'is not well to be forgotten'. He knew well enough the misgivings and the fear which would be aroused in Parliament and people by a Royalist army once more on English soil and he took pains to justify his strategy: his army could not stand another winter in Scotland; if the Scottish army could not be engaged successfully in Scotland then battle must be joined elsewhere. It was now or never; '... if some issue were not put to this business, it would occasion another winter's war', he wrote to Parliament, 'to the ruin of your soldiery, for whom the Scots are too hard in respect of enduring the winter difficulties of this country.' He reckoned that the Royalist army was three days' march ahead of him and he begged Parliament to raise what forces it could to check the young King's advance until their army could catch up with him.[1]

So Cromwell staked all upon an enterprise which was fraught with as dangerous consequences as anything he had yet undertaken. For there was no certainty of the reaction of the English people when they found the young Charles Stuart among them and his marching army might be halfway through England, recruiting as it went, before Cromwell could overtake it. And, once it was in England, its victory or its annihilation were the only possible alternatives. It was win or lose all. Perhaps there was, after all, something of the gambler in Cromwell – the same instinct that had induced him to push forward the Self-Denying Ordinance that might have ended his military career. Or perhaps it was only a way of appealing to the Lord to judge between them.

Oliver left Monck to control Scotland, he sent Lambert and most of the cavalry in direct pursuit of the King, sent Harrison forward by the east coast route to outflank him, and himself followed with the rest of the horse and with the infantry, starting from Leith on the 6th, crossing the border on the east side, marching through Northumberland, Durham and into Yorkshire. Charles, having passed through Carlisle, was marching along the Welsh border, where he hoped to gather support, elated to be on English soil, perhaps pausing to remember that his father had pursued this very route in reverse after Naseby.

But it was Cromwell, not Charles, who gathered support on the march southward. Charles's approach savoured too much of an invasion. Although discipline was tight Presbyterians in England found they were more afraid of a cavalier than of an Independent. Local militia responded to Parliament's call to arms. People like Fairfax who would not have crossed the border to fight in Scotland regarded the situation quite differently when a Scottish army had invaded England. The populace as a whole wanted peace not war and Cromwell seemed more likely than Charles Stuart to provide it. A few ardent Royalists came in to the young King under the banner of the Earl of Derby but Lambert and Harrison had joined forces on the 15th near Warrington and while they followed the King southward Cromwell ordered one of their commanders, Colonel

Robert Lilburne, to remain in Lancashire to deal with Derby and his little band. This Lilburne did effectively at Wigan on August 25. Three days before that Charles had reached Worcester, the only city that had opened its gates to him and offered rest to his sorely fatigued army. But Cromwell was steadily advancing – York, Nottingham, Coventry, Stratford – the names were a death knell to Charles's hopes. On the 24th Cromwell joined Lambert and Harrison at Warwick. Here he found more old friends and comrades – Fleetwood, Desborough, Lord Grey of Groby – all assuring him of the support of the Midlands and of the South, which, indeed, was manifest by the numbers of local militia men responding to the call to protect their homes. On the 27th, when Cromwell took up his headquarters at Evesham, he had some 28,000 men under his command. He was not far from Powicke Bridge where a mere handful of men had met in the first skirmish of the civil war; nor from Edgehill, scene of the bloody encounter that ushered in nine years of internecine strife. The coming battle would be the last. One way or the other the struggle would be over.

With superior numbers Cromwell had no hesitation in sending Lambert and Fleetwod across the river Severn to cut off Worcester from Wales to the west and from Gloucester and Bristol to the south. Another division, of which Cromwell was the head, barred the way to London. These dispensations made, Cromwell's strategy was straightforward. The river Severn flows south from Worcester into the Severn estuary and is joined to the west, some two miles below the town, by the river Teme, the two rivers thus forming a virtual right angle. Just north of the Teme, on the west side of Severn and within this right angle Charles had posted a Scottish force, the rest of his small army being either in the town or to the north. On September 3, the anniversary of Dunbar, Cromwell threw a bridge of boats across the Severn from the east side just above the Teme, thus taking the Scots on their flank, while Fleetwood threw another bridge of boats northwards over the Teme thus taking them frontally. Cromwell was at the forefront of the ensuing attack. 'We beat the enemy from hedge to hedge', he wrote, 'until we beat him into Worcester.'

Charles with his Council of War was watching from the tower of Worcester Cathedral, and seeing Cromwell's main army in pursuit on the west side of the Severn he himself led the bulk of his army, some 14,000 strong, on to the east side of the river in order to attack Cromwell's reserve. Cromwell hurriedly re-crossed the Severn by

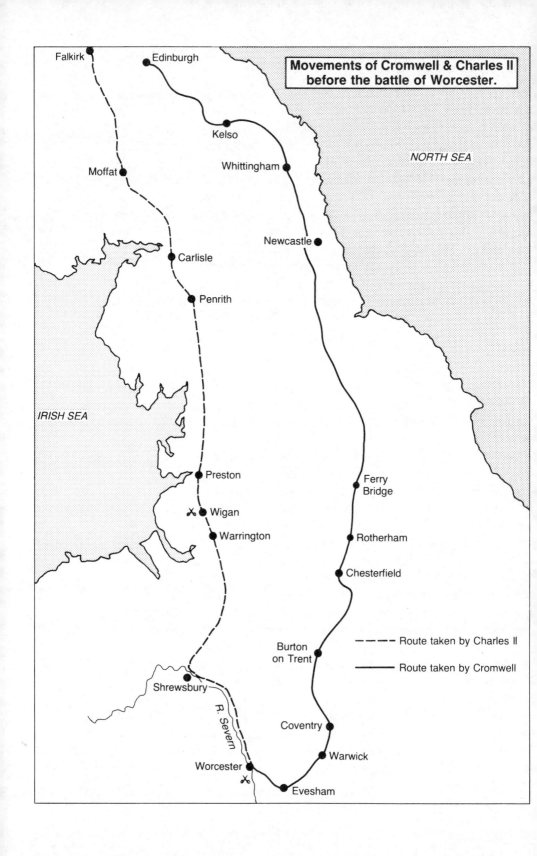

Movements of Cromwell & Charles II before the battle of Worcester.

Falkirk
Edinburgh
Kelso
NORTH SEA
Whittingham
Moffat
Newcastle
Carlisle
Penrith
IRISH SEA
Preston
Ferry Bridge
Wigan
Rotherham
Warrington
Chesterfield
Burton on Trent
Coventry
Shrewsbury
R. Severn
Warwick
Worcester
Evesham

- - - - - Route taken by Charles II
——— Route taken by Cromwell

his bridge of boats with about half his army and the two forces, equally matched in numbers, met in furious combat, often at push of pike, which lasted for some three hours. At last, as Cromwell reported, there came the 'total defeat and ruin of the enemy's army; and a possession of the town, our men entering at the enemy's heels and fighting with them in the streets with very great courage.'[2] Here, again, Cromwell was to the fore. 'My Lord General did exceedingly hazard himself', wrote one of his men, 'riding up and down in the midst of the fire; riding himself in person to the enemy's foot to offer them quarter, wherein they returned no answer but shot.'[3] Cromwell, more than anyone else, knew what had been staked upon this battle. Neither he nor his men thought about it, but it was Old Noll in his last battle. And he did them proud.

It was 'a stiff business', he wrote to Parliament, 'yet I do not think we lost two-hundred men.' Of Charles's army, 6–7,000 were taken prisoner, including many high-ranking officers and Scottish nobility, the most important of whom were sent to London for trial. The Duke of Hamilton died of a broken thigh. Of the thousands of horse and foot who escaped towards Scotland few reached home for they were intercepted by Cromwell's men or by local people. The King was one of the few who escaped, finding a touching loyalty or an unwillingness to betray him among people of many ranks and callings, in spite of Parliament's offer of a reward of £1,000 for the King's person or the threat of high treason against any who helped him. Charles reached France via Brighton on October 22. Meanwhile the clearing of Worcester of its carnage of horses and men continued, men were routed out from their hiding places, hundreds were penned up in the Cathedral.

In his second letter to the Speaker after the battle of Worcester Cromwell specially signalled out the local levies for praise. They had amounted to about 8,000 men, nearly a third of his whole army and 'did perform singular good service; for which they deserve a very high estimation and acknowledgment, as also for their willingness thereunto, forasmuch as the same hath added so much to the reputation of your affairs.'[4] It was certainly of great importance to the Commonwealth that it could call upon local support in time of crisis. The men were immediately sent home after the battle. It had been Charles's weakness that he sought to gain the Crown with the support of an invading army. Nothing could have done more to bring out the local levies in support of their homes and families, as they had done time and again, generation after generation. Not only Cromwell but others were high in their praise. Hugh Peters waxed lyrical in Shakespearean style: 'When your wives and chidren shall ask you where you have been, and what news: say you have been at Worcester, where England's sorrows began, and where they are happily ended.'⁵

Cromwell wrote to the Speaker a brief note at 10 o'clock in the evening after the victory 'being very weary and scarce able to write' but pointing out that it was the anniversary of the victory of Dunbar. He wrote more fully the following day concluding 'the dimensions of this mercy are above my thoughts. It is, for aught I know, a crowning mercy.'⁶

There was no long break this time before his return to London. He sent to the Speaker a hundred enemy colours and came from Worcester through Evesham and Chipping Norton towards Aylesbury where on Thursday September 12, little more than a week after the battle, he was met by Bulstrode Whitelocke, St John, Pickering, and Lister, carrying messages of greeting and congratulation from the Parliament. He relaxed a little with his favourite sport, riding across the fields with a few friends for hawking provided by Mr Winwood, the Member of Parliament for Windsor. They dined that night at Aylesbury, a happy and informal little party, where Cromwell gave each of his friends a horse and a Scottish prisoner. The next day, the 15th, Cromwell rode into London to an enthusiastic and noisy welcome from Members of Parliament headed by the Speaker, by the President and members of the Council of State, by sheriffs, mayors, multitudes of ordinary people 'splitting the welkin with their human shoutings' and volleys of shot, great and small. Parliament voted him lands to the value of £4,000 a year, in addition to those he already held, and begged him to take a residence near to London where he might rest and at the same time attend to public business. Hampton Court was the chosen place.⁷ Whether he would rest was another matter.

Meantime the news from Scotland was good. Stirling Castle had surrendered to Monck on August 14. Dundee had been taken after a ten days' siege followed by a savage massacre of the commander and 800 of the garrison which was as bloody and as pointless as the carnage at Drogheda and Wexford two years earlier. But thoughts were mostly on Cromwell and Worcester, and the Sunday after the victorious general's return sermons of thanksgiving were preached at the churches and Cromwell's letters read from the pulpits. In the euphoria of victory it could be assumed that all would be well and that the peace and plenty, the justice and security for which they had fought would flow down like a mighty stream to refresh the war-weary land. It was some time later that Milton warned Cromwell that 'peace hath her victories no less than war', but even before that Cromwell knew that the struggle was by no means over but had merely changed its form.

For more than ten years he had been a soldier. In that decade he had become the finest soldier in Europe, and was recognized as such. Yet he did not begin soldiering until he was forty-one years old, when most military men were well on the ladder of preferment, and he was then completely untrained and with no experience of war. He began as Captain of a troop of horse, rose to be Colonel of a regiment, Lieutenant-General to the army of the Eastern Association, and finally to total command of the Parliamentarian armies. From the outset he saw the need for discriminating recruitment and enlisted the type of soldier and officer who would go the whole way with him – the 'men of a spirit' who knew what they fought for and loved what they knew. As time passed the recruitment necessarily became wider but by that time the leavening process had done its work.

He showed a gift for organization, insisted upon adequate supply, whether in the form of money to pay his men, of supporting ships for his enterprises, of arms, ammunition, clothing. Above all, he saw the need for strict discipline as every man who served under him was well aware. He never allowed slackness in his men, regular drill kept them in tip-top condition, the continuing care of their horses, upon which he insisted, provided mounts upon which they could rely.

In the tactics of battle he excelled – not through any theoretical training in the art of war but through observation and experience working rapidly on a quick mind naturally attuned to the problems involved. He was quick to perceive the enemy's weakness. His eye, used to travelling over the expanses of his native country, rapidly registered the salient points of the terrain, taking into account such features, typical of the English countryside, as enclosed lands, narrow

215

twisting lanes, and even the furze and rabbit warrens of the hillsides
He mastered the use of cavalry and if in any one sphere he wa
pre-eminent it was in that of cavalry commander. No longer wer
there the shock tactics of Prince Rupert, carrying his horses far beyon
the field of battle where the animals were too exhausted for immediat
return. Instead, even in the flush of victory, he would withdra\
his men from the pursuit and send them in such direction as hi
quick eye perceived to be the vital point of enemy weakness. Quit
often this was a flank attack. He insisted on tight formation in attack
his men riding knee to knee as they charged. He taught them to
preserve their horses. Their pace was probably less than that o
Rupert's horse but they gained in cohesion and, unlike Rupert'
cavalry, could make another charge the same day.

These tactics necessitated a complete rapport with and contro
over his men in which his strict discipline and regular drill bore fruit
They trusted him completely and explicitly, they believed in him
Moreover, he shared the hardships of long, monotonous, difficul
campaigning with them, as well as the exhilaration of victory. Hi
bed was, as often as not, the same cold, wet, inhospitable groun
as theirs; he also had to fight against appalling weather, to suffe
shortness of supplies, to succumb to illness. But overall his certainty
that the Lord was with him conveyed itself to his men. They gav
him absolute obedience and on the field of battle there was neve
any hesitation among Cromwell's troops.

Somehow the trust, the command, the achievement, had now
to be utilized to win the peace.

Part VII

'Peace hath her victories no less than war'

20

England

In spite of sobering reflections the country as a whole was more
flourishing than might have been expected after nine years of civil
war. The population remained steady at about 5,500,000 people most
of whom were dependent in one way or another upon the land.
The destruction and neglect of the civil wars appeared to have left
no deeper scars than those occasioned by years of bad harvests and
to have had rather less effect than the enclosures of the previous
century. The uncertainties of land ownership provided the bigger
problem. Confiscation, compounding, sales; the breaking up of big
estates, the scramble for the spoils; small estates growing bigger in
the hands of thrifty owners; commercial wealth brought in to redress
the balance of decay; and an orgy of speculation by men who knew
how to take advantage of the volatile land market. There were still
many estates, many big and flourishing landowners, many survivors
from the early days of the Long Parliament who had known how
to protect their class by the abolition of the Court of Wards, the
ending of old feudal obligations, by the reform of law relating to
family settlements.

When Cromwell returned from the wars he found himself one
of these landowners of considerable size, though not among the lar-
gest. Even before Worcester his victories had been commemorated
in large tracts of confiscated land – some of the Herbert possessions
which had so munificently filled the coffers of Charles I now raised
the standard of living of the Cromwell family. As a humble soldier
and Member of Parliament Cromwell had invested in Irish lands
and as Lord-Lieutenant of Ireland he had acquired more, and he
still farmed at Ely. His income from the state in money was also
quite considerable with his pay and allowances as Lieutenant-General
and as Lord-Lieutenant of Ireland.

In trade and commerce his interest was less personal, though in common with other members of his class they affected him through family and friends and he had no doubts as to their importance to the country as a whole. The dislocation resulting from the wars had almost righted itself. Overseas trade, in particular, was growing. An observer, a Venetian envoy who described himself as 'the first who has been in London since the abolition of the royal authority', wrote of 'the copious and flourishing trade of London'. 'Ships frequent it in such numbers', he said, 'that on my arrival more than 2,000 were counted up and down the famous river Thames.'[1] Cromwell, like Charles I, could look down upon a veritable forest of masts clustered in the Pool of London, though without the innate enthusiasm for the ships themselves shown by Charles and his family. Cromwell was a land man: even his admirals were 'Generals at Sea'. But he could appreciate well enough the trade, the employment and the successful warfare reflected in his ships. He would have seen a not dissimilar sight in Bristol whose trade with the American and West Indian Plantations was increasing by leaps and bounds. For the Plantations were developing rapidly as sources of raw material and recipients of English manufactured goods, while the growth of the imports of tobacco and sugar was reflected in the rapidly growing re-export trade to Europe which was opening up after the end of the Thirty Years War. Of rising importance, also, was trade to India and the East Indies whose luxury goods like silks and spices flowed into the Commonwealth as they had done into the Court of Charles I. Less glamorous but basically more important was the Northern trade to the Baltic where timber, pitch, resin, tar and other raw materials of ship-building were obtained, while trade with the more distant Russian Empire brought back luxury furs and animal skins. The willingness of Englishmen to venture capital in such overseas enterprise signalled confidence and a growing prosperity. Whatever its shortcomings there was a strong enough interest in the Rump to ensure that commercial affairs were not neglected. Under the influence of Thomas Chaloner a new Council of Trade was established in August 1650, and he had urged Scot, who had visited Cromwell in Scotland in December, to emphasize its importance.[2] All in all, as the Venetian envoy wrote to his employers, 'the facility with which the English increase their fortunes by trade ... has made great strides for some time past.'[3]

Of the manufactures which lay behind this trade the most important was woollen cloth, particularly broadcloth, which constituted some eighty per cent of England's exports and whose prime market was Europe. Woollen merchants had complained bitterly during the wars of the loss of trade and production yet a few years later the export of cloth was described as the 'chiefe and first' of our exports. Tin and pewter, iron and coal, leather for shoes, worsted stockings, added to the extensive export trade while a diversification into the lighter 'new draperies' enabled the cloth export to expand in areas for which broadcloth was too heavy.

This was the not unfavourable commercial and industrial situation which Cromwell found on his return from Worcester. He had been away from England for well over two years with the exception of a short break of barely a month between the Irish and the Scottish campaigns. He left for Ireland five months after the execution of the King, a month after the establishment of the Commonwealth. No one was more aware than he of the unfinished business he left behind, and his hesitation in accepting the Irish command witnessed to his reluctance to leave England at this time. Before his departure a Council of State had been established, several leading Royalists had been executed, the Levellers had been suppressed, the Diggers gently immunized. A new Treason Act, in whose first and second Readings Cromwell had participated, had been passed on 14 May 1649, which included the provision that it was treason for a civilian to stir up mutiny in the army; fresh restrictions on the press were being instituted. He suffered the exasperation of yet another diatribe from Lilburne – *The Legal Fundamental Liberties*: would no prison bars, no press restrictions, restrain the flow of words? It seemed not. Cromwell was not in the country to be forced to stomach Lilburne's *Impeachement of High Treason* against himself and Ireton which issued from the Tower on August 10, nor the highly seditious *Outcry of Young Men and Apprentices*, clearly not the work of apprentices, which appeared three weeks later. He was not in London to witness either Lilburne's trial at Guildhall under the new Treason Act or his triumphal acquittal. Far away in the South of Ireland before Wexford he did not hear the shouts of triumph which greeted the verdict of Not Guilty. It is doubtful whether he would have countenanced Lilburne's consequent liberation on November 8.

Imprisonment for debt and the harsh conditions imposed upon such prisoners had always weighed heavily with Cromwell. He had spoken of these matters in his despatches and the Act of 4 September

1649 was under his influence. So was the Committee appointed in October to consider expenses and delays in the Courts of Justice and to prepare an Act to formulate legal proceedings in English. But legal reform was still sadly lagging on Cromwell's return from the wars and three months later he voted for the appointment of a Commission under the chairmanship of the eminent lawyer Matthew Hale to enquire into 'the mischiefs which grow by delays, the chargeableness and irregularities of the proceedings of the law'. Efforts had also been made in his absence to police the dark little streets of the capital and the no-man's land outside the towns where robbery and crime proliferated. Soldiers were directed to search inns and alehouses and to clear the roads both of impediments and of suspicious persons, but the effect was minimal. In the aftermath of civil war there was too much confusion, too many who were still enemies of the Commonwealth, to make the task possible. Perhaps Cromwell could have put more bite into the operation.

The Act for restricting the press, which had been in preparation before he left for Ireland, became law on 20 September 1649. It required a licence for the publication of any book, pamphlet, treatise, sheet or sheets of news, and differed not markedly from the censorship they had been fighting in the King's time. Did Cromwell's thoughts, as he prepared to leave Dublin for the south, turn to a young man, whipped and pilloried by the Star Chamber, for whose release from prison he had spoken in Parliament seven years earlier? There was also the question of the *Engagement*, modified now so as simply to require loyalty to the Commonwealth, but compulsory on all Members of Parliament and all office holders. Most of the Council of State took the oath, but Fairfax still refused. So did the execrable John Lilburne who had been elected to the Common Council of the City of London after his release from prison and who consequently was debarred from taking his seat, so adding one more grievance to a lengthening list.

Moral issues were not difficult to resolve. The Act for the Observance of the Lord's Day was passed on 19 April 1650 and entailed the seizure of all goods cried or put for sale on the Sabbath, as well as a prohibition against people travelling or innkeepers receiving them on that day. On May 10 incest and adultery were made punishable by death; on June 28 in an Act against Swearing fines were instituted for uttering profane oaths. A proposed Act 'against the vice of painting the face or wearing black patches or immodest dress' failed to gain support. Perhaps even Cromwell's own daughters would have failed to observe it.

On 11 July 1650, when Cromwell was approaching Scotland, the important Act for Settling the Militia, in whose earlier deliberations he would certainly have participated, at last became law. As formerly, contributions were to come from property-owners but taxation was to be at a higher level than before and specially appointed Commissioners supervised the collections in place of the Lord Lieutenant. Again – shades of Charles I – they would have power of questioning under oath, of levying fines, and imposing imprisonment on those who failed to comply. Moreover, the new Commissioners, for a variety of reasons, big and small, were generally less acceptable than the traditional Lords Lieutenant.

The army as a whole had necessarily to be reduced in numbers and the seventy-three garrisons in England and Wales had to be cut down. Parliament had already ordered a Report and shortly after Cromwell's return took action, when twelve garrisons were abolished, five regiments of foot and three of horse were ordered to be disbanded. For Cromwell it was sad but a measure he was bound to support. In spite of some retrenchment the Commonwealth needed money as badly as Charles I had done. The monthly assessments made on the counties during the war continued though now, after Worcester, they were reduced. Customs duties continued. The excise, considered impossible in the King's time but introduced by Parliament in 1643 had remained a growing source of income from a wide variety of goods. Confiscated Royalist and Church lands, compounding with delinquents, had already provided funds for the civil wars; now Crown lands, the Royal palaces, Royal possessions including Charles's valuable art collections, were sold and the screw tightened on more Royalist and Church property. Continued high taxation when the war was apparently won was understandably a source of unrest.

But nothing remained more difficult of solution than the religious issue upon which so many of them had first engaged. Although Archbishop Laud had been executed in January 1645, the episcopacy which was at the root of their trouble had not been abolished until the autumn of 1646, and it took until the end of the year for the Anglican Prayer Book to be proscribed. The Church was not disestablished and the payment of tythes continued. Some Deans and Chapters Lands had been or were being sold, while attempts to dismantle and tear down churches and cathedrals not only as a matter of principle but for the sale of the lead in their roofs and the objects of value within, were pursued only perfunctorily. Bishops had been ejected from the House of Lords, Ecclesiastical courts abolished, ceremonies forbidden, images defaced. Beyond this any reform had from the beginning been circumscribed by entanglement with the Scots and their Covenant. But Presbyterianism had never been fully accepted by the Westminster Assembly of Divines nor by large sections of the population nor, notably, by most of the army. The Directory of Public Worship issued in place of the Anglican Prayer Book won little support. And when a form of Presbyterianism was established in England in June 1646 ultimate authority rested still with Parliament and not with the Presbyters: 'a lame Erastian Presbytery' the Scots called it.

Cromwell's pleas in his despatches from Dundee, Naseby and elsewhere for the regard of tender consciences was in accord with so much general feeling that in September 1650 while he was in Scotland an Act for the Relief of Religious and Peaceable People was passed by Parliament. It repealed the Elizabethan Act of Uniformity and the Act for punishing persons obstinately refusing to come to church, and so made it legal for Independents and, indeed, for Catholics, in fact as it had been in practice, to stay away from church so long as they did not indulge in seditious activites. But the position was neither simple nor easy. How far should or could toleration extend? Cromwell himself cashiered a soldier for declaring 'sin was no sin', and sectarian groups, particularly Fifth Monarchy men and Millenarians, became ever more rabid in their preaching, insisting that the Fifth Monarchy of Christ was about to be established on the ruins of the four earlier kingdoms, and pushing the bounds of toleration beyond the intended limits. Parliament meanwhile made efforts to spread the basic tenets of Christianity to the remoter parts of the country. Their attempts may have been associated with a desire for political stability.[4] If so, the appointment of the militant Monarchist, Major-General Thomas Harrison, to take charge of the scheme for the propagation of the Gospel in Wales, which was already militant enough, was an odd choice.

Equally intransigent were foreign relationships. Catholic France was harbouring Royalists, Catholic Spain, the traditional enemy, was opening its harbours to Prince Rupert and Royalist ships. An alliance with the Dutch Republic, which was a Commonwealth like England, which was Protestant, whose interests in trade and seafaring were similar to our own, would seem to have been straightforward enough. Yet the barrier of regicide stood between. For the King who had been executed was the father of the little Princess of Orange, the wife of William II of Holland, who had been married in London on the eve of the civil wars when she was a shy little girl of nine and he a bright boy of nearly fifteen years old. The childish idyll was destroyed by the events in England but now the Princess Mary was about to bear her first child when her husband fell ill of smallpox and died on 6 November 1650, nine years after their marriage. Their child, a sickly little boy, was born a week later. Not surprisingly there was little personal affection between the House of Orange and the English Commonwealth.

Meanwhile trade and commercial rivalry between the two nations led to conflict. As traders, as carriers and as settlers they had clashed in the East, where the Dutch were first in the East Indies, the English first in India; in the West, where the Dutch, like the English, were settling in America; in the Baltic where both nations sought out and traded in valuable ship supplies like timber, resin, pitch and tar; and on the herring banks where Dutch fishing busses threatened the livelihood of English fisherman. The civil wars had given the Dutch a lead, particularly in establishing supremacy in the carrying trade, and, wisely building upon what they had in common, the Commonwealth, on 14 February 1651, sent a team headed by Oliver St John, now Chief Justice, and Walter Strickland, Ambassador to the States General, to the Hague to negotiate. The discussions were sterile; we were 'rivals for the fairest mistress in the world – trade', as one Member of Parliament put it. Shortly after the return of their envoys the Commonwealth Parliament resorted to legislation in the Navigation Act of 1651 which was introduced in August and became law on November 9, two months after Cromwell's return.

The policy behind the Act of 1651 was centuries old and had been expressed in the first Navigation Act of 1381 which laid down that no merchandise 'going out or coming within the realm of England, in any port' should do so other than in English ships. The Tudor Act of 1485 followed on similar lines. James I in 1622 appointed a Commission instructed to enquire 'how our laws do now stand in force for the prohibition of merchandise to be imported in foreign bottoms'. In 1624 expression was given to their findings in the Act which laid down that tobacco from the colonies should not be carried in foreign ships but only in those of the Plantations or of England. In 1647 Parliament, in the middle of the civil wars, widened the prohibition to include all goods produced in the Plantations. The Commonwealth Act of 1651, while aimed specifically at the Dutch, tried both to codify the existing legislation and to be more specific. It decreed that goods exported from Asia, Africa or America should come to England only in English or colonial ships, and that all goods exported from Europe should come to England, Ireland or the Plantations only in English or colonial ships or ships of the country of origin.

Behind this navigation policy was a Parliament with strong trading interests, as the Venetian Envoy had noted, and the Navigation Acts were part of a policy consciously directed to the furtherance of trade. Like the Stuarts the Commonwealth instructed its Council of Trade to this end and its Directive to its first Council included the provision that it should 'use all good ways and means for the securing, advancement, and encouragement of the trade of England and Ireland and the dominions to them belonging'; while its new Council for Trade, set up in August 1650, while Cromwell was in Scotland, was instructed to consider 'how the commodities of this land may be vented to the best advantage thereof into foreign countries'.[5] The Commonwealth Government may have differed in many respects from that of Charles I but in its trading interests it was at one with the defeated King. That representative of a line of astute observers, the Venetian Envoy, again informed his masters in June 1651: the 'government of the Commonwealth and that of its trade' were 'exercised by the same individuals'.[6]

Ideologies also played their part in Anglo-Dutch rivalry. Charles I had been concerned to uphold the concept of *mare clausum* which John Selden had enunciated in 1619. This claimed British sovereignty in the seas over, roughly, the whole of the North Sea, the English Channel, the Bay of Biscay, and unspecified stretches of ocean north and westward. Sovereignty comprised the exaction of tribute for the rights to fish in these waters, and was expressed by requiring ships of other nations to lower their topsail and their flag when encountering an English vessel. The situation was naturally resented by the high-spirited Dutch and eight months after Cromwell's return from Worcester war broke out between England and Holland. The spark that turned skirmishing into open war was struck in the English Channel when on 19 May 1652 the Dutch Admiral Van Tromp encountered Admiral Blake and refused to dip his flag or lower his topsail.

The Commonwealth's experience of naval warfare was slight. Ships had played an important supporting role in Cromwell's Irish and Scottish campaigns, Major-General Deane and Major-General Robert Blake were Admirals of outstanding skill and courage. They had operated successfully against Royalists in the Scilly Isles and Jersey; in the Mediterranean they had skirmished with Prince Rupert, with French merchantmen, and with the pirates of the North African coast. Now, with the energetic and devoted Vane in charge of the Navy Office, they added thirty merchant ships permanently to the fleet and embarked on a building programme which would provide fifty new ships larger and with heavier guns than those already in use. The number of sailors was still not adequate and impressment continued, but attractive prize money, including £10 for every gun captured, improved morale. When, apart from this fleet, a squadron was specially raised to police the trade routes, more money was needed. The Act for Securing Trade of 31 October 1650 had added fifteen per cent to the customs duties for the specific purpose of providing men-of-war to protect merchantmen. Did the words 'ship money' form on anyone's lips? It was not an exact parallel but close enough for comment while the overt linking of trade and sea-power indicated exactly where the Commonwealth stood. Cromwell himself was sufficiently a man of his time to feel strongly the importance of trade and commerce to his country. His own party had been active both before and during the wars in exploiting the New World and he himself had served on committees and commissions for trade in general and the Plantations of America and the West Indies in particular. When war with the Dutch became open eight months after his return from Worcester he was sorry that a possible Protestant alliance had broken down and would do all he could to restore peace, but nevertheless he regarded the conflict as a commercial necessity. He was undoubtedly pulled several ways: the cost of a war with consequent higher taxation would not help the Commonwealth, the country as a whole needed peace, entrenchment, stability. On the other hand the Dutch ruling classes were more inclined to Presbyterianism than he could wish and he knew that many English sectarians supported the war for this reason. And he had to consider that a successful naval war, that would not be fought over the English countryside, might give the Commonwealth a boost and consolidate its position in the eyes of Europe.

Similarly Parliament and the Council of State had some reservations and even Vane, in spite of his enthusiastic work with the navy, had his doubts. When the Dutch Ambassador left for home there was a feeling of nakedness and some disquiet.[7]

Before the year 1651 was out there came tragic news from Ireland. Henry Ireton had died at Limerick on November 26 of overwork, exposure and fever in the taxing and inclement Irish countryside. He was buried in pomp and honour in London and a fitting settlement made to his wife. Ludlow, who was already in Ireland, took over temporarily as Lord Deputy but it was Major-General Lambert who was appointed to the post on 30 January 1652. Lambert who, as well as being a valiant soldier, had much of the courtier in him, occupied himself with the clothes and furbishments that he considered necessary to his new style. Lady Lambert who, even in Edinburgh, as a Major-General's wife, had paid much attention to her appearance, was even more anxious to deck herself in a style becoming the Lord Deputy's wife. According to report she became so insolent in her new dignity that she claimed precedence over Bridget, Ireton's widow and Cromwell's daughter. But the office of Lord-Lieutenant was abolished – not at Cromwell's instigation but by Parliament after a straightforward assessment of the financial situation. Lambert was offered a subordinate position which he declined. Bridget, on June 8, married Major-General Fleetwood, whose wife had died shortly after her husband, and Fleetwood accepted the Irish post. Cromwell, sorting out the consequent financial tangle, explained that he had drawn no salary since he left Ireland but had remitted it to Ireton, and Ireton had not always accepted it in full. On Ireton's death it was stopped completely and Cromwell now asked that £2,000 should be paid to Lambert for the expenses he had unnecessarily incurred.

21

'Somewhat of monarchical power'?

The death of Ireton was a tragic loss to Cromwell. He missed him as a friend; he missed his controlling hand in Dublin; above all he needed the political sagacity of his son-in-law to help mould a constitutional settlement in England that would complement his military victories. The Rump of the Long Parliament had ably supplied the needs of the armies in Ireland and Scotland, the Navigation Act stood to their credit, their concern with trade and a Council of Trade was evident. But these activities touched their personal interests closely. Constitutionally it was a mere rump of the Long Parliament lumbering on with periodic refurbishment in the form of recruitment to seats that fell vacant, and its executive Council of State appointed by and from itself. There were good men in its ranks: Sir Henry Vane the younger who had done sound work with the navy in spite of suspicions that he was also feathering his own nest; Bulstrode Whitelocke and Sir Thomas Widdrington, Keepers of the Great Seal, sound, probably honest, somewhat timorous; Sir Harry Marten, too volatile for hard committee work but with a reforming zeal that took him to the fringes of the Leveller party. There were men distinguished in their own right like Sir James Harrington, Lord Herbert, Algernon Sidney, Francis Rous, Walter Strickland, envoy to the Netherlands; there were too many vigorous Presbyterians like Sir Arthur Haselrig and like the less assertive Speaker, William Lenthall; but family and friends of Cromwell like Valentine Walton and Oliver St John were effective counterweights. There were too many lawyers in the Rump, which helped to account for its inertia when legal reform was considered. Even with the merchant interest typified by Thomas Chaloner they did not outnumber the rural Members but they were better organized and more influential. But it was often difficult to disentangle a man's interest: landowners with trading connections, merchants who had speculated in land, lawyers connected by family and other ties with land and trade. The military Members of Parliament who might have tipped the scale towards reform were absent on duty for long periods – Cromwell himself, Charles Fleetwood, Nathaniel Rich, Thomas Harrison. Their absence also weighted the scale heavily in favour of the Presbyterians in the House.

Overall it was a body singularly free of any authority outside itself; no monarch, no House of Lords, the army occupied elsewhere, a substantial weight of legal authority within its own ranks. It was not significantly challenged until the army returned after Worcester. But it had responded admirably to the demands of that army and might have expected appreciation if not gratitude. But as a Parliament it was, after Worcester, old and tired. It met normally for only four days in the week and no more than sixty or seventy Members normally attended from whom it was necessary to appoint the Council of State. But the figures fail to take account of the long hours which the most energetic Members spent in Committee nor of its practical achievements in economic matters.[1] But even in the life of a normal government duties of state were liable to pale before the pressing concerns of Members as merchants, landowners, farmers, Justices of the Peace, and family men. In the case of a Parliament which was twelve years old these commitments naturally loomed larger. Such energy as remained to them was employed on their own financial concerns such as land speculation and sale. Recruiters were often men even more prone to speculate in confiscated church or royalist lands. At best, the sense of coherence had gone. Both Vane and Cromwell complained at the difficulty of getting anything done, while over the country as a whole the same old grievances remained: debtors languished, landlords enriched themselves at the expense of their tenants, petty crime and robbery proliferated, the poor and the destitute were not succoured, prisons were full, compensation for war damage was difficult to obtain, legal proceedings were seemingly endless and unnecessarily complicated. The Rump Parliament was not a body with either the muscle or the will to right the familiar aftermath of war. The area in which most had been achieved was the navy, and here the drive, the persistence and the vision had come from one man – Sir Henry Vane. But he had retired in December 1650.

Parliament's gratitude to Cromwell, expressed materially in money and houses as well as property and honour, was dimmed as the danger receded and the god-like General, Jehovah's instrument, was among them again as an ordinary man. They had, after all, managed quite well at Westminster without him. Cromwell's delay in returning from Ireland witnessed to his realization of the advantages of remoteness. But Scotland and Worcester had kept him away long enough: it was a card he could no longer play. He came back with the elation of victory still upon him. Hugh Peter saw it as 'a secret exultation'. Indeed, Jehovah had been so consistently, so manifestly, with him that Cromwell was bound to feel his own power, spilling over now to embrace political, constitutional, social affairs. A man cannot come so far with so much evidence of his own power without chafing at the inadequacies of other men. But, as Clarendon asserted and the Venetian envoy substantiated, Cromwell 'did not find the Parliament so supple and so much to observe his orders as he expected they would have been'.[2] But why should he have expected obedience? For much of the life of the Rump he had been absent, and, in spite of letters, visits, and other contacts while he was away he had not seen the Parliament working at first hand.

He nevertheless topped the list of elections to the Council of State but he still could not be sure of his position nor of what he wanted to do. He lived as quietly as he could in what the Venetian envoy described as 'his unpretending manner of life, remote from all display and pomp. This,' wrote the envoy, 'won him applause, though he was not universally loved'.[3] It no doubt suited his wife who remembered only too well his illness in Scotland and his letters to her; if it was possible to help him back to complete health and strength she was the one to do so. Meantime, although perhaps not universally loved among the Parliament men, he could still count upon the affections and the loyalty of his soldiers.

Cromwell was not a philosopher nor a political theorist like his son-in-law, Ireton. He would not sit long into the night considering the problems of political philosophy. When he did think in general terms, as he had been compelled to in the Army debates at Putney and elsewhere, his philosophy derived from the immediate situation. Similarly now. He had had time during enforced idleness in Scotland, and particularly during his illness, to ponder the general question of government. He realized that all revolutions are about power and he was asking himself who, or what, should exercise that power. He knew, moreover, that whoever or whatever was in control must be strong enough to propel the state in one direction. This he had.

learned from his battle experience. To be successful an army must observe one plan, one directive. It was the very year of Cromwell's return from Worcester that Thomas Hobbes published his *Leviathan*. The state was Leviathan, the greatest creature on sea or land. If it was to go forward it must go 'one way'. Cromwell probably never saw the book – at least not then – though he thought highly enough of the Royalist author to permit his return from exile. But he saw the problem. Leviathan, unless he was to flounder, must go one way. But who was to activate him?

Cromwell went to the heart of the matter and barely a week after his last battle turned his attention to the main instrument of government that would propel the state 'one way' – Parliament itself. On September 18 the Rump Parliament discussed behind closed doors the question of its very existence. A week later, on the 25th, the matter was carried to a division on the motion for a dissolution and a General Election. Cromwell acted as teller for the 'Ayes' who won the motion by 33 votes to 26, and he was one of a committee appointed to draw up a Bill to implement the decision. They worked quickly and a Bill for dissolution was read in the Commons the first time on 8 October 1651. From November 6 onward the House went into committee every day on the subject. On the 14th Cromwell made a long speech. Although the motion for dissolution had been carried the question now was when? Should a date be fixed? Another vote in the House, Cromwell again acting as teller for the Ayes, decided that it should. Finally, and not until November 18, they voted upon the actual date for dissolution and decided it should be fixed for 3 November 1654 – three years hence! The thinness of the House when these important matters were being voted upon indicates the indifference of most Members, while the determination of the few to cling on to power is apparent in the remote date secured for dissolution.

Nevertheless when voting for the new Council of State was taken shortly afterwards – it was installed on December 1 – Cromwell's name again headed the list. With this authority behind he called a meeting early in the month of several MPs and officers of the army. He put it to them bluntly that with the old King dead and his son defeated it was high time they came to a settlement. We must consider, he said, 'whether a Republic, or a mixed Monarchical Government will be best to be settled. And if anything Monarchical, then, in whom that power shall be placed?'

It was a distinguished gathering: Speaker Lenthall, at whose house the meeting was held; lawyers including Chief Justice St John and the Keepers of the Great Seal, Whitelocke and Widdrington; army officers including Whalley and Desborough, Fleetwood and Harrison; important officers of state like Sir Henry Vane. Among them all Cromwell stood out as the most powerful, not only as a victorious soldier, Lord General of the Army, Lord-Lieutenant of Ireland, Member of the Council of State, Member of Parliament, member of many committees including Ordnance, Irish Affairs, Scottish Affairs, Examinations and Legal Questions, but as a man with longer experience of both Parliament and Army than any man there.

After the usual fulsome remarks from Lenthall and Harrison praising the 'marvellous success' of the forces under Cromwell and 'the mercies which the Lord hath given-in to us', serious discussion began. The soldiers generally were against any settlement smacking of monarchy while the more conservative lawyers favoured a mixed monarchy. Widdrington, St John and Whitelocke thought that a mixed monarchical government was most suited to the laws and the people of England. The government of the nation without something of monarchical power in it would be very difficult without shaking the foundations of our laws and the liberties of our people, said St John. The laws of England are so interwoven with the power and practice of monarchy, asserted Whitelocke, that it would be difficult to consider any other form of government. But Desborough thought it better not to have anything to do with monarchy and asked, 'Why not a Republic like other nations?'

Cromwell listened for a while. When he came in it was to agree that the business was one 'of more than ordinary difficulty'. 'But really I think', he continued, 'if it may be done with safety, and preservation of our Rights, both as Englishmen and as Christians, that a Settlement with somewhat of Monarchical power in it would be very effectual.'[4]

His enigmatic contribution to the discussion summed up Cromwell's position. He was not necessarily thinking of either a Stuart or himself, but simply of steering the state 'one way'. Widdrington had suggested Charles's third son, Henry, as a possible ruler. Cromwell was possibly asking himself whether, if it came to the point, he would have enough confidence in himself and be willing to undertake such a position. No one had suggested or even hinted at it. Those who considered 'something monarchical' as essential had done no more than suggest a hereditary ruler. The officers of his army, his staunchest supporters, were for the most part in favour of some form of a Republic. He must still wait upon the Lord. It had not yet been decided whether the settlement should contain 'something monarchical' in it. Until that question was decided the question of 'who?' must wait. But he continued thinking about it and walking with Whitelocke in the Park a little later the question was blurted out: 'What if one man should take upon him to be King?' The inference was startling.[5]

One of the best things the Rump did in the extended period of life it had given itself was to appoint on 26 December 1651, a Committee to consider law reform. Sir Matthew Hale, a distinguished lawyer, was its chairman and Cromwell was a member. On 19 April 1652, an Act for the Union of England and Scotland was read twice and referred to a Committee on which, again, Cromwell sat. Four months later an Act for the settlement of Ireland was introduced. There were struggles over the attitude to defeated Royalists, Parliament on the whole being more severe than Cromwell and the soldiers intended, often failing to observe the terms of surrender and thus violating the soldiers' honour. Cromwell, even in the middle of the Scottish campaign, had been concerned enough to write to Vane on behalf of Sir John Monson: the army considered the terms given him to be just and had 'so formally recommended to the honourable Speaker'. There must be 'no violation of the public faith', he wrote, 'for the Parliament and army's honours!'[6] Soldiers could be more magnanimous than the stay-at-homes. Cromwell would have extended mercy to the gallant Derby, who had been captured after Wigan.

Parliament was making little effort to conciliate the army or the Independents in its ranks. The Act of 29 April 1652 that continued the payment of tythes was an open affront. So, to a smaller section of the army, was its attitude to John Lilburne.

Lilburne, after a series of private quarrels with Haselrig and others, was banished by Order of Parliament in December 1651 and left the country in January 1652 for the Low Countries. This time Cromwell failed to intervene. In spite of his outburst against him Cromwell had been good to Lilburne. On his return from Ireland, though he had little enough time for private affairs, he had managed to secure a grant of sequestered Deans and Chapters lands for the Leveller leader, which was confirmed on 30 July 1650. Lilburne was grateful and had accompanied him northwards when he marched to Scotland. The two men were on visiting terms and Lilburne waited on him at his house in the Cockpit after Cromwell's victorious return from Worcester. They spoke about Royalist intrigue and the attempts of Royalist agents to implicate Lilburne. Cromwell had believed Lilburne's denials then. Now he was uncertain and made no attempt to mitigate the Order of banishment.[7]

Royalist intrigue was, indeed, rising on the one hand while, on the other, petitions were coming in to the General, the Army and Parliament expressing the same desires and demands they had voiced at the height of Leveller activity. But now sectarianism was stronger and Fifth Monarchy preachers supplied the fire previously generated by Lilburne and his friends. As then, the army was active and on 13 August 1652, the officers presented to the House of Commons a comprehensive petition signed three days earlier whose fourteen points indicated not only what they wanted but what they considered to be the failings of the Parliament. It was a mature and thoughtful document obviously emanating from a responsible section of the soldiers. Its fourteen points covered legal and social matters, including the practical request that gild restrictions be relaxed in order to help disbanded soldiers find work; it asked for taxation and financial reform, including the by now generally accepted request for the consolidation of the revenue into a single treasury and the publication of a national balance sheet, and for the appointment of a committee to report on monopolies, pluralities and excessive salaries. The feeling of social inequality that had imbued the Leveller manifestos was still present.[8]

The petition was addressed to Cromwell and he did not sign it. Whitelocke thought that this indicated that Cromwell was getting others to act for him 'in order ... to prepare a way for him'. This accords with the accusation that had been made in 1647. It is more likely that now, as then, he was waiting upon events. This was further indicated when at the beginning of 1653 he partially withdrew from political affairs. He was rarely in the House of Commons at this time, nor did he attend the Council of State at all between March 8 and April 7. Was he ill? No evidence is available; more likely he was seeking the Lord as he had done so many times before, waiting

Oliver Cromwell

for the momentous decision to take shape, perhaps not even consciously sizing up the situation but waiting passively for something to occur that would impel him in one direction. He knew he had it in his power to overthrow the Rump at any time. The soldiers would support him in this. It was not whether he *could* but whether he *should* or *would*. And there remained the still unresolved question of what should go in its place.

Parliament continued its desultory meetings. The Hale Committee made some good recommendations but none were implemented. Officers' meetings in London became more frequent; they circularized regiments in other parts of the country. Sectarian preachers, particularly from London pulpits, became more vehement; the situation was reminiscent of the tumultuous days before the war. The influence of Major-General Harrison, most fanatical of Fifth Monarchy officers, was emphasized by his connection with influential sectaries like Christopher Feake, who was preaching from the pulpit of St Anne's in London and drawing huge and excited crowds, and by his friendship with Vavaser Powell, Morgan Llwyd and other Fifth Monarchy men in Wales. When Harrison was appointed to serve on the Council for the Propagation of the Gospel in Wales his influence was enhanced. He was pushing Cromwell hard. Cromwell complained as much to Ludlow. Harrison 'is an honest man', he said, 'and aims at good things, yet from the impatience of his spirit will not wait the Lord's leisure, but harries me on to that which he and all honest men will have cause to regret.'[9]

The Lord had not yet spoken to Cromwell, but the soldiers began openly to demand a new Representative. This was going too fast and at the beginning of April Cromwell sent a regiment of the most vocal to Scotland, out of the way. And when it was rumoured that the Council of Officers would eject the Parliament Cromwell pertinently asked: By what authority? If they destroyed Parliament in whose name would they be acting? What, he said, would they call themselves, for 'a state they could not be' – by which, presumably, he meant that they had no elected authority behind them. When they said they would call a new Parliament Cromwell was equally emphatic. If you do that, he said, 'the Parliament is not the supreme power but that is the supreme power that calls it'.[10] Clearly he was much concerned with the principles as well as the realities of power and shunned any form of dictatorship, particularly a military dictatorship. He was wrestling with concepts of political obligation with which he was unfamiliar and this in itself accounts for his dilatoriness in taking action against the Rump. If Ireton had been with him it could have been different. As it was he temporarily withdrew from action and sought the Lord.

Royalist news-letters made much of the situation, gleefully linking the army with the Fifth Monarchists: 'Our preaching people rant it very high against the Parliament ... the Army is now higher than ever against the house and are resolved very speedily to pull them downe.' Cromwell was playing the hypocrite. Though he seemed to dislike the army's activity he was 'a great stickler among them'. He protested to the House, with weeping eyes, that he would as willingly hazard his life 'against any whatever that should profess themselves their enemys. Yet most of them know, he hath tears at will and can dispense with any Oath or Protestation without troubling his conscience'.[11] It was 1647 over again!

Parliament could not shut its ears to the common talk and reactivated the Committee considering the Bill for a New Representative. It was suggested either that those Members ejected at Pride's Purge be recalled or that fresh 'recruiter' elections be held to fill vacancies. Vane, who was in charge of the Committee, favoured recruitment. Harrison and some of the officer members were for government by 'moral and religious men', though whether appointed or elected, and if so by what method was not clear. Lambert and other officers favoured full new Parliamentary elections. Outside the house the preachers were openly praying for a new Representative. All factions tried to work on Cromwell. 'I am pushed', he complained, 'to do that, the consideration of the issue thereof makes my hair to stand on end!'[12]

Parliament itself got so far as declaring that Members of a new Representative should be 'such as are persons of known integrity, fearing God and not scandalous in their conversation'. And, most important, it advanced the date for its own dissolution to 3 November 1653. But even seven months now seemed too long to wait and it was rumoured that Cromwell had at last agreed with his Council of Officers to dissolve the Government and constitute another in some way until a new Parliament was chosen. The idea became more specific at a meeting of army officers and Members of Parliament at Cromwell's lodgings in the Cockpit in April 1653. An interim Government of about forty Members should be chosen from Parliament's own ranks by the Rump itself and the Council of Officers jointly which would exercise power until a new Representative was chosen. Discussions went on far into the night of the 19th/20th April. Whitelocke asserted that St John supported the scheme but that he and Widdrington opposed. Further meetings were clearly necessary and Cromwell apparently thought it was agreed that the House would postpone its discussions of the Bill before it until this proposal had been further considered. He was confident that Vane and the Members of Parliament present supported him in this. Consequently the continuation of the discussion next day was to be informal and Cromwell attended in the usual homely garb he wore when not attending official business. He had no thought that matters would be other than they had been agreed the previous evening. He took little notice of a messenger who came to him from Westminster, nor of a second. When a third messenger arrived Cromwell started to his feet in fury and rushed to the House of Commons as he was, without waiting to change his dress. There was only time for a whispered word to Harrison who closely followed him. Cromwell entered the Chamber. Accounts differ as to the exact sequence of events. Apparently he listened to the debate from his accustomed seat for some time – listened until the question was about to be put – then rose, whispering to Harrison, 'This is the time I must do it!'

He started calmly, even praising the Parliament for some of their good works, perhaps remembering the support they had given him in his Irish and Scottish campaigns. Then he got on to their faults and omissions: 'Injustice', 'delays of justice', 'self-interest'. As he worked himself up with his own words Sir Peter Wentworth rose to a point of order. It was strange language, he said, to hear from an honourable Member, highly honoured by the House . . . This was the last straw. Cromwell leapt from his place, clapped his hat upon his head and continued incoherently, stamping his feet upon the ground, a strange figure in his grey worsted stockings and old black coat striding up and down the floor of the House between the formally clad Members with Lenthall anxiously surveying the scene from the Speaker's chair, not daring to interrupt such a Member as Commander-in-Chief Oliver Cromwell, yet more and more perturbed at what he was hearing.

'. . . we have had enough of this . . . it is not fit you sit here any longer, you have sat too long already for any good you have done . . . I will put an end to your prating! Call them in!' he commanded Harrison and some twenty or thirty musketeers of Cromwell's own regiment filed in, grim-faced, ready for business. The flow of words continued. 'You call yourself a Parliament! I say you are no Parliament!'

With the Members on their feet, the musketeers lining the walls, but Lenthall in the Speaker's chair, Cromwell rounded on Member after Member. 'Some of you are drunkards' – and he glared at Chaloner. 'Some of you are lewd livers, living in contempt of God's commandments' – and the accusation focused upon Sir Harry Marten and Sir Peter Wentworth – 'unjust persons, following your own greedy appetities – scandalous to the profession of the Gospel!'

'In the name of God, Go!', he concluded. And, seizing upon the mace, he cried 'Take away this bauble!' thrusting it upon a musketeer. He seized the Order paper with the resolution that was being debated and pushed it into his pocket. Then, turning to the Speaker he summoned Harrison. 'Fetch him down!', he commanded. Lenthall declared with the only vestige of dignity left in the House that he would not come down until forced.

'Come, Sir', said Harrison, 'I will lend you a hand.' And seeing no alternative Lenthall left his chair. There remained the final thrust. As the Members stumbled out Cromwell caught sight of Sir Henry Vane. He cried out that he was a juggler, lacking common honesty, that he might have prevented this. 'Sir Harry Vane, Sir Harry Vane! the Lord deliver me from thee, Sir Harry Vane!'

No mace, no Speaker, the Long Parliament dissolved by the great soldier who had forged its victories over the Royalists and who had been one of its first Members thirteen years before. The key was turned on the empty Parliament House.[13]

The Bill was not seen again. Either Cromwell by seizing it deliberately suppressed it, or merely lost or destroyed it as of no consequence. Marten later wrote to Cromwell assuring him that it contained no 'recruiter' clause;[14] what it did contain remains a mystery. What then drove Cromwell into one of his sudden rages? What did the third messenger tell him that he did not know before? Was it that the Bill was being discussed at all after a promise of delay for further consultation? This would account for his attack on Vane who had promised a postponement of the debate. Or was there something specific in the Bill which became certain only after the news brought by that third messenger? This may have concerned a recruiter clause about which Cromwell may have been wrongly informed or which was being inserted not in the original Bill but in the course of the debate. Cromwell may have been told that Haselrig, whom he imagined to be miles away, had returned to the House and was swinging opinion against the compromise Cromwell was working for. It may have been sheer exasperation which suddenly rose to a climax in the knowledge that the Parliament was still not giving up. 'I pressed the Parliament to period themselves once and again and again and ten, nay twenty times over!', he said later,[15]

But the matter which touched Cromwell closest and could most easily arouse his anger concerned the army. Incredible as it may seem there had already been strong rumours that, so soon after Worcester, Parliament was thinking of replacing Cromwell by Fairfax as Commander-in-Chief of the army.[16] If there had been anything that the third messenger imparted to Cromwell indicating that even then Parliament was discussing, or about to discuss, such a move, it would fully account for Cromwell's blazing anger. The speed with which he acted indicated that time was short. Had Cromwell perhaps not realized until the arrival of the third messengher that the Bill was being discussed at all?

Cromwell returned to the subject again and again, attempting to justify his action in speeches to his Parliaments and in various *apologias* in which he was generally supported by the army: the Rump was making an unwarranted assertion of independence in continuing to discuss the Bill after its representatives had agreed to a postponement; it wanted a hasty passage for the Bill and would adjourn immediately afterwards to prevent subsequent revision. Then, meeting again in November, it would itself be able to supervise the calling of a new Parliament. This possibility aroused fears of the qualifications to be required of electors and candidates: would it not be easy to arrange for a Presbyterian dominance? There was, moreover, an over-riding concern as to the duration of the Parliaments to be elected and a fear that successive Parliaments of two years' duration with no interval between would amount, in fact, to perpetual Parliaments which would act as both legislature and executive with no check upon their activities.

The picture never became very clear. But whatever activiated Cromwell there were enough people to compare his (successful) action in expelling a whole Parliament with Charles I's (unsuccessful) attempt on the Five Members. Was this not 'as great a breach of the privilege of parliament as the demanding the five members?' asked Dorothy Osborne?[17]

22

'Not answerable to the simplicity and honesty of the design'

Central government was not greatly affected by the expulsion of the Rump. Most county committees continued to function and local government affairs proceeded, on the whole, with little break. But constitutionally where did power reside? Cromwell, Commander-in-Chief by Act of Parliament, was virtually the only, certainly the most powerful, legal authority in existence. In constitutional affairs there could be no hiatus. As he claimed, power devolved upon him 'to the end that affairs might not have any interval'. But he needed to explain and he needed to set in train the machinery for a new Parliament. Two days after the dissolution a *Declaration of the Lord General and his Council of Officers* was issued to the country. It had become evident, it said, 'that this Parliament, through the corruption of some, the jealousy of others, the non-attendance and negligence of many, would never answer those ends which God, his people, and the whole nation expected from them.' Copies were despatched to the sheriffs with 'haste, post haste' and instructions were sent to publish immediately. A similar *Declaration* was sent abroad.[1] The army was behind Cromwell. The navy being, as Monck put it, 'engaged with a foreign enemy in a bloody war' had little to say.[2] Royalists naturally welcomed the end of a Parliament that had done them no good, and its expulsion, in signalling a break in their enemy's ranks, was generally reckoned a good thing, though the absolute power that now seemed to rest on Cromwell augured little good for the Royalist cause.

But that power was not so absolute as some people thought, and many who had gone thus far with Cromwell could not stomach his high-handed dealing with the Rump. Vane left the capital for the country, Haselrig and St John made it clear they would take no part in any new constitution-making. Even Bradshaw, who had presided over the King's trial, stayed away, asserting that Parliament was not and could not have been dissolved by Cromwell but was merely interrupted. In the army Fifth Monarchy men pulled one way and carried many with them, declaring for a Parliament of Saints who would rule in the name of Jesus Christ while they waited His second coming. Lambert pulled another way, having prepared a scheme for a more conventional government consisting of a small Council of State, an elected Parliament and a written constitution. An objection to Lambert's scheme was that no legal authority existed to call an election and Cromwell was anxious to keep within the bounds of legality. He himself, on the day after he broke the Rump, nominated a Council of State consisting of seven officers and three civilians which achieved some balance between the various groups who were operating round him. Lambert was its first President, Harrison, Desborough and Cromwell himself represented the army. Walter Strickland, Colonel Bennett, Colonel Sydenham, Major Salwey, had all sat in the Rump. As Harrison wrote to Colonel John Jones in Dublin, they 'resolved to have in power, men of truth, fearing and loving our Lord, his people and interest'. Cromwell agreed. The question remained of choosing or electing that Parliament. Again Harrison posed the question to Jones: 'the difficulty is to gett such; whether my Lord onelie shall call them, or the saints should chose them.'[3]

In the end, as might have been expected, Cromwell came down on Harrison's side. It was to be an Assembly of Saints chosen by Cromwell and the Council of officers. There were doubtless many gathered churches who at one time or another submitted names and whose views were taken into account but basically the selection was that of Cromwell and the officers.[4] There was still a difference of opinion over numbers. Harrison looked to an Assembly of seventy godly men, Lambert to a smaller number, Cromwell favoured a larger Assembly. In the end 140 were summoned and the writs went out in the name of Cromwell as Commander-in-Chief.[5] Meanwhile he carried himself in exemplary manner. He continued his unostentatious way of life and was modest in his demeanour. He made one or two public gestures like pronouncing pardon on a group of prisoners he encountered on their way to Tyburn five days after the dissolution. The only jarring note was when he was walking in St James's Park and demanded that a man he encountered should remove his hat: Buckingham, he exclaimed, had had his hat knocked off when he kept it on in the King's presence![6]

There was naturally talk of the mantle of supreme power in name as well as fact falling upon him. That this was merely to injure him was the conclusion of the Venetian envoy.[7] Yet it was only natural that he should sometimes think of himself, so clearly chosen by success, to wield the supreme constitutional power. There seemed a frightening logic or even inevitability about this, yet Cromwell could not have carried the army, seething with Fifth Monarchy fervour, into such a perilous exercise. Instead he, one of the Saints himself, was willing to govern with a Parliament of Saints and he had a rosy picture of the blessings of such a rule. Meanwhile Royalist letters of Intelligence and news letters buzzed with excited comment and speculation – even that Mazarin had proposed a marriage between Charles and one of Cromwell's daughters. As it happened Cromwell's second surviving son, Henry, who was serving in Ireland, was married on 10 May 1653 to Elizabeth Russell, daughter of Colonel Francis Russell. The marriage cemented a family friendship that dated from the early days of the war but gave no grounds for the accusation of ambition. But if Henry was ignorant of his father's position he was disillusioned when hailed derisively in Spring Gardens with cries of 'Room for the Prince!'[8] More serious was the picture of Oliver himself which was nailed up in the Exchange with a verse beneath beginning 'Ascend three thrones great Captain and Divine!' and ending 'Let all men bare-head cry, God Save the King!'[9]

To the accompaniment of such incidents the 'bloody war' with the Dutch, of which Monck had spoken, was in full swing. Since the spring of 1652 naval battles had raged in the Channel and the North Sea. Blake had been defeated by Tromp off Dungeness in November, 1652; in June, 1653 the Dutch were defeated off the Gabard but the heavy price was the death of Admiral Deane. Cromwell was solicitous in visiting Deane's widow but plans necessarily proceeded for calling the new Representative. By the end of May all was ready. Fairfax, whose name had been put forward, declined, after some consideration, to sit. Similarly Vane, with hesitation, refused a place. But by the beginning of June 129 Representatives of England and Wales with the addition of five for Scotland and six for Ireland had been named. The writs went out on June 6. The one addressed to Praise-God Barebone, leatherseller, of Fleet Street in the City of London, survives and so a humble tradesman gave to posterity a name by which to know this Parliament. It was not

243

wholly an Assembly of Saints, of cranks, of Fifth Monarchy Men or religious fanatics, though some of these were there. Others were men of experience, of learning and of balanced judgment like Francis Rous from Devon, Provost of Eton College; or Richard Mayor, father-in-law of Cromwell's son Richard. Henry Cromwell was there, fresh from Ireland and marriage; Thomas French from Cambridge who had been instrumental in giving Oliver his first step up the ladder by securing his return to the Parliament of 1640; Lawrence, his landlord at St Ives; Henry Ireton's brother, John; such well-known names as Strickland, Monck, Hewson. There were seven knights, two peers, an East India Company merchant. More than a third of them held or had held military office, twenty-four had sat in the previous Parliament. There were seven regicides among them. Socially it was a mixed Parliament. Gentry and lesser gentry predominated, as in previous Parliaments, but there were more tradesmen and artisans among whom the men of sectarian and radical leanings tended to prevail. These, however, were less experienced than the rest in Parliamentary affairs and their proposals were less practicable, their tactics less effective, their efforts at reform less likely to succeed. All in all it was a varied and not negligible body which would hold office until 3 November 1654, having chosen its successor three months before that.

A naval victory over the Dutch was a good omen for the new Assembly when Monck defeated the Dutch off the Texel and Tromp was killed. Less helpful was the return of Lilburne from exile in the Low Countries, his excuse being that the ending of the Parliament that had sentenced him entailed the abroation of its Act of banishment. He was, nevertheless, imprisoned in Newgate and threatened with a new trial, though petitions for its postponement until the new Representative was sitting were signed by thousands of Londoners.

On July 4 the new Parliament was summoned by 'Oliver Cromwell, Captain General and Commander-in-Chief of all the Armies and Forces raised and to be raised within the Commonwealth', to attend the Council Chamber at Whitehall for its official inauguration. The room was small for the 130 or so Members who took their seats or pressed round the long Council table. Cromwell stood with his back to the window facing the middle of the table, leaning lightly upon a chair. His officers crowded round him – as many, one account says, as could be crammed into the room. It was a strange gesture to make to a Parliament of Saints, unless to emphasize that the army would be judge of its saintliness. Cromwell, clearly very emotional, made 'a new, grave and reasonable speech' in 'a grave and Christian-like manner, frequently weeping', taking occasion once again, as he had in his exchanges with Dundas outside Edinburgh, to dwell upon 'events' and the evident hand of God in determining their outcome.

He referred at the outset to 'the scantness of the room, and heat of the weather'. 'Seeing you sit here somewhat uneasily', he said, 'I shall contract myself with respect thereunto.' He spoke of the war – how God had raised up 'a poor and contemptible company of men, neither versed in military affairs, nor having much natural propensity to them' and brought them success. He spoke of 'the most memorable year' – 1648–9. In this, and in all events of the civil wars, he saw 'an evident print of Providence'. After Worcester he and his fellow officers and soldiers 'expected, and had some reasonable confidence that our expectations should not be frustrated, that, having such a history to look back unto, such a God, so eminently visible ... that ... the expectations which were upon our hearts ... would have prompted those who were in authority to have done those good things which might ... have been judged ... worthy of such mercies.'

And so he came to justify the expulsion of the Rump. He and his officers had tried all means in their power to influence Parliament, and he spoke of the meetings between officers and MPs, of the fears that Parliament would perpetuate itself. He made it appear that his chief reason for the expulsion was the promise, not kept, that further discussion in the House of Commons would be suspended until the Committee had met again. He continued at length, regardless of the heat, the crowd, and his promise of brevity, growing more and more fervent

> The Lord hath done this, and the Holy One of Israel hath created it; that He hath wrought all the salvations and deliverances we have received. For what end! To see, and know, and understand together, that He hath done and wrought all this for the good of the whole flock!

And he launched into one of his great pleas for toleration,

> Therefore I beseech you ... have a care of the whole flock! Love the sheep, love the lambs; love all, tender all, cherish and countenance all, in all things that are good. And if the poorest Christian,

the most mistaken Christian, shall desire to live peaceably and quietly under you, – I say, if any shall desire but to lead a life in godliness and honesty, let him be protected.

It was a somewhat bizarre occasion. In front of him were the men selected for their saintliness, in whom he professed to have confidence. Over all was the power of the Lord in whom he professed perfect faith. But he had summoned them, not as a Saint himself but as Commander-in-Chief of all the Armies of the Commonwealth, a strong contingent of whom were visibly supporting him as he made his speech. He was taking no chances. If the Saints proved unworthy of his trust there were other means . . .

Cromwell spoke for another two hours before he recalled his promise of brevity and the conditions under which his audience was listening. 'I am sorry I have troubled you, in such a place of heat as this is, so long,' he said. He commended them and their work to God, assured them that they had the support of the army, the navy, and the Churches of Christ throughout the nation, and told them he had set up a Council of State, eight or nine of its members being from the dissolved Rump: 'I did exercise that power that, I thought, was devolved upon me at that time; to the end that affairs might not have any interval.'[10] This was his fixed belief – the political lifeline to which he must firmly adhere: there must be no hiatus.

The following day the Assembly moved to the House of Commons, elected Francis Rous their Speaker. Cromwell was formally requested to attend, he was elected to the Council of State, the mace was sent for from Colonel Worsley's house where it had remained since the expulsion of the Rump, and on July 12 the nominated Saints declared themselves a Parliament: it was a praiseworthy amalgam of tradition and innovation which would be judged simply by whether it worked or not; and that judgement would be bound up with the question of whose interests it furthered, whose it threatened.

The Little, Nominated, or Barebones Parliament got down to business immediately, addressing itself first to the gargantuan task of bringing all financial affairs into the hands of one body. It was not wanting in courage and almost at the same time it turned to the law. The law constituted a labyrinth no easier to negotiate than the Cretan lair. There were said to be some 23,000 cases of five to ten years' standing lying in Chancery alone. In spite of the fact that there were no lawyers in its ranks, and after only one day's debate, it resolved to abolish Chancery; it instructed a Committee to codify the law and reduce it into the 'bigness of a pocket book'; it called for an equitable, easily understood body of law in English. The intentions were excellent. But to expect to unravel centuries of written law, precedent and practice in the course of a few hours' debate, to expect to silence by a vote in Parliament the vested interests that swarmed thickly round all aspects of the law, showed either an extreme naivety or a fervid belief in a Divine mission; it certainly indicated a sense of the sheer urgency of legal reform which had been bandied about for decades. It is to the credit of the Barebones Parliament that in spite of difficulties it was able to press on to the Statute Book Acts for the relief of prisoners for debt, for the establishment of civil marriages, and for the registration of births, marriages and burials.

On Church matters a resolution abolishing patronage was passed, university endowments were threatened. On the tricky issue of tythes no agreement was reached largely because of the intermixture of lay and ecclesiastical tythe-owners in their ranks. There was a strong feeling against supporting an Established church by tythes, and a condemnatory chorus of Fifth Monarchy Men and their supporters rose outside Westminster from pulpit and press. Cromwell, reverting to his usual panacea, tried to arrange conferences between Presbyterians and Independents on the one hand and Fifth Monarchy Men and Baptists on the other. But he found himself facing a hostile grouping of Saints: 'Who made thee a Prince or a judge over us?' They would have Harrison as Lord General for Cromwell was a 'man of sin' who supported a national church.

Another matter on which the army and Cromwell himself were incensed against this Parliament as they had been against its predecessor concerned the abrogation of the terms which they, the victorious soldiers, had granted to their enemies who had surrendered. Every soldier's honour was involved in keeping faith whether in matters of life, liberty or property. But the Barebones Parliament, like the Rump before it, had different notions of honour where defeated Royalists were concerned and imprisonment, heavy fines and severe terms for compounding in many cases repudiated the terms of surrender.

After seven weeks of this Parliament all was not well. Every issue raised such a diversity of views and interests that action was inhibited and good intentions evaporated. Cromwell's letter to

Fleetwood in Ireland of August 2 spoke all:

> Fain would I have my services accepted of the saints ... but it
> is not so. Being of different judgements, and of each sort most
> seeking to propagate their own, that spirit of kindness that is to
> them all, is hardly accepted of any ...[11]

The issue was put more brusquely by Henry Cromwell in Ludlow's
house at Monkstown in Ireland: The Nominated Parliament, he said
'made a very kickshaw' of his father.

Soon there were danger signs outside Parliament. Not only was
Lilburne back, there was talk of insurrection in Scotland and of
Royalist plots centering upon Portsmouth. By December the more
conservative section of the Barebones Parliament had had enough.
John Lambert, in particular, had never come to terms with this
Assembly and continued to work on his own scheme, as Parliament
was well aware. With a group of officers he had been discussing
once more the idea of a written constitution like the *Agreement of
the People* or the *Heads of the Proposals.* Cromwell had been approached
but had so far refused to countenance the *Instrument of Government,*
as it was to be called, or to accept the title of King which it offered,
or to dissolve another Parliament: this one had yet a year to run.

The plot was well thought out and organized. On the morning
of December 12 the moderates came early to the House when most
of their opponents were at a prayer meeting and tabled a motion
'that the sitting of this Parliament any longer, as it is now constituted,
will not be for the good of the Commonwealth, and that therefore
it is requisite to deliver up to the Lord General Cromwell the powers
which they had received from him'. They adduced as their reasons
that Parliament had sought to overturn the law, the clergy and the
property of the subject and had not made sufficient provision for
the pay of the army. Rous, the Speaker, who was party to the plot,
took no chances. Without waiting for the House to fill, without
even putting the motion to those Members who were there, he rose
from his chair, called for the mace to precede him, and with some
fifty or sixty Members of Parliament hurried to Whitehall. There
they signed their names to a certificate of abdication, obviously previously prepared, which returned their power to Cromwell. Later
in the day two officers arrived at the House of Commons and ordered
out those who were still sitting there: it was necessary for they might
have constituted a quorum. Two files of musketeers enforced the

summons and the Colonel in charge asked the Members why they were still there and what they were doing. 'We are seeking the Lord', they said. 'Then', said the Colonel, 'you may go elsewhere, for to my certain knowledge he has not been here these twelve years.'[12]

Cromwell was pleased they had gone, though he had not himself tried to end their sittings. His later disavowals sound sincere. Though he probably had some idea of what was brewing, of the actual method and timing he was ignorant. 'I did not know one tittle of that resignation, till they all came and brought it, and delivered it into my hands,' he said. It is more likely that Lambert, with his own constitution struggling to be born, would have done something to expedite the departure of the Saints. But Cromwell was disappointed: 'the issue was not answerable to the simplicity and honesty of the design,' he said.[13]

23

'Power over the three nations'

With the demise of the Nominated Parliament Cromwell was once again on his lonely eminence. 'My power', he said, 'was again by this resignation as boundless and unlimited as before, all things being subject to arbitrariness, and myself a person having power over the three nations without bound or limit set, all government being dissolved, and all civil administration at an end.'[1] It was not quite true that all civil administration was at an end, for civil servants kept their places, in the counties the sheriffs and JPs and lesser officers operated, the judiciary functioned, the treasurers of various committees waited to have their authority confirmed by whatever constitution would emerge, the farmers of the customs petitioned for continuity in their lucrative trade, the probate of wills continued, and Henry Scobell was still there – the Clerk to the House of Commons who had retained his office through the vicissitudes of government and now awaited, uncertainly, the outcome of the present upset. But Cromwell's words expressed his fear of hiatus, his doubts of his ability to carry so much upon his own shoulders as it now seemed he must do. More than ever he needed Henry Ireton. Instead of his dead son-in-law he now had Major-General John Lambert, of whose military prowess and enthusiasm he had had ample proof during the wars, but whose political acumen was yet untried.

When Lambert and the officers first presented their scheme to Cromwell in November there were two outstanding difficulties about its acceptance. In the first place the Barebones Parliament was still sitting and Cromwell would not override its authority. When they presented it a second time in December that difficulty had been removed by the resignation of Parliament and Cromwell was free to concentrate on the other problem presented by the *Instrument* which, it seems, was no less than the offer of supreme power to him under the title of King. For three or four days he wrestled with the Lord, seeking guidance. If he accepted was he guilty of self-aggrandisement? Would they not say that this is what he had been seeking, that ambition had been his driving force? Was it? He searched his soul. If he refused was he not, as he expressed it to himself, guilty of 'a desire ... sinful enough, to be quit of the power God had most clearly by His Providence put into his hands?'

He refused the title. When Lambert and the other officers brought the *Instrument* to him a second time not only had the Nominated Parliament disbanded itself but the title of Protector was substituted for that of King. After a further few days of inward struggle Cromwell accepted the title and the authority that went with it. On 16 December 1653, less than a week after the demise of the Nominated Parliament, he was installed as Lord Protector under the terms of the *Instrument of Government*. It was 'the first practical written constitution in English history'.[2]

The *Instrument of Government* provided for government by a single person assisted by a Council of State named and appointed by the *Instrument* and sitting for life, and by a Parliament consisting of a House of Commons without an Upper Chamber which would meet every three years and sit for a minimum of five months at a time. The office of Protector would not be hereditary but would last for life and successors would be chosen by Parliament or by the Council in the intervals of Parliament. The House of Commons would be elected by constituencies which were made more equal in size by the abolition of the smaller boroughs. Borough franchise would remain roughly the same as before resting, generally speaking, in Corporations. In the counties the forty-shilling freehold franchise would give way to a voting qualification dependent upon the possession of property to the value of £200 or more. There was a small gain in uniformity, a more decided bias towards a middle-class Parliament.

Those who had taken the King's part in the civil wars would be excluded from voting for the first Parliament and from sitting in the first four Parliaments called under its authority. Roman Catholics and Irish rebels were permanently disqualified both as voters and as representatives. The terms of the *Instrument* could not be amended by the electors — a protection which had also been found necessary by the framers of the *Agreement of the People* and *The Heads of the Proposals*.

On the vital question of religion the *Instrument* showed the kind of toleration that Cromwell wished: 'That the Christian religion, as contained in the Scriptures, be held forth and recommended as the public profession of these nations.' Both doctrine and form of worship were intended to be comprised within this formula, but popery and prelacy were excluded, and abuse of the freedom granted in licentious or dissolute conduct would not be permitted. On the other hand 'prelacy', in the sense of worship according to Anglican rites, was not, in practice, generally interfered with.

Power to control the armed forces was vested in the Protector, with the consent of Parliament when sitting, otherwise with the consent of the Council. This given, he could 'dispose and order the militia and forces, both by sea and land for the peace and good of the three nations'. The consent of Parliament was similarly required for all taxation but in an emergency in an interval of Parliament the Protector could act with the consent of his Council.

The Council and its relation to Parliament and to Protector was clearly of the utmost importance. After consideration of its size a maximum of twenty-one, a minimum of thirteen was agreed upon. The first fifteen were named in the *Instrument* and until his first Parliament met Cromwell could, with the consent of the majority, add members up to a maximum of 21: his share in selection was important but not overriding. Among the first fifteen there were military men, but civilians predominated. There were Henry Lawrence, Cromwell's landlord at St Ives, Richard Mayor, his son's father-in-law, a man to whom Cromwell seems to have taken a liking. All but two of them had been members of Barebones' Parliament. Among the soldiers were his son-in-law, Fleetwood, though duties in Ireland caused his absence until 1655; the rugged Philip Skippon took a place on the council.

The importance of these men, apart from their own personalities, lay in their independence. They were not a monarch's appointment, like the old Privy Council, nor were they directly responsible to Parliament. Their relationship to Parliament and their own power was related to and to some extent circumscribed by that of the Protector. They nevertheless could, reciprocally, exercise some restraint on him. The intentions of the *Instrument* were in this respect indeterminate; but the Council did remain, when Parliament was not sitting, the most immediate check upon the Protector. There remained also the judiciary and the framework of the law. Cromwell's lawyers, like King Charles's, had already shown a degree of independence that could act as a brake upon the Protector, though how far they could bridle a Protector who was also Commander-in-Chief of the army was a different matter. It all depended upon the Protector himself and the last thing Cromwell wanted was a power based upon force. He closed his eyes to the fact that, in the last analysis, this is what he had achieved.[3]

The *Instrument of Government* was an eclectic document, indebted to Ireton's *Heads of the Proposals*, particularly in tying the right to vote to what amounted to contribution to taxation, and to the *Nineteen Propositions* presented to the King in 1642. To a lesser extent it echoes the legislation which had passed the House of Commons before the outbreak of war. The words that had been poured out since 1640 and earlier had at last been translated into some form of working constitution and Oliver Cromwell was the man chosen to give it life.

> That the supreme legislative authority of the Commonwealth of England, Scotland, and Ireland, and dominions thereunto belonging shall be and reside in one person, and the people assembled in Parliament, the style of which person shall be the Lord Protector of the Commonwealth of England, Scotland, and Ireland,

so read his brief. His title would be His Highness the Lord Protector. His residence would be the Palace of Charles I in Whitehall where many of the King's treasures still remained. It had all been done very quickly. Only three clear days intervened between the end of the Barebones Parliament and Cromwell's installation as Lord Protector on Friday 16 December 1653. He took the oath of office in the Court of Chancery in Westminster Hall wearing the simple clothes of a citizen, except that his suit and cloak were of rich black velvet and there was a broad band of gold about his hat.

But the relation of the Lord Protector to the army was shown by the soldiers who lined the route from Whitehall to Westminster and by the words of his oath as Protector in which he claimed to have been advised by 'several Persons of Interest and Fidelity in this Commonwealth, as the officers of the Army', and by the memorandum which accompanied the Oath which refered to him as 'Oliver Cromwell, Captain General of all the Forces of the Commonwealth, and now declared Lord Protector thereof'. But as he took the oath he was supported not only by his army officers but by state officials and representatives of the City of London, including the Lord Mayor and Aldermen. While Lambert presented him with the civil sword of state.[4] He was a 'rather likely figure',

> some five feet ten or more; a man of strong solid stature, and digni-fied, now partly military carriage; the expression of him valour and devout intelligence, – energy and delacacy on a basis of simpli-city. Fifty-four years old, gone April last; ruddy fair complexion, bronzed by toil and age; light brown hair and moustache are getting streaked with grey. A figure of sufficient impressiveness; – not lovely to the man-milliner species, nor pretending to be so. Massive stature; big massive head, of somewhat leonine aspect, evident workshop and storehouse of a vast treasure of natural parts. Wart above the right eyebrow (and between mouth and chin); nose of considerable blunt-aquiline proportions; strict yet copious lips, full of all tremulous sensibilities, and also if need were, of all fierceness and rigours; deep loving eyes, call them grave, call then stern . . .[5]

At nearly fifty-five years old he was the oldest of the European leaders or rulers. But if at forty, with no military training or exper-ience, he could become the best soldier in Europe, could he not, at fifty-four, albeit with no training and little political experience become at least effective enough to sustain and guide the Common-wealth? He thought he could.

After the inauguration ceremony he was conducted by carriage on the short journey to the residence assigned him and his family in Whitehall along a route guarded by soldiers. There was some applause but it was a decorous and not wildly enthusiastic journey. The City of London signalled its support for the Protector sometime later by a banquet in Grocer's Hall on February 8. It was difficult to judge the general feeling, enthusiasm such as there was being gener-ated by the end of Barebones as much as by the inauguration of a Protector. Those who thought Cromwell was bent on seizing supreme power, those who doubted the ability of the soldier to turn statesman were sceptical. How he would balance the conflicting demands of reform, inertia, and vested interest remained to be seen.

The new Parliament was summoned for 3 September 1654. In the nine months between the resignation of Barebones and the meet-ing of this new Assembly Cromwell and his Council would be, as he said, 'the trustees of the Commonwealth'. The Council which would remain in permanent session and with which the Protector would work closely was named in the *Instrument* itself and, with his help, contained many good names: soldiers whom he liked to work with; kinsmen who bolstered his morale; lawyers with whom he was never happy but whose presence was essential; most of all, perhaps, John Thurloe, a man who had already served him well and who was named Secretary to the Council. Until the new Parliament had assembled Cromwell, together with this Council, was empowered under the *Instrument* to legislate by Ordinance. He had as much power, in a different sphere, as he had as Lord General. But would there be anything equivalent to martial law to keep his civilians in order? Could army discipline, so essential to their martial victories, be imposed now, to win the peace? At least he had control of the armed forces – with his Council now or with the Parliament when it was sitting. He also had a degree of financial control in the intervals of Parliament, though how far a sitting Parliament would circumvent him he could not be sure. Perhaps there would be less talking, more opportunity for action, in the nine months before the new Parliament assembled. There would certainly be more responsibility of a kind he had not known before, not only in guiding the affairs of the nation through his Council but in conducting affairs of state with Ambassadors and foreign diplomats in his role as His Highness the Lord Protector. The Venetian envoy remarked that he looked 'utterly careworn'. He was. He was on a lonely eminence. Many of his old friends and colleagues had gone: Fairfax with whom he had forged those miraculous victories in arms, lived in retirement; St John, the cousin and mentor of the old days, had left the capital for his home in the country; cousin Hampden and many of those clear-eyed young men who first stood against the King were dead; his son, his nephew and a son-in-law were among those who had paid the price of protest. Bradshaw, timorous and querulous, who had nevertheless helped him to that final, irreversible act of regicide, had asserted himself sufficiently to withold support from the Protectorate and was becoming increasingly vocal as a Republican; Sir Harry Vane who had, until that disastrous day in the old Rump Parliament, been his goad and censor, held aloof. Cromwell looked in vain for other faces from the old days – Holles, Stapleton, Ludlow – who had not always been helpful but who had played their part.

He missed the humble men he had trained as soldiers – the 'men of a spirit' who had risen from the humblest walks of life to command and to victory, many of whom, like Harrison, had succumbed to Fifth Monarchy fervour, while others simply did not like this way of government by a Lord Protector and a Parliament, which sounded too much like the government they had overthrown. Among the younger men who were coming up were more of good family, of secure background, less urgent in their demands, less easily swayed by passion. He hoped they would serve his turn. He had trodden a difficult path since Worcester and one which he understood less well than the hazardous ways along which he had led his marching army. But the Lord who had taught him to be a soldier at the age of forty would teach him to be a statesman at the age of fifty-five.

Instinct induced Cromwell to turn to the places and people from whom he might expect trouble. He dealt leniently with the Fifth Monarchy opposition, merely sending Major-General Harrison to his home in the country. The army in Ireland, where his son-in-law, Fleetwood, was in charge, caused little difficulty. Edmund Ludlow remained difficult and refused to return to public life. John Lilburne, who had stormed home from banishment after the fall of the Rump had been brought to trial for a second time on 13 July 1653. He had lost none of his exuberance, none of his popular appeal and both the Royalists and Cromwell watched the outcome with expectation or trepidation. The shouts of joy that announced his acquittal were heard a full mile off; they would have penetrated to Whitehall together with the beating of drums and sounding of trumpets by the very soldiers sent to guard him. With 'scandalous, seditious and tumultuous papers' dispersed every day in the city with full accounts of Lilburne's trial and the speeches he made, Cromwell ordered on August 27 'that John Lilburne should be held prisoner for the peace of the nation'. This time close imprisonment worked. Apart from his wife no visitors found their way to the Tower, no pamphlets issued from his prison room. The Leveller movement had no organization with which to feed its one-time leader, and the guard imposed by Cromwell was more efficient than that of old.

Royalists believed there had been a considerable threat from Levellers in City and country, from gathered churches and from the army. They may have been right. A pamphlet attacking Cromwell was scattered in the streets of London on the night of 14 September 1653, accusing him of high treason to 'his lords the people of England' in not entrusting them with the choice of a new Representative elected by manhood suffrage when he had expelled the Rump. Among the soldiers Cornet Joyce was prominent saying he wished that the pistol aimed at Cromwell on Triploe Heath had been discharged. He was cashiered. The protests died down, though many Fifth Monarchy men were imprisoned, and there was no sign of protest as the Parliament of Saints was tried and found wanting and as Cromwell was installed as Protector.

In the spring of 1654, however, before his first Parliament had gathered, Thurloe and his agents unearthed a serious Royalist plot. Being forewarned Oliver went by water on the first part of his journey to Hampton Court on May 14, the assassination attempt was foiled, and the chief plotters executed. About the same time there occurred a case which Cromwell feared might be a precedent for Lilburne. A certain Captain Streeter, who had been imprisoned by the Council of State in the time of the Rump for publishing seditious pamphlets, appealed successfully for a *habeas corpus* on the the grounds that an Order of Parliament ceased to be in force after a dissolution. On February 11 he left prison a free man. It was so obviously a precedent for Lilburne that Cromwell resolved to remove him where the writ of *habeas corpus* did not run, and Lilburne was sent to a gloomy fortress in Jersey by Order of the Council of State, before he had time to take action. It was a cowardly act on Cromwell's part, out of accord with his general attitude to prisoners and particularly to Lilburne whom he had known for many years – and not always as an enemy. Lilburne, like Cromwell, was spent and had no chance of recuperation in the gloomy Mont Orgeuil to which he was assigned. Cromwell, on the other hand, in his new situation and working only with his Council of State, regained much of his old vigour.

He was to learn something of what governing a country really meant. He had participated briefly in Parliaments as one of many; he had acted in battle as Commander-in-Chief. Now he was to see what it was like to assume the highest political office. A glance at some of the hundred or so Ordinances which passed through his hands and those of his Council of State in the nine months before Parliament assembled indicates the extent and nature of the business they handled.

Procedure varied slightly but in general a preliminary discussion in Council decided where action was needed and a small committee was set up to consider details. Evidence and advice was taken, the legal work put in hand, a draft Ordinance took shape. The Council was fortunate to have Henry Scobell, the clerk to many Parliaments and a man of wide experience, as one of its own clerks. The Lord Protector had other work to do but the presentation of a proposed Ordinance to Cromwell was far from being a formality and he frequently called for amendments or reconsideration.

It is not always easy to understand the Council's priorities. Legal affairs relating to property were obviously important to them and one of their first discussions concerned the Act for the Probate of Wills which had been begun by the Barebones Parliament, and was now concluded. They returned to the vexed question of Chancery with an Ordinance for its 'better regulation', thus avoiding the pitfall which Barebones had dug for itself. They confirmed the establishment of a High Court of Justice. Cromwell retained ten Judges and advanced Matthew Hale to the judiciary, promising to observe Hale's condition that he should not try Royalists. An Ordinance for the relief of creditors and poor prisoners was passed. The payment of soldiers and sailors was attended to in various ways, again following the inconclusive work of the Barebones Parliament. Army accounts were examined, committees appointed to look into the affairs of the navy and Admiralty, the question of lands in Ireland and America which stood as security for loans was examined both from the point of view of public debts and soldiers' pay and for 'the encouragement of Protestants to plant and inhabit in these countries'.

Very necessary was the continued raising of money. The excise was continued on a variety of goods, including the important raw materials, alum and copreras; an imposition upon coals to go towards building and maintaining ships for guarding the seas was continued – without, apparently, a backward glance to Charles I. The disposition of estates under sequestration orders was to be better ordered and, following several earlier proposals, the receipts of the revenue, from a variety of scattered sources, were to be brought into one Treasury.

Cromwell's social policy as expressed through his Ordinances embraced the relief of poor persons who had helped the Commonwealth, the redemption of capitives taken by Algerian and other pirates. Ordinances regulated hackney cabs in an attempt to mediate in their disputes with Thames watermen. They provided for the repair of highways, even laying down the precise speed at which letter post should operate in summer and in winter. They encouraged serving soldiers to learn a trade. Several Ordinances were directed to behaviour. Challenges and duels were forbidden, cock-fighting, horse-racing and similar pursuits prohibited, not so much for the activities themselves as for their generation of rowdy and seditious meetings. Work was continued on the Great Level of the fens, attention given to the improvement and sale of forests and other land hitherto belonging to the King and his family. Efforts were made to clean up 'abuses' on the Thames and Medway: perhaps Cromwell's mind went back to like improvements for the benefit of the fishing and boating on his native Stour.

On the basic question of religion several Ordinances were promulgated carrying on the principles which had been put forward earlier by Independent ministers and supported by Cromwell himself. In March 1654 a Central Commission of 'Triers' was set up to approve the appointment of ministers. Five months later similar commissions were established in the counties to 'vet' ministers and to expel those 'scandalous in their lives and conversations' or in any way guilty of blasphemy, of drunkenness, or even of sanctioning the erection of maypoles or the acting of stage plays. The appointment of the 'triers' and 'ejectors' was a practical attempt to curb the loose living and to control the abuses which had defied central control. It in no way mitigated Cromwell's basic views on toleration.

None knew better than Cromwell that there were wounds to heal. The Engagement Act which made it incumbent on all office-holders to swear to be faithful to the Commonwealth without King or House of Lords was still on the Statute Book. But to Cromwell such 'general and promisary oaths and engagements' were 'burdens and snares to tender consciences'. The Act was repealed and replaced by a Treason Act less irksome but with more bite which simply made it treason to plot or contrive the death of the Protector, to deny his supreme authority in Parliament, or to stir up, or endeavour to stir up, mutiny in the army.

Most of the Orinances promulgated by Cromwell and his Council before the new Parliament met were confirmed with but slight amendment by the second Protectorate Parliament in a Bill which received the Protector's assent in June 1657.[6]

With so much to do at home it could be understandable if the energy of Cromwell and his Council flagged when considering foreign affairs. The contrary was the case. The Dutch war was with them still, although negotiations for a peace treaty had been going on for months. It was Cromwell's achievement not only to bring these discussions to a conclusion in the treaty signed in April 1654, but to procure favourable terms for his country. The English by then had captured over 1,400 ships from the Dutch, including 120 men-of-war, and were masters of the Narrow Seas. No Dutch merchantman dared show himself in the Channel and there were some 140 English men-of-war at sea ready for any emergency. The terms of the treaty reflected this superiority. The English government and the East India Company were at last to receive compensation for the Amboyna 'massacre' which had occurred during a clash between the two powers in 1623; the Dutch agreed to make good losses incurred by English merchants in the Sound; the English flag was to be acknowledged 'in the British seas', the Dutch dropped their demand for a modification of the Navigation Act of 1651, and both nations agreed to expel from their borders the enemies or rebels of the other and to give aid 'when required' at the expense of the country requesting it. By a secret clause members of the House of Orange, so closely related to the English Royal family, were to be excluded from holding office under the States General. At the banquet Cromwell gave to the Dutch Ambassadors in London they all sang the 123rd psalm: 'Behold how good and how pleasant it is for brethren to dwell together in unity.' Cromwell had hoped for an offensive alliance with the Dutch in the interests of European Protestantism. But it was nevertheless a good treaty for him and for the English.

He was also pressing on with negotiations with Sweden, the land of the great warrior, Gustavus Adolphus, whose Protestant fervour had been equal to Cromwell's own. He sent the staid Whitelocke as his Ambassador to Queen Christina of Sweden who received the envoy with the greatest affability, expressing her ardent admiration for Cromwell. A treaty was signed on 11 April 1654, six days after the treaty with Holland. But it did no more than regulate the commercial intercourse of the two nations while the Swedes agreed not to give help to Charles Stuart or his cause. There followed treaties with Portugal in July 1654 and with Denmark in September of the same year. The Danes had already agreed to compensate English merchants for losses in the Sound during the Dutch wars; they now agreed to let English vessels use the Sound on the same terms as the Dutch. The Portuguese also promised reparation to English merchants for losses incurred during the wars, they promised freedom to English traders from interference by the Inquisition, and, of great commercial significance, they gave leave to English merchants to trade with all Portuguese colonies in the East or West.

None of this added up to the grand Protestant alliance that Cromwell had envisaged, but he had shown that he could not only care for the interests of trade and commerce but be eminently successful in doing so. And this, indeed, to many of his compatriots, was equally, if not more important. He had also demonstrated that he and his government had won recognition and respect throughout Europe; a powerful navy, a large and enterprising merchant fleet, an army demonstrably the match for any that Europe could raise, and himself not only the greatest soldier then alive but a man determined to pursue English interests abroad as he had done the Puritan cause at home.

In Europe itself the greatest source of friction was not religious but the enmity between France and Spain, both Catholic countries. How far could England use their antagonism to her own advantage? Both courted her; both refused the conditions she asked in return for her support. With France these concerned the Huguenots whose rights, which had been granted them under the Treaty of Nantes, Cromwell declared he would uphold if infringed. With Spain English demands concerned freedom for English merchants to practise their religion in Spanish ports without molestation from the Inquisition; and freedom to trade in the Spanish West Indies on a friendly basis. There was at that time no agreement with either France or Spain but Cromwell's horizons had widened. The squire of Huntingdon and Ely was now operating on a world-wide stage. But his gaze could not rest solely on the far horizons. At home he had to meet his first Protectorate Parliament.

Part VIII

Oliver Protector

24

'I called not myself to this place'

The election took place in the summer of 1654. It was the first Parliamentary election for fourteen years. There were to be 340 Members returned for England and Wales, 30 for Scotland and 30 for Ireland. This, in itself, was something of an achievement, that the British Isles, for the first time, were sending representatives to the same Parliament. In practice, however, it amounted to less than this. In Ireland Catholics and rebels were excluded which left an electorate of only English and Scottish settlers, while in Scotland there was little enthusiasm for the election at all. The *Instrument* itself had debarred Royalists and Catholics from voting even in England and Wales and returning officers' indentures were to read that candidates should be bound not to alter the government as then constituted in a single person and a Parliament. Cromwell himself was full of optimism as the election campaigns proceeded: 'the dispensations of the Lord', he said, 'have been as if he had said, England, thou art my first born, my delight amongst the nations, under the whole heavens the Lord hath not dealt so with any of the people round about us.'[1]

The elections were keenly contested but, helped by the narrower franchise, the Members elected were mostly 'moderates', many of them Presbyterians but a goodly number of Independents with a few 'Saints' or men of Leveller principles.[2] Cromwell could have taken comfort from the presence of Bulstrode Whitelocke, 'the truly valuable man' who, with Widdrington, still guarded the Great Seal; of William Lenthall, Speaker since the first days of the Long Parliament whose presence gave continuity to the Interregnum Parliaments; of Dr Owen, Cromwell's chaplain in Ireland, Vice-Chancellor of the University of Oxford; of old William Skippon, the rugged soldier who had watched over and led the London trained bands throughout the conflict; of other soldiers including Lambert, Fleetwood and Claypole (the last two his sons-in-law); of his two sons Richard and Henry; of Richard's father-in-law, Richard Mayor; of Fairfax whom he was glad to see back in affairs; of the 'sound' and useful Nathaniel Fiennes, son of old Lord Saye and Sele who had dominated the Puritan movement before the war. A group of constantly angry Republicans led by Sir Arthur Haselrig and including Judge Bradshaw and Thomas Scot he could have done without. He missed, though perhaps he was pleased to miss, his old friend Sir Harry Vane – whose father, nevertheless, took his seat in the House.

No more than a dozen men, probably less, had been excluded by the Council and its committee which had been formed to examine the returns. Cromwell held aloof. Even when petitioners from the Isle of Ely begged him to consider the case of George Glapthorne, a magistrate who had been elected in spite of the fact that 'he was a common swearer, a common curser, a frequenter of Ale Houses and an upholder of those of evil fame . . . a companion of lewd women . . . not fit to be a law maker or Parliament man' and a petition to this effect signed by 400 people was presented to him on August 15, he referred the matter to his Council.

As Cromwell scanned the returns he would have seen about 125 who had been Members of the Long Parliament, 55 who had served in his Nominated Parliament of Saints – though not more than four of these were ardent Fifth Monarchists. There were 55 solid knights of the shire, seven lords, four earls; 107 he could class as 'military' men, three were judges. He noted, he was certain to do so, eighteen Regicides and eleven more who had sat in judgment on the King. In other respects, also, he was satisfied. St John as Chief Justice, the admirable Thurloe as Secretary to the Council. He could, on the whole, be reasonably happy about the future.[3]

The session opened in the afternoon of September 3, Cromwell's lucky day of Dunbar and Worcester. Hobbes thought he was 'a little superstitious' in the choice.[4] Cromwell, like James I, delighted in date coincidence. It was unfortunate that the 3rd was a Sunday, for this offended some Puritans. Only about 500 Members – about three-quarters of those elected – gathered in Westminster Abbey for the traditional opening sermon and this was about the number who actually took their seats. There was little ceremony. The Members talked a little as they made their way to the Commons, then went at Cromwell's summons to the Painted Chamber: ten or twelve, led by Bradshaw, refused to be 'summoned' and stayed away. The rest heard a brief opening speech and then adjourned until the next day.

Monday September 4 followed tradition in the pageantry of the official opening ceremony. Oliver rode in state from his official residence in Whitehall to Westminster Abbey. He was dressed as a citizen, not as a soldier, quite simply in black suit and cloak with his hat upon his head. He was preceded by hundreds of gentlemen and officers, accompanied by his lifeguard, his pages and his lackeys, all richly dressed and bareheaded. His son Henry and Major-General Lambert rode with him in his coach, both bareheaded. His son-in-law, Claypole, Master of the Horse, led the Protector's richly caparisoned steed, the Captain of his Guard, his Master of Ceremonies, the Commissioners of the Great Seal and others, all richly and elegantly attired, went with him and joined the procession into the Abbey, Lambert bearing the Sword of State, Whitelocke the Purse, Commissioners carrying the Great Seal, newly engraved by Thomas Simon who, as Cromwell had requested from Scotland, was now official Engraver to the Commonwealth.[5] After the sermon Cromwell proceeded to the Painted Chamber, the Members returned to the House of Commons and continued their desultory discussions of the previous day. Cromwell's summons, though expected, was again taken wryly; Charles I had never summoned his Parliaments but had come to them when he wished to address them. Nevertheless they obeyed, though they were somewhat affronted to find the Protector on a raised chair of state surmounted by a canopy while they sat on benches round the wall, their heads uncovered.

'You are here on the greatest occasion that, I believe, England ever saw', he told them,

> having upon your shoulders the interests of three great nations with the territories belonging to them. And truly, I believe I may say it without an hyperbole, you have upon your shoulders the interest of all the Christian people in the world.

The object of their coming together was 'Healing and Settling', and not to 'set the wound fresh a-bleeding'. If you do not heal, he said, 'what shall we do?'

He went on to consider the condition of the nation in 'civils' and 'spirituals'. In civil affairs he fastened upon the Levellers in a way that explained his severity towards them and Lilburne. Rather than highlighting a Royalist danger or the conflict between Republicans and Protectorate he seized upon the threat to the established social order from people of 'levelling' beliefs who would have upset 'the ranks and orders of men, whereby England hath been known for hundreds of years'. 'A nobleman, a gentleman, a yeoman', he said, 'the distinction of these ... that is a good interest of the nation and a great one!' This natural magistracy of the nation, 'was it not almost trampled under foot, under despite and contempt by men of Levelling principles?' 'Did not that Levelling principle tend to the reducing all to an equality? ... what was the design but to make the tenant as liberal a fortune as the landlord?' And this was a principle that would have extended not only to all poor men but to all bad men.

Then he turned to 'spirituals' where the situation 'was more sad and deplorable' still. Liberty of conscience and liberty of the subject were 'two as glorious things to be contended for as any God hath given us' yet both had been abused 'for the patronising of villainies' for 'pernicious notions' which, in the name of conscience, the magistrate had been powerless to stem. In the old days, he said, no man could preach unless he had been ordained. Now we seemed to be at the other extreme where only those who had not been trained to religion could do so. He spoke of the Fifth Monarchists. 'We all hope,' he said, 'that Jesus Christ will have a time to set up His reign in our hearts. But for men to entitle themselves, on this principle, that they are the only men to rule kingdoms, govern nations, and give laws to people ... truly, they had need give clear manifestations of God's presence with them, before wise men will recieve or submit to their conclusions!'

The nation, he said, had been rent and torn in spirit and principle from one end to another – 'family against family, husband against wife, parents against children, and nothing in the hearts and minds of men but 'Overturn, overturn, overturn!' There were wars with Portugal, with Holland, with France; we were 'spoiled' in our trade, the 'purse of the nation' could no longer stand it. Cloth manufacture, the great staple commodity of the nation, was threatened by the competition of other countries who had taken advantage of our troubles. 'What a heap of confusions were upon these poor nations!' But 'a remedy hath been applied'. And he spoke a little of what had been done.

He had made peace with the Dutch and with the Dane and a treaty with Portugal was in process. He spoke briefly of some of his Ordinances, referring with pride to the Ordinance on religion. Bills were being prepared to ensure that the Laws were plain and short and less chargeable; Chancery was being reformed; he warned of the serious position of the country's finances – 'forfeited' lands sold, rents, fee-farms, delinquents' lands, all sold and their proceeds spent. That was the reason why taxes still lay so heavily upon the people. He charged his listeners 'to a sweet, gracious and holy understanding of one another' and then dismissed them: 'I shall . . . trouble you no longer; but desire you to repair to your House, and to exercise your own liberty in the choice of a Speaker, that so you may lose no time in carrying on your work.'[6]

It was a confident speech. He felt they were on the right road and on the whole was satisfied with the way things were turning out. He went quietly back to his home in Whitehall leaving the Members of Parliament to return to the Commons Chamber.

Once more Lenthall was chosen as their Speaker; it was a victory for Cromwell that Bradshaw, who was also proposed, was rejected. But as early as September 7 – only four days after Parliament assembled – Haselrig plunged still deeper into controversy by proposing that though government might be in a single person he should be 'limited and restrained' as the Commons should think fit. This was an unnecessary and provocative underlining of what was explicit in the *Instrument*: that the Protector's power was limited by the financial control that remained in Parliament. It also showed scant respect for the Council of State which, by the terms of the *Instrument*, would assist and control the Protector.

But when, on their own in their Chamber, the Members turned to debate it became clear that compliance with the *Instrument* and with Cromwell's position was not a foregone conclusion. The lawyer Hale took up a middle-of-the-road position supporting the idea of government in a single person responsible to Parliament while Parliament was restrained from perpetuating itself, from controlling the militia, or interfering with freedom of worship. But the notion of any restraint at all upon Parliament was not acceptable to the Republicans in the House and more and more the debate hinged on the question of sovereignty: who was the supreme authority – Parliament or Protector? There was logic in the assumption that it could not be both. In many ways the debate was reminiscent of the early days of the Long Parliament with Parliamentary sovereignty measured against Oliver Protector rather than against King Charles I. Feelings ran so high that Bradshaw said that if he must have a master he would prefer Charles to Oliver, while Ludlow bitterly exclaimed that it had seemed that England was about 'to attain in a short time that measure of happiness which humane things are capable of, when by the ambition of one man the hopes and expectations of all good men were disappointed'. But it was left to another Member to ride roughshod over the *Instrument*, setting at nought all its safeguards, by declaring that the Protector's right to rule could 'be measured out no otherwise than by the length of his sword'.[7]

Cromwell had the army behind him, but to be accused of military dictatorship after all his care to create a constitutional settlement with checks and balances between a Parliamentary legislature and a conciliar executive, stung him to the quick. He was further roused when Haselrig cried out for 'one good form' of religion (presumably Presbyterianism) and the suppression of all sects. In fury he again, on September 12, summoned the House of Commons to the Painted Chamber.

He claimed the support of the 'good people of England' in voting for the Parliament and accepting the *Instrument* which was read out at polling stations expressly that they and the people elected should know they did not have power to alter it. 'I told you you were a free Parliament', he said, 'and so you are, whilst you own the government and authority that called you hither. For certainly that word "free Parliament" implied a reciprocity or it implied nothing at all.'

His speech was the great justification for all he had done since his return from Worcester. It reflects all the struggles, all the uncertainties of a soul trying to do the right thing, trying to succeed; not of a man seeking self-aggrandisement but of a man fighting against difficulties – almost a nightmare of shadows and indeterminate shapes and obstacles. He had come through so much, in battle and in constitutional fighting and now – before his proposed solution had even been tried out – in less than two weeks, ten short days, they were turning on him and his settlement to rend it apart.

'I have indeed almost tired myself' was the only admission he made of the strain upon him. He emphasized that this high office was not of his calling. Four times he reiterated the disavowal: 'I called not myself to this place. I say again, I called not myself to

this place. Of that God is witness. And I have many witnesses who
... could readily lay down their lives to bear witness to the truth
of that ... that I called not myself to this place!' Then a little later
he repeated, 'That I called not myself to this place is my first assertion.'
But he required justification fully and completely. 'I must take liberty
to look back: I was by birth a gentleman, living neither in any considerable height, nor yet in obscurity. I have been called to several
employments in the nation, to serve in Parliaments and other affairs.
I will not', he said, refraining of speaking of his military successes,
'recite the times and occasions and opportunities that have been
appointed me by God to serve Him in.'

He had hoped, in a private capacity, to have reaped the benefit,
with others, of their 'hard labours and hazards'. But when he came
to London after Worcester he was 'much disappointed'. 'I had hoped
to have had leave', he said, 'to have retired into a private life', but
what he saw prevented him. He went on to justify his ejection of
the Rump: they intended to 'perpetuate' themselves, he said, giving
the same reason for the expulsion as he had given to the Barebones
Parliament. He justified the calling of that Parliament, referring again
and again to the extent of his own power – 'the authority I had
in my hand being so boundless as it was, I being by Act of Parliament
General of all the forces in the three nations of England, Scotland
and Ireland'. He voluntarily delegated this power to the Barebones
Parliament. After its resignation his power was again, as he put it,
'as boundless and unlimited as before; all things being subjected to
arbitrariness, and myself the only constituted authority that was left,
a person having power over the three nations, without bound or
limit set, and ... all Government dissolved, all civil administration
at an end.'

He emphasized that he himself had had no hand in devising the
Instrument of Government, that he had had to be pressed hard to take
upon himself the office of Protector, that this office put him in no
higher position than he had been in before, but rather limited him.
But he took occasion again to emphasize that he had the armies of
three nations under his command – ' and truly not very ill beloved
by them, nor very ill beloved by the people'.

Then he spoke of 'fundamentals'. Government by a single person
and a Parliament was fundamental (he did not explain the reasoning
that had led him to this basic assumption), so was the provision
that Parliaments should not make themselves perpetual; so was liberty

271

of conscience, and he allowed himself to expand on the subject so close to his heart. Liberty of conscience was a 'natural right; and he that would have it, ought to give it.' Thus simply Cromwell expressed his basic belief, which was there when he recruited his 'men of a spirit' for his first regiment, which he demonstrated time and time again throughout the wars. And now he asks again: 'What have we fought for?' And he answers, 'All the money of this nation would not have tempted men to fight ... if they had not had hopes of liberty better than they had from Episcopacy, or than would have been afforded them from a Scottish Presbytery – or an English either ... if it had ... been as sharp and rigid as it threatened when it was first set up.'

Then, rather more quietly, he turned to his fourth fundamental, the control of the militia. What check is there upon perpetual Parliaments if *they* have complete control? Or upon Protector if *he* should control? Cromwell was groping his way through the principles of political obligation. He had come to them the hard, practical way, unlike Hobbes, for whom such questions were more of an intellectual exercise, unlike the men who considered such matters before the war in the rarified atmosphere of their country houses. But when he came to them they were the basic requirements of democratic government.

Cromwell came then, much more briefly, to 'circumstantials' which he conceded could be modified: income and taxation were subject to circumstances and conditions; even the size of the army could be modified according to needs. It was a long speech. 'I have, indeed, almost tired myself', he admitted. He permitted himself one final, sad reproach: 'You had the affairs of these nations delivered over to you in peace and quietness ... through the blessing of God, our enemies were hopeless and scattered. We had peace at home; peace almost with all neighbours round about. These things we had, few days ago, when you came hither. And now?'

'I have caused a stop to be put to your entrance into the Parliament House', he concluded. 'I am sorry, and I could be sorry to the death, that there is cause for this.'

It was not, however, a dissolution but a demand to sign a *Recognition* agreeing to the form of government as then settled in a single person and a Parliament. There was insolence in his final words: 'The place where you may come thus and sign ... is in the lobby without the Parliament door'.[8] But on the same day he released Fifth

Monarchy Harrison from house arrest and gave him a good dinner with many friendly words, begging him not to persist in those deceitful and slippery ways whose end is destruction. He was making every effort.

The following day, Wednesday the 13th, was a fast day and Oliver kept it quietly with his family at home in Whitehall, possibly much with his mother who was over ninety and in failing health.

On Friday the 15th he turned to the City, summoning the Common Council to a two-hour speech in the Old Council Chamber at Whitehall. He warned them to 'look to three sorts of men' – 'the violent cavalier', 'the rigid Presbyterian' and 'the dangerous Anabaptist'. Thus he encapsulated what he saw as the chief dangers to the state and to religion. Meanwhile some hundred Members of Parliament had signed the *Recognition* of government in a single person and a Parliament. Others took time and met over dinner to decide what they should do. They came in by dribs and drabs but by the end of the month about 300 had signed.[9] It was, after all, a not unreasonable recognition of what the majority had accepted by being voted for as Members of Parliament. But Haselrig, Bradshaw, Scot and about a hundred, mostly Republicans, did not return to the House that session but rode away to their homes in the country.

The followng day he was at his mother's bedside. As she lay dying she gave him her blessing: 'The Lord cause His face to shine upon you, and comfort you in all your adversities, and enable you to do great things for the glory of your Most High God, and to be a relief unto His people. My dear son, I leave my heart with thee. A good night!'

25

'I came with joy the first time, with some regret the second . . . now with most regret of all'

Cromwell was sufficiently relaxed to enjoy a picnic in Hyde Park on the 29th, attended only by Thurloe and a few servants. After the meal he tried out a team of four splendid horses sent him by the Duke of Oldenburgh. He himself took two in hand, a postillion the other two. The animals, in a strange situation, took fright, threw first the postillion and finally Cromwell himself who was dragged some way by the foot in the course of which indignity a pistol went off. There was considerable panic in his entourage and among the bystanders. Thurloe, who was riding with him, leapt from the coach and dislocated his ankle. It was uncertain whether it was his pistol or Cromwell's that went off. But the Protector himself merely brushed down his suit and was later let blood and made to rest. The picture of Oliver picnicking in Hyde Park is pleasant indeed; the accident envisages one of the 'ifs' of history.[1]

Parliament, under the terms of the *Instrument*, had five months to run. It talked a lot but did nothing of importance. It discussed a few reforms, tackled but did not complete a few bills and voted no taxes. There was less money for the army which entailed hardship for the soldiery, more reliance upon free quarter which entailed hardship for the householder. There was a marked reluctance to discuss any kind of Poor Law reform, nor did legal reform arouse much interest. In the absence of the keenest Republicans there were no violent debates, no angry scenes, but there were Members whose dogged criticism of the *Instrument* could be equally damaging and, to Cromwell, equally wearing. If he dismissed Parliament before five months were up he had himself broken the *Instrument*, so they went on, not breaking but whittling down the terms under which they sat; Members of the Council should obtain confirmation of their places from each successive Parliament; no longer would they be appointed for life; the Protector's successor would be chosen by Parliament; the Protector himself would have no vote. This ineffectual Parliament also demanded control of the army for itself, a much reduced standing army, and a return to the militia in the counties under the old Lords Lieutenant. As if this was not enough they signalled their determination to make toleration less basic. Proposals to limit toleration to any degree shook Cromwell hard. Even so mild a stipulation as Baxter's that the Lord's Prayer, the Creed and the Decalogue should be essential requirements of worship aroused his ire and he 'smothered' Baxter in the stream of his wrath.[2]

Cromwell still had support in this Parliament, particularly among the senior officers. Yet opposition was dogged, led by younger, rising figures like Arthur Onslow, Anthony Ashley Cooper, Colonel John Birch. And, what was most bitter to him, in all this talk they made no reference, no approach to him. Not once did they offer consultation or discussion. Outside Parliament, meantime, Fifth Monarchy men still had command of many pulpits, Baptists were active in the army itself, the anti-government press circulated its broadsheets and petitions as it had done throughout the long conflict: neither Royalist, Parliamentarian, Army nor Protectoral censorship could silence the men who wanted to be heard. Royalist invasion and Leveller uprising were rumoured. None of this is what Cromwell had envisaged. Fortunately for him, in spite of its verbal activity, Parliament had enacted nothing and the *Instrument* and his Ordinances still stood intact as they had done on 13 September 1654 when he gave life to this Parliament. It was a maddening situation for Cromwell to come to terms with. Was there any way by which he could control this Parliament? Prize out of them the most essential legislation? Keep them from whittling down and abrogating the *Instrument*? He brooded and decided not. The sooner they went the better. So, obeying the terms of the *Instrument* to the letter and although they had not even voted one penny of supply, he acted at the end of five lunar, not calendar months.

On Monday morning, 22 January 1655, Oliver Protector sent a message to the Commons that they should attend him in the Painted Chamber and leave 'settling of the Government' for a while. The ironic message took them by surprise for they were thinking they were safe until February 3. But they went.

'Gentlemen', he began on the same ironic note, 'I perceive you are here as the House of Parliament, by your Speaker whom I see here, and by your faces which are in a great measure known to me.'

But, as he spoke, sadness and disillusion took over. They had begun in hope and happiness but since the signing of the *Recognition* they had not once been in touch with him. 'I do not know what you have been doing! ... I have not once heard from you in all this time.' Yet discontent, division and danger were threatening from cavaliers, and 'worse ... if worse can be' from 'another sort' who were 'endeavouring to put us into blood and into confusion'.

'I must say', he continued, 'there is some contentment in the hand by which a man falls; so is it some satisfaction, if a Commonwealth must perish, that it perish by men, and not by the hands of persons differing little from beasts! That if it must needs suffer, it should rather suffer from rich men than from poor men, who, as Solomon says, "when they oppress, they leave nothing behind them, but are as a sweeping rain."' The cause of this outburst became apparent as he went on. Men like this had been 'debauching and dividing the Army'. 'They have! they have!', he cried in rising fury. And why were they able to do so? Because of the actions of the Parliament in stopping pay, putting the men to free quarter!

He then came to questions of conscience.

> Is there not yet upon the spirits of men a strange itch? Nothing will satisfy them, unless they can put their finger upon their brethren's consciences to pinch them there. To do this was no part of the contest we had with the common adversary; for religion was not the thing at the first contested for, but God brought it to that issue at last ... and at last it proved to be that which was most dear to us ...'

But those who had won liberty for themselves 'was it fit for them to sit heavy upon others? Is it ingenuous to ask liberty and not to give it?' What greater hypocrisy, he cried, than for those who were oppressed by the bishops to become the greatest oppressors themselves, so soon as their own yoke was removed!

In a three-hour speech he went on to concede that profane persons should be punished by the civil law; he spoke of the militia which must be under the joint control of Parliament and Protector; he disclaimed any desire to make his office hereditary. Several times he returned to their failure to raise supply and the consequent plight of the army – thirty weeks in arrears of pay in Scotland. Were they looking for mutiny? And on free quarter in England. Was this a deliberate provocation? I hope this was not in your minds, he said. I am not willing to judge so. Yet 'you would never so much as let me hear a tittle from you concerning it'.

He spoke of his meetings with this Parliament: 'I came with joy the first time; with some regret the second; . . . now with most regret of all.' Their dilatoriness was unpardonable: '. . . if it be my liberty to walk abroad in the fields, or to take a journey, yet it is not my wisdom to do so when my house is on fire!' Then, in a sudden end to this long speech, 'I think it my duty to tell you', he said, 'that it is not for the profit of these nations, nor for the common and public good, for you to continue here any longer, and therefore, I do declare unto you, that I do dissolve this Parliament.'[3]

Opposition to the Protectorate came from Royalists, Republicans, religious sects, particularly Fifth Monarchists, and from a wide range of people who thought they perceived the shadow of military dictatorship in Oliver Protector: the settlement under which the country was now governed originated with the army; Cromwell's most consistent support came from the army; and he himself had not hesitated to use force or a show of force to get his own way. In such hands political power could easily slip over into military dictatorship. Cromwell had to show that it would not, but the onus of proof was upon him.

There was a contributory cause of dissatisfaction in the style of life he adopted. In conducting foreign affairs, which entailed receiving foreign dignitaries and Ambassadors, it was necessary to uphold the tradition of courtly life observed in Europe. The state of the Protector and his ministers, court officials and servants would be bandied round the Courts of Europe and the standing of the Commonwealth assessed thereby. Although Oliver had no interest in the trappings of attire and ceremony it was inevitable that his dress became more rich and formal, his seat a chair of state, the hangings and furnishings of his audience chamber more costly, his officials more self-consciously grouped around him, bareheaded. For inevitably there grew up what could only be described as a Court with dignitaries, officials, supplicants, foreign emissaries, visitors of all kinds who, with their wives, created a considerable social *milieu*. The actual words 'Court' and 'courtier' began to appear. Perhaps Cromwell went too far.

Warwick complained, 'Now he models his house that it might have some resemblance to a court, and his liveries, lackies, and yeomen of the guard are known whom they belong to by their habit.' Cromwell himself was physically impressive and with the confidence bred of success he carried his position with a regal dignity that surprised visitors. Privately, abetted by his wife, he lived simply, almost frugally. Eggs and 'slaps' were said to be sufficient for his evening meal together with the 'small ale' called Morning Dew. But they made concession to public demand by occasionally dining publicly, as the King had done, though not in so great a state. There was a public dinner every Monday to all officers of the rank of Captain and above, and a table was kept ready for officers who arrived more casually.[4]

The organization of this public life now required a Lord Chamberlain and a Comptroller of the Household, whose very names caused eyebrows to raise. The number of erstwhile royal residences now at Cromwell's disposal also aroused comment. The Cockpit, St James's House and Park, the Mews, Somerset House, Greenwich House and Park (Henrietta Maria's 'Queen's House' built by Inigo Jones), Windsor Castle, Hampton Court were all earmarked for the Lord Protector and his family. Some royal furnishings were re-purchased. Among the treasures of Charles I the magnificent Mantegna's *Triumphs of Julius Caesar* hung in the Long Gallery at Hampton Court, a fitting symbol to Cromwell of his own achievements.

But he tried to preserve the homely touch. At least one Ambassador commented on his simplicity: 'He met me in the middle of the room and on my departure he accompanied me to the door.' He came to meet a deputation from the City of London, stood uncovered, read their petition there and then and asked relevant questions. With old friends he could relax completely. Whitelocke recounts how in the intervals of business he would make them all write verses while he called for tobacco pipes and himself joined in the smoking.[5]

He was never one for dress. Sir John Reresby saw that he was 'plain in his apparel, and rather affected negligence than a genteel garb'. But Warwick could not forget the East Anglian farmer he had first seen in the House of Commons a decade earlier and was surprised at what he now saw: a person 'of great and majestic deportment and comely presence'. This, he added caustically, was 'having had a better tailor, and more converse with good company'.[6] But all is in the eye of the beholder. The soldier Alured was cashiered in December 1654 for saying 'The King did never wear such clothing as the Lord Protector did, being embroidered with gold and silver.'[7]

Cromwell's love of music added a background to Court life which, if not comparable to the masques of Charles's day, dispelled any picture of Puritan gloom. In April 1654 on the conclusion of peace with Holland an entertainment was given to honour the Dutch Ambassador; '. . . music played all the while we were at dinner', the Dutchman recorded. Afterwards 'the Lord Protector had us into another room, where the Lady Protectress and others came to us, where we had also music, and voices and a psalm sung.'[8]

Of the Cromwell sons Richard, the eldest, lived privately, somewhat recklessly and extravagantly, but not upon the public purse. His incursions into Court life were nevertheless strongly criticized. Henry was a well-thought-of serving officer in Ireland. The eldest daughter, Bridget, deeply pious, spent most of her time in Ireland as the wife of Fleetwood and was left out of the gossip. The other three daughters were frequently accused of flightiness, extravagance, and taking too easily to Court life. It ill became them, according to the Puritan and somewhat crabbed Lucy Hutchinson. While she conceded that the Protector himself had 'much natural greatness and well became' his place, court life became his wife and children 'no better . . . than scarlet on the ape'.[9] She did, however, admit that Elizabeth had some natural grace. Elizabeth, Cromwell's second daughter, the 'Bettie' of the letters, loved the life of gaiety which had developed round her father and fitted naturally into its more intellectual side. To her the antagonisms of the civil war seemed so far removed that she had no compunction in using a Royalist friend, Sir John Southcote, who had been exiled after Naseby, to buy damask beds and dress material for her in Paris. She also enjoyed the company of many of the distinguished men who came to her father's Court. With James Harrington, for example, she enjoyed a spirited friendship and was popularly thought to have interceded with her father for the publication of his *Oceana*. Oliver loved her dearly but she worried him at times. He had written to Bridget in 1646, shortly after the weddings of the two girls, of Bettie's 'own vanity and carnal mind'. Writing from Scotland in 1651 he had begged his wife to 'mind [remind] poor Bettie of the Lord's great mercy, Oh, I desire her not only to seek the Lord in her necessity, but in deed and in truth turn to the Lord; and to keep close to Him', he said.[10]

Thomas Hobbes returned to England in 1652 in spite of associations with the exiled Royalists in Paris and took up residence with the Earl of Devonshire. The grim-faced Latin secretary, John Milton, appeared seldom at Court. With Andrew Marvell there were closer connections, though preferment by the Protector was strangely slow in coming. After the publication of his *Horatian Ode* on Cromwell's return from Ireland Marvell retired to Nun Appleton to tutor Fairfax's daughter and later applied vainly for a post in Cromwell's government. He had to be content with acting as tutor to Cromwell's ward, William Dutton, and with him spent much time at Eton before travelling in France. When at last in 1657 he was appointed Latin secretary under Thurloe both Cromwell and Elizabeth were ill. Although so little of his time had been spent at Court Marvell's poems show that he was well acquainted with the Protector and well aware of the Protector's close relationship with Elizabeth.

It was inevitable that Cromwell's Court itself and such harmless contacts as these should help to build up a picture of personal aggrandisement, inevitable also that, in spite of repeated denials, Cromwell should be accused of seeking to restore the monarchy in his own person or, at least, of making the office of Protector hereditary.

26

Swordsmen and Decimators

There was enough opposition and discontent of one kind and another to give rise to the plots and attempted insurrection of which Thurloe kept Cromwell informed through an Intelligence service that intercepted letters and instructions, used spies and *agents provocateurs*, investigated Cromwell's own officials and interrogated prisoners. The Protector heard rumours of combinations of Royalists with Fifth Monarchy Men and Anabaptists, of secret meetings where cartloads of arms were dispensed. He knew of the Sealed Knot, the Royalist secret society which had been founded in 1654 and was now preparing for action. He knew that Charles Stuart was waiting at Middleburg on the Dutch coast to make a concerted attack with the insurrectionists. John Wildman, the erstwhile Leveller, had thrown in his lot with the Sealed Knot and was actually dictating an anti-Government manifesto when he was arrested by a party of horse at Exton near Marlborough in February 1655. He was imprisoned in Chepstow Castle and the planned Royalist rising in which Colonel Penruddock played a leading part was easily suppressed near Salisbury on March 11. It had been rumoured that on February 12 Cromwell was to be assassinated. His response was to send abroad the officers implicated and to replace them by troops newly arrived from Ireland; to treble his guards, seize all horses that could be found in the City and suburbs, and to secure the City and an area four miles around. Two days later he went to the City himself and read out both Wildman's manifesto and a publication from Charles Stuart to justify his actions and demonstrate the reality of the plots against the Government. Major-General Overton, commander in the North who had been brought into the plot, was imprisoned first in the Tower and then sent to join Lilburne in Jersey. Fifth Monarchy Harrison was sent to the King's erstwhile prison at Carisbrooke: it was Harrison who had conducted the monarch to Windsor Castle after he had been brought from Carisbrooke to the mainland at the end of 1648. Royalist leaders, including Penruddock, were executed, many of less note were transported to the Plantations.

Although in no sense panicking the Protector took the assassination attempts seriously. It was said, though probably with little truth, that he frequently changed his route between Whitehall and Hampton Court, that he never slept in the same bed twice, that – and this is more likely – the guards whom he kept around him both by night and by day were armed with pistols as well as swords.[1] Certainly the threats against his person reinforced his determination to stamp out unrest over the whole country. In the novel form his policing took he was also influenced by Parliament's resolution at the beginning of the year to take from him the full control of the militia, which the *Instrument* had vested in him alone. But typically, in the summer, by an act of bravado or of necessity, he agreed to the disbanding of 10–12,000 of his soldiers.

In the immediate aftermath of the insurrections of the spring of 1655 Cromwell tried the experiment of giving his brother-in-law Major-General Desborough, who commanded in the disaffected south-west of the country, a more general brief which included raising and training a militia which would look after the interests of the Commonwealth in that area. A new Parliament was not due until the autumn of 1657 and in the meantime the idea of Major-Generals responsible for designated areas seemed a good one. Well before the end of 1655 twelve had been appointed and their powers were considerable. They not only had control of the existing militia but were given powers of raising an additional standing militia of horse. A new and ingenious if not wholly fair form of taxation raised the money necessary to pay for their enterprise. This 'decimation tax' was a ten per cent levy on all Royalist property of more than £100 per annum. It aroused considerable opposition. Apart from questions of who were Royalists and whether people who had compounded or whose estates had been confiscated should pay again, it created a great unease in areas where wounds were beginning to heal.

The Directives issued to the Major-Generals were detailed.[2] They included the suppression of insurrection, rebellion or tumults (all three terms were used), the prevention of unlawful assemblies, or of 'invasion from abroad'. They echoed the Elizabethan Code against 'idle and loose people', who were to be employed and 'better provided for' or 'sent out of the Commonwealth'. With these ends in mind the Major-Generals should disarm 'Papists and others' who had been in arms against the Parliament; they should ferret out 'thieves, robbers, highwaymen and other dangerous persons as lurk and lie hid' by highways and in lodging houses. They were to have an ear and an eye open for 'the conversation and carriage' of disaffected persons. They were to prevent any activity that might encourage dissaffection. To this end a wide range of activities that attracted crowds of people where 'treason and rebellion is usually hatched and contrived ... and much evil and wickedness committed' were to be forbidden. Horse-racing, cock-fighting, bear-baiting, stage-plays, gaming houses, 'houses of evil fame', and such 'ale houses, taverns, and victualling houses' as were considered likely harbourers of discontent and were not 'necessary to travellers' would be suppressed.

Neither the moral implications of the many prohibitions nor the insistence of Cromwell and his Major-Generals that they were concerned with the maintenance of law and order and not with the suppression of innocent pastimes did much to placate a population which, after years of disturbance, wanted to settle down and enjoy itself. It was all very well that the Major-Generals in their own persons were to 'encourage and promote godliness and virtue' and avoid drunkenness and profanity. But when 'profaning the Lord's Day', which merely meant indulging in sport and recreation on the Sabbath, was made a punishable offence, the example of the Major-Generals hardly mattered. When it was announced that 'if any persons commonly called fiddlers or minstrels shall ... be taken playing, fiddling and making music in any inn, alehouse, or tavern' they should be adjudged rogues or vagabonds, the crusade for law and order seemed to have assumed grotesque proportions. It was, indeed, strangely at variance with the Protector's own love of music that these cheerful minstrels should suffer a blanket prohibition.

The cases that came within the jurisdiction of the Major-Generals included people who were 'drunken and quarrelsome'. One man, an old Royalist soldier, who had been apprehended for this reason had a wife in London but had wandered up and down the country pretending to be a farrier and had 'gone a wooing to two maids' who lent him money on promise of marriage; there were highwaymen; a brewer who brewed without licence, kept a lewd house and harboured highwaymen; there were profane talkers, 'a mad ranting blade' who had attacked others without provocation; a bailiff who had used his position to frighten people and force false statements from them as a means of obtaining money. The Major-Generals were expected to operate the old medieval laws against installing and regrating, all of the Elizabethan Code against sturdy beggars and the like, as well as the newly made laws and Ordinances of the Commonwealth and Protectorate. On the whole they had little support from either the Protector or his Council.

In pursuit of their aims they suppressed 200 alehouses in the hundred of Blackburn in Lancashire alone. At Chester nearly 200 more were shut. Alehouses were, wrote Major-General Worsley, 'the very bane of the country'. The Justices in Shropshire, acting for the Major-Generals, clearly linked morality with disaffection. The regulation of markets also closely concerned the Major-Generals and caused much controversy over such questions as their opening hours or whether Saturday or Sunday markets might interfere with Sunday worship and the sanctity of the Sabbath generally. They had more support in clearing gaols and deporting the worst criminals, though efforts to enforce the Poor Law were taken badly and none of their attempts at social amelioration could compare with the success of Charles I's *Book of Orders*. Controversial, for different reasons, were the attempts made by the Major-Generals to operate the laws against enclosure and the neglect of tillage. They also had to deal with the ejection of 'scandalous ministers' through the Boards of Ejectors appointed under Cromwell's Ordinance of 1654. Walter Bushell, for example, was ejected in this way from the vicarage of Box. It is hardly surprising that, with duties of such wide and varying scope, there was not always uniformity between them. Charles Worsley, on the one hand, prohibited racing in Cheshire, Edward Whalley permitted it in Lincoln. His leniency may have been partly due to what he considered the success of his administration. 'I may truly say', he wrote, 'you may ride over all Nottinghamshire, and not see a beggar or a wandering rogue.'[3]

In carrying out their instructions the Major-Generals had full control of the local militia, horse and foot, that they raised, and they worked with specially appointed Commissioners of the Peace who had powers of fine and imprisonment. A reduction in the standing army to some extent mitigated anger over their policing methods but the new Commissioners of the Peace were bitterly resented as an alien and unnecessary interference with the local magistrates and the traditional and largely independent running of the locality.

The Major–Generals were diligent, most of them regarded their task as cleansing the country from immorality and sedition, as their *Reports* make clear. But they were soon in financial difficulties and the proceeds of the Decimation tax were insufficient to meet their commitments. Attempts to increase the yield by reducing the property qualification for payment came to nothing, but merely built up more hostility against them.

Some of their activities made for greater order and were a protection against revolt but their impact upon the social life of the areas they controlled was considerable. And overall was the disturbing presence of an alien military control insufficiently sensitive to background or to local custom, exercised by men who were often socially and ideologically at variance with the people they should be working with, and less sensitive to local feeling than the former Lords Lieutenant who, whatever their failings, generally had their roots in the area. Appeal from the rule of the Major–Generals was possible only to the Protector himself and his Council. Cromwell's record was good, but London was far away and it was felt that the Major–Generals were the new masters. It was insensitive of Cromwell not to have foreseen such a reaction. Yet he was trying to delegate. In the unsettled state of the country the alternative might well have been a military dictatorship from the centre. But no excuses, no explanation, had any effect. To the country as a whole the rule of the Major–Generals remained a repressive and arbitrary as well as an alien and military régime unknown and unsuited to the people of England.[4]

In June 1655 news reached London of the massacre of Protestants in a Protestant enclave in the valleys of High Savoy. The 'slaughtered Saints' of Milton's sonnet brought tears from Cromwell and a donation of £2,000 from his own purse to the subscription which was immediately raised. To emphasize in an even more practical manner his demand for action he refused to sign the treaty with France which was then ready until the King of France and his minister Cardinal Mazarin had undertaken to expostulate with the Duke of Savoy.

Cromwell had chosen to support France in the long rivalry between France and Spain. He had spoken of peace to his first Protectorate Parliament but as he dissolved that Parliament a fleet of thirty-eight ships under Admiral William Penn, an experienced sailor, with 2,500 soldiers under Robert Venables, a veteran of the Irish service, was on its way to the West Indies, with instructions to attack the Spanish colonies and to make prize of any French as well as Spanish ships he encountered: the instructions indicated that when determining the enemy the issue was not always clear-cut. Cromwell did not have the full support of his Council, Lambert, in particular, being strong against the enterprise. In the event Lambert proved right, for Penn's expedition was not a success and his soldiers proved little better than those who had sailed under Buckingham. The English, however, landed in Jamaica and in October 1655 war with Spain officially began.

Cromwell's colonial policy – the 'Western Design' as his Council called it – was something new. The country was familiar enough with the buccaneering exploits in the Spanish Main of a couple of generations earlier; they all shared with their grandfathers the hatred of Spain and the Inquisition. But colonization was different and the colonies themselves had grown up and had been peopled in Cromwell's lifetime. The same quickness of perception, adaptation and rapidity of action that had brought Cromwell so effectively from farming into soldiery now enabled him to perceive and to grasp another issue which was equally new to him. His natural belligerence helped him. The atmosphere in which he grew up was still redolent of the naval war against Spain; the victories of the English sea-dogs under Elizabeth I were the folklore of his time; he had married in the year the *Mayflower* sailed. He had experienced shame at the puerile policy of James and the naval disasters of Charles. He associated the New World of the Carribean Islands and the American shores with the Protestant religion – Vane was only one of the friends who had lived in the New World and he had himself thought more than once of emigrating; and the valiant settlers had sent him volunteers for his armies.

Parallel to the religious haven afforded by the West were the material advantages of trade and the bonus of raw materials – sugar, cotton, tobacco. He remembered the Providence Island Company of which so many of his friends were members – an ideal combination of economic aims and religious fervour but destroyed by Spain in 1640. With religion and trade went an almost rabid imperialism. England – the England for which and by which and in which he had fought and won – *his* England – was destined to greatness. United with Scotland and Ireland her destiny was to reach out and control the Western oceans. He firmly believed in *mare clausum*. That he was faced by a Spanish trade monopoly made the need for war greater; that he was pitching himself against a power who had controlled the western seas for centuries merely egged him on.

The decision to fight Spain and support France entailed the use of Cromwell's soldiers to fight the Spanish in Flanders. The price of this support would be the cession of Dunkirk to England by the French. Here, again, Cromwell's mind, trained as a soldier, seized on the necessity for England to command the Channel, as she could do with a European land base in her hands, as she had done until the loss of Calais left her open.

These imperialist schemes of Cromwell's required money and the strains on the Protectorate were growing.

It was still necessary to maintain armies in Ireland and in Scotland as well as a force in England and Wales, though the size of the army at home had been reduced by May 1655 and a local militia established in the counties. But there was now also a powerful fleet to support. The cost of Thurloe's efficient Intelligence Service was high, and though kept to a minimum there were still the expenses of Court and foreign embassies to meet. Cromwell could still count on income from the monthly assessments on the counties and from the customs and excise but the Decimation tax served only to pay expenses in the counties where it was raised. Advances on security were hardly possible since many earlier advances were still unredeemed and some well-established City merchants like Vassall and Avery had been driven into debt and lay in prison as a consequence. A few semi-forced loans were made – if ever the spirit of Charles I brooded over the Protectorate it did so now! To add to Cromwell's difficulties and point the resemblance still more clearly, the lawyers were beginning to turn against him. Even Whitelocke, hitherto faithful, resigned the Great Seal because of his objections to Cromwell's Chancery Ordinance. A London merchant named George Cony refused in June 1655 to pay the tax on Spanish wine on the grounds of the invalidity of the Ordinance that imposed it; Sir Peter Wentworth joined in by voicing the old claim that no taxes were valid except by common consent in Parliament, and the lawyers spoke in terms of *Magna Carta*. The two men gave in, having made their protest, but the episode not only underlined the Protector's financial difficulties but revealed the constitutional dilemma. It was not a good time to embark on a costly war with Spain. Like Charles I before him, Cromwell was faced with the necessity of summoning another Parliament. But under the terms of the *Instrument* elections were not yet due and Cromwell and his Council spent long sessions in discussing the dilemma. In the end Cromwell sent out the writs in July, nearly a year early.

The Major-Generals, like Cromwell, could see no alternative to another Parliament. They themselves could not help him financially and they preferred a constitutional settlement to any form of coercion at their disposal. Thomas Kelsey, Major-General for Kent, asserted that he preferred 'the interest of God's people . . . before 1,000 Parliaments' but this sentiment did not help to raise money. As the election campaign proceeded their doubts grew. Their fears were expressed, again by Kelsey, when he wrote to Cromwell that most of the cavaliers in his area were falling in with the Presbyterians against Protector and Government and that the spirit was generally bitter against 'swordsmen, decimators, courtiers etc.' The Venetian envoy was more circumspect. Some say the new Parliament 'will be entirely devoted to the Protector, others foretell the contrary' he reported to his masters.[5]

27

'I beseech you . . . do not dispute of unnecessary things'

Cromwell and his Council were taking no chances. The returns to this Parliament were carefully scrutinized and about a hundred elected representatives were excluded, mainly on Republican grounds, including such well-known names as Haselrig, Bradshaw and Harbottle Grimston, who had been the first to rise in his seat with a list of grievances in the Parliament of 1640. Of the Members who now remained well over 200 had sat in the 1654 Parliament or the Nominated Assembly, 180 were new to Parliament. On the whole they were moderate Presbyterians or Independents; the military had not done very well though the Major-Generals were in evidence. For the first time in sixteen years Lenthall did not preside over the House as Speaker. In his place was Sir Thomas Widdrington who relinquished his role as Keeper of the Great Seal to Nathaniel Fiennes. The President of the Council was Cromwell's old friend of St Ives, Henry Lawrence, while John Thurloe remained as its Secretary; both were appointments which pleased the Protector.[1]

Most of the Members repaired to Westminster Abbey in state on Wednesday 17 September 1656, for the opening sermon by Dr Owen. Cromwell himself made the journey from Whitehall to Westminster escorted once again by his guards, horse and foot, and by members of his Council and his Court, while Lambert rode with him in his coach. The weather was unseasonably hot and when they gathered in the Painted Chamber for the Protector's opening speech he promised to be brief. 'I had been pitying myself', he said, 'but now' (seeing the perspiring faces before him) 'I must turn off that pity and consider the condition you are in.'

His mind was occupied with semi-philosophical concepts of 'words' and 'things' and 'forms'. He assured his hearers he was not much interested in words, the art of rhetoricians, but in things –

in particular the glory of God. Having paid that tribute to the Almighty he plunged into a metaphysical discussion of Being and Preservation which prompted a warning as to the danger of external enemies and, in particular, of the Spaniard. The long fulmination against Spain led on to accounts of dangers at home – Papists, Cavaliers, Fifth Monarchy Men, Levellers. To deal with such perils the Major-Generals had been appointed, 'men of known integrity and fidelity'.

He reminded the Parliament men before him that he had engineered peace with Sweden, with the Dutch, the Dane, with Portugal and France. But, he pointed out, 'our nation is overwhelmed in debts'. But instead of proceeding to questions of supply he could not resist his favourite, most deeply felt subject of toleration. 'That men that believe in Jesus Christ – (that is the form that gives the being to true religion, faith in Christ and walking in a profession answerable to that faith) men that believe the remission of sins through the blood of Christ and free justification by the blood of Christ, and live upon the grace of God... Whoever hath this faith, let his form be what it will; if he be walking peaceably, without the prejudicing of others under another form... If a man of one form will be trampling upon the heels of another form... I will not suffer it in him.'

He continued with 'manners'. 'The mind is the man. If that be kept pure, a man signifies somewhat; if not, I would very fain see what difference there is betwixt him and a beast.'

The law was next under review. There are some 'wicked and abominable laws', he told the Members of Parliament, 'that will be in your power to alter. To hang a man for six-pence, three-pence, I know not what; to hang for a trifle, and pardon murder, is in the ministration of the Law through the ill framing of it. I have known in my experience abominable murders aquitted; and to see men lose their lives for petty matters! This is a thing that God will reckon for.'

'I have little more to say to you, being very weary.' But he still goes on, his promise of brevity again forgotten, as he returns to the subject of the Major-Generals: 'effectual for the Preservation of your Peace'; 'more effectual towards the discountenancing of vice and settling religion than anything done these fifty years'.

With an effort he came back to what was the real reason for summoning them:

'I confess I have digressed much... I would not have you to

be discouraged, if you think the State is exceeding poor. Give me leave to tell you, we have managed the Treasury not unthriftily, nor to private uses; but for the use of the nation and government.' He gave them figures and reiterated, 'You are not so much in debt as we found you.' Still he digressed. When he came to the words: 'I beseech you, I beseech you, do not dispute of unnecessary and unprofitable things', they must have thought it was the end. But he still had more to say, including a recitation of the 85th Psalm – 'Lord Thou hast been favourable to thy land . . .' and an admonition to sing Luther's Psalm: 'God is our refuge and strength.'

At last, after about three hours' talking, he came to the end: 'I have done. All that I have to say, is, to pray God, that He will bless you with His presence . . .'[2]

The speech lacked form or order, it was repetitive, Cromwell jumped from one subject to another. It was the speech of a tired man who for the first time doubted his ability to control the elements round him and who clung with growing intensity to his faith. Nevertheless, as a later commentator wrote, 'The man himself, and the England he presided over . . . are . . . visible in it . . . He who would see Oliver, will find more of him here than in most of the history books . . .'.[3]

It took the Commons a fortnight to approve the war with Spain but on October 1 the vote was given and supplies voted for its further-ance. Not that the war was universally popular. London merchants with West Indian connections, including Lambert, feared the loss of their trade, and all with commercial interests in the New World felt threatened. But Cromwell carried most of the Council with him, and any remaining doubts were scotched by the news that arrived on the day of the Commons' vote that Captain Stayner had destroyed the Spanish treasure fleet off Cadiz and taken large quantities of silver. When thirty-eight wagon-loads of bullion arrived at the Tower of London for coinage into good English money, together with 165 chests of fine silver, sixty chests of coarser silver, and a large quantity of valuable cochineal, the Spanish enterprise was considered to have received Divine approval. When six months later Blake off Santa Cruz captured the Spanish treasure fleet it might have seemed, indeed, that the Lord was smiling on them, except that the gallant Blake died on his way home to England.

It was not an idle Parliament. Apart from approving the war with Spain and voting supplies it annulled the title of the Stuarts to the throne and pronounced it high treason to attempt to overthrow the Protector or his government. Well over a hundred bills were contemplated and over seventy, public and private, went forward for the Protector's approval. They ranged widely. Among Public Bills were Lambert's proposal for a branch court of equity at York which would make the law more easily available in the Provinces; another for making the Merchant Adventurers into a corporation. There was sumptuary legislation and proposals for the reformation of manners and for the observance of Holy Days. The law of probate, so important to the men of property in the Parliament, was to be examined, and state revenues, in a constantly untidy condition, were to be considered. After the troubled period of the wars there were also many Private Bills dealing mainly with people's estates and ownership that needed to be considered. All in all it was an energetic and hard-working Parliament, dividing its days between sessions in the Parliament House and in Committee. The amount of paper they covered, the number of words they produced, were something of a trial to the Protector. He himself was no idler but he remarked of this period that if he rose at four each morning he could not read 'the multitude of bills' offered for his consent.[4]

But whatever sense of purpose they had achieved was rudely shattered in December by James Nayler, an old soldier and sectarian of Quaker views with the ascetic appearance of a Saint and a fancied resemblance to Jesus of Nazareth, who allowed himself to be hailed by devoted disciples as a new Messiah. When he was seated on an ass and escorted into Bristol by women strewing branches in his path the House of Commons was horrified. The rise of Quakerism was already causing concern among them and this was the kind of incident that could quickly work up into a panic of denunciation. Though the extent of their legal power was uncertain the Commons commanded the leading player in this unfortunate incident to be branded, pilloried, whipped and imprisoned at their pleasure.

Cromwell, whose enquiring mind had already led him to a long and tolerant interview with the Quaker leader, George Fox, was shocked at the whole episode both by the blasphemous pageant put on by Nayler and his followers and by the vicious punishment meted out by the Commons. But he was even more alarmed at the assumption by the House of Commons of judicial functions beyond the powers given it by the *Instrument of Government*. The members had, moreover, exercised this function without reference to the Protector. He sent to the Commons to ask the grounds and reasons for their actions and they found it difficult to produce an answer. The Nayler episode was a disturbing enough affair in itself but was even more serious in bringing to the surface a basic constitutional flaw: if the House of Commons could themselves, without reference to any other authority, judicate in the Nayler case, what else could they do and who else could they involve? They had also taken upon themselves, in the very nature of the case, to be judges of the extent of toleration. Cromwell fought on both issues and after a considerable struggle he had Nayler's sentence converted into imprisonment and exile in the Scilly Isles. But Nayler's case remained as a reminder of the problems that were still with him.[5]

At almost the same time another incident broke into the routine of Cromwell's second Protectorate Parliament. On Christmas Day 1656 when, it seemed, even Puritan MPs were overcome by the spirit of Christmas and had joined their families, Major-General Desborough upset the calm of a thin House by proposing that the bitterly resented Decimation Tax be continued and legalized. Since it was this tax that largely supported the Major-Generals and the militia they raised there was more in the motion than the tax itself. As Thurloe wrote to Henry Cromwell in January the opposition were motivated by the 'fear that it will establish the Major-Generals, which they seem to disrelish very much'.[6] It took a month to rally the Members but on January 22, in a much fuller House, Desborough's motion was defeated by 124 votes to 88. The next day the House voted £400,000 for the Spanish war.

Early in the New Year plots against the Protector's life were again the chief concern. Edward Sexby, the gallant agitator of 1647 who even then had been asking bitterly what 'the poor scrubs' had been fighting for, had still found no answer and in his exasperation had written, or jointly written, with Silas Titus, another old soldier, the pamphlet entitled *Killing No Murder*. True to its sentiments he was involved in several plots against Cromwell's life. In January his chief accomplice was Miles Sindercombe, another soldier who had been active in the Leveller movement. Sindercombe was inventive. He tried shooting the Protector from a window as he journeyed from London to Hampton Court. When Cromwell was taking the air in his carriage in Hyde Park Sindercombe made another unsuccessful attempt. Finally, on January 8, he set fire to Whitehall Chapel, hoping to assassinate Cromwell in the confusion that would follow. But a soldier on guard smelt burning, Sindercombe was discovered and sent to the Tower, where he took poison smuggled in to him by his sister.

The Sindercombe affair, possibly the nearness of his escapes, humbled Cromwell. He was touched when the House of Commons not only sent him a message of congratulation but appointed a General Thanksgiving and came to him at the Banqueting Hall in Whitehall to deliver their messages through their new Speaker, 'mellifluous Widdrington'. Cromwell spoke to them there – perhaps this was not the reaction they intended – but it was a short speech full of God's glory and the blessings He had bestowed upon their country. And it was a humble speech. He spoke of 'the inconsiderableness and unworthiness of the person that hath been the object and subject of this deliverance... I confess ingenuously to you', he said, 'I do lie under the daily sense of my unworthiness and unprofitableness.'[7] Oliver invited his Parliament to dinner at Whitehall and afterwards to music at the Cockpit – 'rare music, both of voices and instruments'. Things were not going badly between him and this Parliament. They would not continue the Decimation Tax but by this time his enthusiasm for the Major-Generals had somewhat waned; and they showed a fanatical intolerance over the case of James Nayler, which alarmed him because of its portents. But they spoke of law reform and they had voted money for the Spanish war. As Thurloe had written, 'The Protector and this Parliament do agree very well.'[8]

It was Parliament that was the more dissatisfied of the two, though not at the Protector's expense. When the Address of Congratulation to Cromwell after his escape from assassination was being drawn up in the House of Commons a Presbyterian Member named Ashe moved that it 'would tend very much to the preservation of himself and us that his Highness would be pleased to take upon him the government according to the ancient constitution. Both our liberties and peace and the preservation and privilege of his Highness would then be founded upon an old and sure foundation.'[9] Similar suggestions had been made outside Parliament but were either suppressed or taken little notice of. Cromwell's victories over the Dutch and now over Spain added a lustre to his person that some thought should be matched in his title. The poet Edmund Waller (it is true a kinsman of Cromwell's) wrote at the end of 1656 referring to the capture of the Spanish treasure ships

> Let it be as the glad nation prays
> Let the rich ore forthwith be melted down,
> And the state fixed, by making him a crown;
> With ermine clad and purple, let him hold
> A royal sceptre made of Spanish gold

Others looked to more conventional rule as an antidote against the military rule of the Major-Generals. After the recent assassination attempts the security of a named successor was called for; the people wanted a figurehead and a continuing government they could recognize. It was alleged that the title of 'Protector' was unknown except in a Prince's minority.[10]

The feeling that was welling up took shape five weeks later when Alderman Packe, a Member for London and an ex-Lord Mayor, brought forward on February 23 *A Remonstrance* to be presented to his Highness 'somewhat tending to the Settlement of the Nation'. A deputation of officers, appalled at the report that the *Remonstrance* planned to make Cromwell King, waited upon him on Friday the 27th. Cromwell conceded he had heard of the proposal. But they need not be startled, he said. The Crown had been offered to him before and had been refused. The title of King was as little value to him as to them – 'but a feather in a cap', he told them. The fact is, he said, no settlement had as yet been successful and the *Instrument* needed some amendment. He instanced the proposal now made in the *Remonstrance* for a second Chamber. A check upon the Commons would be a good thing. 'See what they, of their own power and will, I having no power to stop them, have done about James Nayler!' he cried, bringing the case of a simple Quaker to the forefront of the constitutional issue 'May it not be anyone's case another time?'[11]

But the *Remonstrance* was divisive. To the Republicans, who included a majority of military men both inside Parliament and out, as well as a substantial number of influential civilian MPs, its acceptance would entail a sacrifice of all they had fought for. On the other hand civilians in Parliament and in the City included powerful merchants and lawyers who wanted nothing so much as a return to constitutional government and to whom the term 'King' was more satisfactory than that of 'Protector'.

The scheme was presented to Cromwell on March 31 as the *Humble Petition and Advice*. Cromwell's dilemma was very real. 'I am hugely taken with the thing settlement', he declared, and he liked this further attempt at a constitution. He boggled at the name of 'King' but for that there was no necessity; another name would do as well. He knew that many people, including the majority of the soldiers, thought so too. Letters and pamphlets from within and outside the army were urging him not to 're-edify' the old regime. But the proposals had come at a bad time for him. He was deep in consideration of a more formal treaty with France in place of the Agreement of 24 October 1655. The long balancing in his calculations of France against Spain, in the course of which the one-time squire of Huntingdon was involved in the 'night-realm' of Thurloe and his spies to such an extent that he was writing to the great Mazarin of 'a person' and 'No. 200', had long since given way to open warfare with Spain. The formal treaty with France came on May 23, a month after Parliament and Cromwell were faced with Alderman Pack's *Remonstrance* for a new constitution.

He was also deep in marriage negotiations for his two youngest daughters – 'the little wenches' about whom he had so frequently voiced his concern in his fighting days. Both he and his wife were particularly worried over the proposed marriage of Frances, his younger child, to Robert Rich, son of Lord Rich, and grandson and heir to the Earl of Warwick. Frances and Rich had been desperately in love for some time and Oliver and the Earl of Warwick were involved in the usual negotiations for settlement. The Warwicks and the Richs were good Puritans, and their possessions included house and lands in Essex where they had known the Cromwell family since before the war. There may, however, have been some hitch in the marriage discussions for according to a member of the Russell family these affairs considerably troubled Cromwell and his wife. But Frances's sister, Mary, believed that their father had heard stories of ill-repute concerning young Rich – that he was 'a vicious man, given to play and such-like things' – as she wrote to their brother, Henry, in Ireland – and would not sign the marriage contract until he was satisfied on this point. Frances, for her part, set about proving such reports to be false and was able to satisfy her father on this matter. But there was still the health of the young man to be taken into account, for he was known to be weak and sickly.[12]

But *The Humble Petition and Advice*,[13] would wait neither for foreign treaties nor for family commitments and debates went on vigorously in the House of Commons with the Republicans and the soldiers
fighting it tooth and nail. Not until 25 March 1657 was it passed
by 123 votes to 62. It was presented to Cromwell in the Banqueting
Hall on March 31 complete with its offer of a Crown, the right
to name his successor, and a second Chamber to help or plague him.
Fleetwood, Lambert, Desborough, threatened to lay down their commissions if he accepted. He replied that he must ask counsel of God
and his own heart.

Three days later he sent a delaying reply: 'some infirmity of body
hath seized upon me'. Was it the familiar sign of stress? Was he
playing for time? Committees and discussions continued until April
13 when a deputation met Cromwell at Whitehall. He was under
much pressure from the army to refuse, though the City and his
own family, particularly Henry Cromwell, were urging acceptance.
Thurloe unearthed a Fifth Monarchy plot engineered by one, Venner,
a wine-cooper, calling upon supporters to assemble at Mile End
Green. Chests of arms and pamphlets were seized, Venner was sent
to the Tower, and Harrison, the Fifth Monarchist Major-General,
was imprisoned. Not surprisingly Cromwell's speech to the deputation on April 13 though long, was inconclusive. He would meet
them again the following afternoon. But again he was ill. On Thursday the 16th they all met again and adjourned until the following
day when Cromwell was absent through illness. On the 20th he
met the Committee, again on the 21st when he made a speech but
still gave no definite answer. Then, nearly six weeks after the offer
was first made, on 8 May 1657, he met the gathered Parliament
in the Banqueting House and refused their offer of a Crown.

He realized that the business had put the House to a great deal
of trouble and time. 'I am sorry', he said, 'It hath cost me some
too, and some thoughts.' But he believed the *Humble Petition* without
the title of King would serve them well in civil rights and liberties
and in liberty of conscience – 'the great fundamentals' of government.
Whitelocke believed that, left to himself, he would have accepted
the Crown but that the pressure from Republicans and particularly
those of the army, had been too strong. And he had always been
susceptible to the views of the soldiers: they were still his own, part
of himself, and to act against their wishes was too great a burden
to bear.

When the *Petition* was presented to him yet again on 25 May 1657 with the title of Protector in place of King, Cromwell accepted it and on June 26 was installed as Lord Protector for the second time in Westminster Hall, this time with considerable pomp and ceremony. The chair of state was placed at the upper end of the Hall, round it stood or sat the dignitaries of the realm and visiting Ambassadors. The Protector came this time by water to Westminster and stopped at the House of Lords before going in procession to Westminster Hall to have the purple robe of state placed round his shoulders, to receive a richly embossed bible, the sword of state and the sceptre of massive gold. He took the oath, delivered him by the Speaker, and as he sat in the chair of state, the sceptre in his hand, the trumpets sounded and the people cheered lustily. The Ambassadors of Europe, except for Spain but including mighty France, sat round him as well as his own statesmen and household officers and signalling, indeed, that he and the country he ruled were among the mightiest if not the mightiest themselves.[14] Oliver Protector had felt it right, though not to adopt the title of King, yet to participate in a ceremony that was as ritualistic and symbolic as the crowning of any king or queen of England who had sat on that same chair.

By the *Petition and Advice* Parliament was to meet every three years or more frequently if necessary; no amendment was made to the franchise or to the constituencies and the exclusion of elected Members would no longer be possible. The Council of State was to have less power than before, Parliament having the right to veto its membership; and there was to be an Upper House nominated by the Protector of some forty to seventy members, subject to the approval of Parliament. The Protector would have the naming of his successor. Parliament had gained at the expense of the Council but Cromwell also had gained, particularly in obtaining a permanent fixed revenue which would be raised mainly from the customs and excise in addition to an immediate supply for the next three years to cover the cost of the Spanish war. All in all, on the credit side was the fact that the amended constitution had originated in Parliament and that it took the form of a statute. Also in his favour was the virtual demise of the Major-Generals who, though 'not politically murdered', had 'almost, but not quite, committed suicide'.[15] Now at last he had thrown off the accusation that his rule rested upon force. But more of his old comrades had gone: Ludlow, Harrison,

Joyce had all left him. Lambert, who had produced his own constitution, had opposed the Spanish war and supported the Major-Generals, now opposed the *Petition and Advice*. He objected in particular to the creation of a second Chamber, to the new terms of the succession, and altogether to the greater power which he felt the *Petition and Advice* would give to the Protector.

As Cromwell urgently considered the composition of his new Council in the days following the adjournment he received letters from Henry Cromwell and from friends urging him to exclude Lambert. He did so. Lambert, the soldier with whom he had served in war and victory, was omitted from the new Council. There was little outcry. 'Never was any man less pitied or lamented after'; 'he was all for himself; he hoped to be next Protector', it was said. Even his own officers wrote in support of the Protector. But Lambert was a gallant soldier and might have expected better things from the peace.[16] Cromwell's action, in bringing his somewhat profligate and apolitical son, Richard, on to the Council in December rubbed salt into the wound.[17]

In choosing the members of the second Chamber the Council gave Cromwell virtually a free hand. There were to be not more than seventy members, not less than forty. Thurloe said that the Protector 'hath the opinion, and deservedly, of knowing men better than any other man'. But Cromwell had difficulty in making his choice – perhaps in the light of Thurloe's further sage observation that 'a mistake here will be like that of war and marriage; it admits of no repentance'. In the meantime he governed with his Council which met for the first time on July 3, and the business of the state went on. Cromwell wrote congratulations to Blake and sent him a fine jewel before he knew of his tragic death. Troops were despatched to the French Netherlands to help fight the Spanish armies there; ships were instructed to cruise up and down the Channel 'taking care of the safety, interest and honour of the Commonwealth', as Cromwell wrote to General Montague on board the *Naseby* on August 11. In July Edward Sexby, who was the brain behind the attempts on Cromwell's life, was captured and sent to the Tower. John Lilburne, who had at last been allowed home from exile and was quietly preaching pacifist Quaker views in place of his earlier strident tirades, died quietly and little noticed in August. Sexby, his mind deranged, died in January 1658. So those brave voices for freedom who had fought by his side and argued with Cromwell round the Council table in those heady days of war and victory left the scene. Cromwell made no sign. But when Lilburne's widow appealed to Cromwell two months after her husband's death for support for herself and her three children, he immediately authorized the continuation of Lilburne's pension, with arrears; and professing, as he always had, great tenderness towards Elizabeth, he arranged that she should take possession of the lands in Durham which had for long been in dispute between her husband and Haselrig.[18]

28

'Let God be judge between you and me!'

On 11 November 1657, nearly five months after her father's second inauguration as Lord Protector, the Lady Frances Cromwell at last was married to Robert Rich. A civil wedding ceremony was performed by a Justice of the Peace, Cromwell's chaplain made 'a godly prayer'. There was nothing niggardly about the wedding festivities which got into full swing the following day in Whitehall. Cromwell's love of music and dancing, learned at Hinchingbrooke half a century earlier, was expressed in the forty-eight violins and fifty trumpets which he ordered for the occasion. There was mixed dancing, not usual in Puritan circles, in the course of which Cromwell's wife, now termed 'Her Highness', danced with the Earl of Newport. Altogether there was 'much mirth and frolic' which continued until five o'clock the next morning, after which the wedding party adjourned to the Warwick home for another three or four days of festivity. The Countess of Devonshire, the grandmother of the bridegroom, presented the bride with £2,000 worth of plate. Even if 'the most Illustrious Lady, the Lady Frances Cromwell' took it all for granted Oliver and Elizabeth might well have paused to consider the 'little wench' born seventeen years before to the squire of Ely.

If contemporary accounts were correct his reaction was not unusual. 'Cromwell loved an innocent jest' wrote one of his soldiers in Scotland as they watched the man with the milk churn on his head. So now Frances's wedding was marked by a great deal of horse-play from her father. It would seem to be carrying 'an innocent jest' too far to throw about sack-posset among the ladies to soil and spoil their fine clothes, to daub the chairs with wet sweetmeats as they were about to sit down, and finally to pull off his son-in-law's peruke, making to throw it into the fire and, when prevented, sitting on it.[1] The antics may have resulted from release of tension: for good or ill his daughter had had her way and married young Rich; he himself had accepted the *Petition and Advice* and been installed for the second time as Protector after the long and nerve-wracking dilemma over the kingship; the Levellers were silenced, Lilburne was dead, Sexby imprisoned, the Royalists impotent. Foreign affairs were going well. Just so, after signing the King's death warrant, Oliver had splashed ink about over the signatories. He and Ludlow had thrown cushions at each other at the end of a serious political meeting. The story of an even more disreputable incident in his youth may have been exaggerated but points to a similar strain of boisterousness carried to excess, of manic reaction to release from tension.

The following week in a far quieter ceremony at Hampton Court the Lady Mary was married to the Lord Fauconberg, a member of the Bellasis family who were strongly Royalist: so far had outlook and reaction changed that there was little wonder at the union. Marvell wrote a poem for the occasion in which Cromwell was referred to as Jove. Fauconberg was said to be Cromwell's favourite son-in-law whom he kept by his side at all audiences to foreign dignitaries. This could have been for several reasons: to use his son-in-law's fluency in foreign languages, perhaps to show that he could muster Royalist connections, perhaps simply because the elegance of the young man was likely to impress.

After a six-month recess the day for the opening of the second session of Cromwell's second Parliament approached. It was the first meeting under the terms of the *Petition and Advice* and Cromwell was reported with 'a world of fears and jealousies in his breast'. On Christmas Day 1657 and the day following he caused several persons to be arrested, including some at sermons or receiving communion in their own houses. He and his Council had assigned many prominent people to the new second Chamber. The military men included Skippon, Pride, Desborough, Whalley, Hewson. Among prominent Parliamentarians were Whitelocke, Lenthall, Rous – even Haselrig. His two sons were there. Six members of the peerage were named, including Cromwell's new kinsman, the Earl of Warwick who, however, refused to serve with such low-born men as Major-General Hewson who had started life as a shoemaker. It could be that the gulf between Royalist and Puritan was easier to cross than that between class and class. Sixty-three men were summoned in all to Cromwell's second Chamber of whom some forty sat. As most of these were from the House of Commons the move proved detrimental to Cromwell for he thereby lost support where he needed it most. At the same time the Members excluded from the Commons in the previous session, who were not Cromwell men, came trooping back, taking the oath according to the new constitution. Cromwell had weakened his position in two respects, and it soon became clear that the men who filed in after the recess were less inclined to take the new constitution uncritically than those who had passed it into law the previous session.

On 20 January 1658, on a cold, frosty day, Cromwell sat in the House of Lords (as it was still called) awaiting the Commons. He was again 'somewhat indisposed in health' so he left the main speech to Nathaniel Fiennes, still in charge of the Great Seal. 'I have been under some infirmity', he told his audience, and 'therefore dare not speak further to you'. But five days later he summoned them to the Banqueting House, recovered enough and concerned enough to make one of his long speeches.

'I reckon this to be the great duty of my place', he said, 'as being set on a watch-tower to see what may be for the good of these nations'. He saw danger abroad to the Protestant cause, he saw Charles Stuart gathering another army, cavaliers organizing in England to support him, sectarianism spreading at home, each sect striving against the others. He feared 'it would all make up one confusion'. We 'should have another more bloody civil war than ever.' Only the government as established by the *Petition and Advice* together with the army could prevent this. Again he affirmed he did not want his position of supremacy – 'You sought me for it, and you brought me to it.' It was the speech of a worried man. When the Commons asked him for a copy he said he could not remember four lines of it and could not do so.[2]

The Republicans in the House were unimpressed by talk of dangers. The excluded Members who had now returned carried on their work of destroying the *Instrument of Government* under the general assertion that 'We who were not privy to your debates upon which you made your resolutions should have liberty to debate it over again.' 'Unless you make foundations sure, it will not do your work,' piously added Haselrig. They denounced in particular the new Upper House with its preponderance of officers, officials and

303

Cromwell's relations and spent seven periods of discussion time arguing whether it should be called the House of Lords or the Other House. Scot distinguished himself by a speech which took the whole morning, attacking the new Upper House by going over the misdeeds of the old. Haselrig – 'his speeches were shorter though more numerous' – made the high-sounding assertion, though its relevance was not altogether clear: 'I can suffer to be torn in pieces, I could endure that; but to betray the liberties of the people of England that I cannot.' On the other side it was asserted: 'We know what the House of Lords could do. We know not what this "Other House" may do.' On the general question of a second chamber someone brought in Harrington's theory that secure government must rest on a balance of property. It was not known what 'balance' the new House would provide; it did not have an 'interest' in society; here they were taking the stand that Ireton had made years before at the Putney debates. But Major Beke intervened disconcertingly, sounding the note that Cromwell hoped had been silenced: 'The sword is here. Is not that also a good balance?'

More practically Republicans in the City and army joined with those in the Commons to prepare a petition demanding the recognition of the House of Commons as the supreme authority. What was worse they questioned the Protector's power over the army and proposed to limit it. If necessary Fairfax would be reinstated as Commander-in-Chief. Here they were on dangerous ground. There was no doubt of the unrest in the army, not only among Republicans but among the more sectarian rank-and-file. Even the Protector's own regiment of horse was said to be affected. But no Parliament, no petitioners, could deal thus with Cromwell. The threatened cohesion between Republicans in the House, the City and the army was dangerous, and army matters always touched him on the raw, especially when his own authority was questioned.[3]

On February 4, fifteen days after Parliament had assembled, Black Rod arrived, summoning the Commons: 'His Highness is in the Lord's House, and desires to speak with you'.

'What care I for Black Rod!', cried Haselrig.

'Black Rod stays!', shouted others.

In the end they went. Cromwell was in a towering rage. The whole nation, he said, had run into more confusion in the fifteen or sixteen days they had been sitting than ever before. He had told them the truth at the Banqueting House ten days previously: the King of Scots had an army at the water's edge for invasion; tumults were preparing at home. He had not sought the position they had put him in but having put him there they must support him and join him in settling the nation. If this is all they could do 'I think it high time', he said, 'that an end be put to your sitting. And I do dissolve this Parliament! And let God be judge between you and me!'[4]

They were the last words he ever spoke to a Parliament.

Part IX

'For to be Cromwell was a greater thing than ought below, or yet above a king'

29

'If these the Times, then this must be the Man'

Cromwell had not managed his Parliaments successfully. There was no constitutional achievement to stand beside his military success. In five years he had seen the end of four Parliaments, three of them dissolved by him, one of them ending with a resignation which had his approval, if no more positive impetus. Before that he had been privy to a purge of the Long Parliament and had not hesitated to use a show of force to eject MPs who opposed him. His record was no better than that of Charles I, who had, perhaps, been wiser in managing for eleven years without a Parliament at all. Cromwell might, nevertheless, be credited with the higher aim of seeking to govern constitutionally. He wanted to be a representative, constitutionally appointed ruler and he said many times that government in a single person and a Parliament was 'fundamental'. Though, as he had made clear at Putney, he did not want representation to extend so widely as to disturb the distinctions of class, his Parliaments were elected, they were to meet at agreed intervals, and a number of checks and balances between Parliament, Council and Protector were embodied in the constitution. Moreover the *Petition and Advice* – and this to him was of the greatest importance – was a constitutional document that emanated from an elected Parliament. Nevertheless, his record told against him. Actions counted, not motives.

Particular circumstances, also, were unhelpful. By the time his last Parliament met he was faced with a House of Commons denuded of many of his supporters in order to man the new Upper House, and augmented by the return of several powerful Presbyterians who had been ejected, or who had taken themselves off, from earlier Parliaments. The presence of new, younger men as MPs also made his task more difficult. They were not 'with him' as his old colleagues had been, they had not been through it all, they did not understand, almost they began to ignore him. Opposition was being expressed, not only in attacking the *Petition of Advice*, which they did with considerable verve, but in developing what was almost an inertia when it came to tackling social problems.

Above all, though it might seem that there were checks enough upon the Protector, Oliver's Parliaments could never believe in their reality so long as he had control of the army. If they had all seen eye to eye with him on important issues the situation might have been accepted, but there were many Presbyterians in his Parliaments to whom his wide toleration was unacceptable, groups of Fifth Monarchy Men who believed that his very attempts at toleration were a betrayal of the cause, Republicans on both sides of the religious divide who objected to a Protector on principle.

Cromwell considered that his own authority as Protector had been approved by the people and that therefore, though the Parliament might alter 'circumstantials', it must stand by the 'fundamentals' of the constitution as laid down in the *Instrument of Government* and the *Petition and Advice*. The question remains whether a little more tact on Cromwell's part might have helped. It has been said that he was a natural back-bencher, not understanding the subtleties of politics.[1] But he played his game well enough in his opposition to Manchester, in finessing round the Self-Denying Ordinance and in the formation of the New Model Army. But then he was certain of himself. Now he was full of constitutional doubts. Long ago when the officers had suggested the ejection of Parliament he had asked 'by what authority?' And when they said they would call a new Parliament he had told them that in that case not the Parliament but he that called the Parliament would be the supreme power. More recently he had asked Ludlow, who had been pressing him for government of the nation 'by its own consent': 'Where shall we find that consent?' He had given the answer himself to Calamy who had told him when he became Protector that nine in ten of the people would be against him. 'Very well', he had said, 'what if I should disarm the nine and put a sword in the tenth man's hands?' This, as much as anything, was the problem. Parliament was afraid of the tenth man.

Cromwell's approach to his Parliaments was very much that of the General to his army. But he could not be sure whether he was facing the enemy or dealing with insubordination in his own ranks. If there had been more of the tactician who won his case against

Manchester, piloted the Accommodation Order and the Self-Denying Ordinance through the House of Commons, he might have succeeded better. He had seen deeply into the nature of Parliaments then but the knowledge did not help him when he faced his own Parliaments. He needed common sense, which he possessed, finesse, which had deserted him.

There was no basic difference of class or social standing between Cromwell and his Parliaments. Their regard for property was as deep-rooted as Cromwell's own. Religion was a source of contention and there were many Presbyterians in the Protectorate Parliaments who feared Cromwell's toleration both for its own sake and for the social anarchy they thought would ensue. But the biggest division of all between Cromwell and his Parliaments was between Protector and Republicans. His being there at all, as Protector, was an affront which to them denied the basic nature of the struggle which ended with the execution of the King. The Protectorate was in substance, as Ludlow said to Lambert, 'a re-establishment of that which we all engaged against.'

Cromwell had wanted action from his Parliaments but did not get it. The constant bickering, talking and intriguing infuriated him and enfeebled him – more than the hard military campaigning when his word was law. The summer of 1658 when he ruled without a Parliament gave him some satisfaction. But this was not what he wanted. He wanted to be a constitutional ruler governing through and with an elected Parliament. It was ironic that the contradictions in the situation were such as could be solved in his favour only if he employed the very force he had sought to avoid. A tantalizing question is whether Ireton, had he lived, could have affected the issue and brought to heel such antagonists as Haselrig and Scot, Onslow and Challoner, even Ludlow. As it was, Cromwell was very much alone as he faced his Parliaments. If anyone could have taken Ireton's place it was Thurloe, of whom Cromwell was fond. But Thurloe, for all his assets, was not a constitutionalist. In the shadowy world of intelligence and the informer he was comfortably at home. He was less help to his master in the cut-and-thrust of politics.

There is evidence throughout his career that the toleration of which Cromwell spoke in his despatches was something real and urgent to him. He showed it in recruiting his army and in retaining good soldiers whose religious convictions were not quite in accord with his own. He showed it in his attitude to the Fifth Monarchy Men who were a perpetual goading irritant. He talked with the preachers John Simpson and Christopher Feake. He dealt gently with the rough and earnest Harrison, he stepped between Nayler and the angry Parliament. He received John Rogers, another exuberant Fifth Monarchy preacher, with a group of his followers at Whitehall. When his disciples complained that Rogers was being persecuted for conscience' sake Cromwell was moved to cry out that he suffered as a railer, a seducer, and a stirrer up of sedition. 'God is my witness', he exclaimed, 'no man in England doth suffer for the testimony of Jesus.' Here was the difficulty: to differentiate between the action and the word. There were some beliefs, however, which could on no account be tolerated. John Biddle was a Unitarian and, in Cromwell's words, 'If it be true what Mr Biddle holds, to wit, that our Lord and Saviour Jesus Christ is but a creature, then all those who worship him with the worship due to God are idolators.' But when he sent Biddle to prison in the Scilly Isles it was to save him from what would have been a more severe punishment.

Nayler was a Quaker, a group of people with whom Cromwell felt particular sympathy. They had gone further than any of the sects in refusing to recognize the authority of the magistrate or minister and in discarding even the simplest religious props of the Independents. They rarely entered a 'steeple house', as they called churches, or propounded the Scriptures. They had much in common with the Seekers or Family of Love in coming together in silence until the Spirit moved them to speak. They were basically pacificist in spite of brawls with magistrates and noisy scenes with clergy which led to arrest and persecution. Their leader was a man who, a generation earlier, might have been one of Cromwell's soldiers. George Fox was the son of a weaver and apprenticed to a shoemaker. For four years he wandered the country seeking the satisfaction he failed to find in any of the sects. He found it in the guidance of the 'inner light'. His followers called themselves the Society of Friends but they were frequently known as Quakers, possibly because of the physical trembling that accompanied their revelations by the Inner Light.

Fox himself was involved in various disturbances which led to his arrest and early in 1655 he appealed to the Protector. Cromwell admitted him to his bedchamber one morning while he was being dressed. 'Peace be on this House!' exclaimed Fox, in no way abashed, and he proceeded to speak of the light from above and the dark from below. 'That is good.' 'That is true,' Oliver frequently interjected, according to Fox. As the business of the day opened and various officials arrived, Fox made to withdraw; but Oliver caught him by the hand begging him, with tears in his eyes, to come again, for they had much in common.

The Quaker took him at his word. Some time later he came upon the Protector in his carriage at Hyde Park Corner and was able to make his way through the guards to the carriage window to receive a further invitation from Oliver. The interview next day was informal, with Cromwell sitting casually on the edge of a table chatting pleasantly of truth and of religion. Fox was disappointed that the Protector spoke 'lightly' to him. But on the practical side Cromwell had released not only the Quaker leader himself but also many of his followers from prison. A little casual lightheartedness was probably no bad way to deal with George Fox.[2]

Cromwell's attitude towards the Jews was more complicated. For two centuries they had not been allowed legal settlement in England yet they offered no opposition to his government, nor were they likely to. He himself was interested in the Hebrew Scriptures, he respected their success as traders and even wondered whether in this regard they might be made to benefit England. When Manessa Ben Israel, a Jewish physician settled in Amsterdam, petitioned for permission for Jews to live in England Cromwell was sympathetic. But the conference he called to consider the question did not share his views, the members being afraid not only for their religion but for their trade. The utmost that Cromwell could achieve was permission for Jews to reside in England without any legal bar and to practise their religion in private houses.

Cromwell's toleration was exercised within the framework laid down by the *Instrument of Government* and his Ordinances establishing 'triers' and 'ejectors'. Tythes continued to support the ministry, but many of his associates, and they included such powerful figures as Vane and Milton, still denied the role of the civil arm in relation to the church in any respect. It was an uneasy compromise that Cromwell had reached but it was the best that he could do. Presbyterians, Independents and Baptists continued to worship within the mantle of the Church; outside its aegis liberty of worship was permitted to 'all such as do profess faith in God by Jesus Christ'. Cromwell's fanatical hatred of Catholics had somewhat dimmed and, though legal toleration was not achieved, he claimed that they fared better under him than they had under the Parliament.

Clarendon said that Cromwell's 'greatness at home was but a shadow of the glory he had abroad'. Though he had failed to achieve his heart's desire of a grand European Protestant alliance which included England, he and his government had prevented an alliance of European powers against the regicide Republic. The Dutch war had ended favourably and a treaty with the Dutch had been followed by treaties with Denmark, Sweden and Portugal. Soon France and Spain were bidding for his support. 'There is not a nation in Europe,' he told his Parliament, 'but is willing to ask a good understanding with you.' He intervened successfully on behalf of the Protestants in Savoy; he saw England once more acquire a base in Europe with the ceding of Dunkirk; English ships dealt with the pirates who infested the Mediterranean, the Sovereignty of the Seas was successfully maintained and the English flag deferred to. It could be questioned whether it was not a mistake to continue the old animosity against Spain while failing to assess the rising dominance of France. But economically Cromwell was justified and his attitude to the New World, which was dominated by the settlement of Puritans in Newfoundland, in the West Indian islands, and on the east coast of America, was strongly influenced by the mercantilist policy, of which he heartily approved, with its emphasis on trading relations between Britain and the Plantations. Cromwell's colonial policy was primarily westward-looking but to the east beginnings were being consolidated with trading posts in India and the East Indies. Although Mun's treatise *England's Treasure by Forraign Trade* was not published until 1664 its sentiment was fully understood and endorsed by Cromwell. In the same way that he had grasped the necessities of war and politics, so he was well on the way to understanding the necessities of an expanding world of trade and commerce. Merchants, Members of Parliament, commercial interests of all kinds combined to further and to take advantage of this expansion to east and west. If Cromwell was not thinking of the foundation of a British Empire his Protectorate marked a move in that direction.

His insensitivity outside the limits of his Puritanism is illustrated by his use of the native population of Jamaica who were deported to other West Indian islands and to mainland America to serve the colonists there. Prisoners, especially Catholics, were similarly shipped to the Plantations. In the same way the legacy Cromwell left to Ireland stands against him. Irish Catholics lost much of their land, they were not represented at Westminster, many were deported to the West Indies, others remained to serve Protestant landowners who had acquired land under the 'settlements' or who claimed it in return for loans made to Parliament, a few departed to remote parts of Ireland where the land was poor and the surroundings inhospitable. Nor to Scotland had Cromwell's rule accorded any benefit. The country remained poor, reaping little advantage from England's expanding trade. Even her representation in the English Parliament under the *Instrument of Government* did her little good.

There was much that Cromwell enjoyed in his position as Lord Protector. At Hampton Court he hunted, went hawking, and played bowls. He rode hard – 'he was a bold jumper' – he had needed to be in his military career, but he alarmed more timid guests. He had more time for his horses. His chief extravagance, comparable to Charles I's love of pictures, was in procuring horses both for their own sake and for breeding. As Charles's agents had scoured Europe and the Near East for works of art, so Cromwell's scoured the area for horses. In June 1655 an agent was reporting from Leghorn that he was in touch with a friend in Naples. Cromwell's commission for two horses and four mares was complete and he promised not only an invoice but 'a description of each; their race, or pedigree, colour, age, height, quality, and condition'. Clearly the Lord Protector would not accept a pig in a poke. About the same time the man sent to Tripoli to redeem the English captives there was instructed to procure a mare. But she proved unfit for breeding and the agent was told to look for something better. Two years later the Ambassador at Constantinople was informed that Cromwell wanted some good Arabian horses for breeding. All the Protector's public appearances were associated with good horses: the six Flanders mares that drew his coach when he left for Ireland in 1649; the six white horses which drew his coach in 1655 and of which it was remarked 'Certain it is that none of the English Kings had ever any such'. Foreign dignitaries knew what presents the Lord Protector would most gratefully receive, like the Barbary mares presented by the Duke of Oldenburgh which so ungallantly threw their new master in Hyde Park. Cromwell's excitement at the prospect of a new animal is evidenced by Ludlow who records that a deputation to Cromwell begging him to accept the Crown was kept waiting for two hours while he went to inspect a Barbary horse in the gardens of Whitehall.

Hampton Court was well suited to the music he enjoyed and he had a second organ installed in the Great Hall where he would listen to the playing of his organist, John Hingston, a pupil of Orlando Gibbons. A pleasant story tells of a young student of Christ Church, Oxford, who had been expelled by the Puritan Visitors to the College. Friends brought him to sing to the Protector, who was impressed by his deep, bass voice. 'What can I do for you?' he asked. The answer was obvious. Cromwell readily helped him and the young man was restored to his place.[3]

There were some discordant notes through the summer of 1658. Thurloe was doing his work well with *agents provocateurs* in addition to less questionable forms of intelligence. At the end of May two of the most influential of those arrested were brought before a special High Court of Justice which had been set up the previous month. Dr Hewett was an Anglican minister whose church services Elizabeth Claypole had often attended and who had officiated at the wedding of Mary Cromwell and Fauconberg. Sir Henry Slingsby had been caught up in the toils of an *agent provocateur*. Cromwell had to withstand impassioned pleading from both his daughters before the execution of the two men went forward in June.

But deep personal sorrow was coming closer to Cromwell. Elizabeth Claypole, the bright, vivacious Bettie, who had been ill at the time of her sisters' weddings, grew worse and Oliver brought her and her family to apartments in Hampton Court for the benefit of fresher air. At the same time family bereavements were taking their toll. Elizabeth's little son, Oliver Claypole, died in June at the age of one year. Robert Rich, who had been married only four months earlier to Frances, had died in February. The bewildered and sorrowing Frances needed her father's comfort. Three months later her father-in-law and Cromwell's old friend, the Earl of Warwick, also died. Thurloe fell ill. Elizabeth grew worse. Oliver spent long days and nights at her bedside trying to uphold her. She died in great pain on August 16. Her death, for all his trust in the Lord, was a blow he found hard to bear. At the same time his wife was ill. He himself had bladder trouble; he was wracked by gout; a boil on his neck worried him and was evidence of his poor health. George Fox, who met him by chance near Hampton Court about the time found him much changed.[4] The doctors ordered him to Whitehall, for a change of air. But the bouts of chill and heat persisted. His family gathered round him. As he grew weaker he was heard murmuring passages of Scripture. Friends, members of his Household, the courtiers, the politicians came, all those for whom government was a continuing concern. Who did he name as his successor? Something was said of a sealed envelope at Hampton Court. It was never found. Someone asked a name. It was thought to be 'Richard'. Considering his father's concern over Richard's way of life it seemed an unlikely choice. But Cromwell had recently been at pains to bring him onto the Council and to familiarize him with affairs of state. There was no time for more. The Lord Protector was heard praying for Puritanism and the Protestant Cause and at four o'clock in the afternoon of Friday 3 September 1658, he died. It was his lucky day of Dunbar and Worcester and of his first Protectorate Parliament.

If Cromwell had succeeded it was as a soldier; if in bequeathing to his country a stable government, he had failed. He died with no Parliament sitting and murmuring the name of a successor who had been a constant worry to him and was unlikely to be less so to the country. Yet generally speaking he had maintained the form of ordered government, anarchy had been prevented and disorder kept down. There was a military presence behind this and Cromwell's past use of force or a show of force was not easily forgotten. But there were too many of the props of constitutional government remaining to support the accusation of a military dictatorship. Only if it came to downright inability to rule with Parliament might force have again been brought in. Cromwell died before this could be put to the test. A permanent religious settlement still eluded him though he had achieved a wider toleration than had existed under Laud and the bishops. He might claim that he had achieved that other goal for which they had fought: no taxation without representation. Yet the level of taxation was generally unacceptable and it could not be said that all those taxed were represented. If he had allowed himself a more open use of force he might have done more, more quickly. But that was the dictator's path and apart from alienating his old comrades he himself was too deeply imbued with the desire for constitutional settlement to venture down it. He was warm-hearted and compassionate and, as a dictator, could have improved the condition of the poorest members of society. Like Charles I, he would have done 'what's for their good, not what pleases them'. Dictator's words, but there had been no time . . .

When all has been said, he accomplished much. His armies beat the King's men, he played a big part in securing the King's execution. He shone for a while as Lord Protector, recognized not only in England but throughout Europe as the companion of kings. His constitutional settlement failed, making possible a Stuart Restoration, but the restored monarchy was not the monarchy he had done so much to overthrow. The Restoration Settlement of 1660 restored 1640 rather than 1639 and retained the early legislation of the Long Parliament. In so doing it maintained the power of Parliament against monarch and consolidated the position both of the men who had been the opposition in 1640 and of those who had succeeded them during the struggle. It was Cromwell's achievement, not to have initiated or to have won the struggle, but through his victories in battle to have consolidated and made it secure. There had been no substantial shift of class power, nor did he wish such or expect there would have been. The men who had won through to 1660 were with him in this. As he had put it to them, what he wanted was stability. What he complained of was the irresponsible urge to 'Overturn, overturn, overturn!'

To the question whether he had participated in a rebellion or a revolution he had no answer: the question to him would have been meaningless. Whether he had taken part in a continuing historical development of class power from feudal to-monarchical to aristocratic, to bourgeois to proletarian, and at which point of the process he himself stood, would have been a consideration of arid irrelevancies in which the terms themselves were barely understood.

Nor did he carry much of the stock-in-trade of the polemical constitutionalists: Norman yoke, laws of Edward the Confessor, even *Magna Carta* were not, for him, part of the argument. Still less did he want to interfere with the existing social hierarchy: distinctions of class, degrees of wealth were a necessary part of the fabric of society to be interfered with only in cases of hardship, and then within the prevailing pattern. But he never denied there were good men in every walk of life, and he accepted them as such, used them and worked with them – unlike the Earl of Warwick who refused to sit in Cromwell's House of Lords along with a man risen from humble beginnings. To Cromwell 'stability' was the key word. No form of snobbishness influenced his attitude to class. He merely feared the 'confusion' – to use his own word – that a disregard of social niceties might bring about.

In the various crises of war and peace he was sometimes accused of hypocrisy, actions belying words, ready tears to disguise real motives, acceptable means used for unacceptable ends. The human mind is unfathomable and none more so than Oliver's – even to himself. His appeals to the Lord were complex processes and the interaction of the man himself with some outside power is difficult to evaluate. What is certain is that he was deeply religious in the accepted sense of the term and that his actions, in his own mind, were not at variance with his faith or his commitments. Similarly he was accused of ambition. He had been driven by circumstances to high office in the state as he had been in the army, but it was not ambition but merely expediency that drove him forward. An ambitious man could have become king, founded a dynasty and sat with the crowned heads of Europe. That he did this without the aura of kingship says much for the dynamism of Oliver Cromwell but does not support the charge of ambition.

For some of his actions no excuses are adequate. The carnage of Drogheda and Wexford, his gloating letters to the Speaker, stand against him eternally. His hatred of Roman Catholics, the manic exhilaration of conquest, help to explain but do not excuse him. The ruins of castles he destroyed in Ireland and Scotland witness against him, but these were strong points, generally defended. The destruction of churches and their contents which, in spite of strict discipline in other respects, he too often allowed, has probably been exaggerated; the stabling of horses in churches can be excused as a wartime necessity. But in Ireland, hidden in a small valley near Kilkenny, stands intact a little church whose claim to fame is that Cromwell 'missed it'. Such a legend speaks volumes.

To his enemies Oliver Cromwell had been relentless. He was terrible in battle as he cried for 'One charge more!' or as he exulted 'I profess, they run!' But he was a gentle and painstaking son, a loving and considerate husband and father. In the midst of the most arduous campaigning, as in Scotland, his thoughts were constantly with his family and he found time to write and advise them. He helped friends in the material things of life like a new post or promotion. He protected those who were suffering for the sake of their conscience. He knew compassion – to the fenmen, to the poor of Ely. His letters to many people envisage a wide sympathy and understanding. He protected John Lilburne beyond the bounds of normal expectation and sprang instantly to help Lilburne's widow when she needed financial support. Those who knew him personally testified to his greatness of heart, his basic simplicity. 'A larger soul, I think', wrote his steward, John Maidstone, who knew him as intimately as anyone outside his family and who was with him at the end, 'hath seldom dwelt in a house of clay.'

On the whole Oliver Cromwell was strong and healthy, campaigning with his men, sleeping rough, capable of long and rapid marches, and of incredible feats of endurance. His terrifying elation in battle or when he was excited was coupled with periods of withdrawal and inertia for which modern medicine has found a name. Oliver's own doctors spoke of him as 'a most splenetic man', 'melancholic'. Modern physicians use the term 'manic depressive'. Descriptions of him in battle support one aspect of the condition. At Worcester an eye-witness reported 'that Oliver was carried on as with a divine impulse. He did laugh so excessively as if he had been drunk, and his eyes sparkled with spirits.' At Naseby 'the same fit of laughter seized him just before the battle'.

But while Cromwell showed some of the marks of the manic depressive in his alternating bouts of action and inertia, there are differences. The manic depressive loses his will when in a state of depression. For Cromwell the periods of inertia were formative. He was 'seeking the Lord', coming to grips with a problem, deliberately absenting himself from affairs in order to make the greater impact when he had reached the decision which he never doubted was the correct one. There was too much of deliberate withdrawal in Cromwell to label him with the 'depressive' part of the modern term.

It is possible that as a young man there was somewhat (to use his own turn of phrase) of the hypochondriac in him. Such a tendency, if it ever existed, was rapidly lost in the demands of battle and campaigning. But Cromwell soon learned to use an indisposition, or supposed indisposition, as a period of preparation for action. When he emerged it was with the confidence that God had counselled him; when he was victorious or successful it was clear that Providence was on his side. This Providence which played so big a part in shaping his actions and in justifying his career was as well known to his Puritan contemporaries as to himself. To them it was manifest in small, more homely ways, but the same 'dispensations' were there. The workings of Providence needed no explanation to his contemporaries. To them, as to him, it was justification by success.[5]

To some extent success generated success. Could he fail when it was so evident that the Lord was with him? But Oliver Cromwell himself was a natural leader. He foresaw the necessity for action – as he did even before the fighting started. Men responded to him; he had a natural *rapport* with people of all walks of life; he had the orator's gift of rousing his soldiers to action, though this was not so manifest when addressing his Parliaments. He knew when to stay silent. Waller observed in the army Councils 'Cromwell's disposition to draw men out and to reserve his own opinions'.

The term 'charisma' is hardly appropriate to so rugged a character as Oliver Cromwell. In some respects the indefinable quality reflected in the term is his. Yet he lacked the finer points of culture – he hardly had time for them. It was, indeed, the coarser side of Cromwell that provided the common touch that endeared his soldiers to him. He was a man whom it was easy to love, easy to hate, for his emotions were so often on the surface. The 'ready tears', which to some people spelt hypocrisy, were as genuinely emotional as his elation in battle. He himself found it easy to love, easy to hate, and so has posterity.

The forces that shaped this complex man lie partly in the times in which he lived. Without the calls of religious persecution and constitutional wrongs he might have remained a vigorous East Anglian farmer attending to his property and his family in unremarkable style. Similarly, without the influence of Dr Beard he might have been less certain of his destiny, less able to commune with the Lord. The influence of his mother throughout her long life was profound. That strong-minded woman had guided him through his disreputable youth to marriage, had seen him settled in her own Isle of Ely, and had accompanied him to the splendour of Whitehall. His short relationship with Henry Ireton was also important. Here was a man, hard, single-minded, razor-sharp, the perfect foil for Cromwell's instinctive reasoning. And perhaps as important to a man as the times in which he lives and the people around him is the land where he spends his youth. The strange, inscrutable features of the fenland landscape in which he grew up, owing little to man, outside man's provenance, dependent only on the Lord, were a fitting introduction for Oliver Cromwell to the world of imponderables he entered at the age of nearly forty.

As he lay in his bed in the Palace of Whitehall eighteen years later, far from the spreading fields and the quiet delights of his boyhood and his early married life, murmuring disjointed passages of scripture – the words and images that had upheld him and determined his conduct – there broke the greatest storm of thunder and lightning in living memory. It was a fitting accompaniment to the exit of that proud spirit, that tortured soul, that man of action, compassion and humility. In the last years he had known little rest except in the Lord. Now it was over and he went out with all the hosts of heaven blazing and all their trumpets sounding to find peace at last.

He was honoured both in his public funeral and in his burial with kings in Westminster Abbey. His praises were sung in prose and verse. But it was soon over. In a few years the Stuart line wiped out, so far as it could, the image of Oliver Cromwell. His disinterred body was reburied at Tyburn, like a criminal's; his head was displayed over Westminster Hall, like a traitor's. His dust now lies beneath the roar of traffic at Marble Arch where once the gallows stood; his head, three centuries after his death, has found a resting place in the ante-chapel of his old College, Sidney Sussex, at Cambridge. More pleasantly the grammar school in Huntingdon, where he learned his lessons from Dr Beard, is now a museum devoted in name and contents to his memory. The citizens of his native Huntingdon refused a statue to his memory at a time when the majority were opposed to his record. But in the market place at St Ives he is fittingly commemorated in this way. Hinchingbrooke, the focus of so much of his boyhood activity and who knows of what youthful aspirations, has been partly restored and houses the sixth form of a modern comprehensive school. The grounds and gardens are somewhat changed, are less extensive, but much of the old building with its impressive façade remains, its situation unaltered. On a warm spring evening the boy Oliver plays again on the spreading lawns among the rabbit warrens or broods beneath the trees on questions of salvation and free will. Here, where it began, Oliver's story might fittingly end. But the historians would not let it rest there. In the nineteenth century when the wheel had come full circle and Cromwell was hailed as the great Parliamentarian, another statue was somewhat incongruously erected outside the Houses of Parliament at Westminster. His hand on his sword he broods over the Parliament he could not control as though asking himself 'Why?' Or whether, in the end, it had made any difference?

Notes

Chapter 1 (pp. 3–13)

1 Hinchingbrooke House – see Bibliography. Entertainment of King James – Nichols *Progresses*, I, pp. 98–101. Cromwell ancestry – most of the *Lives* listed, particularly *Noble*; short version of genealogical table in Dickinson *Cromwell*, full version from Cromwell Museum.
2 Church register of St John the Baptist now in church of All Saints, Huntingdon.
3 Cromwell's early life is based upon contemporary works listed in the bibliography.
4 Letters to Mayor, to Richard in Abbott II, p. 236, Carlyle I, p. 451.
5 Robert Cromwell, Abbott I, p. 13.
6 Heath and other *Lives*.
7 *Lives*
8 Marriage entry in Guildhall Library, MS 6419/2.
9 Firth, *Cromwell*, pp. 7–8; Abbott I, p. 37.

Chapter 2 (pp. 14–23)

1 For Huntingdonshire and the fenland in Cromwell's time see Camden's *Britannia*; Dickinson, *Cromwell*.
2 Weyman, 'Cromwell's Kinsfolk'.
3 Warwick, p. 249; Simcotts, p. 76.
4 Abbott I, pp. 50–51.

Chapter 3 (pp. 24–30)

1 Mayerne, Sloan MSS, 2069 fol. 96B
2 Abbott I, pp. 81–2 summarizes what is known of this strange and unlikely incident.
3 Notestein and Relf, *Commons Debates for 1629*, pp. 139, 192–3; the preacher was Dr Alabaster.

Chapter 4 (pp. 31–39)

1 C.S.P.D. 1629–31, pp. 402–3 and Preface viii–xix.
2 *ibid*. 1631–3, p. 23.
3 Abbott I, pp. 71–2.
4 *ibid*, p. 81; Heath, p. 17.
5 Abbott I, p. 80.
6 Noble I, p. 352.
7 Camden; V.C.H. Cambridgeshire.
8 Abbott I, pp. 82–3.
9 *ibid*. p. 96.
10 *ibid*. pp. 96–7.
11 *ibid*. 95.
12 Hill, *God's Englishman*, p. 46.
13 Fuller I, p. 221.
14 C.S.P.D. 1637–8, pp. 438, 500–1, 503–4; Dugdale pp. 459–60.
15 Abbott I, p. 107.

Chapter 5 (pp. 43–54)

1 Visitations of Laud in Gardiner, *History* VIII, pp. 106 ff.

2 Gregg, *Free-born John*, pp. 64–7.

3 *supra* p. 32.

4 C.S.P.V. 1636–9, pp. 110–111, 124–125; Gregg, *King Charles I*, pp. 299, 301–2; Hill, *God's Englishman*, p. 47.

5 See, e.g., Zagorin, *passim*.

6 Heath, p. 23; Abbott I, pp. 107–8.

7 Cooper III, pp. 296–9.

8 *ibid.* p. 304.

9 Keeler, Brunton and Pennington, *passim*.

Chapter 6 (pp. 55–65)

1 Warwick, pp. 247–8.

2 Roots, *Great Rebellion*, p. 29.

3 See, e.g. Abbott, I, pp. 120–5.

4 Clarendon, *Life*, p. 89; Hill, *God's Englishman*, p. 59.

5 Gardiner, *History* IX, pp. 285–7

6 Abbott I, 127–8.

7 *ibid.* 135–6. pp. 126.

8 Hill, *God's Englishman*, p. 59.

9 Abbott I, p. 136.

10 *ibid.* p. 125, 146.

11 Gardiner *Constitutional Documents* xxxv–vi, pp. 202 ff., Clarendon, *History* IV, Section 51, 52; Warwick, pp. 201–2.

Chapter 7 (pp. 69–81)

1 Abbott I, p. 149.

2 *ibid.* pp. 164–5.

3 *ibid.* pp. 155–6.

4 *ibid.* p. 163.

5 Carlyle I, p. 114.

6 I am indebted for this information to Professor Ivan Roots and to Michael Silverman of Henry Sotheran Ltd who, at the time of writing, possess the book.

7 Gardiner, *Documents*, xxxvii–viii, pp. 249 ff.

8 Abbott I, p. 150.

9 Cooper III, pp. 328–9.

10 Bramston, p. 86.

11 Abbott I, pp. 190–1.

12 Firth, *Cromwell*, p. 74.

13 Firth, 'Raising of the Ironsides' *passim*.

14 Gardiner, *Civil War* I, p. 30; Fiennes's Report E.126/38; and see Bibliography.

15 Abbott I, p. 204.

16 *ibid.* pp. 209–10.

17 Firth, *Cromwell* p. 91.

18 Abbott I, pp. 210, 225–6.

19 Warwick, pp. 251–2.

20 Firth, *Cromwell* pp. 92–3.

Chapter 8 (pp. 82–92)

1 Letter to Parliament, Abbott I, pp. 228–9.

2 Abbott I, p. 230.

3 *ibid.* pp. 231–2

4 *ibid.* p. 239; Gardiner, *Civil War* I, pp. 188–91.

5 C.J. III, p. 186.

6 Abbott I, pp. 259–61.

7 *ibid.* pp. 265–6; Gardiner, *Civil War* I, p. 241.

8 Abbott I, p. 270.

9 Manchester *Quarrel*; Firth, *Cromwell* p. 91; Abbott I, pp. 256, 261–2.

10 Abbott I, p. 248.

11 *ibid.* p. 278.

12 Gregg, *Free-born John*, pp. 108–9.

Chapter 9 (pp. 95–103)

1 Marston Moor, see Bibliography.

2 Abbott I, pp. 287–8

3 Gregg, *Free-born John*, pp. 110–11.

4 Quarrel with Manchester, *Camden Soc.*, 1875, pp. 71–7

5 Abbott I, p. 292.

6 Clarendon, VIII, §184–5.

7 2nd Newbury, see Bibliography; Abbott 297–301

Chapter 10 (pp. 104–114)

1 C.S.P.D. 1644–5, p. 125.
2 Gardiner, *Civil War*, II, p. 5.
3 Quarrel with Manchester.
4 Whitelocke, p. 34.
5 Kishlansky, ch. 2; Firth, *Army*, ch. 3.
6 Seward, *Anecdotes*, pp. 357–8; Abbott I, p. 333.
7 Gardiner, *Civil War* II, p. 192.
8 Cromwell's movements round Oxford are traced in detail by Abbott I, pp. 339 ff.
9 See Bibliography.
10 Abbott I, pp. 374–8 – 'the longest letter Cromwell had yet written'.
11 *ibid.* p. 386.
12 Gregg, *King Charles I*, pp. 405–7.

Chapter 11 (pp. 117–127)

1 Abbott I, p. 412.
2 *ibid.* p. 410.
3 *ibid.* p. 416.
4 *ibid.* p. 428.
5 Gregg, *Free-born John*, 158–71; Woolrych, *Soldiers and Politicians* for slightly different and far more detailed account. Both Kishlansky and Woolrych in their detailed work attach less importance than I have done to the influence of Lilburne and the Levellers in the army at this time.

Chapter 12 (pp. 128–140)

1 Gregg, *Free-born John*, pp. 159–78; E.392/9.
2 Fairfax, A Short Memorial in *Maseres Tracts*, vol. I, p. 444; Berkeley, Memoirs, *ibid.* p. 364; Clarendon MSS. vol. 30, f. 134; *Clarke Papers*, vol. I, pp. 214–5; *Free-born John*, p. 187 and note 6.
3 Gregg, *Free-born John*, p. 192; *King

Charles I, pp. 414–16; Woolrych, *Soldiers and Statesmen*, pp. 174–81; Gardiner, *Civil War*, III, p. 316.
4 Gardiner, *Constitutional Documents*, pp. 316 ff.
5 Gregg, *Free-born John*, pp. 193–6
6 Gardiner, *Constitutional Documents*, pp. 333 ff.
7 Putney Debates: *Clarke Papers*, vol. I; Woodhouse, Part I and *passim*; Woolrych, *Soldiers and Statesmen*, ch. IX.
8 *Letter of the Agitators*, E.414/8.
9 Kishlansky, 'What Happened at Ware'; Woolrych, *Soldiers and Statesmen*, 280 ff; Gregg, *Free-born John*, pp. 222–3.

Chapter 13 (pp. 141–150)

1 Gregg, *King Charles I*, pp. 418–20.
2 Huntington, *Sundry Reasons . . .*, p. 11 (E.458/3).
3 Gardiner, *Civil War* IV, pp. 26–31.
4 *Memoirs*, pp. 185–6.
5 Abbott I, pp. 428–9.
6 William Allen, *Faithful Memorial* (1659).
7 Abbott I, p. 621.
8 Gardiner, *Civil War* IV, p. 178; E.457/21.
9 See Bibliography.
10 Abbott I, pp. 696–9, and an earlier letter pp. 676–8.
11 Underdown, *Pride's Purge, passim*.

Chapter 14 (pp. 151–163)

1 Muddiman; Wedgwood, *Trial*; Gregg, *King Charles I*, Ch. 35; Underdown, *Pride's Purge*, pp. 182 ff.
2 C.J. VI, p. 159. Gardiner, *Commonwealth* I, p. 11.
3 Whitelocke, p. 71.
4 Gregg, *Free-born John*, pp. 266–72

Chapter 15 (pp. 167–172)

1 Abbott II, pp. 38–9.
2 Gregg, *Free-born John*, pp. 278–82 and refs on p. 412.

Chapter 16 (pp. 173–186)

1 See Murphy throughout; Abbott II, chapters II, III, IV.
2 Gardiner, *Commonwealth* I, p. 96; *Moderate Intelligencer* 5–12 July 1649 (E.565).
3 *Perfect Diurnal*, 23 August 1649 (E.532).
4 Abbott II, pp. 124–8; Murphy.
5 Abbott II, pp. 140–3; Murphy.
6 Gardiner, *Commonwealth* I, p. 156.

Chapter 17 (pp. 187–199)

1 Whitelocke, pp. 460–2.
2 C.J. VII, p. 142; C.S.P.D. 1651–2, June 26.
3 E.604/4.
4 Ludlow, pp. 245–6; Gardiner, *Commonwealth* I, p. 266.
5 *ibid.* p. 251, 267; C.J. VI, pp. 428, 441.
6 Abbott II, p. 281.
7 *ibid.* p. 289.
8 E.607/20.
9 Gardiner, *Commonwealth* I, p. 270; E.608/5.
10 *ibid.* p. 275.
11 Hodgson, p. 130.
12 *idem*; Abbott II, p. 293.
13 Abbott II, p. 300.
14 Hodgson, p. 142.
15 Fleetwood, qu. Abbott II, p. 311; E.778/22.
16 Abbott II, pp. 302–3.
17 *ibid.* 314–15.
18 Ambrose Barnes, qu. Abbott II, p. 317.
19 Abbott II, pp. 315 ff. and Bibliography.
20 *ibid.* p. 325.

21 *ibid.* p. 329.
22 *ibid.* p. 327.
23 *ibid.* p. 330.

Chapter 18 (pp. 200–208)

1 Abbott II, p. 327.
2 Correspondence with Dundas, Abbott II, pp. 335–41.
3 Carlyle II, p. 127 note 7.
4 Abbott II, p. 346.
5 Nickolls, *Original Letters*, p. 40.
6 Abbott II, p. 391.
7 Worden, *Rump*, p. 254.
8 Abbott II, p. 392.
9 *ibid.* p. 394.
10 *ibid.* pp. 396–7.
11 *ibid.* pp. 397–8.
12 *ibid.* pp. 404–5.
13 Coltness Collections, pub. Maitland Club, Glasgow, 1842, p. 9. Reproduced Carlyle II, pp. 197–8. And see note 3 p. 198.
14 Abbott II, p. 412.
15 *ibid.* p. 421.

Chapter 19 (pp. 209–218)

1 See Bibliography; Abbott II, p. 444.
2 *ibid.* p. 462.
3 *ibid.* p. 460.
4 *ibid.* p. 462.
5 *A Perfect Diurnal* (E.641/15).
6 Abbott II, pp. 461, 462.
7 C.J. VII, pp. 13, 15; E.641/14.

Chapter 20 (pp. 219–228)

1 C.S.P.V. 1655–56, pp. 299, 308
2 *supra*, p. 203
3 C.S.P.V. 1647–52, pp. 187–8.
4 Worden, *Rump*, p. 235.
5 *supra*, p. 220
6 C.S.P.V. 1647–52, p. 188.
7 Whitelocke III, pp. 195–6; Worden, *Rump*, pp. 301–6.

Chapter 21 (pp. 229–240)

1 Worden, *Rump*, pp. 30–32, 88–92.
2 C.S.P.V. 1647–52, p. 270.
3 *idem.*
4 Worden, *Rump*, p. 276; Whitelocke, pp. 516–17.
5 Whitelocke, pp. 549–51.
6 Abbott II, p. 296.
7 Gregg, *Free-born John*, p. 305.
8 Gardiner, *Commonwealth* II, p. 224–26.
9 Ludlow I, p. 346.
10 Gardiner, *Commonwealth* II, p. 245.
11 Firth, 'Expulsion of the Long Parliament'.
12 Ludlow I, p. 346.
13 Newsletter 18 March 1653 (Hist. Rev. 1893, p. 528).
14 Worden, *Rump*, pp. 332 ff.; C. M. Williams, 'Political Career of Henry Marten'.
15 Worden, *Rump*, esp. Part five.
16 Gardiner, *Commonwealth* II, pp. 246, 255.
17 *Dorothy Osborne to William Temple*, 23 April 1653, ed. G. C. Moore Smith (1928).

Chapter 22 (pp. 241–249)

1 Abbott III, pp. 5–9.
2 *ibid.* p. 10.
3 Woolrych, *Commonwealth*, p. 111.
4 *ibid.* Chs. IV, V, *passim.*
5 Abbott III, p. 34.
6 Gardiner, *Commonwealth* II, p. 280.
7 C.S.P.V. 1653–4, p. 78.
8 Gardiner, *Commonwealth* II, p. 279.
9 Abbott III, pp. 28–9.
10 *ibid.* pp. 52–66
11 *ibid.* p. 89.
12 Buchan, *Cromwell*, p. 438.
13 Woolrych, *Commonwealth*, Ch. X.

Chapter 23 (pp. 250–261)

1 Abbott III, p. 136.
2 Roots, *Great Rebellion*, p. 170.
3 Gardiner, *Constitutional Documents*, p. 405 ff.; Kenyon, *Stuart Constitution*, No. 94; Woolrych, *Commonwealth to Protectorate*, pp. 353 ff.
4 Abbott III, p. 455.
5 Carlyle II, p. 315.
6 Roots, 'Cromwell's Ordinances', ch. 6 *The Interregnum*, ed. Ayler.

Chapter 24 (pp. 265–273)

1 Gardiner, *Commonwealth* III, p. 117.
2 Cf. an interesting letter in Cl. MSS xlix, fol. 56 qu. in Gardiner, *Commonwealth* III, p. 177 note 1.
3 Gaunt, pp. 11–13; Roots, *Great Rebellion*, pp. 181–2.
4 *Behometh* in *Maseres Tracts* II, p. 631.
5 Whitelocke, p. 582.
6 Abbott III, pp. 434–43.
7 Gardiner, *Commonwealth* III, pp. 181–7; Abbott III, pp. 445–50; Ludlow I, p. 343.
8 Abbott III, pp. 451–63.
9 Gardiner, *Commonwealth* III, pp. 184; 203 note 3; Abbott III, p. 466.

Chapter 25 (pp. 274–280)

1 Firth, 'Cromwell and Sport'. Abbott says Cromwell was kept in bed for three weeks (III, 474).
2 Baxter I, p. 197.
3 Abbott, III, pp. 579–93.
4 *Court and Kitchen*; Firth, 'Court of Cromwell'.
5 Firth, *ibid.*
6 *Memoirs*, p. 248.
7 Firth, 'Court of Cromwell'.
8 *ibid.*

9 Hutchinson, *Life of Colonel Hutchinson*, p. 370.
10 *supra* p. 205; Firth, *Cromwell*, p. 461.

Chapter 26 (pp. 281–288)

1 Loudon to Ormonde, 8 March 1656 in Carte, *Original Letters* II, pp. 80–1.
2 Directives were several times issued to the Major-Generals. For those of October 1655 see Firth and Rait II, pp. 813–22. They are summarized in Kenyon, *Constitution*, No. 95.
3 Gardiner, *Commonwealth* IV, pp. 29 ff. For Reports of the Major Generals see Thurloe IV, pp. 215–391.
4 Roots, 'Major Generals' in Parry.
5 C.S.P.V. 1655–6, p. 261.

Chapter 27 (pp. 289–300)

1 Roots, *Great Rebellion*, pp. 198–9.
2 Abbott IV, pp. 260–79.
3 Carlyle ii, p. 554.
4 Roots, 'Lawmaking' p. 134 and *passim*.
5 Roots, *Great Rebellion*, pp. 205–9.
6 Firth, *Last Years* I, pp. 123–4.
7 Abbott IV, pp. 388–90.
8 Firth, 'Court of Cromwell'.

9 Burton I, p. 362. Firth, *Last Years*, Ch. V.
10 *ibid*. Ch. V.
11 Burton I, p. 378.
12 Carlyle II, p. 497.
13 Gardiner, *Constitutional Documents* No. 103; Kenyon *Constitution*, No. 96; pp. 337–8.
14 Whitelocke, pp. 661–2.
15 Roots, 'Lawmaking', p. 133.
16 Firth, *Last Years*, pp. 61–5; Thurloe VI, p. 609.
17 For full list of counsellors see Thurloe VI, p. 669.
18 Gregg, *Free-born John*, p. 347.

Chapter 28 (pp. 301–305)

1 Harl. MSS No. 991 (Richard Symonds).
2 Abbott IV, pp. 705–8; 712–20.
3 Firth, *Last Years* II, pp. 6–31 *passim*.
4 Abbott IV, pp. 728–32.

Chapter 29 (pp. 309–323)

1 Trevor-Roper, 'Oliver Cromwell and his Parliaments', p. 45.
2 Gardiner, *Commonwealth* III, pp. 264–7, IV, pp. 5–6; Fox, *Journal* (1836 ed.) I, pp. 265–6, 381.
3 Firth, 'Cromwell and Sport'.
4 Fox, *ibid*. I, pp. 485–6.
5 Worden, 'Providence . . . in Cromwellian England'.

Bibliography

As Carlyle surveyed the piles of manuscripts and other material he was intending to publish as Cromwell's *Letters and Speeches* he reminded himself that 'a great man does lie buried under this waste continent of cinders' and he asked 'Canst thou not unbury them, present them visible, and so help, as it were, in the creation of them?'

The 'unburying' has gone on for 300 years since Cromwell's death, gaining momentum from Carlyle's work which was published in 1845, and accelerating in the last half-century. Steadily and surely the facts, the interpretation and reinterpretation have strengthened the outline of seventeenth-century history and brought its leaders into sharper focus.

This short bibliography seeks merely to indicate some of the most immediately useful books and articles: their own bibliographies will guide the reader further. A full bibliography would be as long again as this book itself, as W. C. Abbott demonstrated when he published an, at that time, complete Cromwell bibliography in 1929. Bearing in mind Richard Fleckno's remark in 1659 that 'those who write Books ought to have more regard to their leisure who read them than to their own in writing them', I have refrained from adding more pages to this book than the present selective bibliography entails.

The Letters and Speeches of Oliver Cromwell with elucidations by Thomas Carlyle edited by S. C. Lomàs with an Introduction by C. H. Firth, 3 vols 1904 (first published 1845).

The Writings and Speeches of Oliver Cromwell ed. W. C. Abbott, 4 vols. 1937–1947. (Cambridge Mass.).
With regret I have abandoned in the references Carlyle's racy and evocative *Letters and Speeches* for Abbott's later edition, mainly in the interests of simplicity for there are other references I need to quote from Abbott. But it is Carlyle who, for me, brings to life the man, Oliver Cromwell. He who would know Cromwell in all his guises should read Carlyle straight through – all three volumes – from cover to cover.
Abbott, on the other hand, links the documents with a full narrative of events which presents a virtual biography of Cromwell.

Bibliography

Bibliography of Oliver Cromwell: a list of printed materials by W. C. Abbott, 1929 (Cambridge Mass.), with a supplement to 1944 in vol. iv of the *Writings*; further supplemented by P. H. Hardacre in *Journal of Modern History* 33 (1961)

The chief bibliographical guide to the whole period is *Bibliography of British History, Stuart period, 1603–1714*. The 1st ed. of Godfrey Davies, pub. in 1928, was brought up to date in 1970 by Mary Frear Keeler, but publications have continued thick and fast since then and supplements are published in the annual Bulletins of the Historical Association and the Royal Historical Society.

For consultation throughout see Peter Gaunt, *The Cromwellian Gazeteer*, 1987.

Background

S. R. Gardiner's monumental narrative history:—
    Vols VIII–X of *History of England*, 1886–1891,
    The four volumes of *The Great Civil War*, 1886,
    The four volumes of *The Commonwealth and Protectorate*, 1894–1901.
    After Gardiner's death continued in 2 vols by C. H. Firth as *The Last Years of the Protectorate*, 1909.

Equally monumental, though in a different way is Edward, Earl of Clarendon, *The History of the Rebellion and Civil Wars in England*, edited in six volumes by W. Dunn Macray, 1888.

A selection of biographies of Cromwell in chronological order

Richard Fleckno, *The Idea of His Highness Oliver late Lord Protector*, 1659.
Henry Fletcher, *The perfect politician, or a full view of the life and actions ... of Oliver Cromwell*, 1660; the 'only early life of any value'.
James Heath, *Flagellum*, 1663; extreme Royalist.
Mark Noble, *Memoirs of the Protectorate House of Cromwell*, 1784.
M. Guizot, *Life of Oliver Cromwell*, 1868.
H. Church, *Oliver Cromwell A History*, 1895.
John Morley, *Oliver Cromwell*, 1901.
C. H. Firth, *Cromwell*, 1901.
John Buchan, *Oliver Cromwell*, 1934.
R. S. Paul, *The Lord Protector*, 1955.
M. P. Ashley, *The Greatness of Oliver Cromwell*, 1957.
Christopher Hill, *God's Englishman: Oliver Cromwell and the English Revolution*, 1970.
C. V. Wedgwood, *Oliver Cromwell*, 1973.
Antonia Fraser, *Cromwell, our Chief of Men*, 1973.
M. P. Ashley, *Charles I and Oliver Cromwell*, 1987.

The young Cromwell

P.G.M.Dickinson, *Hinchingbrooke House*, 1970.
P.G.M.Dickinson, *Oliver Cromwell and Huntingdon*, 1981.
C.H.Cooper, *Annals of Cambridge*, vol. 3, 1908.
C.W.Scott-Giles, *Sidney Sussex College, A Short History*, 1950, revised with additions 1975.
O.Weyman, 'Cromwell's Kinsfolk' in *E.H.R.* VI (1891) pp. 48–60.

Interesting Studies of Cromwell

Anon., *The Court and Kitchen of Elizabeth Cromwell*, 1664; satirical but useful. Available from Cromwell Museum, Huntingdon.
C.H.Firth, 'Cromwell's Views on Sport', *Macmillan's Magazine*, Oct., 1894.
C.H.Firth, 'The Court of Cromwell', *The Cornhill Magazine*, 1897.
Percy A.Scholes, *Puritans and Music in England and New England*, 1934.
F.N.L.Poynter and W.J.Bishop, *Beds. Hist. Record Soc.* Vol. XXXI. *A Seventeenth Century Doctor and his Patients: John Symcotts.*
Alan Smith, 'The Image of Cromwell in Folklore and Tradition', *Folklore*, Vol. 79, 1968.
Blair Worden, 'Providence and Politics in Cromwellian England', in *Past and Present*, Nov. 1985.
Blair Worden, 'Oliver Cromwell and the Sin of Achan', in *History, Society and the Churches, essays in honour of Owen Chadwick*, ed. Derek Beales and Geoffrey Best, 1985.

The changing image of Cromwell

'For the war of Pens continues longer than the war of Swords, and grows commonly more sharp and cruel after death, until time gives the deciding blow at last . . .' (Fleckno)

W.C.Abbott, 'The fame of Oliver Cromwell', Vol IV of *Writings and Speeches*, 1947.
D.H.Pennington, 'Cromwell and the Historians', *History Today*, vol. 8, 1958.
R.C.Richardson, *The Debate on the English Revolution*, 1977.

Biographies of people close to or associated with Cromwell

Cromwell's family
R.W.Ramsey, *Henry Cromwell*, 1933.
  Richard Cromwell, 1935.
  Studies in Cromwell's Family Circle and other Papers, 1930.
  Henry Ireton, 1949.

Bibliography

King Charles I
Pauline Gregg, *King Charles I*, 1981.

Fairfax
John Wilson, *Fairfax, General of Parliament's forces in the English Civil War*, 1985.

Lambert
W.H.Dawson, *Cromwell's Understudy ; the life and times of General John Lambert*, 1938.

Sir Henry Vane
J.K.Hosmer, *The Life of young Sir Harry Vane*, 1888.
Violet Rowe, *Sir Henry Vane the Younger*, 1970.

Thurloe
D.L.Hobman, *Cromwell's Master Spy, A Study of John Thurloe*, 1961.

Lilburne
Pauline Gregg, *Free-born John*, 1961, paperback 1986.

Whitelocke
Ruth Spalding, *The Improbable Puritan*, a life of Bulstrode Whitelocke, 1975

Wildman
Maurice Ashley, *John Wildman, A Study of the English Republican Movement in the Seventeenth Century*, 1947.

Contemporary Memoirs

Edmund Ludlow, *Memoirs*, 2 vols. ed. Firth, 1894.
John Rushworth, *Historical Collections*, 7 vols. 1659–1701.
John Thurloe, *A Collection of State Papers*, ed. T. Birch, 7 vols, 1742.
Sir Philip Warwick, *Memoirs of the Reigne of Charles I*, 1701
Bulstrode Whitelocke, *Memoirs Biographical and Historical*, 1860.

Constitutional Documents

S.R.Gardiner, *Constitutional Documents of the Puritan Revolution*, 3rd ed. 1906.
J.R.Tanner, *English Constitutional Conflicts of the Seventeenth Century 1603–1689*, 1928.
J.P.Kenyon, *The Stuart Constitution, 1603–1688, Documents and Commentary*, 1966.

Military Affairs

Peter R. Newman, *Atlas of the English Civil War*, 1985.
T.S.Baldock, *Cromwell as a Soldier*, 1899.
A.H.Burne and Peter Young, *The Great Civil War. A Military History of the First Civil War 1642–1646*, 1959.
A.H.Woolrych, *Battles of the Civil War*, 1961.

Bibliography

Peter Young and Richard Holmes, *The English Civil War: A Military History of the Three Civil Wars* 1642–1651, 1974.

Peter Young, *Edgehill*, 1967.

Peter Young, *Marston Moor*, 1970.

Peter R. Newman, *The Battle of Marston Moor*, 1981.

D. Murphy, *Cromwell in Ireland. A history of Cromwell's Irish campaign*, 1883.

C. H. Firth 'Battle of Dunbar' *Royal Hist. Soc. Trans.* XIV, pp. 19–52.

C. H. Firth, *Cromwell's Army*, 1902; paperback with intro. by P. H. Hardacre, 1967.

C. H. Firth, 'The Raising of the Ironsides', *Royal Hist. Soc. Trans.* vol. XIII, pp. 17 ff.

C. H. Firth and Godfrey Davies, *The Regimental History of Cromwell's Army*, 2 vols, 1940.

Mark A. Kishlansky, *The Rise of the New Model Army*, 1979.

The Army Debates

The Clarke Papers ed. C. H. Firth, 4 vols. Camden Soc. 1891–1901.

A. S. P. Woodhouse, (ed.) *Puritanism and Liberty*, substantial selection of the debates with supplementary documents, 1938.

Austin Woolrych, *Soldiers and Statesmen, the General Council of the Army and its Debates 1647–1648*, 1987.

The Navy

J. R. Powell, *The Navy in the English Civil War*, 1963 (Hamden, Conn.).

Particular studies

David Underdown, *Pride's Purge*, 1971.

Blair Worden, *The Rump Parliament*, 1974.

Austin Woolrych, *Commonwealth to Protectorate*, 1982.

Ivan Roots, 'Lawmaking in the Second Protectorate Parliament' in *British Government and Administration*, ed. H. Hearder and H. R. Loyn, 1974.

Ivan Roots, 'Cromwell's Ordinances: the early legislation of the Protectorate', in *The Interregnum: the Quest for Settlement 1646–1660*, ed. Gerald Aylmer, 1972.

Peter Gaunt, 'Cromwell's Purge? Exclusions and the First Protectorate Parliament' in *Parliamentary History*, Vol. 6, pp. 1 ff, 1987.

Other good secondary sources

Ivan Roots, *The Great Rebellion, 1642–1660*, 1966.

G. E. Aylmer, *Rebellion or Revolution? England 1640–1660*, 1986.

Christopher Hill, *Puritanism and Revolution*, 1958.

Christopher Hill, *The World Turned Upside Down*, 1972

P. Zagorin, *The Court and the Country*, 1969.

Collections of Essays

Richard Pares and A.J.P. Taylor (eds) *Essays to Namier*, 1956, includes H.R. Trevor-Roper, 'Oliver Cromwell and his Parliaments'.

E.W. Ives (ed) *The English Revolution 1600–1660*, 1968.

R.H. Parry (ed) *The English Civil War and After*, 1970, includes Ivan Roots on the Major-Generals – 'Swordsmen and Decimators'.

Donald Pennington and Keith Thomas (eds), *Puritans and Revolutionaries*, 1978.

John Morrill (ed) *Reactions to the English Civil War*, 1982.

Ivan Roots (ed) *Into Another Mould: aspects of the Interregnum*, Exeter Studies in History, 1981

Colin Jones, Malyn Newitt and Stephen Roberts (eds), *Politics and People in Revolutionary England: essays in honour of Ivan Roots*, 1986.

Index

337